Enjoy the book!

Joe Mezzga

THE CAROLINA PANTHERS

THE CAROLINA PANTHERS

The First Season of the Most Successful Expansion Team in NFL History

Joe Menzer and Bob Condor

Macmillan • USA

*For Sarah, Andrew, Elizabeth, and the
baby to be named later.*

—J.M.

*For Mary, my soulmate and precious love—
always and more than ever.*

—B.C.

MACMILLAN
A Simon & Schuster Macmillan Company
1633 Broadway
New York, NY 10019

MACMILLAN is a registered trademark of Macmillan, Inc.

A catalogue record is available from the Library of Congress.

ISBN: 0-02-861396-1

10 9 8 7 6 5 4 3 2 1

Contents

Looking Back
A Season to Remember

The Carolina Panthers had just completed their first season in the National Football League, losing 20–17 to the Washington Redskins at RFK Stadium, a creaking, crumbling structure that seemed a depressing place to be on a chilly Christmas Eve.

But the mood in the visitors' locker room was surprisingly upbeat and decidedly positive, with hopeful thoughts already cast toward a promising future that would continue next season in Carolinas Stadium, a 72,685-seat, state-of-the-art facility in uptown Charlotte.

Jerry Richardson, principal owner and founder of the team, worked the room quietly, offering words of support. Rather than consoling players about the loss, he chose to thank them for a wonderful season, making it a point to stop at the lockers of key veterans like Sam Mills and Brett Maxie, and star youngsters like rookie quarterback Kerry Collins.

As Richardson walked from the locker room a short while later, he turned to a reporter and said, "Have you seen our new stadium yet? It will blow you away."

Mike McCormack, team president, stood in front of the locker stall of rookie offensive tackle Blake Brockermeyer for a long moment, telling the promising lineman not to worry about an injury he sustained during the game. "Focus on the future; it's bright", the Hall of Fame offensive tackle said to the young offensive tackle. Brockermeyer nodded in agreement.

"We surpassed all the expectations of everybody—the media and all the other teams in the league," said Brockermeyer, nursing a left foot he feared might be broken. The injury did not temper his enthusiasm as he talked on.

"I feel like we're just as good as 95 percent of the teams in this league," he added. "I mean, you've got San Francisco and who knows which Dallas team shows up . . . but there are only two or three teams that really stand out as being better than us. Any given day, I just feel like we can go out and beat whoever we play. That's a credit to us."

Across the room stood Collins, who along with Brockermeyer and others such as rookie cornerback Tyrone Poole are considered the cornerstone on which the future success of the Panthers rests. Collins was surrounded by a throng of reporters, which was not unusual.

"Even with this loss," said Collins, "it was an incredible season for an expansion team. . . . I can speak for every guy in this room when I say we are disappointed with this loss, but we are extremely pleased with the season as a whole. There were a lot of good things

1

about this football team that we established this season that are going to carry on through for a number of years."

The Panthers finished the season with a record of 7–9. No other team in NFL history had ever won more than three games in its first season of play. Even more impressively, the Panthers won seven of their last 11 games after beginning their history with five consecutive losses. They even toyed with making the playoffs late into the season.

"When we were 0–5," said Coach Dom Capers, "I don't know if I would have believed we'd finish with seven wins."

Brockermeyer smiled through his personal pain.

"Now we have something to build on," he said.

Five weeks after the end of the season, Dom Capers sat behind a large, clean desk in his office at the team's temporary headquarters in Rock Hill, South Carolina. His desk was always clean. So was his car, a dark blue Mercedes-Benz so spotless it was suspected he had a cloth run over it on the hour. Certainly the automobile could be easily located; he parked it in the same spot outside Winthrop Coliseum shortly before 6 A.M. most days during the season, and usually did not move it until 11 P.M. or later.

By all accounts, Capers is an organized man. He keeps a series of leather-bound notebooks detailing the daily events of his life locked in a credenza to left of the desk in his office, and it was a rare day when he failed to jot down notes before leaving for home at the end of what routinely was a 17-hour workday. He had been keeping this record since 1981.

"If you get even two or three days behind, it's hard to remember what you did on those days. And to me, that just reinforces why I do it in the first place," Capers said. "So I generally try to write some things down before I go home for the night. It's like brushing your teeth."

The Panthers' first season was filed away in one of those notebooks, and what a season it was.

Seven wins.

A victory over the defending Super Bowl champions—on the road, no less.

Victories at home over the Indianapolis Colts, who would go on to play in the American Football Conference championship game against Pittsburgh; and against the Atlanta Falcons, when a final thrilling goal-line stand kept the Falcons from clinching a playoff berth.

Four wins in a row at one point.

But all of that was in the past for Capers. There was much to do. The coach had to shape the 1996 roster by deciding which of his own free agents to attempt re-signing, which free agents from other teams he wanted to pursue, and who among the 400 or so collegiate draft prospects might fit in best in the Panthers' system.

As he reflected on the first season, though, Capers put off for a moment his agenda for the day and the coming months. He smiled. He savored the season gone by.

He recalled how the Panthers began the season 0–5. Some cynics wondered then if they might just go 0–16.

"I think our players really believed going into every game that they had a chance to win," Capers said. "But when you start out 0–5, it's only natural for them and everyone else to begin wondering if this isn't your typical expansion team."

The typical expansion team might have expected to start out 0–5. There were six franchises who preceded the Panthers down the NFL expansion path, beginning with the 1960 Dallas Cowboys, who went 0–11–1. The Cowboys were followed by the 1961 Minnesota Vikings, who went 3–11 their first year, as did the 1966 Atlanta Falcons and the 1967 New Orleans Saints.

And except for Dallas, those were the expansion overachievers.

The last two teams to join the league in 1976—the Seattle Seahawks and the infamous Tampa Bay Buccaneers—combined to win two games and lose 26 their first season. The Seahawks won both contests and went 2–12; the Buccaneers went 0–14 and eventually lost 26 consecutive games before winning one.

From the start, however, the Panthers never expected to be like "your typical expansion team."

Capers remembered the disappointment that gnawed at him after the fifth loss in a row, 31–27 to the Chicago Bears at Soldier Field. He was frustrated, angry and a little heartbroken after the game slipped away in the final two minutes. But he was determined to present a different image to his players in the postgame locker room.

"Hey, we aren't going to change," he told his players. "Whether we're winning or losing, we believe in what we're doing. It's the right way. The way to win is to do things right day in and day out—to set a high standard of consistency and work to that standard every day."

The Panthers won the next week and the week after that, too. In fact, they won their next four games.

Months earlier, no one quite knew what to expect of the first-year Panthers. Sure, some of their veterans—brash guys like cornerback Tim McKyer and linebacker Lamar Lathon— were predicting a big season. But no one paid them much attention.

History showed an expansion team should expect to struggle. Most of them had spent their first NFL season getting outscored by an average of more than two touchdowns per game. The Tampa Bay Bucs, everyone's expansion laughingstock, lost their first five games by the combined total of 120–26, getting shut out three times.

Much of the Panthers' offensive future was pinned on the arm of rookie Kerry Collins, the quarterback from Penn State whom they had selected with the fifth overall pick in the previous April's college draft. But he wasn't necessarily expected to help out at all during the inaugural season; yet he became the starter by the fourth game, injecting life into a moribund offense.

Many of Capers' high hopes for a defense bolstered by multiple signings of veteran free agents were dependent upon the 36-year-old legs and nimble mind of linebacker Sam Mills, plucked from the hands of Capers' former employers in New Orleans. A gamble to be sure, all Mills did was craft the finest all-around season of his 10-year career, one that had included four previous Pro Bowls while with the Saints.

There were the high-profile free agents like defensive end Mike Fox, who along with Mills and defensive back Brett Maxie anchored what would become the seventh-ranked defense in the 30-team NFL.

And there were unsung free agents like Derrick Moore, a running back released in the preseason by San Francisco, who went on to gain more yards than any expansion back in NFL history.

Then there were all the unknowns, the lunchpail players who would become heroes—guys like Willie Green, Eric Guliford, Greg Kragen, Curtis Whitley, Mark Dennis and Matt Elliott—players who were unwanted by their previous teams and looking to find a home, or guys merely looking to extend their playing careers by a year or two.

Green, in many ways, embodied the first-year Panthers. He was one of the Original 10, which is to say he was one of the first 10 free agents the team signed in December of 1994. If any other teams had wanted these guys, they would have already been finishing out the 1994 season in somebody else's uniform.

In the locker room, Green would say just about anything.

"And say it loud, too," mused teammate Dwight Stone. "But Willie's heart is in the right place."

A Muslim, Green would debate the virtues of his religion endlessly. Usually he argued with placekicker John Kasay, a devout Christian who moved his locker from across the room to be next to Green, where they passionately pursued their good-natured debates. When Green felt his points were being misunderstood by Kasay and others on the team, he ordered a box of 20 Korans—the Islam equivilant of the Bible—from the Saudi Arabian embassy and distributed them to those who had questions about it.

"When people want to talk about Christianity, that's fine," Green said. "But when someone wants to talk about Islam, all you hear about are the terrorists who want to blow stuff up. That's not what being a Muslim is about."

Green was out to smash that perception and a thousand others about African Americans, fellow Muslims and professional athletes. He relished being a role model and was a solid citizen, even if his sometimes zany antics in the locker room might be misleading. He wasn't about perceptions; he was about being real.

"I went to the mall one day and some guy who recognized me came up to me and said, 'Where are all your bodyguards?'" Green said. "I suppose some guys may feel like they need them, but even if people knew who I was, I wouldn't want to be like that. I want to be just a regular guy that anyone can come up and talk to. We might be professional athletes, but we're really no different from anyone else when you get right down to it."

Green is always trying to learn, and was taking a night class in English literature at Winthrop University as the Panthers' first season unfolded. When he was 45 minutes late for the class one Monday evening after catching a 44-yard touchdown pass to send the Panthers' regular-season opener at Atlanta into overtime, Green's teacher admonished him.

"I don't like people who are tardy to my class, Mr. Green," Professor Dorothy Thompson said.

Then she looked him over and noticed he was dressed a little fancy for her class. Green was wearing a suit.

"Why are you dressed up? You didn't schedule a job interview for my class time, did you?" she asked.

"No," replied Green, "I didn't have an interview. I was *being* interviewed. On TV."

"On TV? For what?" Thompson pressed.

Willie Green, the mild-mannered student who sat in the back of class, paused while he tried to decide whether to reveal his alter ego, Willie Green the wide receiver and locker-room conversationalist for the Carolina Panthers.

Finally, Green asked: "Did you see the Panthers' game Sunday?"

"Not much of it," she replied. "I only saw the part at the end where this guy made a great catch. His name was Willie something. . . ."

This time, Dorothy Thompson was the one who paused, her eyes growing wide.

"Are you that Willie Green?" she asked.

"I am," Green said, smiling. "And I'm late because I was on Dom Capers' TV show. I'll try not to be late again."

In the Carolina locker room, everyone knew Willie. His locker stall was the place to stop for lively conversation, funny stories, and thought-provoking tidbits. Once, Green talked about homosexuals in the locker room.

"You know what Greg Louganis said: 'There are two in every locker room.' So I'm always looking out," said Green, laughing.

Willie Green is loose, exciting, verbose and fun to be around. He also is far more talented on the football field than any other NFL team had thought possible.

Just like the first-year Panthers.

For Capers, days during the season began promptly at 5 A.M. Each week, the Panthers crafted a game plan that was placed in a binder, a copy of which was handed out to each player. Offensive players received one binder; defensive players another. Each usually contained between 400 and 500 pages of information and weighed approximately four pounds. It contained a "ready-list" that detailed every single offensive and defensive call that might need to be made during the coming game, complete with diagrams and a "script" that could be followed on various videotapes during meetings with coaches, so players could visualize what would be happening on the field.

As Capers idly fingered through the defensive game plan from the week of the Indianapolis contest—which produced a 13–10 Carolina victory—he slipped into coachspeak:

"Here's a 3–4 package, then you get into a 4–3 package, and then you get into a substitution of personnel and your red-zone stuff and your dime packages, your different fronts . . . zone calls, man calls, blitz calls . . . another front . . . a Hail Mary situation . . . Jumbo, which is a short-yardage situation . . . and your goal-line package."

Capers chattered on about the players' need to understand the significance of "OKIE-SAM-WILL with a RIP-LIZ call" and displayed how this was cross-referenced in a back section of the game-plan binder, complete with a diagram and written explanation. He talked about different formations, like TENS, which is a two tight end set; and FLUSH, which is a set that includes four wide receivers. He also talked about FLUSH GUN, ACE and JACKS.

"It's a different language," he said. "It's like a deck of cards."

He paged through the binder some more, and showed how every mental error from every practice and every game during the season was documented. He thumbed through a section on the Colts' offensive tendencies, gleaned from taking every single play Indianapolis had run from the previous five games and punching them into a computer. Every single play the Colts ran over the previous five weeks, in fact, was diagrammed.

"You've got three- and five-step drop-pass plays, play-action passes, screens, first- and second-down passes, third-down passes, red-zone passes, short-yardage and goal-line passes, dogs and blitzes and notes," Capers rattled on as he turned the pages.

There was a review of the previous week's game, including a list of every single play on offense and defense and whether it was judged a "win" or a "loss" from the Panthers' perspective.

"If we hold the other team to three yards or less on a run, that's a win for us," Capers explained.

There also was a section on Colts personnel, typewritten notes from each team meeting pertaining to the game and a list of "alerts" and "musts" that was hammered home during a final pregame team meeting Saturday night at the Ramada Inn in Clemson, South Carolina, where the Panthers played their first season of home games.

The binder was, in a word, incredible.

It illustrated why someone like Sam Mills, who not only understood and comprehended the volumes of information, but had the knack to convert that knowledge to usefulness on the field and relay it to others, was so valuable to everything the Panthers tried to accomplish on defense.

"He's like a Rhodes scholar," Capers said. "You can see as you go through this, it's like preparing for a test—and your test is on Sunday."

The binder also illustrated Capers' belief in preparation down to the tiniest detail.

"You're trying to reinforce the things you tell them," Capers said. "If we're going to state that attention to detail and the little things are important and are what wins games, then we have to monitor those things very closely.

"The whole key, to me, is to provide constant feedback. If I'm going to go off on this journey, every so often I want to know where I am on the journey—and if I'm on course or not. As you go through a season, there is always a tendency to get knocked off course. So you always have to try to bump yourself back on course, and this is a tool that enables you to accomplish that."

Capers' attention to detail was evident not only in the grandiose game plans he and his staff produced every week, but in the very makeup of the roster itself.

Sure, everyone knew acquiring a talent like Collins would be important. But Mills? Some thought he was almost finished when the Panthers signed him for two years. And Mike Fox, the important "push guy inside" on the Panthers' defense, the guy who made it extremely difficult for opponents to run the football? Many critics thought the Panthers totally blew it by signing him for $9 million over five years.

"He was the first free agent we signed," said Capers, "and if I had it to do all over again, he'd be the first free agent we'd sign again."

And what about guys like long-snapper Mark Rodenhauser, a player Capers really wanted? Rodenhauser was 34, had been left exposed by the Detroit Lions in the expansion allocation draft, and only took the field when his team either was punting or attempting a field goal. Surely an expansion team had more pressing needs, but Capers made it a priority to make certain someone with experience, like Rodenhauser, was on the inaugural roster.

"There's no quicker way to lose a ball game than to have a snap go over the head of your punter or your placekicker during the heat of battle," Capers said.

That never happened once during Carolina's first season, thanks to Capers' foresight and Rodenhauser's exceptional devotion to his singular duty. The first time in Panthers ' history a snap goes over the head of a waiting punter or placekicker will be a surprise to Capers.

"I don't like surprises," Capers said.

Yet Capers was the first to admit he is capable of making mistakes. During a team meeting the first week of training camp at Wofford College in Spartanburg, South Carolina, he made one he would be reminded of often by a certain player throughout the coming season.

"Listen up, guys," he told his players that day. "Many of you come here from successful college programs where it may have been easy for you to win certain games. But this is the NFL. There are no Penn States versus Northwesterns here. Every week is a tough struggle."

Toward the back of the room, fullback Bob Christian, a Northwestern alum, cleared his throat loudly.

"There will be no easy games, no weeks off, like when a Penn State might play a Northwestern in college," Capers continued.

Christian cleared his throat again. Louder this time.

"Hey, take it easy on Northwestern, will ya Coach?" Christian blurted out.

Later, a smiling Capers said of the incident: "Everybody in there kind of looked at Bob and started giving him a hard time. Then I realized what I had said. I never thought about us having a guy from Northwestern sitting in there."

The coach also didn't think Northwestern would shed 25 years of mediocrity, rise as high as number three in the national rankings, and represent the Big Ten in the Rose Bowl for the first time since 1949.

In many ways, then, the 1995 Panthers were to professional football what the 1995 Northwestern Wildcats were to college football. They were a surprise to everyone but themselves; they were refreshing; and they grew to believe they were laying the foundation for great success in the not-too-distant future.

THE BEGINNING

Chasing a Franchise

The 10-year promise started long before the Panthers became the most successful expansion team in NFL history. Just two days after finishing six and a half years of hard work to secure an expansion franchise for his home region, team owner Jerry Richardson was making his next pledge. He was standing on a dusty lot in uptown Charlotte, which by the opening kickoff of 1996 would be graced with a state-of-the-art football stadium.

"We didn't get into this for funsies," said Richardson on Friday, October 29, 1993, to a crowd of some 50,000 Panthers fans who were celebrating the previous Tuesday's announcement that NFL owners voted unanimously to place a team in the Carolinas. "Our goal is to put together an organization and coaching staff so that one day we're going to be standing here in this same area celebrating our first Super Bowl."

The crowd erupted into hoots and hollers and applause.

Richardson politely stood until it was quiet.

"Wait a minute. You missed the best part. . . . Our first Super Bowl victory within 10 years."

There were more whoops and cheers, even if most people in the crowd considered such a championship wishful thinking.

Who could blame Richardson for his enthusiasm? As he told the fans, "It might be all right to puff our chests out for a couple of days."

Mike McCormack, the eventual team president who served as adviser to the bid, followed his boss to the podium.

"Jerry, is nine years within 10?" he asked, still not quite believing what he had just heard.

"Scared me to death," McCormack said later. He told one reporter, half-jokingly, "Don't believe a word I said on stage."

For his part, Richardson denied being swept up by the week's triumphant events, which seemed to include standing ovations everywhere he went.

"No, it wasn't spontaneous," he said about his bold prediction. "It's right here in my notes."

Nobody dared point out that the last two expansion teams, Tampa Bay and Seattle (McCormack's former employer), hadn't made the Super Bowl in their 17 years in the league. The Atlanta and New Orleans franchises, soon to be division rivals, had participated in more than 60 NFL seasons between them and were still waiting to make pro football's ultimate game.

For at least a couple of days, touchdowns and blitzes and the competitive reality of the NFL didn't matter. It was time for Carolinians to puff out their chests a bit.

The drive is an easy one from Charlotte to Jerry Richardson's house in Spartanburg, South Carolina. It takes a little more than an hour, a straight shot about 70 miles west on the interstate highway.

Back in April of 1987, Richardson pointed his car on the familiar route, but somewhere over the state border his whole life took a turn that would bring him to a new and uncharted destination. In fact, the scenic part of the trip has just started.

"As I was driving on I-85, I heard on the radio Charlotte had been selected as the first city to get a new NBA expansion franchise. Not only selected, but the first city selected. I was shocked," said Richardson.

"I was one of the people who had bought season tickets prior to the selection of the city. Only a few thousand people did so, but I was supportive of bringing a professional sports franchise to the Carolinas. I really was not optimistic they would get the team."

Yet the Hornets had pulled it off. Now Richardson was thinking, "Why not a football team, too?" He realized it was a bit crazy, and maybe not the ideal fit for his substantial investment portfolio. A longtime personal goal was to be free of debt by age 50, something Richardson had just accomplished the previous summer.

"We started my business when I was 25 [funding a Hardee's franchise with $4,864 in playoff winnings he earned as a rookie wide receiver for the Baltimore Colts in 1959]. Over time, we had to borrow a large sum of money to grow our business [now called Flagstar, with more than 1,500 company-owned and franchised Denny's, 600 Hardee's, 211 Quincy's, and 210 El Pollo Loco restaurants]. The year before, on July 18, I recalled sending a letter to Hugh McColl [chief operating officer of NationsBank] saying I'm 50, and we achieved our goal. I was real proud."

This didn't stop him from dreaming as the radio played.

"I thought about things for a couple of days, then I went to see Hugh. It was sometime in April. I told him I would very much like to try to get an NFL franchise for the Carolinas. I needed his help to do it because I didn't want to have to ask taxpayers to help pay for the facility. He and I talked about it over the phone and in person for a couple of months."

Even more important discussions were taking place in the Richardson household.

One Sunday afternoon Richardson and his youngest son, Mark, fresh from earning a master's in business administration at the University of Virginia, were rocking on the front porch at the family vacation home at Lake James.

"I'm thinking about trying to bring an NFL franchise to the Carolinas," said Jerry. "We need somebody to manage it and work it on a daily basis. Would you be interested in doing that?"

Well, uh, yeah, sure, Mark told his dad. He had never heard his father say one thing about wanting to own a pro football team. The two shared an intense interest in football—Mark played linebacker at Clemson during the 1981 national championship season—but watching games on the weekend is a long way from operating an NFL franchise. The two decided Mark, 27 at the time, would handle the day-to-day operational details and be based in Charlotte.

"I'm not sure if he hired me or assigned me," Mark said in 1992. "We understood going in that what we're trying to do is a big gamble and risk, that you put five years [it turned out to be six and a half] of your time, effort, and money into a project that may never come to fruition. We understood and accepted that."

Mark was excited by the possibilities but not without some fear. He didn't even tell his wife-to-be, Joan, about the possible bid for three months.

The reaction of Jerry Richardson's other son, Jon, was as vastly different as the distance from the Lake James home in South Carolina to Duck Beach at the upper easternmost reaches of North Carolina's seashore near Nags Head. Duck Beach is where Jerry and Jon took a stroll in the sand a few weeks after Mark first heard his father's latest brainstorm.

"Why would you want to take on a football team?" asked Jon, who had completed his MBA degree at the University of North Carolina and, along with his wife, Kathleen, developed a successful home services business in Chapel Hill. "It's so risky. You don't need to take on something that big."

Jerry listened to his son and appreciated the honesty.

"It's important for the family to understand what we're doing. I wanted you to know," said Jerry.

It wasn't that Jon didn't love the game of football. He was a star wide receiver at North Carolina and was even invited to try out with his father's old team , the Baltimore Colts, in 1982. He simply worried that his dad was taking on too much.

Nonetheless, six months later, by January of 1994, Jon joined his father and brother as director of the new stadium construction project in Charlotte. Jon and Kathleen sold the Chapel Hill business.

While the two brothers are different—Mark seeks the media spotlight and drives a Dodge Viper, Jon is happy to work behind the scenes and comfortable in his Ford Bronco—they have displayed a common denominator their father most appreciates.

"The team is probably the only way the two boys and I could be working together," said the elder Richardson. "Mark works on the business side, Jon is responsible for the stadium, and I spend a lot of time on league affairs. We have our own areas. It gives me a firsthand look. I can see that both boys are very hardworking and conscientious. It's the most rewarding part of the whole process for me."

Jon Richardson's skepticism was shared in the early days of the Carolina Panthers by marketing consultant Max Muhleman, widely credited with generating the impressive fan-base statistics (more than 9 million people in a 150-mile radius) that wooed the NBA to bring the Hornets to town. When Jerry and Mark Richardson came calling for a similar workup of the marketing numbers—at the recommendation of banker McColl—Muhleman was intrigued but not overly impressed.

"I thought they were nice people, but I didn't think they could get it done," Muhleman recalled. "I didn't think they understood the magnitude of what had to be done."

Said Richardson: "I remember he wasn't as enthusiastic about it as I was."

The Richardsons and Muhleman at least agreed to meet again.

"Have you thought about a stadium?" asked Muhleman at the second get-together.

"Yeah, we've thought about it. We've decided we'll build our own," said Jerry.

Ouch, Muhleman remembered thinking.

"It had never occurred to me people would take on both a private stadium and a franchise that was probably going to cost them $100 million. As far as I know, it's never been done," he later explained.

As it turns out, Muhleman was underestimating the actual cost of the franchise and stadium. So did Richardson and others when he met with son Mark, Muhleman, McColl, attorney Richard Thigpen Jr. (now the Panthers general counsel), and John Lewis of Arthur Anderson and Company.

The group of friends and businessmen figured the stadium would cost $85 million (they spent nearly $100 million above that before the grand opening in late summer 1996). Since the NFL hadn't actually formalized plans for expansion—and certainly hadn't committed to a price per franchise—Richardson and the others estimated a franchise might cost $50 million.

Wrong. The franchise fee in 1993 was $140 million. Plus, the Panthers accepted three years of reduced television revenues, totaling a loss of $69 million, and agreed to delay participation in the league's highly profitable licensing arm, NFL Properties, for 18 months. The team paid another $10 million in interest on a loan to cover the entry fee after the expansion announcement and abandoned its original proposal to ask for a break on revenue sharing of special club seating to help retire the stadium debt quicker. Total bill: more than $220 million.

"If I thought it was going to cost $220 million for the franchise and $183 million for the stadium, I never would have started going after a team. The cost is so overwhelming," Richardson said.

Lucky for the football fans of North and South Carolina, Richardson was locked into doing something special for the region. Like an all-star receiver not afraid to risk a hard tackle when going into the middle part of the field for a pass, Richardson kept his focus on the end result. His business associates were anything but surprised.

Born in Spring Hope, North Carolina, Richardson played football at Wofford College in Spartanburg, South Carolina, where he still lives today with his wife, Rosalind, and where the Panthers attend summer training camp. He was good enough to make the NFL champion Colts as a rookie in the 1959 season. He even caught a Johnny Unitas touchdown pass in the title game (and keeps a game ball and pair of Johnny U's cleats on display in his Spartanburg home).

Yet he fashioned bigger things—and greater financial rewards—for himself. His salary for his third season in 1961 was planned to be $9,750. He decided football was holding him back. He walked out of training camp and invested $4,864 of his playoff winnings from 1959 in the first franchise of the rapidly growing Hardee's hamburger chain. He was partners with his Wofford roommate and team quarterback, Charlie Bradshaw, opening a restaurant on Kennedy Street in downtown Spartanburg.

The original franchise still stands, but there have been hundreds more since then, along with other restaurant chains and several different corporate structures. Flagstar is presently the largest publicly held corporation in South Carolina and employs more than 100,000 people nationwide. Richardson resigned as CEO in May of 1995 to concentrate on football matters, but not before gaining the reputation as a masterful manager who relates well to his workers. For years he started some days by arriving at various company-owned Hardee's and pitching in to make biscuits, pour coffee, or take orders at the drive-through window.

"When I first met Jerry, he wouldn't say a word about football or business until he told me how he did business," said Muhleman. "He said, 'We always tell the truth. We're always on time. We always do what we say we're going to do, and we believe in teamwork and harmony.' "

Perhaps Richardson's finest moments as a businessman came during what could have been a public relations nightmare. As Richardson was in the final stages of bidding for the Panthers franchise, 32 African-American customers of Denny's outlets in California filed a class-action lawsuit charging racial discrimination in the form of refusing services, putting minorities in segregated areas, and making African-Americans pay for food in advance. Two days later, six African-American Secret Service agents were denied service at an Annapolis, Maryland, Denny's restaurant while white colleagues were quickly provided meals.

Within two months, Richardson took action by reading an accord with the NAACP to oversee a program to randomly check all Denny's restaurants for any discriminatory practices. Plus, Richardson agreed to create more minority opportunities in franchises, vendor contracts, and training. The NAACP was planning to present sensitivity training programs to Denny's employees, and more blacks would be used in advertisements. There was a hot line already in place to report any discrimination incidents.

"I'm hoping the content of the agreement will serve as a future model for corporate America to improve a relationship with the African-American community and other communities throughout the United States," said Benjamin Chavis, director of the NAACP at the time of the agreement on May 30, 1993. Chavis added that Flagstar and the NAACP had been discussing such programs since early 1992.

Richardson had somehow turned a negative into a positive.

By September, when he first met face-to-face with a dozen NFL owners in Chicago, he started by addressing the Denny's situation. There was no fretting about image or possible repercussions for the Carolina bid. Richardson simply wanted to clear the air.

"I shared my point of view," said Richardson. "I asked them if they had any questions about it; I would prefer we discussed that before we went any deeper into the presentation. There weren't any questions about it. They understood my point of view."

In May of 1994, more than six months after the franchise was awarded, Denny's agreed to pay $54 million in damages to thousands of customers in the class-action suits in California and Maryland. It was the largest racial discrimination settlement in history.

In a press conference, Richardson said settling was preferable to expensive legal fees and bad publicity. He emphasized that it was no admission Denny's ever had a policy or practice of discrimination.

"It is not our intent to treat anyone other than with dignity and respect. . . . I will continue to apologize as much as you would like."

The Panthers were almost called the Cougars, but Mark Richardson favored Panthers. He had always liked the animal. His father also wanted his son's suggestions for a color scheme to be used on everything from team uniforms to school backpacks to hats and sweatshirts. Mark jumped at the chance to combine black, silver and blue.

Jerry loved the color choices but wasn't quite sure about the name. NFL Properties, which was worried about too many teams wearing black, suggested purple as the team's dominant colors. The league marketing people offered two alternatives to the name derby: Rhinos and Cobras.

No thanks, said the Richardsons, we'll stick with Panthers and the black-blue-silver color combination. Jerry grew so fond of the name—which wasn't supposed to be made public until the franchise was officially rewarded—that he ordered a special vanity license plate, PNTHRS.

Though Richardson Sports was still four full years away from NFL expansion pay dirt, 1989 was a year of accomplishments. In April, the hiring of Mike McCormack, a Hall of Fame offensive tackle and former NFL head coach and general manager, added even more credibility to an operation that was already getting high marks because Jerry Richardson was making it a point to visit and schmooze with NFL owners at every opportunity. In his first month, McCormack had called contacts at every NFL club at least twice. He prompted a considerable buzz about the quality of the Carolina bid, which had a bit of a late start compared to some of the other cities.

McCormack, whose contract with the Seahawks expired in January, met with Richardson when the prospective owner flew to Seattle. McCormack admits now he first thought Richardson's bid was merely a "pipe dream." After spending some time with Richardson, who can be quite persuasive, McCormack changed his mind.

"I'm here for two reasons," said McCormack at a Charlotte news conference just weeks after the initial meeting. "The first is Jerry Richardson. I think he, his family, and his group represent the type of ownership the league is looking for.

"My second reason is the demographics of this area make this the best potential new market for the NFL."

In August of 1989, the Richardsons hosted a preseason game before a sellout crowd of 52,855 at Raleigh's Carter-Finley Stadium between the New York Jets and Philadelphia Eagles. NFL officials attending the game were impressed with the football fever of fans in this "basketball country." Sure, North Carolina is the home of Michael Jordan and a fistful of college basketball powers, but its denizens are equally passionate about fall football weekends.

By early September of 1989, Richardson had filled out his core group of partners (he later added Charlotte insurance executive William E. Sims, the first minority member of the ownership group). Family partners included Jerry, Rosalind, Mark, Jon, and daughter Ashley Allen. Other announced investors were retailers John and Tom Belk, real estate developers Howard "Smoky" Bissell and John Harris, food distributors Jerry and Steve Wordsworth, and Century 21 Real Estate CEO Dick Loughlin. Leon Levine, chairman and CEO of Family Dollar Stores, later joined what is now an 18-partner group.

In the early going, Richardson corresponded regularly with the partners, especially to keep them optimistic about the bid's chances of landing a team in the Carolinas. Perhaps attempting some form of male camaraderie, Richardson used various acronyms to punctuate his own enthusiasm.

Letters often arrived with w.g.g.t.f.f. scrawled or typed toward the bottom of the page. It was code for "We're gonna get that fucking franchise."

Another common set of initials was "B and B" to signify "black and blue," the colors Richardson wanted all along. The purple uniforms touted by the NFL were the real pipe dream here.

NFL commissioner Paul Tagliabue first announced formal plans for expansion in April of 1990. He said the league would add two teams for the 1993 season, making it an even 30 with five clubs in each division. Sounded simple enough—until labor unrest was layered over the scenario. Stalled negotiations for a new collective bargaining agreement with the players ultimately cost Carolina fans two seasons. After cutting the field of competitors from 11 to 5 (Charlotte, Jacksonville, Baltimore, St. Louis, and Memphis) during 1992, the NFL decided late in the year to postpone expansion until the 1995 season. This timetable was cinched when a seven-year labor agreement was reached in early January 1993.

A few weeks later, during Super Bowl week in Los Angeles, the Richardsons met with former NFL commissioner Pete Rozelle, who was still calling the shots when this whole dance got started in 1987. He had agreed to be a special adviser to the Carolina franchise, keeping tabs on owner sentiment toward the expansion cities.

The news from Rozelle was not encouraging.

"I don't think you're going to get a team," he told Mark and Jerry Richardson. "You've got to figure out a way to get the taxpayers involved."

This seemed an odd concept, but apparently owners were convinced the other expansion cities would have more stable and loyal fans because stadiums were being publicly funded. This troubled Richardson, whose plan all along was not to burden the Carolina taxpayers. He was also facing the problem of escalating costs. The partnership group had already spent more than $5 million in lobbying efforts alone (they budgeted $500,000), and it was clear by now that expansion fees and stadium costs were going to be much higher than anticipated.

Another problem: Other cities were emphasizing taxpayer nonparticipation as a negative aspect about the Carolina bid, and some owners were buying it.

"People seemed to spend a lot of energy on why we shouldn't get it rather than concentrate on why their cities should get a team," said Richardson.

Even so, the Panthers group had a problem and needed to solve it.

That's where Louis Howell comes in.

"The first time I ever heard of the concept of permanent-seat licenses (PSLs) was from Louis Howell, who was general counsel of Spartan Foods, our company at the time," said Richardson. "Back when we first started the expansion effort, he said, 'What I think we should do, when we start selling season tickets, I think we should charge $1,000 for the right to purchase a season ticket.'"

Richardson contemplated the notion but didn't think much about it until mid-1992 when it appeared the stadium costs would be more than double the original plan. He got to thinking about Lewis Howard's idea and whether it would fly. PSLs moved past the thinking stages when it was clear the NFL was fretting about the Carolinas' lack of taxpayer participation.

"As costs escalated we had to think about ways to raise more money," said Richardson. "I noticed Hornets tickets were already sold out and newspapers were running [classified] ads asking up to $8,000 to buy the right to purchase someone's two season tickets.

"Plus, in the South, as you know, it's not unusual to have people be members of the Wolfpack Club or IPTAY (Clemson's booster club) or on and on. They make annual contributions and get privileges in return, like premium season tickets."

The concept actually worked on many levels. It would show a fan commitment—one even stronger than the taxpayer argument because fans were laying out anywhere from $600 to $5,400 of taxable dollars to get a seat in the new Carolinas Stadium—and what's more, the PSL brainstorm would generate significant funds to cover construction costs.

Richardson saw one more benefit.

"The fans will take care of the stadium. They're not going to trash it. These fans will be off the charts. You hear about all these other teams with fan clubs of 30,000 or 50,000 or 100,000 members. That pales next to 50,000 people willing to put up this kind of money.

"We believe the fans who come to our stadium will have an investment far beyond any other in professional sports. Their expectations are going to be high, and they should be. They're going to expect us to do well on the field."

The Richardsons had trouble selling the NFL on permanent-seat licenses. An ironic twist when you consider division rival St. Louis, which lost out to Carolina and Jacksonville for an expansion franchise, later wooed the Los Angeles Rams by selling PSLs to its new Trans World Dome. Moreover, Jerry Richardson is now head of the NFL stadium committee and is widely praised for his state-of-the-art facility built with private money.

The Panthers group kept lobbying and urging, finally getting the go-ahead to start selling PSLs on July 1, 1993. "It was no small task," said Richardson. "It had never been done before."

The original sales program was a wild success. Panthers fans bought 48,500 PSLs in two months—41,632 in the first four days—purchasing the transferable right to buy season tickets for life. Some companies opted for large blocks of PSLs so employees could buy season tickets as a job perk. In all, the initial PSL campaign raised $54 million, and NationsBank and Wachovia banks committed to buying any remaining PSLs (62,000 in total were available and 7,272 tickets will be available for individual games without any rights fee) on July 1, 1996, for up to $30 million.

The banks might be doing more than a community service in picking up any slack in PSL sales. Some observers think the Panthers PSLs will only appreciate over time.

Fans in Greensboro/Winston-Salem/High Point bought the second-highest number of PSLs, following Charlotte residents. Greenville-Spartanburg was third, supporting the two-state argument, while Raleigh-Durham was fourth highest and Columbia fifth. Some 1,000 PSLs were sold as far away as Roanoke, Virginia (Washington Redskins country), and Bristol, Tennessee.

The PSLs basically sealed the deal for Carolina. A large group of league officials visited Charlotte in September simply to learn more about the seat-licensing setup. Jerry Richardson had turned another negative into a positive.

On the night of October 26, 1993, Jerry and Mark Richardson and Max Muhleman were sitting in a meeting room in the Chicago O'Hare Hyatt Regency Hotel. Next door were the 28 NFL owners who had just voted on expansion teams.

"You realize where we are, don't you?" Mark Richardson asked his father.

It was the same room where the Richardsons and Muhleman had made their final 15-minute pitch earlier in the day. Mark was smiling; he knew victory was near.

"Do you think they would bring us here to tell us we lost?" asked Jerry.

"No way," said Mark. "We're here so they can tell us we won."

The son who had worked so many long hours on his dad's dream was right, of course. He couldn't stop smiling.

Jerry told him to stop it, he looked like the Cheshire cat. "We've got to be humble," he added.

Then Ed McCaskey, the 74-year-old president of the venerable Chicago Bears, walked into the room.

"Jerry, well done," said McCaskey.

Then the jovial Bears executive turned to Muhleman, the marketing whiz who had delivered an impromptu and moving speech about Jerry's upstanding character at the final owners presentation before the vote.

"Max, if I ever have a heart transplant, I want you to talk to my doctor."

Mark Richardson couldn't get the grin off his face no matter how hard he tried.

"I can't believe it," said Jerry. "I just can't believe. Can you believe we got this thing?"

It was only fitting that Ed McCaskey was the first NFL official to deliver the good news. His father-in-law, the late and legendary George Halas, was the first former NFL player to own a franchise. Jerry Richardson is the second.

Where to start. Maybe with the 72,685 extra-wide cushy seats, all of which have been installed by hand and positioned to face the middle of the field. Or maybe the bronze panther statues at each of the $1 million entrances. Perhaps the cutting-edge sound system and two huge scoreboards with 24-foot by 36-foot color replay screens for optimal viewing at any place in the facility. Possibly just the fact that Carolinas Stadium is open-air and sports natural grass.

This stadium is clearly Jerry Richardson's pride and joy. One way to slow down this man on the move is ask him about the Panthers' new house, with adjacent practice facilities and team offices.

"We visited almost every stadium in country," said Richardson. "We went to all the special places, like Camden Yards in Baltimore. We took all the good ideas and put them in our stadium.

"It will be a fan-friendly and player-friendly place. I'm not aware of any dressing room that is any larger than ours. It is 45 yards long and 15 yards wide.

"We have never done anything to compromise the fans. Take the Jacksonville franchise. Our stadiums were built at the same time but theirs is $134 million and ours is $184 million. Why? Because ours has more fan features.

"Can you imagine how a 10-year-old will feel walking into this place for the first time? It's going to be quite a thrill. It's going to be wonderful."

The Architects

When team president Mike McCormack persuaded Bill Polian to join the Panthers as general manager in January 1994, he hired a guy with definite designs on the top job.

McCormack wanted it that way.

The master plan, as McCormack explained to Polian during the interview process, was to build a team together. Two veteran NFL minds—greatly respected around the league and similar in work ethic and ability to judge talent, if not personality—building a winner from scratch. It would be the chance of a lifetime.

Then they would run it together for a while before McCormack, 64 at the time, stepped aside and let Polian become number-one man on the football side. It was all quite civil and a sound business plan.

But on the night of January 8, 1994, even before Polian's hiring and McCormack's promotion from GM to team president could be announced to the media, the plan appeared to be in serious jeopardy.

After a leisurely Friday evening dinner with friends, McCormack and his wife, Ann, retired for the night at their Charlotte home. Everything was falling into place, McCormack thought, as he fell asleep.

But a short while later, McCormack awoke and could not go back to sleep. Maybe it was something he ate? Maybe a little heartburn? The discomfort lingered, and McCormack had to admit to himself that something was wrong.

"I just felt funny," he recalled. "So I got up, fuming."

His wife sat up with him.

"What's the matter with you?" she asked.

"I don't know," McCormack said. "I just feel strange."

A glass of milk, which worked the trick on other sleepless nights, didn't help matters. Within the hour, Ann convinced her husband that maybe he'd better call a doctor or even visit the emergency room at Presbyterian Hospital.

About 18 hours after that, McCormack lay on an operating table, his chest cut open as physicians scrambled to complete quadruple bypass heart surgery.

He never actually had a heart attack, but he was dangerously close to having a massive one, according to his doctors. When he awoke Sunday morning, one of the doctors who performed the operation was waiting bedside with a message for him.

"You were two hours away from us reading about you in the newspaper," the doctor said. "It's a good thing you came in."

Mike McCormack, a bear of a man who stands six-four, has never smoked and has always stayed within a few pounds of the weight he played at as a 248-pound tackle for 10 seasons in the National Football League. He is accustomed to life going according to plan—as long as you have a good plan. So is Bill Polian. Together, they are the architects of the Carolina Panthers.

A friendly Irishman with a reddish complexion accentuating a full, round face and a head of white hair that by 1994 made him resemble Norman Rockwell's all-American vision of a gregarious grandfather, McCormack was born in Chicago on June 21, 1930. He was barely one year old when his father, Michael, decided to move the family to Kansas City, Missouri, where he felt he had a better chance of keeping a steady job as a heat-pipe insulator. Once there, three more children followed. Mike McCormack was the oldest in a family that must have seemed small to his father, who was one of 11 children himself, and who had emigrated from Ireland when he was 16 years old.

One of the first things Michael McCormack did upon arriving in the United States was adopt the Notre Dame Fighting Irish as his football team. As a youth, Mike McCormack would sit with his father around the radio on Saturday afternoons and listen to Notre Dame games.

"I'm not sure I knew all the nuances of football when we started doing that," McCormack said. "But it seemed like he enjoyed it so much that I got a kick out of it. I had never seen a football game. It wasn't like you watched it on television. You listened to it, and you might see some highlights on a newsreel at the matinees and things like that, like the Movietone News. Even that wasn't a regular thing, but that was about the only time I saw it."

Nonetheless, it wasn't long before young Mike McCormack started imitating the plays he heard described each Saturday afternoon during the football season. And when he wasn't doing that, he was playing baseball or basketball with other kids in the neighborhood.

"We had vacant lots on almost every other corner, so there was always a baseball game, a football game or something else going on in one of those lots in our neighborhood," McCormack said. "It was an active life. . . . We didn't have the finest things in life, but we always seemed to be able to do what we wanted to do."

By the sixth grade, Mike McCormack was playing football in the Catholic Youth Organization. He was a little bigger than the average size for kids his age, with strapping shoulders and powerful legs. By the time he was in high school, he already was six-three. He played center on the school's basketball team and played fullback and defensive tackle on the football squad.

His father didn't get to see his first live football game until Mike was in high school. One of the first games he saw, Mike, playing fullback, took a handoff on a fake-punt play and attempted to run with it. He didn't get far. The opposing team was not tricked and tackled him quickly.

Afterward, Michael McCormack sought out his son.

"Boy, you really did that well," he said of the particular play. "I could follow where the ball was going real well the whole time."

Mike McCormack simply nodded.

"I didn't have the heart to tell him that you're not supposed to be able to follow where the ball is going on that play. That wasn't the idea," he said nearly a half-century later, chuckling at the memory.

From high school, it was on to the University of Kansas and more football. The sport paid for his education via a scholarship. He had heard of professional football, but didn't know much about it.

The *Kansas City Star* newspaper and its celebrated sports editor, one C. E. McBride, did not have a high opinion of professional football in 1951, when McCormack graduated from Kansas. On McBride's direction, scores from the pro games were never printed. The only time he mentioned the sport on the pro level at all was when players from area colleges were drafted, and even then he permitted only a small box under the heading "Area boys drafted," followed by their names, the teams that drafted them and nothing else.

"Not a single sentence," McCormack said.

The list wasn't always produced in a timely manner. McCormack was drafted by the old New York Yanks in 1951 and didn't even know it until a phone call came from a scout, Jack White, saying he was in town to offer McCormack a contract.

"The draft was right after the first of the year, and I didn't hear anything," said McCormack, who was working as a graduate assistant on the Kansas coaching staff at the time. "Then I got the phone call. I didn't know anything about it. So I just said, 'Sure, come on by and we'll talk.'"

White dropped by and offered McCormack $6,000 to play for the Yanks in the up-coming 1951 season. One week prior to that, McCormack had been offered a contract to teach and coach at a high school on a nine-month deal for $2,700, or $300 a month.

"And on that, I had to go to school in the summer to work on my master's at my own expense," McCormack said.

The math was easy, the way McCormack figured it. The $6,000 would be for three or four months work, no more.

"Well, I ought to try it then," he said to himself, figuring he would play three years to get a financial headstart on whatever his real life's work would be.

"Thirteen years later," said McCormack with a laugh, "I retired."

McCormack played for the 1951 College All-Stars against the Cleveland Browns in Chicago, and the next day he was in Ripon, Wisconsin, to scrimmage with the Yanks.

"I didn't know what to expect," he said. "But it was football. I was projected as the starting right tackle. They plugged me right in there, so I started playing."

He played right through the Korean War, although he was drafted into the army in 1952. Shortly after arriving at Fort Larry Wood in Missouri, where they couldn't find a uniform shirt big enough to fit him, McCormack was ordered to see a colonel who asked him if he wanted to play football for the base team.

"I played football that season and took my basic training after the season," McCormack said. "Then I stayed and played the next year, too. I really think if it hadn't been for football, I would have been in Korea.

"I was in the Army Corp of Engineers. They built things like the Inchon Reservoir. . . . It was not a [good] place to be. We had a Captain Kelly in our outfit who did a tour in Korea. He came back and said, 'Man, it was so cold there were a lot of soldiers who wouldn't even get out of their sleeping bags.' They were getting overrun and they didn't even get out of their sleeping bags. They were being bayoneted (to death) right there. Man, hearing that was scary."

McCormack stayed out of Korea by playing football against other base teams, like the one coached by Al Davis, the feisty future owner of the Oakland Raiders, at Fort Jackson. Competition was fierce.

"The post commanders at each one of these bases was tied into their teams," McCormack said. "I don't know if they gambled or not, but they wanted their teams to win."

McCormack's did. They were the Fifth Army champions both years he played, and he was runner-up for the All-Army Player of the Year award to Ollie Matson, who later would be inducted into the Pro Football Hall of Fame after playing 14 NFL seasons as a halfback with the Cardinals, Rams, Lions and Eagles.

Meanwhile, the rights to McCormack as a professional football player were being transferred all over the place. The Yanks' franchise moved to Dallas, then sold McCormack's contract to the Baltimore Colts—all while McCormack continued playing for Fort Wood and drawing a paycheck from Uncle Sam.

Even before he returned to civilian life in 1953, after serving his two-year hitch in the army, McCormack discovered he had caught the eye of Paul Brown, coach of the Cleveland Browns, and a man who would go on to have the biggest influence in McCormack's career. Brown first took a liking to McCormack during the 1950 East-West College All-Star Game, where McCormack was one of only about six players to play both offense and defense, helping the West to an upset win over the heavily favored East.

By 1953, Brown was willing to send 10 players, including a young defensive back named Don Shula, to the Colts for McCormack and two others, defensive tackle Dan Colo and linebacker Tom Catlin. He consummated the trade while McCormack was still in the service.

In early December of 1953, Brown had McCormack fly to Cleveland.

"He wanted me to sign a new contract," McCormack said. "I didn't realize it, but at the time, if you were in the service, your contract expired. So I could have become a free agent and signed with anyone. So that's why he wanted to sign me before the season was over that year."

The Browns had clinched the Eastern Conference title and a spot in the NFL championship game with a win the previous week against the Chicago Cardinals, giving them a 10–0 record heading into the last two games of the regular season, which essentially were now meaningless. McCormack met Brown face-to-face for the first time the night before the Browns hosted the New York Giants in their next-to-last regular-season game.

"Well, we clinched it last week, so I don't know how good we're going to be tomorrow," Brown told McCormack right off. "But you can come and sit on the bench if you like."

McCormack took him up on the offer and watched in amazement as the Browns destroyed the Giants, 62–14, in front of an enthusiastic crowd of 40,235.

"That impressed me, needless to say," McCormack said. "He was very magnanimous. He gave me the same contract I would have had with Dallas when I was drafted [into the army]. I thought, 'Oh, boy, he's a great fella.'"

McCormack didn't come to find out that he could have become a free agent until he was chatting with some of his new teammates during training camp the next summer. He was surprised, but not bitter.

"Hell, looking back on it, that would have been the worst thing I could have done—to become a free agent. . . . I might have ended up in Green Bay," McCormack said. "I enjoyed every minute of my career with the Browns."

McCormack played nine seasons under Brown in Cleveland. In his first season, 1954, McCormack actually started at middle guard on defense, and the Browns won their second NFL championship. In 1955, Brown moved McCormack to starting right tackle, having him anchor the offensive line, and the Browns won another championship. From 1956 until his retirement in 1962, McCormack served as team captain, although the Browns did not win another championship during that time.

Along the way, McCormack blocked for the likes of Jim Brown, Otto Graham and Marion Motley and grew to greatly admire Paul Brown. He later would compare his coach, to Dom Capers, whom he and Bill Polian would agree to hire as the first head coach in the history of the Panthers.

"Paul was a great teacher," McCormack said. "You could go back to Paul's second week of training camp, the third hour of the fourth day—and you were going to be doing the same thing. You were going to be taking a step with your left foot, right foot . . . very similar to Dom.

"[Brown] used to have us write out why we were doing calisthentics, night after night after night. The purpose was to improve our condition, be physically sharp, get mentally ready to play football. We wrote that out longhand every night at the lecture. Then we'd draw up our own plays."

Those lectures are the stuff of legend. Players today might have trouble sitting still for even one of Brown's nightly monologues, which could go on for hours, but he expected his players then to pay attention and take detailed notes of everything he was saying.

"The first lecture was three hours long," McCormack said. "I joked that I was going to have to get my hand in shape to take notes all year long. My legs were fine; it was my hand that needed the work. But he was a great teacher."

Training camps under Brown, decades before the days when the length of camp was dictated by a collective bargaining agreement between players and owners, lasted eight or nine weeks. The days were long. After an early-morning breakfast, the morning practice would be devoted entirely to the running game—but the team would take on only one running play per day and attempt to work it to perfection. After a break for lunch, the team would take on one pass play and attempt to do the same.

The practices were detailed and well organized, and not a minute was squandered. But they weren't as lengthy as the lectures. Most morning practices lasted a little less than two hours and the afternoon sessions rarely went longer than two and a quarter. They would be followed by meetings and the dreaded skull session at night.

"In those days, you have to remember that we didn't have the off-season work, so a lot of the time was devoted to getting us back into shape," McCormack said. "We had three weeks of which you might have 18 days of two-a-days. Then the fourth week, you'd play your first preseason game—and you'd play six preseason games."

By his third season with the Browns, McCormack was a fixture on the offensive line and was making a salary of $9,000. Brown pulled him aside.

"Mike," said the coach, "one of these days you're going to be a five-figure ballplayer. Keep up the good work."

It took McCormack three more seasons to become a five-figure ballplayer. Brown called him in after each of the next two seasons, told him what a great job he was doing, and offered him only one $500 raise.

"Go ask your dad when he ever got a $500 raise in one year," Brown told McCormack when the player protested.

"I can remember Dad coming home as a union man, talking about a two-and-a-half-cent per hour raise," McCormack said. "So [Brown's] logic sounded good to me."

McCormack's last season as a player was 1962, which also was the last year Brown coached the Browns. Art Modell bought the team from a group that included Paul Brown in March of 1961, and then fired Brown after a season filled with disputes.

"It was a shame," McCormack said. "What happened was Paul was one of the owners. They sold out and made a lot of money. But Paul didn't want Modell to have anything to do with the football team. It was almost as if it was still Paul's team. And I remember Art saying one time, 'I didn't pay $800,000 for this team for four season tickets.' He wanted to be involved.

"I retired the same year Paul was fired, but not for that reason. . . . We had three children. When I left for training camp, Ann seemed to be pregnant every year. I was 32, and I told her if she got pregnant again I would retire. So I quit for family reasons. I could have played maybe a year or two longer."

His salary at the time of his retirement was well into five figures at $18,000. Upon his induction into the Hall of Fame in 1984, Brown called him "the finest offensive lineman I have ever coached." And when *USA Today* named its all-time 75th anniversary All-NFL team a decade later, McCormack was listed as one of the three finest tackles to ever play the game.

About the time McCormack was graduating from Kansas and embarking on his lifetime in professional football, William Patrick Polian, born one year and one day after the bombing of Pearl Harbor initated U.S. entry into World War II, was a young boy already making a name for himself in the Bronx. Polian was eight when McCormack played his final season at Kansas, and every spare moment was spent playing sports. Football and baseball were his favorites.

"It was really sort of an idyllic existence," Polian said. "The Bronx of my day has no relationship to what people think of the Bronx today. It was a borough of closely knit neighborhoods, largely broken down along ethnic lines. My neighborhood was pretty much Irish and Jewish. I don't know how many people it consisted of, but it couldn't have been any more than five or six square miles, at best.

"Your life revolved around the school, the [Catholic] church and sports. And, of course, we were fortunate anough to grow up during a time when the second Golden Age of Sports in New York was taking place. I'm sure you've heard the song, 'Willie, Mickey and the Duke,' . . . well, we got to see them play every day.

"You played sports all the time. You talked sports all the time. You went to Yankee Stadium. You went to the Polo Grounds . . . occasionally to Ebbets Field, although that was a long train ride. People didn't have cars in those days, so you took the subway train wherever you went. And you played ball all the time."

"Everybody played every sport. There was no specialization," Polian said. "You played basketball in the wintertime. If you didn't play for the school team, you played CYO ball. You played baseball in the summertime—80 or 100 games. . . . And, of course, with football, once you got to high school, that's where your focus was. That was our existence. That was what we did."

Polian was the oldest of three children borne by his mother, Bernice. His father was Bill Sr., and for a while his maternal grandmother and maternal aunt lived in the same apartment. Then they lived right next door.

"It was a way of life that is entirely unknown to my own children," said Polian, "and perhaps to many people in the country today, except maybe in small towns. The nuclear family was an extended family."

Polian met his future wife, Eileen, when both were in eighth grade, enrolled at Our Lady of Mercy grade school. Upon graduating from high school at Mount Saint Michael Academy, a Catholic school in the Bronx, Polian attended nearby New York University, where he was a starting strong safety and captain of the football team, as well as a member of the wrestling team. It was at NYU where he met and was coached by Bob Windish, whom Polian later would call "without a doubt, the biggest professional influence on my life."

Polian had decided by the time he was a sophomore in high school that he wanted to follow in the footsteps of guys like Howard Smith and Al Kull, football coaches at St. Michael when he played there. And after graduating from NYU in 1966, that's what he did—working for 10 years as an assistant at Manhattan College, the United States Merchant Marine Academy and Columbia University.

He was making about $13,000 a year, Eileen had just had their third of what would be four children, and Polian was becoming frustrated with the profession because he didn't feel he was progressing up the ladder fast enough. It was about this time that Windish, who was by then working for BLESTO, a pro scouting combine, gave Polian a call that began turning his life in a new direction.

Windish and another friend, Jim Garrett, were both working for BLESTO at the time. They invited Polian to go with them on a number of scouting trips.

"You know," Windish told Polian, "you really have an eye for talent. You really ought to think about becoming a talent evaluator on the pro level."

Shortly after Polian began digesting this thought, Windish landed a job as personnel director for the Montreal franchise in the Canadian Football League. Windish called Polian again.

"Look, I can't pay you much more than expenses," Windish said. "But if you'd like to try your hand at it, I've got a job for you as a scout."

Polian already had begun to dabble in the advertising sales business in New York and was doing quite well in that new endeavor, so he jumped at the chance to stay involved in the game he loved, even though he was essentially scouting for free at first.

The head coach in Montreal was Marv Levy. Polian's new path in professional football, though it would be a winding one, was set in motion.

McCormack did not stay out of football for long after retiring from the Browns. He took a two-year break, worked in the insurance business and at first turned down a chance to get into coaching with Lou Saban in Buffalo. In 1966, though, he did not turn down former teammate Otto Graham, who asked him to join his coaching staff in Washington.

Graham was fired after three seasons, but McCormack was retained as offensive line coach and received the opportunity to work one season under Vince Lombardi, the NFL legend who made his mark with the Green Bay Packers by winning five titles in 10 seasons, including victories in Super Bowls I and II. McCormack found Lombardi entirely different from Paul Brown, yet brilliant in his own way.

"He made you believe that you were going to be in such great physical condition that the only way you could lose a game was to let the clock beat you," McCormack said. "If the game went on long enough, you were going to be in such better physical shape than your opponent that you would win the game.

"He drilled them in practice. I was early enough in my coaching career, and not that far removed from my playing career, that I felt sorry for those guys. I mean, he pushed them. He drove them. It was all an act with him. But he was able to do that and get it across to them."

Like Brown, Lombardi could be charming away from the field. McCormack said stories he tells of the off-the-field Lombardi are hard for those who played under him to believe.

For instance, attendance at meals during camp was mandatory for coaches and players. But after the first week, Lombardi would give players Wednesday nights off to go to the movies or do whatever they wanted to after dinner. McCormack suspected right away that it was because Lombardi wanted a night off, too.

The first Wednesday the players had off, Lombardi told his assistant coaches, "I'm giving the players tonight off. Go in and mess up a salad."

"What?" asked McCormack.

"Just go in and mess up a salad. Just eat a tomato off it or something. We're going out tonight," whispered Bill Austin, another assistant who knew what was going on.

"Lombardi would take us out," McCormack said. "We'd go in, check in at the training table for dinner, get a salad, maybe put some salad dressing on it and take a bite. And then we'd go out to a place called Lombardo's—not Lombardi's, but Lombardo's. And he would have a table ready for the whole staff. There would be an Italian dinner and some wine, the whole bit."

That wasn't all. After a little wine, Lombardi would loosen up. He would tell jokes and stories to his staff and laugh heartily. He would even dance.

"I remember there was an older waitress there who would always come up and kiss him on the cheek," McCormack said. "He loved that. He'd get up and dance with her."

Those who played for Lombardi were never permitted to see this side of him. The Redskins struggled, too, and Lombardi was not used to coaching a struggling team. As the up-and-down season approached its conclusion, the 'Skins defeated the Eagles 34–29 to improve their record to 6–4–2 with two games left in the season. This at least clinched a .500 record, but Lombardi wasn't happy.

As the players and coaching staff gathered in a meeting room the Wednesday before their next game, Lombardi was obviously steamed. He was getting more steamed by the minute when he realized everyone was in the room but Vince Promuto, one of the offensive linemen coached by McCormack.

"[Lombardi] went back to the locker room to get him," said McCormack, "and there, to the amusement of the trainers, was Vince Promuto imitating Lombardi. Promuto was imitating Lombardi. Well, Lombardi walked in on him and all hell broke loose.

"I'll never forget the sight of Promuto as he came running into that meeting room, trying to pull his jockstrap and his pants on at the same time with Lombardi right behind him, just chewing his ass. Then Vince just carried it right on over and started chewing on the whole team."

It was quite a speech.

"You guys think it's great that we won last week, but let me tell you something," Lombardi said, spitting out the words. "We haven't clinched anything yet. I've never had a losing season, and I'm not going to have a losing season this year. And I don't want just a nonlosing season. I don't want to finish break-even. I want a winning record. I've never had anything less. You shouldn't settle for anything less, either, but sometimes I think you guys just don't care enough!"

Later, after the players had departed and Lombardi was alone with his assistant coaches, he broke into a big gap-toothed grin that had become one of his trademarks over the years and said, "Boys, I was really a bitch today, wasn't I?"

"He loved it," McCormack said. "He was always looking for that edge. Promuto gave him a reason to go off that day, and he loved it. It was just the thing he needed to get the players all worked up. We went out and won the game that next Sunday to clinch his winning record."

It was the last winning record Lombardi would have as an NFL coach. He passed away from cancer the following September.

Much the same way McCormack grew to admire and be influenced in his career by the likes of Lombardi and Paul Brown, Polian soon would find his intertwined with Marv

Levy. After guiding the Montreal Alouettes to their second Grey Cup championship in five seasons in 1977, not long after Polian began helping with the scouting, Levy was named head coach of the Kansas City Chiefs in the NFL.

It hadn't taken Levy long in Montreal to take notice of the scouting reports Bill Polian was sending in on a regular basis.

"They were the most detailed, complete, reliable reports we were getting," Levy said.

So when Levy left for Kansas City, he did not hesitate to ask Polian to come along with him. He even offered him a decent salary, something Polian still wasn't yet earning in Montreal. For the next five years, life was grand for Bill and Eileen Polian, but they were just beginning to get their first taste of employment in the NFL.

They discovered how tenuous a life it could be when Levy was fired after the strike-shortened 1982 season. When the head coach goes, oftentimes so does most of his staff. Polian landed on his feet, though, as pro personnel director with Winnipeg back in the CFL.

This represented a new leap of faith for the family. Until then, Polian's scouting had permitted him to keep the family home in Cornwall, New York, traveling wherever he needed to go for the Chiefs or for his now-booming advertising business. But this time, it was a full-time football gig. It meant uprooting the family and moving to an uncertain situation in Winnipeg.

During one hectic year there, with Bill working 18- and 20-hour days to help keep the team afloat, Levy came calling again. But not with an offer to return to the NFL. Levy had taken the head-coaching job with the Chicago Blitz of the fledging United States Football League, and wanted Polian to be his pro personnel director.

Shortly after they both came on board, Levy and Polian learned that the entire team was traded—every last player.

"It's fun to look back on now," Levy said recently, "but it wasn't fun to live through. The first thing we learned was that there had been a franchise switch from the owner who had previously owned the Blitz and had a pretty good team, a team that had won 12 games the year before. I had no prior knowledge of this, nor did Bill, but he bought the Arizona franchise the day we arrived on the contingency that the entire rosters be traded.

"So one day after we arrived on the job, we traded a roster that had gone 12–4 for one that had won two games the year before. That was a big trade."

And not one of the better ones in the history of professional football.

A few weeks later, on the day the Blitz broke training camp, the new owner of the team decided he did not like the prospects of the new season. So he walked into the team's offices and made a simple but startling statement.

"I quit," he said. "I told the league they could have their franchise back. I don't want it."

In retrospect, Polian later said, this should not have surprised anyone.

"He took one look at that team and said, 'That's it.' I don't blame him."

The league, which was having its own problems staying in business by that time, took over the team—leaving Polian and Levy with a shoestring budget to take care of basic financial needs.

"We took dilapidated school buses to the airport," Levy said. "We had no money at all. We couldn't stock the washrooms with toilet paper. At Christmas, one of the [assistant] coaches gift-wrapped toilet paper and gave a roll to everybody in the organization."

Later, Polian discovered a few hours before kickoff on the final day of the season that there was toilet paper but no towels in the locker rooms at Soldier Field. So he cooked up another trade.

"I had to trade all the footballs I could get my hands on, a couple jerseys and some leftover helmets to a local hotel near Soldier Field in order to have towels for the last game of the season against the Michigan Panthers. That's a fact," Polian said.

"I did it on the morning of the game. I came in, it was a hot day, and we had no towels. So myself and the assistant equipment manager high-tailed it off and made a trade. We didn't care. We knew we needed the towels more than those helmets if we were going to wrap it up."

Life got much easier for both Levy and Polian the following year. When Levy became head coach of the Buffalo Bills in the NFL, he took Polian along with him as pro personnel director. There, they would join forces to help build a team that went to an unprecedented four consecutive Super Bowls. But no one can say they didn't pay their dues in the profession.

———————

After Vince Lombardi's stunningly swift death, McCormack stayed on with the Redskins for three more seasons—one under Bill Austin and two under another legendary head coach, George Allen, who also left an impression and once called McCormack "the best assistant coach I have ever had." One of Allen's other assistants in Washington was Marv Levy, who was in charge of special teams the last two years McCormack coached the offensive line.

Regardless of Allen's lofty praise, Brown and Lombardi are the two coaches McCormack would remember most, the two who would shape his own philosophy as he later became a head coach himself in Philadelphia and briefly in Seattle. The memories of both great men would also be called upon to serve him well when it came time to build franchises in Seattle and the Carolinas.

In Seattle, the Seahawks had 51,000 season-ticket holders and had yet to make the playoffs when McCormack took over as president in 1983. By the time he left Seattle in 1989 to join Richardson's bid for the Panthers' franchise, the Seahawks had reached the playoffs in four of their last six seasons, had sold all 61,000 of their season tickets and had a waiting list of more than 29,000 fans who wanted them.

Polian, meanwhile, was in the process of building the Buffalo Bills into a title contender about the same time. When he was promoted to general manager there in 1985, the Bills were coming off consecutive 2–14 seasons and attendance was pathetic. Three years later, the Bills had developed into one of football's best teams and Polian had come to be regarded as one of the NFL's shrewdest judges of talent—as well as a man with a temper.

"I don't think anyone in the world can scream as loudly into a telephone as Bill," said Bob Ferguson, who used to negotiate contracts with Polian in Buffalo, and by 1995 was directing football operations for the Denver Broncos. "My favorite Bill line, and one I still borrow occasionally, is this: 'I'm going to come through this telephone and tear your tonsils out!'"

When it came to absorbing personal criticism, Polian seemed to care little. When it came to criticizing the players who made up his team, Polian could get defensive in a hurry. When it came to watching games from the press box, Polian's ruddy complexion could turn a brighter shade of red in a hurry and he could rarely restrain himself from blurting out whatever came to mind, whether it be a high-decible dissertation on the poor quality of the officiating, or a volatile disagreement with someone nearby who had written or said something derogatory about his team. His outbursts were often laced with profanity.

McCormack was more mild-mannered. Both were good Irish Catholics who sometimes attended Mass together on Sundays. But whereas Polian could be explosive, wearing his emotions on his sleeve, McCormack was more reserved, patient, contemplative. If he was going to let a swearword slip, it would most assuredly be under his breath.

They worked well together from the start. When Jerry Richardson told McCormack to go out and hire the best personnel man he could find, he turned immediately to Polian, who had just been let go by the Bills after engaging in an unwise front-office verbal dispute involving owner Ralph Wilson's daughter, who was the Bills' marketing director.

McCormack set up a golf match at the 1993 league meetings in Palm Springs that included Mark Richardson, himself and Polian. The younger Richardson did not know Polian at the time.

"I made sure I put Mark and Bill in a cart together," McCormack said.

Polian had just been hired by the league office to help out in various matters, such as ironing out problems pertaining to the salary cap.

"Do you want to stay in the league office, or would you like to get back into being involved in the day-to-day operations of a team?" McCormack asked point-blank.

"Oh, I want to get back with a team," Polian replied.

"Well, we don't officially have a team yet. But we think we're about to get one, so we'll stay in touch," McCormack said.

Once the team was awarded six weeks later, negotiations with Polian began in earnest. Polian was also talking with three other teams at the time.

"I need the title of general manager," said Polian, "because that's what I was in Buffalo and that's the capacity I would work in if I went to another team. But I don't want to step on your toes. What do we do?"

McCormack replied: "Look, we both want the same thing. We don't have egos here. Besides, I'm not going to be here much longer. I'm sure we can work something out."

Richardson eventually solved the problem by saying he would promote McCormack to team president and Polian could have his title of general manager. This was just before Christmas in 1993.

"I'll think about it over the holidays and get back to you," he told McCormack and the Richardsons.

"Well, if you don't choose us, we hope you have a terrible Christmas," they joked.

On January 5, Polian said he was coming on board.

Three nights later, McCormack was in the hospital preparing for bypass surgery.

"I didn't mean for Bill to take over so quickly," McCormack later cracked.

McCormack recovered quickly, however, and spent the Panthers' inaugural season very much involved in day-to-day personnel decisions.

"We work very well together," McCormack said. "I don't prevail all the time and Bill doesn't prevail all the time. When we disagree, we usually go home and sleep on it for a night and try to come to some sort of agreement when we get together the next day.

McCormack and Polian believed in the same things when it came to building a team. And even though neither man had presided over construction of an expansion team, both felt they had built solid teams essentially from scratch in Seattle and Buffalo, respectively. It was done by forming a top-notch scouting staff, hiring a head coach and a staff with experience and communication skills, and by establishing a front office that was going to be stable and supportive, with the backing but not the constant meddling of a strong ownership.

For both men, the Carolina Panthers seemed a perfect fit.

The Capers Caper

I t takes precisely 47 seconds to drive from one end of Buffalo, Ohio, to the other, providing the speed limit of 35 miles per hour is observed. Most motorists ignore this suggestion, breezing through the town of 800 on their way to nearby Senecaville Lake as if they can't leave it behind fast enough.

"Be careful," said a housekeeper at a hotel giving directions to Buffalo from what is considered the nearest real city, Cambridge. "Blink and you will miss it."

Blink and you would miss the Buffalo Grill, which proudly serves "things grilled and distilled," according to the sign out front. You would miss two other bars—the VFW and the T&L Tavern—two gas stations, a Subway sandwich shop, two bait-and-tackle shops (one sells guns, too), Weber's Grocery, Adams Country Store, the Somewhere in Time resale shop, a post office and the two homes in which Dom Capers grew up.

Capers is Buffalo's most famous ex-resident. He understood early that you had to leave town to make a mark in life.

"I always knew Dominic would leave," said his mother, Jeanette Capers. "I knew he'd never stay home."

Most residents don't leave, or at least they don't venture too far if they do. One was asked recently if most people left Buffalo after growing up there or stuck around.

"Oh, most of us leave," said the man. "Like me. I moved away to Pleasant City for a few years before I moved back."

Pleasant City is located less than two miles up the road from Buffalo, just under the Interstate-77 overpass. This is where Dominic Capers' mother now lives, less than half a football field away from Pat Willis' family diner. Willis is Dom's cousin and a man who has served as cook, mayor and a musician at local wedding receptions, often simultaneously.

Capers stopped in Willis' diner while visiting his brother and mother in June of 1995. The new coach of the Panthers was a little taken aback when one of the waitresses, whom Dom had known for years, refused to acknowledge him at first and then just kept shaking her head at him, refusing to speak to him.

"What's wrong with her, Pat? She won't talk to me," Dom Capers said.

"Well," said Pat Willis, "you know she's a die-hard Steelers fan."

Finally, the waitress could hold her tongue no longer.

"Just keep your hands off our Steelers!" she said, smiling but in an altogether serious tone. "You already stole Gerald Williams and Dwight Stone from us, and then you go out and trade for Barry Foster! Are you going to come after Rod Woodson next? Promise me you won't steal Woodson, too. Promise me you'll quit taking all our good players, Dom, and I'll speak to you. I'll even bring you some food, whatever you want."

As for the food, the trim, muscular Capers long ago had sworn off french fries and virtually everything else on Pat Willis' menu. Yet he couldn't swear to the waitress that he would remove the Steelers from his suddenly ravenous player-acquisition diet.

Dominic Capers, whose real first name is Ernest, was not the first choice for head coach of the Panthers—not by owner Jerry Richardson, not by Mike McCormack, and not by Bill Polian. Their joint first choice was Joe Gibbs, former coach of the Washington Redskins and a resident of Charlotte who quit the Redskins after three Super Bowl championships in 11 years because he felt burnt out.

To the Panthers, and to Richardson especially, Gibbs seemed the ideal fit. The Panthers contingent spent the better part of a week with Gibbs early in 1994 and offered him the job. Talks grew serious when Gibbs met with Panthers officials, including owner Jerry Richardson, for more than four hours at the Ritz-Carlton hotel in downtown Atlanta the day after Super Bowl XXVIII. Gibbs had been out of coaching for only one season, however, and was hesitant about jumping back in. Though he lived in Charlotte and wouldn't have to move, he already was deeply involved in auto racing. He owned one team with the National Association of Stock Car Auto Racing and two drag-racing teams, which he was running at a much more leisurely pace than he had run the Redskins—and with the help of his two sons. He also was making a name for himself in television broadcasting as an NFL analyst for NBC, which he enjoyed immensely.

Eventually, Gibbs decided he couldn't make the commitment to return to coaching. He couldn't do it to himself or his family.

"I think if I ever was going to coach again, this probably would have been the job," Gibbs said later. "It was going to be close. I had already moved here. Those kinds of things were very appealing. And I thought Mike and Bill and Jerry were great when I talked to them.

"But I think after I got out of coaching and started analyzing everything, I finally realized what I was like when I was coaching. It really didn't matter how many times I won; I wanted to win the next time just as bad. So I knew I was going to drive myself the same way, because you just don't like the losing."

He no longer relished the thought of 18- and 20-hour workdays. He remembered all the sleepless nights on a couch in his office at Redskin Park. Yet this type of workaholic nature was in large part what drove Polian, in particular, to so greatly admire Gibbs. No one could outwork Joe Gibbs. No one could possibly have a team better prepared come Sunday.

This was exactly the type of coach the Panthers wanted—someone who would work tirelessly and without distraction to build a better future for the franchise.

Richardson even hinted to Gibbs that he didn't need to be quite as obsessive about the job as he was by the end in Washington. But deep down, both men seemed to know that if Gibbs took the job, he would approach it the only way he had ever known.

"They tell you that you can back off, take it a little easier," Gibbs said. "Well, I wasn't going to do that. I think all those things started registering with me. Plus the fact that my kids were working with me in the racing thing and the fact that I was with my wife more. All of that made me finally realize, 'Hey, I'm not coaching again.'"

Richardson was disappointed. So were McCormack and Polian, although they were less surprised. Along with Mark Richardson, who was also involved to a lesser extent in the hiring of a coach, they quickly turned elsewhere to find the man who could lead them to a Super Bowl within Jerry Richardson's mandated 10-year timetable.

It didn't take long for the short list of candidates to be whittled to two names. Steve Spurrier, the head coach at Florida, was never seriously considered—even though this was reported repeatedly. At first McCormack considered Spurrier a brilliant offensive mind and a potential NFL coaching star; Polian was less enthused. When the two administrators and Mark Richardson met with Spurrier for a round of golf and a feeling-out session at a charity event in Durham, North Carolina, Polian came away unimpressed. A brilliant mind, maybe, but Polian wondered if Spurrier would be willing to put in the long hours this particular job of building from ground zero would require. Talks with Spurrier, who coached at Duke before going to Florida, never went any further.

The Richardsons were disappointed again and felt a little uncertain about where to turn to next. Polian and McCormack, veterans of the NFL game, calmed them. They continued flying around the country, talking with potential candidates. They talked to Joe Bugel and Raymond Berry and eight or 10 others, but none warranted a second meeting with the Richardsons.

"What happened was, Joe Gibbs didn't slam the door shut after our first meeting the day after the Super Bowl," McCormack said. "He closed the door, sure, but he didn't slam it shut. He said, 'Maybe I'll feel differently later. Maybe, by next Thanksgiving, I'll feel differently.'

"With that as a security blanket, guys in the media and fans left us alone. We were able to go out and do the legwork we wanted to do with nobody bothering us. We told everybody Joe Gibbs was our first choice, and he would let us know around Thanksgiving. Meanwhile, Dom's star was rising. We did our homework on all these other guys so, sure enough, when Joe told us he hadn't changed his mind around Thanksgiving, we had a pretty good idea what direction we wanted to go."

Separately, both Polian and McCormack offered Jerry and Mark Richardson essentially the same advice: "When you meet the guy who is going to be your coach, you'll know. You won't come out of the interview saying, 'Geez, I don't know. This might be the guy and it might not.' You'll know."

They wasted no time in contacting Rich Kotite, who was fired as head coach of the Philadelphia Eagles the day after Christmas 1994. The Panthers interviewed him three days later. Kotite was a New Yorker through and through, much like Polian. They had known each other for years, and both McCormack and Polian greatly respected Kotite's abilities as a coach, despite his fall from grace in Philadelphia, where the Eagles lost their last seven games the previous season after a 7–2 start, resulting in Kotite's abrupt dismissal by first-year owner Jeffrey Lurie.

The other possibility on the Panthers' short list was Dom Capers, whose name was not a household one. But within NFL circles and even collegiate ones, he long ago had been annointed as a Future Head Coach. It was only a matter of time before someone hired him in that capacity.

The problem for the Panthers was this: They wanted to move quickly to name a coach, but Capers had not yet completed his third season as defensive coordinator for the Pittsburgh Steelers. The Steelers, by virtue of their 12–4 record, which was the best in the American Football Conference, were waiting to see who their first playoff opponent would be when Polian placed separate phone calls to Tom Donahoe, the Steelers' director of football operations, and Bill Cowher, the team's head coach.

"Would you have any objections to us talking to Dom?" Polian asked both men.

"No, not as long as it isn't disruptive to our team," they replied in kind. "We'd like to see him get the job."

Polian later said, "They gave him glowing recommendations. We said we wouldn't be disruptive, and we weren't."

Yet Polian knew as well as anyone that contacting Capers while the Steelers' season was still on—even if he had the Steelers' permission—was expressly forbidden by NFL rules: It's called tampering. As a result, the Panthers fretted at first over whether to immediately pursue Capers or to simply wait until the Steelers had either won the Super Bowl or were eliminated from the playoffs.

Polian pushed for them to move ahead immediately. Rumors were surfacing that Capers might accept a different head-coaching position—possibly at Louisiana State University, possibly with another NFL team. Capers would later admit he had already received feelers from "two or three other clubs." He had heard through the coaching grapevine that the Panthers might be interested, too, but he wasn't sure.

"That was our principal motivation behind the whole thing," Polian said. "We thought that if we didn't express our interest, he might take the LSU job or another job somewhere else."

In a meeting with the Richardsons and McCormack, Polian said, "Look, if there's a penalty to pay, the greater good is still being served as long as the Steelers are not upset. We've talked to them. We can't risk letting [Capers] walk away and go somewhere else without finding out first if he might be our guy."

McCormack and the rest agreed. They had to at least let Capers know they were interested in him.

"We wanted a coach who was a teacher all along," McCormack said. "We wanted a coach who was current in the game, who could pretty much take care of one side of the ball. Not a complete isolationist, so to speak . . . a guy who knew both sides, but someone who had strength on one side of the ball. We also wanted a young one—a young guy who could communicate with the players.

"Communication is very important. And, as much as we could tell, we wanted someone who had the ability to try and get along with the media."

Capers felt open communication with players, the front office and, to a lesser extent, even the media was important for today's NFL head coach.

"To me," said Capers, "the whole key is honesty. One of the biggest jobs as head coach is as communicator. You can't just tell a player something. You have to make sure he's hearing the same thing you're saying, because sometimes he might hear only what he wants to hear. And what you have to say may not always be what he wants to hear."

Capers was only 44, young by coaching standards. He was considered a defensive genius, having developed a method of "zone blitzing" out of the Steelers' unique 3–4 base alignment that had other coaches throughout the league scrambling to the film room in the off-seasons to copy what he was doing. And he was considered a guy who painstakingly communicated with his players, so they were never surprised by a person-nel move he might initiate as defensive coordinator.

It was during Capers' second interview with the Panthers that McCormack was struck by Capers' similarities to Paul Brown.

"We found out that he would be patient, that he wasn't a screamer, a loud type," McCormack said. "I was raised with Paul Brown. The more I see Dom, the more I compare him to Paul. He says things the way they are. That's the way he was when we sat there in the interviews.

"He said, 'I believe this. I believe that. This is what I would do in this situation. This is how I would handle that situation.'"

After the second interview, McCormack sought out Polian.

"Boy, he sure reminds me of Paul," McCormack said. "That was Paul. Paul would just tell you things like, 'I don't like what you're doing. You've got to do this to correct it.' There was no kicking and screaming."

Polian laughed. He had been struck by a similar vision while sitting through the interviews with Capers.

"Marv [Levy] and Dom Capers," said Polian, "philosophically, emotionally and in terms of approach, are twins. . . . It's ironic, but also reassuring. It's just as though you've seen it all before. Marv is without a doubt the greatest teacher I've ever been around.

"He'll publicly downplay this if you tell him I said it, but he's also the greatest motiva-tor I've ever been around—and the two go hand-in-hand. He and Dom Capers are the two best-organized coaches I've ever been around—and not organization for organization's sake, but organization to win."

The choice, then, was simple. Nonetheless, Polian, McCormack, Mark Richardson and Jerry Richardson all slept on it. McCormack left for Seattle to see his grandchildren. The next day, the four men met via the wonders of a teleconference call.

"Write down a name," Jerry Richardson commanded.

All four men wrote down Dom Capers. Hammering out a contract was easy, and within a few days the Panthers had signed the first head coach in franchise history to a five-year contract worth approximately $450,000 annually. Not a bad salary, but certainly a bargain compared to what the Panthers would have had to pay Gibbs.

Shortly thereafter, they had to settle up with the league on a tampering charge leveled by the commissioner's office. It cost them $150,000 and two 1995 draft choices, and they caught hell, so to speak, from the religious right in the Carolinas for their admission to breaking the rules to make sure they got the man they wanted.

Newspapers, particularly the *Charlotte Observer,* were flooded with letters of complaint.

"This incident is a slap in the face to the many honest supporters of the Panthers," wrote Rennie Biggers of Charlotte.

Reverend Dana A. McKim of Hickory, a minister with the Christ United Methodist Church, wrote, "The moral of the latest parable of Richardson Sports is consistent and succinct: 1) If you have money, you can do whatever you want, whenever you want with whomever you want and you will get exactly what you want—and the fans will pay the bill. 2) Everyone else is doing it and that makes it right.

"The morality of the parable of Richardson Sports stinks."

And from Wayne Harbin of Lincolnton: "When the Carolinas were awarded the Panthers, we were told that it would be a first-class operation. Instead, the Dom Capers deal shows what we have is business as usual. I have lost my respect for the organization. I will stay a Redskins fan."

Polian, who at first tried to blame the media for disclosure of the tampering but later admitted it was a calculated risk accepted all along by management, probably didn't help matters when he went on a local radio talk show and treated the matter nonchalantly.

"Look," said Polian on the air, "to us we realize there is a technical violation of the rule and there is a penalty to pay. But we're looking at it as a recruiting violation."

Later, he added: "They don't get that upset when Clemson is put on probation, or when North Carolina State is put on probation."

McCormack was more repentent, at least publicly.

Speaking on the team's weekly radio call-in show, he said, "We were wrong in what we did. There's no doubt about it. We admit that. I guess there's no excuse for it. And we were taken to the woodshed for it."

Around the league, front-office types snickered. The new kids in school had been caught with their hands in the cookie jar.

"The Panthers are the new kids on the block and they stubbed their toes a bit," 49ers president Carmen Policy told the *Observer.* "But I don't think the Panthers had a lot of criminal intent here. I think it was more like they were getting antsy, having to sit back and wait for a coach. I don't think they really intended to fly in the face of the league.

"We're not going to try to kick them out of our division or anything like that. You could say the Panthers were being barred from dating, let alone from holding hands or necking. And they wanted to be aggressive and go ahead and get started with things. So they trampled on a few rules in the process."

Polian was certain, as were the Richardsons and McCormack, that all would be forgiven as soon as the people of North and South Carolina got to know Dominic Capers.

Almost everyone these days calls Capers either Dom or Coach. But his mother, Jeanette, still calls him by his middle name, which is Dominic. And his brother, Julius, often calls him Doc, a nickname from Dominic's prodigious Little League days that stuck to a certain degree in tiny Buffalo, despite the fact no one quite remembers how or why he got it.

Even though he essentially moved out of Buffalo for good when he left in 1968 to attend Mount Union College, located in Alliance, Ohio, precisely 73 miles up Interstate-77, just past the Pro Football Hall of Fame in Canton, Capers has always held his hometown close to his heart. He still speaks fondly of O'Connor's Restaurant, where as a kid he said "the big treat was to go right across the street from where I lived and get a scoop of ice cream for a nickel. If you were lucky, you could get a dime and get two scoops."

He visits whenever he can in the NFL off-season, finding plenty of reason to go back even though O'Connor's has long since closed. His mother lives in Pleasant City, just off what she calls the main drag. Julius, four years younger than Dom, lives right across the street from Jeanette with his wife and two children, Dom's spirited nieces, who like to play practical jokes on their good-natured and suddenly famous uncle. Pat Willis runs the diner two doors down from Jeanette and also serves as Pleasant City's mayor, something nearby Buffalo does not have.

"It's the largest unincorporated town in Ohio," said Jeanette of Buffalo. "That means you can do just about whatever you want there. There is no city hall, and there really aren't any local laws."

It's hard to imagine Buffalo being the largest of anything in Ohio or anywhere else. When Capers was growing up there, most of the streets were dirt or gravel. Some off the main street still are.

But a few folks, such as Dom's parents and one Albert Andrews, laid down some laws of their own. Andrews owned and operated the Buffalo Grill for 47 years and was such an institution that many people still call it Albert's, even though the man passed away quite some time ago. Get out of hand in there while Dom was growing up and Albert had a surefire way of calming things down. He kept a shotgun behind the bar and would fire it into the ceiling or the opposite wall.

Pellet holes poorly hidden by a new menu sign on the wall offer proof of Albert's Law, and his willingness to enforce it.

The Capers family—which also includes younger sister Nina—lived, at one point, just a few doors down from Albert's. But Jeanette never had to worry about Dominic going in there and getting into trouble.

"The bars were there," said Dom, "but I knew that if I ever set foot in one of them, the wrath of my mother would come down upon me. I stop in now every once in a while if I'm back with a buddy or two, but I still think about my mother not approving of me. I used to think maybe I would have the worst reputation in the world if I stepped foot in one of those bars."

Instead, his parents guided him toward athletics, school and the Lutheran church, all the while preaching the virtues of hard work. Dom excelled at baseball, in the church choir, and in the classroom, where he earned straight As. His father, Eugene, would examine the homework of his sons each night and was a stickler for neatness, right down to precise penmanship. If he didn't like the look of the homework, he would rip it up and make Dom or Julius do it again.

"But that didn't happen often," Jeanette said. "I think it only happened to Dom one time."

About the only time Dom ever got into trouble was one day when he broke the windshield on the automobile of the local barber, Jackie Davis. It was an accident, Dom having made a wild throw with a baseball as he and a childhood friend tossed out in front of Davis' establishment. As soon as Capers threw the ball, he knew he was in trouble and considered running from the scene, to the point of starting around the corner.

"But I came back because I knew I had to face the music," he said. "I knew it would be tougher with my father if I didn't. My father didn't really ever need to do anything other than raise his voice. If he raised his voice, you knew you were in trouble, and that's all he ever needed to do."

Eugene Capers was a project engineer who worked on finally getting Route 313—the main drag in Buffalo, now called Claypike Road—paved in the 1950s. Eugene was proud of his work as an engineer and as an accomplished carpenter on the side who helped remodel kitchens in various Buffalo homes. But he was more proud of his eldest son.

Eugene would often attempt to hustle home from work early to drag and line the field on those nights when Dom played for the Buffalo Bisons in Little League. Later, when eight schools consolidated and Dom finally had the opportunity to pursue organized football at newly formed Meadowbrook High School, Eugene helped design and build the football stadium that is still used today.

"He was a man who believed you got back out of things what you put into them," Dom Capers said of his father, who died after a heart attack at age 57 in 1982. "I was as close to him as anybody could be."

And close to him in personality, too, according to Julius Capers.

"To me and my little sister," said Julius, "Dom was as much a father figure as a big brother. We respected him that much."

"I could always depend on Dom," Jeanette added. "I could depend on him to take care of things like a man since he was 10 years old."

So could the Capers' neighbors. Accounts of Dominic's work habits and devotion to detail while growing up abound in Buffalo.

Across the street from the two-story, three-bedroom Capers home then were three widows who took delight in watching young Dominic's progression into adulthood. He cared for their lawns during the summer, meticulously finishing the edges with a fork. He shoveled snow from their sidewalks in winter. He even darted down to Weber's on occasion and did some of their grocery shopping for them.

Two days before Capers coached his first game for the Panthers, a preseason affair against the Jacksonville Jaguars to be played, appropriately enough, right beside the Hall of Fame just up the interstate from Buffalo, Jeanette Capers gave four reporters from the Carolinas a tour of Buffalo. She insisted on stopping by at the homes of two of the three widows, who still lived across the street from the old Capers home.

"Dominic was a wonderful, wonderful boy," said Patsy Miller, 86, who shuffled to her porch to talk effusively about him even though eye problems had left her almost completely blind. "I always knew he was going to make something of himself."

Another of the widows was Estie Wycoff, now deceased. When she was 86, she fell and broke her wrist. Her daughter, who lived two hours away in Mansfield, Ohio, drove to Buffalo and told Estie she would have to return to Mansfield with her.

"Forget it," Estie Wycoff told her own daughter. "I'll stay right here. Dom will take care of me."

And so he did. For the next several weeks, while Wycoff's wrist slowly healed, Capers, then in his teens, would gather his pillow, a sheet and a blanket and head across the street to tend to the old widow's needs before bedtime. Then he would sleep on Wycoff's couch.

The third widow who lived across from the Capers household was Eva Robins, who was 91 when Jeanette stopped by to say hello with her troupe of reporters. Robins displayed the remnants of a quick wit—although she obviously hadn't made a habit of keeping up with all the details of Dom's coaching career.

"He's got a pretty good job now, doesn't he?" Eva Robins asked Jeanette Capers. "Is he going to get a better one?"

Trying to suppress a smile, Jeanette gently shook her head, rubbed Robins' slight shoulders and said, "No, dear, I think he'll keep the one he's got for a while."

Capers may have had other thoughts, however briefly, upon flying to Charlotte and being introduced as the first head coach of the Panthers on January 23, 1995. Most new head coaches in the NFL have a pretty good idea of what they're walking into; they've studied the roster of the team they're about to coach and they know which members, if any, of the coaching staff they wish to retain.

When Capers arrived, the Panthers had no roster to speak of. They had only 11 players under contract. He didn't have much of a coaching staff with which to commiserate, although two assistants, offensive line coach Jim McNally and receivers coach Richard Williamson, had been hired before him when it became apparent both men, each highly respected throughout the NFL, were going to be available because their previous employers, the Cincinnati Bengals, were more concerned with pinching pennies than retaining their services.

Barely one month before Capers' arrival, even as they stepped up the coaching search, Polian and McCormack and assistant general manager Joe Mack had taken a moment to sign a group of "street free agents" that nobody else would have. They would come to be called the Original 10, and they were introduced at a lavish news conference in uptown Charlotte.

Willie Green was there—a tall, hopelessly skinny wide receiver who actually had four years of NFL experience but hadn't been signed by another team after his release the previous October by Tampa Bay.

Randy Cuthbert was there—a Duke graduate hoping to put off becoming a high-school mathematics teacher for at least one more year.

Big Kevin Farkas was there—the only member of the Original 10 to attend the news conference in a casual golf shirt that barely stretched over his 380-pound frame. Most of the rest, which included tight ends Matt Campbell and Lawyer Tillman, running back Tony Smith, wide receiver Eric Weir and offensive linemen Mike Finn, Carlson Leomiti and Darryl Moore, wore suits and ties or at least donned sport coats for the big event.

"The Panther logo didn't look real up there that day," Farkas would later say. "The whole day didn't really seem like it was real, to tell you the truth. No one was used to the logo or anything else yet. It didn't look or feel much like you were signing with a real NFL team. We didn't even have a coach yet."

The Panthers actually had the players sign their contracts in front of the media at the news conference, something they weren't likely to do with future top draft picks.

Afterward, the fun continued when Leomiti, a huge offensive line prospect who weighed in the neighborhood of 400 pounds, began playing a piano and singing the Commodores' hit "Easy" while the bemused media looked on.

"Music is a very relaxing thing to me," Leomiti later said. "Football sometimes frustrates me when my body is not functioning the way I want it to. So music is the way I unwind."

From the looks of Leomiti, he spent a whole lot more time relaxing and unwinding from being frustrated about football than he did at anything else, except perhaps eating.

Joe Mack harbored no illusions about this group. He felt if they could get one or two players who actually made the team and did something, the Original 10 would be considered a smashing success.

"The NFL was still in season then," said Mack, "so in theory, everybody able to play in the league was already playing in the league. These were guys nobody else wanted."

Three weeks later, an 11th player was signed as a free agent prior to Capers' arrival. He was Matt Elliott, another offensive line candidate. He hadn't played in a year, since being cut by the Redskins during the 1994 preseason. He spent the previous year working part-time at a gym and as a broadcaster for Cablevision in Loudoun County, Virginia, where he served as a color analyst on the Loudoun County High School Game of the Week and was a sideline reporter at Redskins home games.

The great irony of Dom Capers growing up in Buffalo was that it almost robbed him of a chance to ever play organized football. As a boy, Capers was a baseball standout throughout Little League and Pony League. His exposure to football was almost nonexistent.

Buffalo did not have organized football at any level. It wasn't until eight small schools from places like Buffalo, Pleasant City, Senecaville and Derwent combined to make one high school in 1963 that Capers finally got to play the game he would grow to love very quickly.

"I had some cousins and an uncle who played football," he said. "They played in a little town called Hopedale, which was toward Steubenville. That's where my father grew up. I would go over and watch them practice, and I really liked it. But the first time I ever played organized football was when I was a freshman in high school."

Capers played quarterback at Meadowbrook High and was the team's leading scorer as a junior. He also excelled in basketball. But baseball was still his best sport and his first athletic love. A right-handed hitter with power, he played first base in high school and outfield in college at Mount Union, where he also played defensive back in football.

"One of the things I liked about going to Mount Union was that I could go there and play both football and baseball the first year," Capers said.

From there he went on to Kent State as a graduate assistant under Don James, who later would go on to great success as head coach at the University of Washington. College coaching stops at Hawaii, San Jose State, California, Tennessee and Ohio State preceded Capers' pro career, which began under Jim Mora with the Philadelphia/Baltimore Stars in the old United States Football League and continued under Mora as coach of the defensive secondary with the NFL's New Orleans Saints before Capers went to Pittsburgh as defensive coordinator in 1992.

Capers' life was football. His first marriage of 17 years was a casualty of the long hours of coaching, but he remained amicable with his ex-wife even after their divorce in 1991. They had no children.

"Seven months out of the year, when you're spending all your time [coaching], it takes a little bit of a toll," Capers admitted. "It's just one of those things where you make a decision and as you invest time in one area, you aren't investing time in the other area. It happens a lot in this business."

He remarried to his current wife, Karen, an airline stewardess, in June of 1994.

It was while Capers was at Ohio State that his father passed away shortly after giving his eldest son a leather-bound notebook. Capers began recording the date, time and details of every event in his life in this notebook, which he replaced a year later with another one. To this day, he religiously records everything that transpires during his day in one of these leather-bound notebooks.

The first time Charles Chandler, a reporter for the *Charlotte Observer*, met Capers at Three Rivers Stadium in Pittsburgh, early in January of 1995, he asked to see one of these notebooks. It was the day after the NFL had fined the Panthers $150,000 and taken away two draft picks for "improper contract discussions" before the Steelers' 1994 season had ended. Everyone knew Capers would be the Panthers' head coach, even though the Steelers were busy preparing for their upcoming playoff game against Cleveland and Capers wouldn't officially be named Carolina's coach for 19 more days.

After about 45 minutes, the talk turned from football to jogging. Chandler mentioned that he jogged and also kept a daily log of how far he ran and how fast. Capers, a muscular fitness buff who also is an avid weight lifter, said he did, too.

"In fact," Capers told Chandler, "my records are so complete that I can compare my times on any given day against the time I ran on the same day in any of the past 14 years." Then Capers mentioned that he also wrote down everything he did each day, prompting Chandler to ask to see one of the notebooks.

"Capers went to his office and brought out his 1994 book to show it to me," Chandler later wrote in the *Observer*. "The handwriting was perfect. His notes were neat, organized, and incredibly detailed.

"If he went to a movie, it was in the book. If the Steelers practiced, every exercise was in the book. If he had a meal with a friend, it was there. . . . His recordings seemed a bit obsessive, but I remember being impressed and thinking, 'The Panthers might really have something in this guy.'"

At Pat Willis' family diner in Pleasant City, they were already convinced the Panthers really had something. The only worry for Pat was finding enough Panthers' paraphernalia to replace the stuff he had covering a small but rapidly expanding area on one wall. There, next to a picture of the 1955 Pleasant City basketball team, the first team from Guernsey County to go to the state championships in Columbus, were several articles pertaining to Capers and the Pittsburgh Steelers. There was only one article about Capers and the Panthers.

Traditionally, the area's pro football loyalties were split between Pittsburgh and Cleveland, with the two cities close to being equal distances away. Capers himself grew up a Browns fan, occasionally attending a game at old Cleveland Municipal Stadium while in high school and college.

Now he had waitresses in his hometown hassling him about plucking too many Steelers from Pittsburgh's roster.

But was Barry Foster, the oft-injured running back acquired at the end of May, still a good player? Would Dwight Stone, a valuable special-teams player and a receiver of limited means in Pittsburgh, who signed as a free agent, even make the Panthers' roster? Wasn't Gerald Williams, a defensive lineman plucked off the Steelers' roster in the expansion allocation draft, coming off an injury-plagued season of his own and on the decline at age 32?

Capers intended to find out. In some ways, his upbringing had a direct bearing on how the first roster of the Carolina Panthers would shape up.

"It's funny, because I've been through the college coaching," Capers said. "I spent 9 or 10 years there, where I was often in the larger cities recruiting or coaching. I was fortunate because I had a great family. You realize that more as you go along, when you've been in so many different homes recruiting.

"Buffalo was a town where everybody cared about one another. If somebody had a problem, everyone was concerned about it. You grew up with a lot of trust in people, where you feel that everyone trusts or cares. And I think that's good, because I feel that many times if you grow up not trusting anyone or anything, thinking that somebody always had an ulterior motive, that can be bad.

"I never, ever felt that way because I wasn't treated that way growing up. You judge people for what they are, and you give everybody a chance."

Scout's Honor

When Dom Anile first visited Fort Valley State in Georgia during the fall of 1993, the Panthers weren't even an official NFL franchise. Yet Anile's work that day promises to pay off many years ahead for the Carolina defense.

Anile, the Panthers' director of player personnel, was at the tiny school to scout a player for his former employer, the Cleveland Browns. He never did see the player who prompted him to make a special weekday trip, but his time was far from wasted.

"It was my last year with Cleveland," said Anile, whose considerable heft is matched only by his largess of good stories. "My area scout had given a really high grade to a defensive back by the name of Joe Best. The grade was high enough for me to say I'd better go see this guy. I decided to go early during two-a-days, knowing if liked him I would get back there to watch a game."

Anile's logic was something only a pro football scout could fully appreciate. Game films put together by small schools are often inferior to major college programs. The film might be grainy or shot without enough light (or into the sun for too much exposure). The camera angles often aren't high enough to catch all 22 players moving around the football field because smaller stadiums are less tall.

"You've got to attend a game to check out a small-college player at the skill positions like defensive back, halfback and wide receiver," explained Anile (pronounced "ah-neal-lee"). "You might be looking at films and the camera guy is following the ball and suddenly the kid being scouted is not in the picture anymore. Then your kid comes back in the picture and might or might not make a play. But you don't know what happened in between.

"A lineman I can probably check on tape. A skill player, we have to go to the game."

Back to the Fort Valley story: "It turns out Joe Best wasn't there. He was ill or something. So Coach [Douglas] Porter, he's a super guy, he invited me back to his office to watch some film of Joe Best. Coach Porter has all these tapes and I'm sitting there trying to find Joe Best.

"But tapes are shot from bad angles and I can't even read the players' numbers. All I see is some guy making great plays."

Porter was sitting right there; Anile asked him for some help.

"Coach, is that Joe Best?"

"Oh, no, that's our other cornerback," said Porter.

Then Anile watched another pass play busted up by a Fort Valley defender.

"Now, Coach, is that Joe Best?"

"No, that's our other cornerback."

Anile had seen enough.

"So, Coach, is it OK if I stay and watch practice anyway, even though Joe Best isn't here?"

"Of course," said Porter.

"Who's this other kid at cornerback?" asked Anile.

"Tyrone Poole. He's a junior."

Anile, an NFL scout since 1982 and prodigious talker, practically since birth, knew precisely when to keep quiet.

"Once I hear a kid is a junior," Anile said later, "I try to stay away from inquiring too much. Coaches get nervous. They think we influence a kid to come out, but we don't do that at all."

Anile kept a low profile at practice. He watched Poole work and liked what he saw— a lot. He would keep an eye on this cornerback over the next two seasons.

"I went back to Cleveland and said I don't know who the hell Joe Best is, I don't know if I'll ever find out who Joe Best is, but there's another kid there who is going to be one hell of an NFL player."

Nearly two years later, with the 22nd pick of the 1995 college draft, and their second selection in the round acquired in a trade with Green Bay, Dom Anile and the Panthers made Tyrone Poole the first defensive back chosen and first-ever first-rounder from Fort Valley State, a school that has also produced perennial all-pro linebacker Greg Lloyd of the AFC champion Pittsburgh Steelers and all-pro safety Eddie Anderson of the Oakland Raiders.

Judging from his rookie season with the Panthers, it won't be long before Poole joins his Fort Valley predecessors among the league's elite players.

Bill Polian has a theory about first-year players in the NFL. He expects them to make their biggest jump in progress during their second season. If that holds true in 1996, the Panthers will be reaping some eye-popping benefits from the team's first-ever college draft on April 22 and 23, 1995. On the strength of three separate draft-day trades, Carolina put itself into position to select its starting quarterback, two starting offensive linemen (and maybe a third), a starting cornerback, a frequently used pass rusher and a solid special teams player heading into the second season of both these players and the franchise.

The first five players picked by the Panthers—quarterback Kerry Collins, offensive tackle Blake Brockermeyer, Poole, defensive end Shawn King and offensive guard-center Frank Garcia—all played regularly. Fifth-round choice and offensive guard Andrew Peterson started two games. Safety Chad Cota, a seventh-round selection, was among the statistical leaders on special teams coverage and made the first tackle in Panthers history when he downed Atlanta's Roell Preston at the Falcons' 23-yard line on the first kickoff of the season.

The Panthers' front office was pleased after their wheeling and dealing with Cincinnati, Green Bay and San Diego led to four picks among the first 36 players but fewer overall than most teams. It seemed perhaps an odd strategy for an expansion team needing to stock up on players, but Polian didn't think so.

"We thought if we could get four first-rounders, at almost any price, it would be a successful draft," said Polian at the team's temporary headquarters at the Winthrop University Coliseum in Rock Hill, South Carolina. "The idea isn't to win the draft and get a lot of extra picks, it's to win on Sundays."

The day worked out beautifully for Dom Anile and his college scouting staff. Carolina's top four picks were rated highly on their draft board, which ranks players by position rather than round quality. Collins, though the second quarterback picked behind the Houston Oilers' Steve McNair, was first overall on the Panthers board. Poole was also their top-rated defensive back, and they made a trade with Green Bay to get him. Brockermeyer was rated second by Carolina behind Jacksonville's number-two overall pick, Tony Boselli. But by the time Brockermeyer was grabbed at number 29 he was the fifth offensive lineman selected. King, fourth on the Panthers board among defensive linemen, was actually the ninth such player taken.

Furthermore, both Garcia and Peterson, teammates at the University of Washington, were still available in later rounds. Anile had both offensive lineman ranked much higher than other NFL clubs, which were likely swayed by the lack of an invitation for either player to the league's annual scouting combine for 300 college prospects in mid-February at the Hoosier Dome in Indianapolis.

"Once preseason games started, scouts from other clubs were coming up to us and saying how much they liked Garcia and Peterson and how they were just about to pick them when we grabbed them," said Anile. "I don't know if I believe that."

Of course, the big trade of the day was Carolina giving up the first pick of the draft to the Bengals in exchange for the number-five selection in the opening round and fourth turn in the second round (number 36 overall). Some NFL general managers were surprised at the exchange, based on conversation with Panthers officials who were holding out for two first-round picks.

But team president Mike McCormack, Polian, Anile and everyone else in the "war room" at Rock Hill were happy with a move that basically swapped everybody's all-world, can't-miss running back Ki-Jana Carter for Collins and King. The trade looked even better in preseason when Carter, a teammate with Collins on Penn State's unde-feated 1994 team, tore an anterior cruciate knee ligament before ever playing in a regular season game.

McCormack, who allowed Polian plenty of room to operate in personnel matters, was quite vocal about making what was considered a bold move. He lobbied both Polian and coach Dom Capers during the weeks leading up to the draft.

"There's an axiom in pro football: You never pass up a quarterback," said McCormack on draft day. The Panthers' top football man looked relieved after several weeks of deflecting the queries of NFL executives, media people and friends alike.

"Mike reminded me many times he played on some great teams that had the greatest running back arguably of all time, Jim Brown, and they didn't win enough champion-ships because they didn't have a quarterback," Polian said.

Capers was in sync with his bosses.

"When you look around the NFL and talk about the number of teams who do not have a top-notch quarterback and you look at the number of starters over 30 [16 going into the 1995 season]," said Capers, "it's astounding."

Team officials weren't unimpressed with Carter. Polian, not prone to flatter, called him "magnificent," but privately worried about whether the gifted running back would take a beating behind a young and inexperienced offensive line.

As for Collins, he wouldn't be scheduled to play right away. The Panthers executives simply fell in love with the Penn State quarterback. Other teams were less enamored with him, leading some observers to believe Collins might drop as low as the middle or late part of the first round if Carolina didn't pick him.

Instead, owner Jerry Richardson and Collins were talking by phone after the fifth selection of the first round.

"Young man, congratulations," said Richardson from Rock Hill. "We're thrilled to have you join the Panthers. Do you know what the Lombardi [Super Bowl] Trophy is?

"Yes, sir," said Collins from NFL draft headquarters in New York.

"Have you thought about it?"

"I just started thinking about it."

The message was received. Collins, who flew down to Carolina that same day, mentioned "Super Bowl" six times in the first minute of his press conference.

"This has been a dream of mine since I was a little boy," said Collins to a packed room of reporters. "Now to be part of a team so committed to going to the Super Bowl is such a thrill.

"I know it's not going to be good enough to just get the Super Bowl either. I won't be satisfied until we win this thing."

According to Anile, many NFL teams lost interest in Collins at the annual Senior Bowl game played in January at Mobile, Alabama. He threw an interception during practice early in the week and the majority of scouts on hand figured the defensive back had anticipated the alleged hitch in Collins' passing motion. Anile didn't think so. What he saw he figured to be simply a bad throw.

"I'm not sure Kerry Collins is a great practice player," said the Panthers' chief evaluator of college talent. "He's what you might call a gamer. His competitive juices flow on game day and his abilities take over."

True enough. During the 1993 and 1994 college seasons, both Anile and Polian had personally watched Collins lead Penn State to several wins with late-game heroics against ranked teams (one during Collins' junior year in a victory over Tennessee and prized quarterback Heath Shuler, another coming from 21 points back versus an Illinois defense that had six players eventually drafted by NFL teams).

Anile said he felt no differently about the young quarterback's practice tendencies after watching him in training camp with the Panthers.

"One pass he throws in the dirt and you think, 'pheeew.' Then he might throw one over a guy's head."

Collins didn't have a good practice the entire week at the Senior Bowl. But he was making the right impression nonetheless with Anile, Polian and other Panthers executives in Mobile. They figured him to be a leader who would win games.

"We took him out to dinner and talked about the things you and I might talk about," said Anile in late October after watching Collins go 3–2 in his first five NFL starts. "We liked everything about his character. Our ideal situation was to let him learn under [Frank Reich and Jack Trudeau] until the offensive line got better. We didn't want to throw him in the fire too soon.

"But it's working out because Kerry is mentally tough. We're excited. He is one strong guy. When he has bad moments, he doesn't let them bother him. Some moments will be shining, and others will be 'Holy Moly.'"

The hitch did concern Polian and Anile enough to warrant watching hours of film after the Senior Bowl week. They watched in slow motion and super–slow motion. They took out stopwatches and compared Collins' pass release to other quarterbacks playing in the NFL. They had special videotapes of plays when Collins was especially pressured by the opposing defense.

"Our conclusion is it was not a problem," said Anile. "He's got a bit of baseball throw like a catcher. It's a certain cocking of the ball. But you only see it when Kerry has time to throw the football. When somebody is coming fast on him, pooomf! There's the release, there goes the pass without any cocking of the wrist.

"We decided people in our business look for negatives instead of positives," said Anile. "But nobody's perfect. God didn't make anybody perfect. I think other scouts were nitpicking with Kerry Collins."

Player agents were less skeptical about the quarterback. Leigh Steinberg, with the league's most impressive group of clients, recruited Collins hard and used some big-name influence.

Collins was back at school and on the telephone one Wednesday night in January, talking to his father about Sunday's upcoming NFC showdown between the San Francisco 49ers and Dallas Cowboys. The call was interrupted by call-waiting.

"Hello?"

"Kerry, this is Steve Young."

"Yeah, right."

Collins said later he thought a friend was playing a practical joke. He had talked a couple times with Steinberg but nothing was mentioned about any phone calls from NFL superstars to discuss how the agent negotiated such favorable contracts.

A couple hours later, the phone rang again.

"Hello?"

"Kerry, this is Troy Aikman."

Collins couldn't believe it. He was laying on his bed, looking at his Troy Aikman poster on the wall.

"Steve just called."

"Oh yeah? Well, you call him back and tell him we're gonna kick their ears in this weekend," Aikman said.

The first official meeting of the Panthers' front office on February 1, 1994, was lightly attended. Not for any reason except only three people represented the entire football operations group at the time: McCormack, Polian, and newly hired assistant general manager Joe Mack. With no coach, no players, not even a place to practice, what could the three men possibly accomplish?

"Go out to buy pencils and notepads," said Mack, laughing at the memory. "Actually, we had a lot of decisions to make. We had to get a computer system established, a player grading system established. We had to hire scouts and video people. We had to get our organizational chart in place."

A much bigger project was discussed that day: how to build the Panthers on the field given the off-the-field parameters of today's league rules. McCormack, Polian, and Mack during the weeks and months that followed would talk long hours about the pluses and minuses among signing unrestricted free agents, other free agents, waived NFL players, expansion draft selections, and college draft choices.

The days are gone when the college draft lasted 17 rounds and players were basically bound to their teams unless traded. Now only 64 percent of this past season's Pro Bowl players were drafted by their teams out of college. Only four of a total 85 all-stars were acquired in trades. The rest were free agents. Most were unrestricted free agents who switched teams for better contracts during the off-season; some had been released by one team and signed by another.

While Dom Anile is responsible for evaluation of the college talent, Joe Mack supervises pro scouting and helps Polian and McCormack with contract negotiations. His crunch time begins in January, just about when most NFL employees are breathing easier after the just-completed season. His first task is to finalize his list of about 40 to 50 unrestricted free agents who could help the Panthers win more games. These are players who other teams don't want to lose, but usually go to the highest bidder beginning with the first signing day in mid-February right through the start of training camp in July.

"It's part wish list and part needs list," explained Mack. "We're not going to sign everybody, but there will always be certain positions we're looking to improve each winter. "

Before Carolina's first season—even before the expansion and college drafts—the needs and wishes were many. In all, the Panthers signed 123 players before the end of the 1995 season, starting with the group of street free agents on December 15, 1994. Two of those players, wide receiver Willie Green and tight end Mathew Campbell, finished the season on the team's roster. Another player, offensive lineman Kevin Farkas, was part of the practice squad, and two others, tight end Lawyer Tillman and running back Tony Smith, finished the season on the injured reserve list.

In fact, Green developed into the team's big-play receiver. He finished with a career-high 47 catches for 882 yards and a team-high six touchdowns, including an 89-yard completion from Collins to clinch a thrilling win over the Falcons in the final home game at Clemson.

Green was one of 18 free agents on the roster for the season finale on Christmas Eve against the Washington Redskins who were either veterans released by other teams or rookies undrafted and subsequently signed by the Panthers.

None of these players approached the Panthers with much leverage in the form of offers from other clubs.

Nor did sizable contracts go to many of the players chosen in the expansion draft. Twelve Panthers, including six starters, were on the final game roster out of the 35 veterans picked from other NFL teams on February 15, 1995. There were some astute picks recommended by Mack: wide receivers Mark Carrier (team leader in receptions and yardage) and Eric Guliford (a clutch player among the conference leaders in punt return, including a touchdown against Chicago); cornerback Tim McKyer, the incessant talker who backed his gift of gab with solid play and returned an interception 96 yards for the only touchdown in the San Francisco win; center Curtis Whitley, a backup San Diego lineman and former Clemson Tiger who made *Sports Illustrated*'s All-Pro Team in his first season as a starter; and nose tackle Greg Kragen, seemingly old at 34, who was "still a good football player even if he wasn't a prototypical defensive lineman at this point in his career," said Mack.

Kragen was the perfect example of how Mack and his pro scouting staff could sift through some 2,000 to 3,000 videotapes—they call it "grinding down the film"—to find a handful of players who would eventually help the Panthers.

"Greg was a little bit older but what I noticed on film was his enthusiasm and instinct for game," said Mack, who watches about six to eight hours of film nearly every day from mid-July to May.

Just how can anybody judge "enthusiasm" and "instinct" from game films?

"Maybe the way he tries to fight through blocks," replied Mack. "Maybe how he chases a play even if he doesn't have the best chance of catching it. Maybe at the end of a play he is excited not only about a play he made but also those of his teammates."

Unlike Jacksonville, which selected several former first-round college draft picks with large salaries on expansion draft day, Carolina was saving its money for unrestricted free agents. It wanted as much room as possible under the league-imposed salary cap for all teams, which was $37 million for the 1995 season.

"We didn't think there were a lot of guys worth big dollars and forcing us to squeeze the salary cap," said Mack, who filed a report on every expansion-draft prospect and even traveled to the NFL offices in New York on occasion to clarify what was a changing set of rules for how other teams would be required to make players available. "One problem was we didn't know if some players we might choose would be willing to rework their contracts to keep us under the cap."

So the big money went to unrestricted free agents and top draft choices. Given the blessing of owner of Jerry Richardson, Polian and Mack set an aggressive strategy for pursuing NFL veterans. They were especially interested in meeting the needs of the 3-4 defensive scheme planned by Capers, who used the alignment in Pittsburgh to lead the AFC in fewest points allowed for three straight seasons. Unlike the more popular 4-3 alignment, the 3-4 utilizes only three down linemen and four linebackers—as opposed to four down linemen and three linebackers.

Not long after he was hired on January 23, 1995, Capers sat down with Mack for a let's-get-better-acquainted meeting. It was instantly clear to Mack that Capers was not like other promising young head coaches, such as Dave Wannstedt in Chicago, who desired total control of football personnel decisions.

"Coach, what kind of defensive players do you need?" asked Mack, who to that point had based most of his work anticipating the 4-3 scheme used by most teams in the NFL.

"Well, if we can't get 3-4 players, I can adjust and use a 4-3 [defense]," said Capers.

"No, Coach, we want to get who you want. OK, what is the critical part of your defense?"

"The outside linebackers have to be able to rush the passer."

Mack realized this was a tall order.

"That type of player is a tough combination," said Mack. "It means someone who is big, powerful and strong, but also fast. It made for a much smaller pool of free-agent linebackers."

This made them more expensive acquisitions. Cleveland Browns coach Bill Belichick said that is one reason more teams don't use the 3-4. "You don't pick up these good outside linebackers at K-Mart," he said during the preseason.

Truth is, Houston's Lamar Lathon and New Orleans' Darion Conner were about the only two on the short list. Lathon weighed enough (about 250 pounds) to encourage the Oilers to convert him to defensive end in 1994, a season in which he recorded 8.5 sacks. The Panthers loved his speed—as did many teams—and intended to turn him loose at outside linebacker. Conner was also fast and about 240 pounds; he recorded 10.5 sacks (fifth in the NFC) in 1994 while playing for Vic Fangio, the Panthers defensive coordinator who was then coaching linebackers for the Saints.

"We figured Lamar and Darion were going to be our linchpins as outside linebackers," said Mack. "We concentrated on them real hard."

The Panthers succeeded in signing both players, primarily due to a realistic approach which assumed players would be inclined to join more established clubs if the money offers were about equal. Polian and Mack figured they would have to spend more to earn some credibility with players and their agents. Lathon would become the Panther with the highest 1995 salary, a cool $3.1 million, and Conner would pull down $1.5 million.

"When you chart pass rushers to what they are getting, it's big money," said Mack. "If one team is willing to pay that, it knocks you out of the box. You have to have the mindset to be aggressive."

Some NFL general managers thought the Panthers were aggressively foolish by agreeing to pay former New York Giants defensive lineman Mike Fox $9 million over five years, including a $2 million signing bonus. They were mostly concerned that their own teams' defensive lineman would be comparing statistics with Fox, who had averaged less than two sacks each of his five seasons in the NFL—roughly a million dollars per sack according to some cynics.

But Carolina saw his value in stopping the run, collapsing the pocket and stacking up blockers so linebackers could make quick tackles. The team offered the sweet deal to Fox on the first morning of the free-agency period and he accepted by midafternoon, forgetting about the visits he was supposed to make to other NFL teams.

"We saw a tough guy and a hard worker," said Mack about Fox. "We needed a big defensive lineman who could stop the run. But there was also the context of the moment. We were an expansion team. We had very few players and no one of note.

"So it was a leap of faith for established players to come with us. We felt, rightly or wrongly, that we had to be more aggressive than other teams. We had to establish ourselves with everybody from the players to the fans.

"Negotiations with many of our free agents were pretty quick. We were decisive. The players and their agents thought they were fair offers and, in some cases, more than fair market value."

At the press conference announcing the signings of both Fox and placekicker John Kasay (who got a five-year deal worth $4.3 million), Polian was less willing to talk economics—"I don't believe in market value," he said, scowling. "What is market value, really?"—and more interested in notifying the league's other 29 general managers of the acquisitions.

"We told people today we're in business," he declared. "We're serious. We're not going to wait for the bus to leave. We're getting on board very early.

"We're not the San Francisco 49ers. We can't hang out the championship banners and sell Super Bowl rings. What we can sell is a commitment to winning. If there's a spilloff effect and other players see what we're doing and think we're serious—well, that's great."

Of course, a big chunk of money can always attract serious attention. Kasay said the Panthers' offer "blew me away."

"It was like when I saw my wife for the first time," said the man who would become leading scorer during the inaugural season. "It really didn't matter what everyone else looked like. She was the one."

Polian and Mack were just getting warmed up. They eventually signed 13 unrestricted free agents, plus 18 other veterans who were cut or released from other NFL teams. Although they wouldn't dare admit it to the media, Polian and Mack only truly regretted giving $6 million for four years to offensive tackle Derrick Graham, who lost his starting job during the seventh week of the season, and perhaps overpaying wide receiver Don Beebe ($615,800) for a season of 14 total receptions for 152 yards and one touchdown.

On the other hand, Carolina's open checkbook stole linebacker Sam Mills right from under the noses of his longtime team and division rival, the New Orleans Saints. Mills and his agent were insulted by the initial Saints offer but impressed with the numbers offered by Panthers executives: $2.8 million for two years. Such numbers warranted a trip to Charlotte.

"We did a big sales job on Sam," said Mack. "We knew he had warm feelings for [Saints head coach] Jim Mora. He was the only pro coach Sam had played for. We were very aggressive financially and showed him how much we wanted him here."

Mills toured the Panthers' Rock Hill facilities and, like every free agent, was given a detailed tour of the new stadium under construction in Charlotte. Mack emphasized the planned natural-grass playing field, which is a major selling point for highly paid athletes looking to avoid injuries and extend careers.

"The evidence [associating injuries with artificial turf] is more anecdotal than hard research," admitted Mack. "But it does make a difference for players."

After the tour, Mills went to dinner with Panthers defensive coordinator Vic Fangio, who was his position coach in New Orleans.

It was a productive day for Carolina. The Saints eventually offered to match the Panthers contract, but Mills had already been won over. He signed with the expansion team a few days later, and by season's end was considered the Panthers' 1995 most valuable player by most anyone following the team—including star broadcaster John Madden of the Fox Network, who named Mills to the highly visible and talent-laden All-Madden Team.

The Panthers' seven wins and flirtation with playoff possibilities was a credit to the entire organization, not the least of which included Joe Mack and pro scout Chris Polian (the general manager's 24-year-old son), plus Dom Anile and his two regional college scouts, Ralph Hawkins (a former NFL defensive coordinator) and Jack Bushofsky (player personnel director of the Colts for 11 years), who would double-check the work of area scouts Hal Athon (western United States), Boyd Dowler (the Green Bay Packers great who played on the first two Super Bowl championship teams and now covers the Southeast for the Panthers), Bob Guarini (Midwest), Jerry Hardaway (East Coast) and Tony Softli (Texas, Oklahoma, Colorado and other states between the Midwest and West Coast). Together, the 10-man group represents one of the largest scouting staffs in a league that includes teams with as few as three full-time scouts.

"This is a really tough business in some ways," said Mack, who was once successfully and intensely recruited by an assistant coach named Bill Polian to play linebacker for the U.S. Merchant Marine Academy in Kings Point, New York. "You're under the microscope. People are checking your performance all the time. It's tough on your family, your wife. You are away from the kids a lot."

Yet Mack asks for no sympathy.

"Oh, I wouldn't want to do anything else. I enjoy going to work. The hours are long and there's lots of them. But more than once I ask myself, 'I get paid for this stuff?'"

At one time, in his late 20s, Mack wasn't paid all that much. He earned $50 a school (including expenses) evaluating college players for the BLESTO scouting service. He supplemented his income with a bartending job in Philadelphia at a place called Jimmy's Speakeasy.

Then he got his break. BLESTO hired him full-time for the princely sum of $17,000, plus expenses.

Anile would lay awake for part of almost every night between late January and the college draft in late April, pondering the countless scenarios that might affect the 120 to 140 prospects listed on the team's draft board and another 50 or so listed as "medical rejects" or "DND" (Do Not Draft) due to character flaws uncovered during psychological testing, team security checks or discussions with college coaches. His staff had arrived at this list after starting with about 400 names of college players before the 1995 season.

The process did have one obstacle not present for the first Panthers draft: Anile tore his right Achilles tendon while stepping out of the way of an errant pass during a

University of Nebraska practice in October; he didn't go on the road—weekdays to various major college practices and Thursday nights and Saturdays to games—for the last two months of the season (despite trying without success and against doctor's orders one week). He recovered in time for bowl games and all-star games, but relied on game films and his staff reports until then.

But Anile didn't let it bother him. He has been at this gambit since 1982, when he left an 84–33–1 college coaching record to become a scout. He spent eight seasons with the Cleveland Browns before joining the Panthers. In his final draft with the Browns, his recommendations resulted in the number-nine overall selection of cornerback Antonio Langham, who started every game during his rookie season and had team-high 29 deflected passes and two interceptions. The Browns had a compensatory pick that season, selecting Derrick Alexander as the 29th and final first round choice of the 1994 draft. Alexander finished as the team's leading receiver, tying Paul Warfield's rookie mark of three 100-yard games. The pair of Browns rookies were two of only eight first-rounders who made an immediate impact in the NFL.

Anile's draft results in 1994 and, of course, 1995, were the envy of most every NFL front office. Plus, Polian is known as one of the league's shrewdest judges of college talent—and a master wheeler-dealer on draft day. No wonder most team general managers were grumbling all off-season about the extra picks awarded to Carolina and Jacksonville in the 1996 draft.

The extra choices—one each in rounds three through six and two additional players in round seven—were rubber-stamped at an owners meeting without any significant discussion in September 1994. Green Bay general manager Ron Wolf was the most vocal critic. He was on the Tampa Bay staff when the Bucs joined the NFL in 1976. Tampa and fellow expansion team Seattle only received extra picks in the first year, when they were awarded one additional choice in rounds two through five of a 17-round draft. That made for 11 picks in the first seven rounds, compared to 14 for the Panthers and Jaguars.

The top three rounds are what matter most, said Anile, who nonetheless found Frank Garcia, Andrew Peterson and Chad Cota in rounds four through seven.

"Make a busted pick in the top three rounds and your organization doesn't recover for a couple of years," explained Anile. "You're in trouble if you don't hit on those guys.

"The players you pick in the fourth and fifth round should be competitive and make a good run at your football team. Whether your sixth- and seventh-round picks make an impact is a matter of how hard [the scouting staff] is working. The majority of good players are gone by then. There is some sort of hole in those players."

One more war story among dozens from Anile: He always tells his scouts to work out any kid who shows up for a tryout. "Never turn a kid away," he preaches.

Before the 1995 draft, Anile accompanied regional scout Ralph Hawkins on a visit to see defensive line prospect Hugh Douglas at tiny Central State University in Wilberforce, Ohio. Douglas had an agent who set up the workout for several NFL scouts at the Central State gymnasium. A big kid by the name of Brandon Hayes showed up with his own agent to show scouts his potential as an offensive lineman. But Douglas' agent said no way, he paid for the gym and special liability insurance. He told Hayes and his agent to get lost.

As Anile tells it, Hayes sort of just shuffled into a corner while Douglas impressed the scouts with skills that would soon enough make him Defensive Rookie of the Year in the NFL with the New York Jets.

After the session with everybody safely gone, Anile told Hawkins, "Let's check out this other kid. We know all we need to know about Hugh Douglas."

The Panthers scouts liked what they saw after putting the appreciative Hayes through the paces outside the Central State gym. He was eventually signed to a free-agent rookie contract and had a promising preseason until he tore the anterior cruciate ligament in his right knee and was put on the injured reserve for the 1995 season.

"What clinched it for us was when Ralph and I hustled back to Hugh Douglas' agent's office, who had invited anyone to come over to look at more practice films of Douglass," recalled Anile. "Well, we went and said, 'Gee, can we look those practice films?' He said sure, great, and we watched Hayes for about two or three hours. The agent never knew, and we kept it quiet."

THE
PRESEASON

Getting Started

This was not a typical NFL minicamp, which is often treated with indifference by the media and sometimes even by players themselves. This was the first time the Panthers took the practice field as an entire team. The local media was out in force at Winthrop University, and even some national media paid their respects. The New York Times *dropped by one day and a reporter from a Japanese magazine dropped by another. Even the MetLife blimp circled the practice fields behind Winthrop Coliseum the first day, giving the whole scene a feeling of NFL authenticity for the first time.*

S ure, the Panthers had been working out at Winthrop during a 12-week off-season conditioning period for veterans that was designed to give them a jump on the rest of the league. Sure, these same veterans had been diligently attending classes at the same time, trying to grasp the offensive and defensive systems Professor Dom Capers intended to implant in their brains by the following September.

But now the rookies, their identities a mystery until only 10 days earlier, were taking part as well. It offered the first extended look at Collins and the rest not only for the media but for the coaching staff as well. As the Panthers took the field that first day and began lining up to do stretching exercises, Frank Reich turned to locate the player directly behind him and shook his head in mock surprise.

"I never, ever thought I would be doing calisthentics in the NFL and turn around to see another guy from Lebanon, Pennsylvania, right behind me," he said.

Yet there he was—not only another guy, but another quarterback. And not just another quarterback, but the quarterback Reich was supposed to tutor so he could one day take Reich's job.

Incredibly, Collins, the quarterback of the future, grew up in the same hometown of 24,800 as Reich, the quarterback of the present. Other than producing quarterbacks for the Carolina Panthers, Lebanon is famous—or so its citizens like to think—for producing lots of Lebanon bologna.

"The red kind, which is much better. Not the pink," reminded Audrey Brubaker, executive secretary of the Lebanon Chamber of Commerce.

Like most Lebanonites, Brubaker was well aware of the city's newfound ties to one of the NFL's expansion franchises not after the draft but upon Reich's free-agent signing with the club a little less than a month before the draft.

Something of a hero in his hometown, when Reich was with the Buffalo Bills in 1992, he engineered one of the biggest comebacks in NFL history, and sweatshirts bearing his likeness and touting the achievement suddenly became a hot item in Lebanon.

"I felt lucky to snatch one up, they went so fast," Brubaker said. "That Frank, he's a heartthrob around here."

Yet Collins, 22 years young the day he was drafted, was the eligible bachelor of the two. Reich was 33, married and the father of two young daughters.

Nonetheless, as of April 1995, Collins had not yet attained Reich's celebrity status in Lebanon—partly because Collins was an unestablished NFL rookie, despite being a high draft choice, and partly because Collins transferred from Lebanon High to West Lawn High in nearby Reading, Pennsylvania, after his sophomore year in high school. Folks don't quickly forget or forgive those kinds of things in small towns.

Reich's parents still live in Lebanon, so he has visited often each NFL off-season. His father, Frank Sr., was a teacher in the Lebanon school district and a football captain at Penn State. His mother, Pat, was a longtime physical education teacher at Cedar Crest Middle School. Even Collins was well aware of the legendary Frank Reich's pull on the community.

"I kind of started following Frank when he went to Maryland and pulled off that big comeback there [erasing a 31–0 deficit to Miami in 1984]," said Collins, who was 11 years old at the time. "And then, of course, after he went to the Bills. Everyone in Lebanon knew who Frank was."

Collins had fond memories of his own childhood in Lebanon.

"It was good for me," Collins said. "There were a lot of kids around, always playing sports. I would have been hard-pressed to find a better situation than the one I had when I was growing up. There was a playground right across the street from where we lived, and it had a basketball court, a baseball field and a place to play football. What kid could ask for more?"

Conversely, Collins didn't really catch Reich's attention until 1994, when Collins was directing Penn State to a 12–0 record and a Rose Bowl victory as a senior.

"I knew he was a big-time prospect coming out of high school," said Reich, "but I didn't really follow him until this year. He's impressive."

As they met in the locker room at Winthrop Coliseum shortly after the draft and before the first minicamp, Collins said he and Reich spent "at least 20 minutes just talking about mutual people we know from back home. It was kind of funny."

"I think it's hysterical," Reich added. "To think we're from the same hometown, let alone play the same position for the same NFL team . . . well, the odds for that happening must be astronomical."

The Panthers were giving everyone plenty to talk about in the NFL, the way they were pursuing unrestricted free agents. Lamar Lathon, an outside linebacker considered a key in the 3-4 defensive alignment favored by Capers, was the highest-paid Panther during the inaugural season. In five previous years with the Houston Oilers, he totaled 14 sacks—eight of which came in 1994, his last season there.

As time progressed, it became obvious the Panthers' strategy was to instantly construct a veteran-laden defense through free agency.

Capers valued the presence of veterans. He also wanted several players who understood his concept of zone-blitzing and believed in his motives of bringing pressure from the 3-4 defensive alignment that, by 1995, only three other clubs utilized.

Lathon, a six-three, 252-pound mass of sculpted muscle and somewhat questionable psyche, was considered a key to the success of the 3-4. So was six-two, 242-pound Darion Conner, another outside backer signed as an unrestricted free agent for one season only. Their jobs as "speed rushers off the corners," as Capers put it, were to bring constant pressure on opposing quarterbacks.

Capers' defenses in Pittsburgh earned the nickname Blitzburgh. Yet they were successful not only because they blitzed often, but because opposing offenses could rarely detect where all the pressure was coming from. In addition to Lathon and Conner, for instance, the Panthers might shoot an inside linebacker right up the middle on a blitz—or they might send a cornerback barreling in at the last instant, undetected and therefore unblocked. Behind these creative blitzes, the defensive secondary would settle into coverage zones, not the man-to-man coverage favored by most other teams.

Capers believed this way of playing defense, which was considered somewhat revolutionary by many of his NFL brethren, gave defenders better vision of the football on most plays and therefore prevented big plays from happening with much frequency.

He also believed the best chance it had of succeeding in the first year with the Panthers was to have as many skilled and experienced veterans playing it as possible.

No one was more skilled or experienced, in Capers' estimation, than Sam Mills. Nor was there any player available via free agency with whom Capers was more familiar. He had been an assistant coach for two seasons with the Philadelphia/Baltimore Stars in the old USFL and for six more with New Orleans while Mills was establishing himself as one of the hardest-hitting, most consistently productive linebackers in all of professional football.

Lawrence Taylor, the great linebacker for the New York Giants and former University of North Carolina star who has since retired, once looked at Mills across the locker room at a Pro Bowl and told a reporter, "Just once I'd like to make a hit like he does. It's got to be better than sex."

But would Mills come to Carolina? He had spent all nine of his NFL seasons with the Saints. He had never had a head coach besides Jim Mora in 11 professional seasons, counting the USFL.

It wasn't easy convincing him, but in the end Capers sold Mills on the idea that this represented a rare opportunity to be part of something special from the start. He assured Mills that he would in essence be the "quarterback on defense," making all the defensive calls throughout the course of games. Convincing Mills to sign a two-year, $2.8 million contract with the Panthers turned out to be a coup. And even though Mills turned 36 years of age on the final day of the Panthers' first three-day minicamp, it already was becoming clear what his addition to the roster meant—on the field and off. Mills might not say much in the locker room, but he commands attention when he does speak up.

"It's like those old E. F. Hutton commercials," receiver Willie Green said. "When Sam does talk, we all listen."

Mills also led by example, spending countless hours poring over film. He regularly came in on the players' rare days off to watch film. Capers knew no one would prepare more carefully or more completely than Sam Mills.

Mills' arrival meant instant respect for the defense. It meant basically having another coach on the field for Capers, although Mills resented it when he was referred to as "a coach on the field." He wanted to be known as a player who made plays—all plays, big and small. A coach on the field, to him, represented someone whose finest playing days were behind him.

Mills is only five feet, nine inches and barely 225 pounds, although there isn't an ounce of fat on his squat, powerful frame.

ESPN broadcaster Chris Berman once called Mills a nickname he did not like: Field Mouse.

"Call me a field general or call me General Mills, but don't call me a field mouse," Mills later said.

His teammates often preyed on his lack of height, too—but only verbally. No one could abuse him physically.

"They used to tease me all the time," Mills said of his early teammates. "We'd be in the huddle and they'd say, 'Where's Sam? We've only got 10 guys on the field.' Then one of the bigger guys would look down at me and say, 'Oh, there you are.'

"It was all in fun, though. Even now it goes on to some extent. If a pass goes over my head during practice, I'm gonna hear a short joke. I just tell everybody that I've never had the height, so I don't know what I'm missing."

Mills almost missed out on a career in pro football. Unlike Kerry Collins and some of the others on the Panthers' roster who were former high draft choices and therefore had a smoother path paved to the NFL, Mills was not drafted after a decent but not spectacular college football career, at Division II Montclair State in New Jersey. At Montclair, basically anyone who wanted to play on the football team did. Mike Fratello, who would go on to gain fame as a coach in the National Basketball Association, actually played nose tackle for one season at Montclair—and at five feet, six inches, Fratello is even shorter than Mills.

The Cleveland Browns did give Mills a tryout right out of college, but it didn't last long. The Browns cut him in a move the franchise regrets to this day.

"I was just excited to have a tryout, to get my shot," Mills remembered. "That doesn't always happen for guys from a small school like I was. I wanted to see how I could do against the Division I guys. I felt good about my performance. I felt bad that I got released, but I felt good about my performance.

"The worst time was flying back home. When you're flying back, you're sitting on that plane, and there are no other players around you. You're just sitting there with a bunch of people from the regular working world, and it finally hits you. You think, 'Well, this is it—at least for now.' That's a bad feeling, a real bad feeling."

Mills experienced it again shortly thereafter when the Toronto Argonauts of the Canadian Football League also cut him.

The ninth of 11 children, Sam Mills Jr. nonetheless did not consider himself a failure. He was the first in his family to graduate from college, and he took pride in that. He had an alternative career planned as a high-school teacher and possibly a coach if his playing career hit a dead end, but even after being cut by the Argonauts, with whom he had tried out while on a leave of absence from his teaching job in New Jersey, he didn't figure that was the end.

After Toronto cut him, he kept teaching photography and woodworking at a New Jersey high school, where his salary in 1981 was $13,600. He drove a 1969 Jaguar back and forth to work, saving his money to provide as best he could for wife Melanie and their five-year-old son, Sam III.

Then the United States Football League came calling.

When the chance for a tryout with the Philadelphia Stars presented itself, Mills was told by his superiors at the high school that he was doing a good job and was due for a raise—but they simply could not grant him another leave of absence to chase his football dream. He could take the teaching job or leave it, but he couldn't leave and plan to come back to it.

Mills left.

There were about 80 players at the tryout he attended. Among the coaches watching the tryout was Joe Pendry, then an assistant coach for the Stars and, ironically, now the offensive coordinator for the Panthers. Mills caught Pendry's eye and also impressed the other coaches in attendance.

Afterward, Mills was invited into the back of Pendry's beige Chevrolet conversion van—where he was offered a contract for $25,000.

"Obviously, there was no negotiating," Mills said. "I signed the contract right there in the back of Joe Pendry's van. I was ecstatic. If they had offered me $18,000, I would have taken it.

"Heck, I probably would have played for free if they would have asked me and if I could have afforded it."

The head coach of the Stars at the time was George Perles, but he never coached Mills. He left to become head coach at Michigan State University before the next season began and was replaced by Mora, who later would call Mills "the best player I've ever coached." In 1984, Mills' second of three USFL seasons, the Stars added a young defensive secondary coach named Dom Capers.

Mills did not play in his first NFL game until he was 27, after Mora and Capers brought him with them to the Saints in 1986. He made up for it quickly, however, by being named to four Pro Bowls in his first six seasons with the Saints.

"I took the scenic route to the NFL," Mills said. "Everything that happened to me early in my career turned out to be a blessing in disguise.

"When I see a rookie heading for the parking lot with his bags packed or just handing in his playbook, I know what he's feeling. Some of them may not think I do because a lot of them just know me as a four-time Pro Bowler and all that—but I do. I've been on that other side, too."

If Sam Mills best exemplified what a coach liked to see in a player, then Barry Foster might be described as a guy who exemplified what a coach feared most in an obviously talented player.

Surly. Didn't like to practice. Wouldn't play hurt.

Those were some of the criticisms of Foster when, two days before the opening of their first minicamp, the Panthers attempted to address one of their more serious offensive trouble spots by trading for Foster, the enigmatic running back whom Capers had known during his years in Pittsburgh.

The cost of acquiring Foster, a former Pro Bowler who led the American Football Conference in rushing just two seasons earlier, was not great—a sixth-round pick in the 1996 college draft, plus a conditional fourth-rounder in 1997 should Foster meet certain incentives based on his production on the field in 1995. The reason was obvious. The Steelers were looking to dump the oft-injured back and his $2.45 million 1995 salary.

The Panthers, desperate to upgrade their nondescript backfield, were willing to accept the risks that accompanied a player like Foster.

"This was an opportunity we didn't feel we could pass up," Bill Polian said. "Barry Foster is a proven back who can get you yards when you need to get them. Along with Randy Baldwin and Derrick Lassic, we think we now have three backs with distinctly different styles that will give us the ability to change up on offense and throw different looks at opposing defenses."

Asked where Foster fit in among those backs in terms of style, Polian laughed and replied, "He's a bash-and-crash back. He's a pure power guy."

Since leading the AFC in rushing in 1992, Foster mostly had been a hurt guy. Ankle and knee injuries limited his availability to just 36 percent of Pittsburgh's offensive plays in 1993 and 1994 combined. Polian said it was because of nothing more than "the usual nicks and bangs" that a back of Foster's style must endure, but there had been an ugly dispute in Pittsburgh over the seriousness of an ankle injury in 1993. Basically, Pittsburgh's team physicians insisted the injury was not serious enough to keep Foster from playing; Foster sought a second opinion independent from the team and against the club's wishes, and surgery was recommended, ending his season.

Polian shrugged all that off. He was willing to take a chance on Foster. He also did not buy the criticism that Foster was a bad guy, although his reputation had been sullied in Pittsburgh over the dispute with team doctors and an adverserial relationship with the media there.

"We just got a guy who can carry the mail," Polian said, beaming. "He's only 26 years old. We think he's got plenty left."

As for Foster's personality, Capers was quick to jump to Foster's defense. He said Foster was just a quiet, somewhat introverted person. He also made it clear that he didn't much care what kind of relationship Foster developed with the media in the Carolinas, as long as he, as Polian put it, delivered the mail in large volumes and with a consistency rate equal to that of the U.S. Postal Service.

"Many times the past three years I sat up in the press box [as Pittsburgh's defensive coordinator] and watched defensive backs from other teams come up to try to tackle

Barry—and then I would see him run right through them," Capers said. "I always said I was glad he was on our side. I'm happy to say I can stand before you and say the same thing again now."

Foster downplayed his recent history of injuries and reports of his terrible relationship with media and even fans in Pittsburgh. And he said he was ready and determined to produce like he had two years earlier.

"I feel like on any given day, I can go out and put up 100 yards [rushing]," Foster said. "If I'm healthy, I feel I'm one of the best."

The first minicamp lasted only three days, but revealed a great deal. Naturally, much of the focus was on Collins. He did not much resemble a glamorous first-round pick all of the time; in fact, more often than not, he didn't.

There were times when he hit receivers on the numbers with sharp passes, much like one would expect considering his resume and draft status. There were more times, however, when his passes wobbled, hung in the air, and ended up either in the dirt or somewhere downfield, well beyond the mystified and frustrated receiver.

By his own admission, he was struggling to comprehend a complex offensive system and was given so much to learn in the three days that he suffered somewhat from information overload. The Panthers decided it was better to have it that way— giving him as much or more than he could handle and letting him learn from his mistakes on the field—than trying to spoon-feed him along at a slower pace. After all, what did they have to lose? Collins was already showing he wasn't the type of young man who would get down on himself or lose confidence in his abilities over a few poorly thrown balls.

"When Kerry knows what he's doing," said offensive coordinator Joe Pendry, "he's good. When he doesn't know what he's doing, anything can happen. He's liable to detonate anywhere. He's a little like a time bomb right now. You don't know when he's going to go off. When he does, it can look pretty bad. You'll look at him after one of those bad reads or wild throws and think, Where did that come from?

"But it's all part of his growing process as a rookie quarterback. There isn't a rookie quarterback out there who doesn't go through this. . . . Kerry gets mad at himself, but he is what I call unflappable. If he messes up and it bothers him, it only bothers him for a few seconds. A quarterback has to have that kind of attitude."

Capers said what impressed him most about Collins in his very first workout was "the way he handled himself at the line of scrimmage. I think he has good field presence."

No one seemed worried that Collins wasn't sharp overall, least of all Collins. With Reich and Trudeau, two veterans with 19 years of NFL experience between them, already in the Panthers' fold, the plan for the time being was to let Collins gain a better grip on the offensive system before trying to get behind the wheel and drive.

"Being a young quarterback, this is really an ideal situation for me," Collins said. "I'm going to make some mistakes and it's going to take some time. . . . I can't go out there acting like this is my team, because it's not. But I feel confident that one day I can lead this team."

Whether it was Collins or someone else at quarterback, someone would have to lead the Panthers against the defending Super Bowl champions, the San Francisco 49ers, not once, not twice, but a total of three times. The Panthers were scheduled to play the 49ers in the preseason at San Francisco and, as NFC West divisional rivals, twice in the regular season, home and away.

When Hideki Okuda, a Japanese reporter for *American Football Magazine,* visited Winthrop one afternoon for his first look at the Panthers, one of the first questions he fired at one of the local reporters covering the team was, "How bad do you think the Panthers will get beat by the 49ers the first time they meet?"

The local reporter's honest reply to Okuda's query: "Forty-two to six."

The first minicamp in the history of the Carolina Panthers ended in appropriate fashion when a pair of high-spirited scuffles broke out between players during the last five minutes of the final workout.

"Now that's fuckin' football right there! It's gettin' nasty!" shouted offensive line prospect Mike Finn as the first skirmish broke out between center Frank Garcia, who was proving to be a fiesty rookie, and nose tackle Mike Teeter.

Later, as he trotted off the field, Teeter shrugged and mentioned there was bound to be a whole lot more of that kind of thing in a few weeks when the team held its second mincamp over nine days instead of three.

"Any time you get a bunch of guys together, there's a lot of testosterone flowing," Teeter said. "When you get guys together, there is a tendency for them to get really aggressive after a while. The first couple days are fine, but I can't even begin to tell you what's going to happen in our nine-day camp."

One day earlier, the Panthers had been surprised by what happened during an autograph-and-workout session at Furman's Paladin Stadium in Greenville, South Carolina. An estimated 6,000 fans showed up, stunning even the most optimistic Panthers officials.

The Panthers split up into groups by position and took up residence behind long portable tables for what was supposed to be a 45-minute autograph session, only to be deluged by the number of folks who wanted their signatures. At one point, it was estimated there were 1,000 fans in the quarterbacks' line alone. The very first fan in that line told a reporter he arrived at 10:30 A.M., even though the signing session wasn't scheduled to begin until four hours later.

Eventually, the Panthers had to cut off the autographs—announcing over the public-address system that fans could still obtain the signature of their favorite Carolina quarterback by sending a self-addressed, stamped envelope to the club. Cynics joked that maybe Barry Foster could carry the mail back to Winthrop University and then deliver the autographs back to the fans.

Collins was so popular with fans at Furman that he already was looking to Reich for advice on how to make it through such an ordeal without having the writing—and also throwing—hand cramping badly.

"I'll bet I signed between 200 and 300 autographs in a span of 45 minutes," Collins said. "I'm surprised I could throw a ball after that."

Reich told him to get used to it.

"Playing in Buffalo and going to four Super Bowls, my arm is well-conditioned to that sort of thing," said Reich, smiling. "But if I had to take penmanship, it would not be a pretty sight. I would not be passing. My autograph is kind of a big *F* and a big *R* and a number 14. The key to signing your autograph is to always put your number down, too. Otherwise, they'll never know who you are."

Signing in that manner, basically leaving all letters in between the *F* and the *R* illegible by executing a quick scribble, was proven to conserve arm strength and prevent hand cramps. These were the kinds of important things Collins needed to remember.

After the first minicamp concluded, Collins looked briefly for a place to live and then took off for a short vacation at Hilton Head, South Carolina. Then he returned to State College, Pennsylvania, and worked some with Bill Walsh, the former NFL head coach, on improving certain techniques.

Bill Polian was quick to point out to the media that the informal workout with Walsh was Collins' own idea, but the team had given its blessing. He was adamant in adding it had nothing to do whatsoever with Walsh trying to get the supposed "hitch" out of Collins' throwing motion, which, as Dom Anile freely admitted, was rather obvious when Collins had extra time to deliver a pass.

"Kerry Collins has no problem throwing the football. That's not even an issue. Forget about it," Polian said.

As far as finding a place to live near Rock Hill, Collins didn't figure money would be much of an issue either—even though contract negotiations between his agent, Leigh Steinberg, and Polian had yet to begin.

"I have a pretty good idea of what I'll be able to afford," said Collins, grinning broadly.

Prior to the opening of the second minicamp at Winthrop at the beginning of June, Capers was asked to serve as the grand marshal of the Red Dog 300 NASCAR Grand National race at Charlotte Motor Speedway on May 27. It was the first race Dom Capers had ever attended, and he made no secret of the fact that he wasn't sure what was going to transpire.

"I hope I don't mess it up," Capers said of being grand marshal. "I'm just going to go where they direct me and do whatever they tell me to do."

While Dom wasn't a racing fan, his brother, Julius, was an avid follower of the NASCAR circuit. Julius drove down to Charlotte for the race with his family, and was asked about Dom's knowledge of automobile mechanics.

"He knows where the gas nozzle is and that's about it," Julius Capers joked.

Dom Capers was aware of his brother's interest in racing, but was a little uncertain of the specifics.

"He's got a guy he likes, a favorite driver, but I can't remember who it is," he said of Julius one day.

After naming several drivers, someone offered, "Dale Earnhardt?"

"Yep, that's it. That's the guy he likes," Capers said.

The head coach of the Panthers may not have known what was going on at the Charlotte Motor Speedway, but he did know his stuff at Winthrop, and he was beginning to like much of what he saw during the conditioning workouts for veterans and during the second minicamp.

So was Lamar Lathon, the outside linebacker who was liable to say anything on those days when he wanted to talk. Players were often asked how many games they thought the Panthers could win in their inaugural season, and they almost always, following Capers' lead, answered the question the same way: by politely talking their way around it without providing a definitive answer. But not Lathon.

Following a workout toward the end of the second minicamp, Lathon boldly predicted the expansion team could win as many as 10 games in its first season. He pointed out that between himself, Sam Mills, Darion Conner, Frank Stams and Carlton Bailey, all signed as free agents, they had five linebackers who had started elsewhere in the NFL the previous season. Those five also had a combined total of 27 years NFL experience between them.

"You look at the guys we have right now," said Lathon, "and there's no reason we can't say that we're the best linebacking corps in America. I know we haven't played a game yet, but we've got a makeup of veteran linebackers who know what we're doing. . . . When you've got guys like that, you've got the leadership it takes to win football games.

The prediction came unprovoked. It surprised even the small contingent of media who had gathered around Lathon as he gained steam in his spirited monologue.

"Do you really think 9 or 10 wins is possible for an expansion franchise?" a reporter asked.

"I know a lot of people have tried to downplay the possiblity of us being very good," Lathon said. "They think we'll be like other expansion teams or whatever and win maybe four games.

"I hate the word 'expansion,' but that's what we are—until we establish ourselves and win some football games. Then people will start calling us the Carolina Panthers instead of 'the expansion Carolina Panthers.' I think the possibilities with the veteran corps that we have are unlimited. . . . We're going to be able to shock a lot of people."

Lathon's comments clearly surprised Dom Capers.

"I certainly appreciate Lamar's optimism," said Capers, shaking his head when told of Lathon's prediction. "But being that Charlie Dayton [Carolina's director of communications] gave me some alarming statistics about the best any expansion team has ever done is three wins, it's interesting. So I guess if we set a record for expansion wins with four, we'll all be tremendously disappointed now, huh?"

For Capers, the minicamp was an indoctrination of sorts into the fishbowl world of being a head coach. Every comment he made of any consequence showed up in the papers, often in the headlines. Even the words uttered by his players, which he could not entirely control, could cause headaches, he was learning.

His life was changing.

Asked how it was changing one day, Capers related a story about how he was in line at Wendy's late one night on his way home from Winthrop in Rock Hill. He was still wearing his coaching outfit, complete with Panthers hat, Panthers shorts and Panthers golf shirt.

"Wow," said the woman standing in line in front of him, "you must really be some Panthers fan."

It wasn't until another man standing in line recognized Capers that she realized he was the head coach of the Panthers. Once the humorous story hit the newspapers, Capers found he had to explain why he had elected to eat a grilled chicken sandwich (no fries) at Wendy's over Hardee's, the fast-food chain from which the restaurant empire of Jerry Richardson had grown.

"I'll have to talk to him about that myself," Richardson joked next time he visited Winthrop.

The work Capers really enjoyed was on the field. And by the end of the second minicamp, it was becoming clear that his veteran players were beginning to develop the feel of an actual team, and his rookies—not just Collins, but also Tyrone Poole, Blake Brockermeyer, Shawn King and a couple of pleasant later-round surprises in Frank Garcia, Andrew Peterson and Chad Cota—were a promising bunch.

Now all the Panthers had to do was sign them to contracts prior to the opening of training camp on July 15.

It was not an easy task, but then it never is. Polian's contempt for agents was well known, and he did little to hide the fact he did not much respect Leigh Steinberg, the high-powered player broker who was negotiating Collins' contract. Polian resented the fact agents had become so powerful, and none was more so than Steinberg.

It was a two-way street. Steinberg, like Polian, would never say anything disparaging about the Panthers' general manager on the record; but privately, there were times when he let slip true feelings of his own contempt. He respected Polian for his ability to judge talent but felt the Panthers GM was too inflexible and hard-nosed when negotiating the more complex contracts.

Negotiating a contract, especially one of such a magnitude as Collins', usually is somewhat like a ritual dance. The sides circle each other and size each other up before moving in close and taking action. Even then, they fire warning shots they don't really mean and make initial offers they know the other side can never accept in good conscience. All the while, they won't hesitate to take their case to the media quickly if they feel the other side is treating them the least bit unfairly.

So it was early on, when Polian announced to the media that "Jerry Richardson has made it very clear he is totally against voidable-option contracts. We will do no voidable-option contracts."

Steinberg was the NFL's greatest proponent of voidable-option contracts, in which a player, if he reached certain incentives, could void the last several years of a long-term contract and essentially become a free agent if the team that drafted him didn't ante up after a certain season, usually his second or third year.

When the Panthers closed shop for nearly a month of vacation after their second minicamp, Steinberg and several of the other agents who represented Carolina draft picks were stunned the Panthers executives actually did go on vacation. For nearly a month, Polian had no contact with them; the agents took this as a sign of arrogance, and in some cases offered the opinion it was downright stupid if the Panthers truly expected all of their rookies to report to camp on time.

Eventually, Collins signed a complex deal that contained no voidable-option years for the player. It did, however, contain a voidable option for the team—and it cost them a record $7 million signing bonus to get Steinberg and his client to agree to it.

The seven-year deal was designed to void after the third year, assuming Collins became the player everyone expected him to become. All Collins had to do was lead his team in passing or throw for 1,600 yards in one of his first three seasons.

Of course, he's already achieved the incentives based on his 1995 performance. But instead of him becoming a free agent upon reaching these incentives, it triggered a buyback clause in the contract at the Panthers' option. In other words, the last four years of the deal became void—but the Panthers could buy back three years at a predetermined price, and by paying an additional $6 million bonus at the time they exercised the buyback clause. The bottom line: Collins was set to receive a $7 million signing bonus to be paid in two chunks, $3 million immediately and $4 million after his first season, and eventually would get $21.6 million over six years.

Polian was pleased. So was Steinberg, and therefore Collins, who signed the deal the day camp opened and missed some introductory meetings, but no practice time.

Polian was happy because, according to his calculations, the contract was only six percent above what was paid to Trent Dilfer by Tampa Bay, the sixth pick in the previous year's draft. Steinberg was pleased because the $7 million signing bonus was a record for a rookie, at least until Steinberg flew to Cincinnati to hammer out the contract of Ki-Jana Carter, the would-be Carolina number-one pick who went instead to the Bengals. Collins was pleased because he was now free to do what he wanted to do all along: forget about the contract and concentrate on playing football.

The Panthers were willing to pay the huge signing bonus because for salary cap purposes it would be spread out over the life of the contract.

"It's not an outrageous contract," Polian said. "The reason we got it was because we were willing to pay the signing bonus. If I'm going to be given the choice of when we need the money five years down the road or six years down the road . . . having a cap number [for Collins] of over $5.5 million when we're getting ready to go to the big dance or paying a big signing bonus up front and having a cap number of 4.7 in the fifth year, I'll take the 4.7 anytime. Plus, next year when we're going to have another high draft choice, his cap number is only $1.8 [million]."

All Collins and his teammates knew was that the kid from Lebanon was suddenly very wealthy. Collins said he intended to do some things for his mother and father with the money, and also planned to help out his older brother, Patrick.

"My brother has already bought a car with the notion that I was going to give him some money, so I'll help him out a little bit," Collins said.

Collins didn't need a new car. He had bought a sports utility vehicle for himself prior to completion of the deal.

"I got the payments deferred," he said. "I have a little bit more money now than I did then."

Prior to taking the field at Wofford College for his first training-camp workout, Collins was talking in the locker room with Jack Trudeau about his good fortune—or his sudden fortune.

"Jack, I just can't believe this," Collins told Trudeau.

Trudeau, who was sitting next to Collins, turned and pinched the rookie's arm. "Believe it. It's real," Trudeau said.

Later, Trudeau added, "I've never sat around with a $7 million signing bonus in my pocket. I guess no one in this league has. But it's an awesome thing to go, in one day, from being broke and in debt to being wealthy beyond your wildest dreams."

Some of the players joked with Collins, calling him Deep Pockets and asking for cash handouts.

"Everybody wants a loan," Collins said. "I have to admit it seems a little weird to be going in a few months from a college student scrounging for money to buy a pizza to someone who is going to have all those zeroes behind one little number in his bank account."

Center Curtis Whitley recounted to reporters how he thought it was pretty righteous that he received an automatic $10,000 bonus for being one of 30 players selected in the expansion allocation draft who reported to camp—until he heard of Collins' deal. Then he, too, wanted to apply for a loan from Deep Pockets, Inc.

"I lead a relatively simple life," he said. "I don't need a whole lot. I just need food, shelter and clothing."

Whitley said he didn't expect the big money Collins was suddenly making to be a problem with anyone on the team.

"The only problem I have with his contract is that my name wasn't on it," he added, laughing.

Collins did plan to spread some of the money out, but not to teammates. Saying he relished the opportunity to be a positive role model for children and young adults, Collins intended to donate generously to a number of charities in the Carolinas and elsewhere. He revealed plans to make a $1 million donation to begin the Kerry Foundation in Charlotte, which would provide financial aid and guidance counseling to disadvantaged youths. He also said he intended to donate a total of about $150,000 to establish a scholarship fund at Penn State, his college alma mater, and to underwrite the cost of building a new locker room at Wilson High School in Reading, Pennsylvania, his high-school alma mater near Lebanon.

"By giving me this contract," said Collins, "the Carolina Panthers have pretty much made a long-term commitment to me. That means a lot. . . . I want to show people that I intend to give something back to the community, plus something to the communities who helped make me what I am."

As for Collins on the field, Sam Mills tried to put the whole signing episode into perspective.

"Anytime you're drafted where he was and you play the position he plays, you're going to get that big contract," Mills said. "He's going to be under a lot of pressure. When you're making that kind of money, people expect you to be Superman. I just hope everyone evaluates him as a player, like any other player, and gives him time to develop."

The same day the Panthers closed the deal on Collins, they also signed top draft picks Tyrone Poole, Blake Brockermeyer and Shawn King. It was time for some serious football, and the rookies were in the fold. Everyone in the organization seemed excited, but Polian tempered the euphoria by insisting it wasn't a good sign that the Panthers would be relying so heavily on rookies their first season.

"Marv Levy said it best when someone once asked him who the best rookies in the league were," Polian said of his old mentor. "Without hesitation, Marv answered, 'The best rookies this year are last year's rookies.'

"A rookie is a rookie is a rookie; from here on in, they're all rookies," Polian added in his own words. "They're going to cause you to lose games. They're going to fumble. They're going to make mistakes. All these guys who have been so highly touted from February on—every one of 'em in the league—will fall on their faces sometime this season."

Camp Capers

Players began arriving at Wofford College for the Panthers' first training camp the afternoon of July 14, toting television sets, stereos and, in some misguided cases, golf clubs that would never be used. One player who turned heads upon arriving was big Kevin Farkas, the offensive lineman who weighed in at the minicamp in May at a whopping 383 pounds. He looked decidedly slimmer. Another player impossible not to spot was huge Carlson Leomiti, the piano-playing offensive lineman who appeared even heavier than when he left minicamp weighing close to 390.

By the next morning, Leomiti, who weighed in at nearly 400 pounds during his physical, was gone, one of the first players cut. Farkas, who weighed in at 343, was gearing up for the afternoon's grueling test of conditioning under the searing sun on one of Wofford's three well-groomed practice fields.

The test consisted of 14 consecutive 40-yard dashes in what, at its peak, was 102-degree heat. The drill is designed for groups of players to complete their series of sprints within a designated time—ranging from 5.1 seconds for defensive backs and running backs to 6.5 seconds for linemen—with a period of rest ranging from 30 to 45 seconds in between each one.

Farkas went last by design. Noting that Farkas kept his word by shedding 40 pounds since the previous minicamp, Coach Dom Capers arranged for him to run with the final group of players, which consisted of three other offensive linemen weighing more than 300 pounds each. Capers correctly assumed that the rest of the team, having already completed their conditioning tests, would be watching the group very closely and that Farkas' progress could become a rallying point—providing the gathered individuals their first real chance to begin bonding as a team.

Capers was correct. On the far side of the field away from the prying eyes of the media, Baron Rollins, like Farkas a free agent and a longshot to make the team, struggled to complete his sprints within the designated times. On the near side, Derrick Graham, the team's highest-paid offensive lineman and supposedly its best hope at the key position of left tackle, wasn't much more impressive. He looked plodding and woefully out of shape. In between Rollins and Graham were Farkas to the far side, and Brandon Hayes, another aspiring rookie, to the near side.

The rest of the players giggled at Rollins, mocking his peculiar running style of almost high-stepping it down the field, but in painfully slow motion. They gently chided Graham, the veteran, and Hayes, the nondescript rookie. But the man they watched with the most interest was Farkas, who suddenly resembled, at least physically, a bona fide NFL player.

John Kasay, the team's average-size placekicker, removed his shirt and used it to fan the six-nine Farkas in between each 40-yard effort, which at first went smoothly enough *for the big fella. Earlier, Kasay had completed the drill with perhaps the greatest ease of anyone. He may be a kicker, but his father, John Sr., is a strength-and-conditioning coach at the University of Georgia—so Kasay knew all about getting and staying in top physical shape.*

Farkas, on the other hand, once got kicked out of Liberty Baptist, a Bible school in Lynchburg, Virginia, "for breaking a lot of little rules." Mostly, he liked to drink beer and eat. One of his favorite meals was spaghetti; he would cook the entire contents of a one-pound box for one sitting. "I would use low-fat sauce, but that's a lot of damn spaghetti," Farkas admitted.

On this scorching day, Farkas was determined to not only survive Camp Capers' first test, but to also make each of his 40-yard sprints within the designated time, some-thing that many others had failed to do earlier in the day. Wide receiver Richard Buchanan, for instance, stumbled to one knee after the 11th of his 14 sprints and almost was unable to finish at all on his last three. Vince Marrow, a tight end, was timed at 7.83 seconds in his final sprint, literally staggering across the finish line a full 15 yards behind the others in his group and long after the air horn wailed, signaling expiration of his designated time.

The 14th and final sprint was Farkas' sternest test.

With Kasay and Tim McKyer, the vocal veteran cornerback, shouting encouragement into his ear, Farkas leaped off the starting point and chugged past the 20-yard marker, sweat pouring down his face, cheeks bulging. He hit the 30-yard marker, his face beet red, legs still churning.

Just . . . 10 . . . more . . . yards.

"Get it, Farkenstein!" called out one teammate.

"Go big fella! You can do it!" shouted another.

Farkas crossed the line just ahead of the horn sounding. The rest of the players let out a loud celebratory cheer, making it seem as if this was their first small victory as a team. Farkas was so pumped up that he turned and kept right on trotting back to the starting point, which he was not required to do. Most players walked back slowly, hands on weary hips. Some very nearly crawled.

Then, suddenly, Farkas almost collapsed. He fell to one knee and had to rest for a moment, gulping water between gasps for air, before moving over to rejoin teammates for stretching exercises that marked the end of the day.

The first training camp in the history of the Carolina Panthers had commenced.

The modern-day NFL training camp does not much resemble the training camps of years past. For one thing, players in Mike McCormack's day did not earn enough money in football to make it their year-round occupation. So the players had to work regular jobs during the off-season. Then they used a prolonged training camp to whip their bodies into shape.

In McCormack's day, training camp was designed more than anything else to trans-form bodies softened by physically inactive off-seasons into ones that could withstand the rigors of a violent and demanding game. This was not the objective of Dom Capers' training camp. Capers expected his players to report in shape. His objective was to hone the players' mental toughness more than anything else. He aspired to sharpen their concentration levels to a point where fatigue never entered their minds, and to drill offensive and defensive schemes into their heads to a point where designated assignments would be carried out as if they were second nature. It would take time, Capers knew.

The head coach met with his players the night before the conditioning test to painstakingly map out rules and regulations, talking for roughly 45 minutes.

"You will all be treated the same," he told his players. "I don't care who you are, where you've been or what you've accomplished. These are the rules, and if you break them, here is how you will be punished. It's all spelled out for you ahead of time.

"The rules are the same for everyone, and I can assure you that the coaching staff will be consistent in these matters, no matter who you are. Consistency in everything is important to us. We want to be consistent in everything we do, on the field as well as the way we approach things off the field. It's the way we intend to do business."

After some opening comments, Capers gave way to team owner Jerry Richardson, who spoke for about 20 minutes to the players.

"It's hard to believe that in 1959, about this same time of year, I was showing up in Baltimore for my first training camp," Richardson told his captive audience. "I had a pregnant wife back home at the time, so I know all the uncertainties and stress y'all can be under as players. Don't think I don't understand about that."

After Richardson, Charlie Dayton, the Panthers' director of communications, stood and spoke for 25 minutes, stressing over and over to the players the importance of being cooperative with the media. Being a first-year team, establishing favorable impressions with the press was a priority with the organization, and the players needed to be made aware of this.

Capers then wrapped up the first meeting of camp. Ever the organizer, he produced a book that detailed plans for not only each minute of every single day of camp, but for virtually the entire season. Each assistant coach, each player—even Richardson—was issued one of these detailed books.

To Capers, the man who had recorded the date, time and detail of every event in his life in a series of leather-bound books since 1981, this was nothing unusual. But Richardson was astounded—and impressed.

"Dom has a plan for everything," Richardson said. "That book showed everything we were going to do from Friday night when camp opened through December 24 [the last day of the regular season]. Now we didn't go over every day, but I can go get my book and I can tell you on October 7 what we will be doing. I can tell you what we will be doing on October 7 at nine o'clock in the morning or at ten o'clock at night. He's got a plan."

McCormack was equally impressed. He also was excited. He always enjoyed the opening of training camp because this was when the hitting began. Minicamps were fine, but no hitting was permitted without pads. It is an NFL rule. As offensive line coach Jim McNally liked to say, there was only so much you could tell about players—particularly oversize offensive linemen—when they were practicing "in their pajamas."

McCormack relished the sights and sounds of players in full gear ramming into each other.

He was enthusiastically relating this fact to a group of reporters the night camp opened, positively glowing about the fact that the team had managed to sign its top four draft choices in one 24-hour flurry of activity that day, when a UPS deliveryman appeared at the entrance to a reception room near the front of Wofford's Physical Activities Building, which overlooked the three temporarily darkened practice fields that would be filled with large, busy men the following morning.

"Delivery for Alan Haller!" the man shouted out, entering the room cautiously. "Alan Haller? Is there an Alan Haller here?"

The man was carrying a set of golf clubs. Haller, a cornerback who by no means had a spot on the team assured, was nowhere in sight.

Noticing the parcel that was being delivered, McCormack shook his head in disgust. "I hope that man is joking," he said. "Alan Haller will have no use for those here."

As Farkas and the rest sweated through the conditioning drills, Barry Foster, the team's newest acquisition, sat on the sidelines watching silently. He did not participate. Capers said it was because the coaching staff did not want to run the risk of having Foster's right ankle, which had been operated on the previous year, swelling up on him.

Foster didn't say much of anything. To anyone. As was his habit in Pittsburgh, where he posted a sign on his locker that read POSITIVELY NO VISITORS, Foster was not talking to the media and, in fact, rarely spoke to any of his teammates or even members of the coaching staff. Dwight Stone, a former Steelers teammate, was about the only one in the Carolina locker room with whom he spoke.

Each day, without fail, someone in the media would request an interview with Foster, either formally filling out an interview request form and handing it in to the public relations department or by approaching Foster separately or by attempting to have a member of the PR staff approach him. Each day, without fail, Foster would refuse to talk.

This happened each of the first five days of camp. On some of those days, members of the Panthers' PR staff would not even attempt to ask the surly Foster to consider the interview requests. His answer was always the same.

"You kind of have to pick and choose your spots with Barry," Charlie Dayton explained one afternoon.

Foster even made avoiding the media into an art. The practice fields at Wofford are located in a small valley, some 500 yards downhill from the locker-room facilities. After a long practice—the Panthers usually practiced at 9 A.M. and 7:30 P.M. every other day, and at 3:30 P.M. on the days in between—oversize golf carts with seating for six or more players would be dispatched down the hill to bring up weary veterans first, and a few rookies later if they were fortunate enough to catch one of the last shuttles.

After each practice, Foster grabbed a seat in one of the first carts down the hill. And he always sat in the front seat, next to the driver—so that when the cart pulled up near its destination, he would be on the opposite side of where the media dutifully stood watch, only a few quick steps from the sanctuary of the locker room. Some joked that the quickest moves Foster exhibited each day were when he bounded out of the cart and darted out of sight.

In reality, though, Foster looked formidable on the practice field at first—when he practiced. When the team held two-a-day workouts, Foster rarely participated in both. In fact, he rarely practiced two days in a row at all under any circumstances.

Foster finally did agree to talk to a group of the media on July 20, the sixth day after arriving at Wofford. His decision caught Coach Capers by surprise.

Capers was walking up the hill from the practice fields toward the locker room with Bill Polian, when he saw a mob of media scurrying over to the interview tent that sat on a hill overlooking the fields.

"I don't know who they're going to talk to, but they're in a big hurry," Capers told Polian. "Whoever it is, he must be important."

Later, the coach added: "I saw the press all taking off, and I was worried about someone pulling a hamstring."

It wasn't going to be Foster. He lifted himself gingerly from the golf cart and ambled slowly over to the interview tent, following Dayton almost like a kid being led to the dentist's office for a dreaded checkup. Once there, one of the first questions asked was, Why did he decide to talk?

"Well, Charlie, the PR guy, kept bugging me about it," Foster replied with admirable honesty. "So I thought I'd better come on out and talk to you guys because I've been dodging you. I've just been so tired after practice that I haven't had any interest in it."

Foster went on to explain that he simply has never been comfortable talking with the media, especially en masse.

"I think this is uncomfortable for anyone," he said, staring out at what resembled a wheat field of tape recorders, cameras and microphones held by about 40 anxious members of the media. "It's not something I do, or any player does, every day."

But on this day, Foster did talk. He talked about how he was very enthused about the upcoming season. He said he felt better than he had heading into any preseason, in fact, since 1992. It was in 1992 that Foster led the American Football Conference in rushing with 1,690 yards and powered his way to 11 touchdowns.

The most any back had rushed for with an NFL expansion team was a mere 722 yards, accomplished by some fellow named Junior Coffey with Atlanta in 1966. Foster bluntly said that he planned to obliterate that record.

"My goals are to stay healthy and gain 100 yards every day I play," he said. "If I haven't gained 500 yards after five games, something's wrong."

The problem with Foster was that something always seemed to be wrong with him. Knee and ankle injuries limited him to just 19 of a possible 32 regular-season games with the Steelers in 1993 and 1994, which is partly why Pittsburgh was willing to part with him in the trade with the Panthers. He also was slated to make an awful lot of money in 1995, which was another reason the Steelers were happy to be rid of him.

On those special occasions when he did practice early in training camp with the Panthers, Foster looked impressive. During one 11-on-11 night scrimmage, Foster ran over his former Steeler teammate, cornerback Tim McKyer, and then enthusiastically high-stepped his way to a hypothetical touchdown.

"That's what I do," Foster said. "I run the football, and sometimes guys get in the way." McKyer told reporters afterward that Foster looked like, well, vintage Foster on that particular play. "I got trucked," McKyer added.

Told of McKyer's comment, Foster laughed and said, "I don't consider that a good 'truck.' I wasn't even running very hard. Tim McKyer, that's not someone to be too proud about running over anyway. He only weighs about 110 pounds."

Truthfully, McKyer weighs 178.

But Foster was actually making a joke—with the media! He also commented that he spent much of the five weeks leading up to camp changing the diapers of his 10-month-old son, Barry Jr.

Could this be the same moody Barry Foster everyone had come to know and hate?

Toward the end of his coming-out news conference with the media, however, Foster parted with a not-so-subtle reminder that he was going to be paid $2.4 million that season to run the football, not his mouth. A reporter asked Foster if he was hoping for a fresh start with the media as well as on the field in his new football home.

Foster hedged.

"I don't know," he replied. "I've been avoiding you guys, and it won't be the last time. I guess I'll try to be more accommodating, I just don't know. Give me a little time."

Talking with the media for the first time since the day after his acquisition apparently exhausted Foster. He sat out the next two days of practices.

On the practice fields, the battle for the starting nod at quarterback commenced quickly and heated up with each pass of each passing day. Kerry Collins was the bonus baby, the guy who had just secured a $7 million signing bonus; but that didn't mean much to the veterans, Frank Reich and Jack Trudeau. At least for the time being.

Reich kept insisting to everyone that he did not have the starting job won, despite the impression that it was his to lose because of his longtime Buffalo connection to Polian, who signed him to a lucrative free-agent contract. Capers kept repeating that the job was wide open, but was always careful to point out that Collins was a distant third for the moment behind Trudeau and Reich.

On the surface, it seemed an awkward position for Reich and Trudeau to be in. Prior to camp, they often played golf together, forming the kind of deep friendship that can only take root when you're harrassing someone as he stands over a short putt. Reich's squeaky-clean image took a beating as Trudeau explained some of the low-class antics Reich was known to pull on the golf course. Worse yet, when informed of Trudeau's accusations, Reich did not deny them.

"Out here," said Reich, gesturing to the Wofford College practice fields, "we have a deeper respect for each other's football game. Out on the course, we have no respect whatsoever for each other's golf game. We'll do whatever we can out there to get the other guy to hit a bad shot."

Trudeau is the better golfer of the two, boasting a 2-handicap.

"But he should be better," Reich pointed out. "He owns his own golf course."

Indeed, Trudeau does own a nice little place called Wolf Run, an 18-hole course in Indianapolis. He admittedly plays far more often than Reich, who describes himself as "an 8- or 10-handicap."

Trudeau also comes from a long line of golfers within his family. His mother's grand-father once owned a nine-hole course in Forest Lake, Minnesota, that somewhat tragi-cally was turned into a turkey farm during World War II—a bit of history gleaned from the family tree that Trudeau at least in small part attributed to his desire to own a course today. Despite the golfing ancestry, Trudeau said no one should feel sorry for Reich when they are playing together. He insisted Reich is a master at bush-league tactics designed to rattle his opponents at the most inopportune moments, such as in the middle of a backswing on a drive or just before the putter connects with the ball on the green.

"His big thing," said Trudeau, "is to pick up the flag and wave it real hard right behind your head while you're putting. He'll do that, or he'll jingle his keys in his pocket when you're getting ready to putt a 2-footer for birdie.

"That's a Boomer Esiason tactic. Boomer always said that if you couldn't make a 2-footer for birdie no matter what was going on around you, you don't deserve it."

It should come as no surprise that both men have played golf in the past with Boomer Esiason, the Arizona Cardinals quarterback whom Reich played behind at the University of Maryland. Trudeau served as Esiason's backup in New York with the Jets. Both agree that Boomer is to blame for most of their low-handed habits on the golf course—and both agree that Reich seemed to learn the most, which is to say the worst, from Boomer.

"It's kind of embarrassing for Frank, really," Trudeau said. "To start off with, he stands on the first tee begging for strokes every time, and then he has to pull all that other stuff, too. Even with all that, I think he's only beaten me once. That's all I'll admit to, anyway."

On the football field, it was a different story. And this was all about football now, for neither intended to pick up a putter during camp. The two men insisted again and again that they were pulling for each other, even though one's success meant the other's certain downfall.

Throughout the first two weeks of camp, Capers was careful to make certain that Reich, Trudeau and Collins each received an equal share of the snaps taken during practice. Each got to work with the first offensive unit roughly the same amount of time. Trudeau, at the outset, looked the sharpest. Reich was only so-so. Collins, as expected, struggled at first, wildly throwing passes in the dirt or in the vicinity of no discernible receiver. He often threw the ball where he expected receivers to be but where they weren't, because he expected them to run routes that existed exclusively in his own confused head.

To make matters worse for the rookie, he was, well, just a rookie. And rookies are subject to some mild fraternity-like hazing in the NFL. Collins was required to fetch newspapers for the two veteran quarterbacks and deliver them to their doorstep each morning. At first, Collins did it himself. Then he smartly paid another rookie to do it for him. Collins and Jerry Colquitt, another rookie QB chosen in the sixth round of the draft, were required at dinner one night to sing a rendition of the song "Ebony and Ivory."

Collins is white; Colquitt black. There also were days when Collins and Colquitt were not permitted to talk to the veteran quarterbacks until they addressed him first, and even then they had to refer to them as Mr. Trudeau and Mr. Reich.

Trudeau seemed to revel in this sophomoric rookie hazing the most. But in truth, both he and Reich recognized that before long, Collins would be the man at the helm of the Carolina offense. They also realized that this might be their final chance to steal a little more time in the NFL spotlight during the fading twilight of their careers.

"We're in kind of a unique situation here," Trudeau said. "I've been a starter with other teams before coming here. Frank never had that opportunity because he backed up Jim Kelly all those years in Buffalo. We both realize that this would be the ideal year to step in and start here, because Kerry is the quarterback of the future—and realistically, he's probably going to have the job by next year."

As camp progressed, word emanated from Stevens Point, Wisconsin, that the Panthers had it made no matter how hot it got in Spartanburg. That word kept coming from the camp of the Jacksonville Jaguars, the other NFL expansion team and the Panthers' opponent in the upcoming Hall of Fame preseason opener in Canton, Ohio, on July 29.

Despite insistence throughout the organization that they did not care to compare themselves with the other expansion entrant, comparisons were inevitable. There also was a pervading thought process that could not prevent players from inquiring about the latest horror stories to come out of Stevens Point, where the Jaguars had gone to escape the heat of Florida but had run into one of the worst heat spells to ravage the Midwest in years. The players weren't supposed to care about what was going on with the Jaguars, but in truth, they could not hide the fact that they did. They cared deeply. So did management, even though they proclaimed not to whenever asked to comment publicly on whatever the Jaguars were doing.

By the second week of camp, obvious differences in the way the two teams approached the regimens of training were surfacing. Jacksonville practiced twice a day on every day of the week except Sunday. The Panthers went twice a day on Mondays, Wednesday and Fridays only—and even then scheduled the second practice for 7 P.M. to avoid the heat. The Jaguar players were not permitted to sit on their helmets on the field and were instructed to never "take a knee" even when there was a break during a workout. They weren't so much as allowed to remove their helmets at any time during practice; in fact, they weren't even permitted to unbuckle their chin straps from the moment they stepped onto the practice field until that wonderful moment when they finally were able to escape it. They also were forbidden from taping their cleats in the manner that had grown popular amongst NFL players, on the outside of the shoe. Panthers players were allowed to do all of the above, as long as they always paid attention to what was transpiring in front of them on the practice fields.

There were rules in Camp Capers. Tight end Vince Marrow, for instance, broke one when he relieved himself in the corner of the end zone of one of the practice fields during a midday workout at Wofford—in full view of the media, teammates and even a smattering of bemused fans who watched from the far hillside and a closer tent for VIPs. Marrow would not last long at Wofford before being released.

Capers did not like players who were late, players who did not practice regularly, players who could not or would not give every ounce of effort in their bodies day after day, or players who urinated in the end zone during practice.

"We have some rules, but only what I consider important ones," said Capers, who was not immediately aware of Marrow's training-camp transgression. "I don't want to be a policeman. I want to be the coach. If I'm out there being a policeman all the time, trying to enforce a bunch of rules instead of trying to coach the players and make them better, we're missing the point somewhere."

Many Panthers simply could not hide their disbelief for what was happening in Stevens Point.

"Those things Jacksonville does are silly," cornerback Tim McKyer told Scott Fowler of the *Charlotte Observer*. "It kills morale. I might have gone there in the expansion draft, and now I thank God every day that Jacksonville didn't draft me.

"Coach Capers is walking a nice line. He's working us hard, but he's not killing us."

Fowler, in fact, solicited opinions from several Panthers one afternoon in Spartanburg, and the players seemed unanimous in their belief that Coach Tom Coughlin of the Jaguars was riding his players too hard.

"You can get away with that kind of stuff in college," said center Matt Elliott, "because you're dealing with boys who you have to smack upside the head with a two-by-four every now and then. But not in the pros."

At the same time, others acknowledged that the hard-line approach sometimes produces positive results; although they did not believe it could be a long-term benefit.

"I had Bill Parcells in 1993 at New England," said cornerback Rod Smith, "and he just wore us down to the ground. He told us every day, 'I want to find out who is going to crack.' We had two and a half straight weeks of two-a-days, and during that time we had more than 50 guys miss at least a day of practice because of injury. Practically everybody got hurt."

"That approach can work for a while," said Reich, "but the longevity of it is where you really get in danger. . . . You can drive a team or organization for a little bit of time, and it may bring out the best in the short run. Maybe that's the plan [for Jacksonville]."

As members of the Bills in Buffalo, Reich, wide receiver Don Beebe and tight end Pete Metzelaars had become somewhat spoiled, so Camp Capers did not seem quite like the vacation to them that it did to others who had just escaped the thumb of Parcells in New England or some other tyrant in another NFL camp. The Bills rarely practiced twice a day during camp under Coach Marv Levy, leaving plenty of time for rounds of golf in the afternoon.

Metzelaars, however, said it wasn't always like that in Buffalo. He said the Bills earned easier camps over the years by first becoming more successful on the field when the games counted for real. They did, after all, win four consecutive AFC championships, even if they never did win a Super Bowl.

"I remember one camp when the most pressing issue for all of us was whether or not Bruce Smith would break 100 in golf," Metzelaars said. "We had a little outing toward the end of camp and it came down to the very last hole. He needed to par something like the last two holes to come in with a 99, so a bunch of us were out there in our golf carts following him around. He did it, too."

Of the Panthers' camp, Beebe added, "The ones I experienced in Buffalo were like Club Med compared to this. You could play 18 holes of golf a day [in Buffalo] with no problem. Frank, Pete and I used to do exactly that. This camp is too demanding to even pick up a golf club."

Unlike Mount Coughlin, who erupted long and often in the Jacksonville boot camp, the commandant of Camp Capers rarely displayed raw emotion on the practice fields at Wofford. But there were times when even Capers lost his cool in the Spartanburg heat. Less than two weeks into camp, after 13 productive but largely uneventful workouts, Capers exploded on his charges one hour and 15 minutes into an afternoon workout that began under sunny blue skies as the temperature inched toward 100 degrees.

The team had just begun the 11-on-11 phase of practice, and did not look sharp. The defense jumped offsides. The offense fumbled the football. Capers abruptly interrupted the workout and wasted no time in letting the players know that their effort and concentration levels were unacceptable. He accused the players of giving into the heat.

"When you give in to the heat," said Capers, "you stop learning. You stop growing as a football player. You stop getting better. And if you aren't going to get any better, what's the point of practicing?"

Besides, added Capers, the heat and humidity are excuses for failure.

"Excuses are for losers," Capers reminded his players. "Winners win, and losers make excuses."

Nonetheless, it was hot in Spartanburg. Day after day after sweaty day. There was no denying that fact.

"I'm glad I pray a lot," said offensive lineman Mike Finn, "because if hell is any hotter than this, I know I wouldn't be able to stand it."

One player who welcomed Capers' emotional outburst on the field was Paul Butcher, a reserve linebacker and self-professed special-teams maniac.

"We hit a little lull," Butcher said. "It's hot and humid out there. We're all tired, sore and dragging a little bit. It's that time of training camp. But he's absolutely right. There's no excuse for not coming out ready to practice hard."

Butcher was McCormack's kind of guy.

"I love to hit," Butcher said. "My favorite time of practice is when we do nine-on-seven running drills, where there is no reading [of the play] involved whatsoever and you just get to look for somebody to hit. That's pure smash-mouth football. I love that."

Butcher, 31, was entering his ninth NFL season. He played previously for the Lions, Rams and Colts, and he was named most valuable special-teams player at each stop. The day he was selected off the Indianapolis roster in the 27th round of the expansion draft, he guaranteed reporters that he would become a special-teams captain with the Panthers.

"How can you guarantee something like that?" a reporter asked.

"Because I've been one everywhere I've been. Just watch," Butcher replied.

Butcher was tabbed Dr. Psycho in college at Wayne State in Detroit, and spent his entire NFL career trying to live up to the nickname. He lived and breathed to play designated wedge-buster on kick-return teams, which most players detest. Even when reporters' questions weren't about hitting, Butcher liked to turn the conversation in that direction. He enjoyed nothing more off the field than describing what he enjoyed most on it—like the time he hit an opposing player so hard that both their helmets flew off.

"We blew each other up," he said. "But you want to know what the worst part of it was? We were both offsides on the play. We had to line back up and do it all over again."

Butcher said he and the other player were wandering around in a daze after they got up from the initial hit. But when his coach asked if he wanted to come out, Butcher refused.

"I did tiptoe down the field the next time, though," Butcher said.

Butcher did not tiptoe often on a football field. He isn't all that big for an NFL line-backer—six feet tall, 240 pounds—so he always figured he has to hit harder than the average player to stick around. At Wayne State, he weighed a mere 210 pounds while establishing the Dr. Psycho legend. Since that's barely acceptable weight for a defensive back in the NFL and Wayne State isn't exactly known as a collegiate football powerhouse, it's somewhat remarkable he even got a pro team to take a flier on him.

It almost didn't happen.

"I had some teams looking at me, but no one had invited me to training camp. So I was all irritated," Butcher said. "The Lions had a couple of linebackers who were holding out, though, and they finally called me. They started camp on a Sunday, and they called me on Monday morning at nine o'clock and said, 'How soon can you get up here?'"

Butcher was 90 minutes away. He hopped in his car and sped to the Lions' camp.

But being Dr. Psycho at tiny Wayne State and keeping the nickname alive with the Detroit Lions are two vastly different challenges. Butcher had to prove himself a maniac all over again.

"I know they just thought of me as camp meat," said Butcher, "but I just started hitting people as hard as I could."

After five or six days of "knocking some heads pretty good," the Lions' linebackers squared off in a one-on-one drill agains the Lions' offensive tackles and guards. "It's a really stupid drill designed to see who's tough," Butcher said.

Just the kind of drill Butcher loved. But when his turn to hit came, the linebackers coach noticed the fellow rookie opposite him and said, "Butch, not yet."

Butcher, who knew fresh meat when he saw it, responded angrily.

"What's up? It's my turn," he protested to the coach.

"Not yet," the coach replied firmly. "Wait off to the side for a minute."

Two players later, massive Keith Dorney, a two-time All-Pro offensive lineman and team captain for the Lions, stepped to the line on the offensive side. Dorney weighed 295 pounds and sported a full beard.

"He looked like a big ol' grizzly bear," Butcher said.

"Butch," said the coach, "now it's your turn."

Nearly 10 years later, Butcher still pointed to what happened in the next instant as the defining moment in his career—when Butch became a reborn Dr. Psycho.

"If I had gotten in there and gotten knocked on my butt, it would have been over for me," Butcher said. "But if I didn't, I could earn some respect. So I hit him so hard I broke his facemask, knocking his head back, everything. All the defensive guys started going nuts, high-fiving me and yelling."

A stunned Dorney nodded at Butcher through broken facemask and said simply, "Good hit, man."

Butcher made the Lions that year and kept the nickname. He later moved onto the Rams in Los Angeles, where he became, for a while, the Tasmanian Devil. He then spent two seasons with the Colts in Indianapolis, where he was known as Wild Man and had a small fan club comprised of guys who would show up for games brandishing rubber meat cleavers and wearing blood-stained butcher's gowns with BUTCHER stamped on the back in red block lettering.

With the Panthers, however, he had a problem. Despite the fact that he appeared to be challenging for one of the two starting inside linebacker positions, in addition to his exploits on special teams, too many people were still calling him Paul.

"I like to have a nickname, but I don't have one with this team yet," he said as camp progressed. "I have to establish myself first."

Obviously, Butcher wasn't the only player in Panthers' training camp who loved to hit. All the linebackers enjoyed giving somebody a good jolt.

The first day players were allowed to hit each other, in fact, Carlton Bailey absolutely leveled Don Beebe, his former Buffalo teammate. The 6-3, 235-pound Bailey drilled the 5-11, 183-pound Beebe after the wide receiver ran a pattern across the middle of the field and briefly clutched a pass thrown by Reich. When Bailey hammered him, instantly flipping Beebe on his back, the ball bounded away.

This was on the fourth day of camp, and Beebe did not appreciate being Bailey's punching bag.

"I tell you what," said an angered Beebe, "Carlton hit me like it was full gear out there and we were playing in a scrimmage.

"And he's an ex-Buffalo guy. It doesn't matter anymore, I guess."

Immediately after the hit, Beebe, bounded up and screamed at Bailey: "What are you doing?!"

Bailey's response: "I didn't follow through on the hit. If I had followed through, Beebe, they would have had to come out and get you [off the field]."

Later, Bailey had a photographer who printed a picture of the tackle in an area newspaper make him an oversize print of the photo. Then he took it to Beebe and good-naturedly asked the receiver to autograph it for him. Beebe obliged, proving there were no hard feelings over the hard hit.

On another part of the field earlier the same day Bailey crushed Beebe, Lamar Lathon was busy embarrassing Derrick Graham, Carolina's highest-paid offensive lineman, who outweighed Lathon by some sixty pounds. Twice during a one-on-one pass-rush drill, Lathon charged Graham and knocked Graham flat on his back.

In later describing his obvious domination, Lathon said, "I shouldn't be giving away my secrets, but I faked him on the counter, then hit him with what I call the club."

Capers and his coaching staff monitored the hitting carefully. The danger of this particular phase of training camp, when guys like Butcher, Bailey and Lathon were itching to take someone's head off, was that the only potential victims on the practice fields were their teammates. The coaches talked with the defense about holding back slightly when it came to hitting running backs and receivers—and quarterbacks were completely off limits. But at the same time, the coaches wanted to begin molding the defensive unit into a tough, aggressive, hard-hitting unit.

"If you want to be a physical football team, you have to start establishing that in training camp," Capers said. "You never want anyone to get hurt foolishly on the practice field, but football is a physical game."

McCormack, naturally, was loving it all. So was Farkas, who was happy to be someplace where he could be one of the guys and eat all he wanted for free. Well, at least much of what he wanted. The big guy was determined not to eat himself off the roster like he did the previous year in Denver.

Farkas, who played collegiately at nearby Appalachian State in Boone, North Carolina, after getting kicked out of Liberty Baptist, said he couldn't believe his eyes the first time he saw the training-table layout in Denver's camp.

"We had steak, lobster, pasta, chicken, hamburgers . . . you name it and they had it laid out there for you," Farkas said. "I thought I was in heaven. My problem was that I ate and ate and ate every day until I was stuffed full. They'd have butter sauce out there for dipping your lobster and stuff into, and I'd pile that on, too. I paid no attention to what I was putting into my body at all. I just figured I'd work off whatever I put on during the practices."

The butter sauce wasn't all he was piling on. He piled on the weight, too, as his theory of working it off did not compute.

"I ate like a dang pig," Farkas admitted. "The problem was that where we trained, they didn't have a scale that went over 350 pounds. So it wasn't until we got back to Denver [just before the final preseason game] that we found out I weighed 388."

The Broncos cut him shortly thereafter.

The Panthers, however, were willing to take a chance on guys like Farkas. They were willing to feed them, too, but Panther players were expected to exercise moderation even while tempted by a huge training-table layout that for lunch routinely included 200 pounds of turkey for sandwiches, 250 pounds of chicken halves, 100 pounds of fish filets, 100 pounds of assorted cooked pastas, dozens of hamburgers, turkey burgers and vegetable burgers, 150 pounds of fresh fruit, a 10-foot-long salad bar with all the fixings and five-foot-long twin freezers filled with ice cream, frozen yogurt, ice-cream sandwiches and an assortment of ice-cream bars. There also were large standup coolers filled with dozens of gallons of milk, bottled water, sports drinks, soft drinks and fruit juices.

And that was for lunch. For dinner, a typical daily menu might include much of the above plus 400 10-ounce choice steaks, 400 13-ounce lobster tails, 200 pounds of breaded shrimp and more.

A normal human being will take in an average of 2,600 calories per day. An NFL player will take in an average of 7,500—or roughly three times that of the normal person. When players are practicing in severe heat, like in Spartanburg, where the average midday temperature hovered in the mid- to high-90s and often creeped over 100, replacing lost body fluids and eating large meals are essential to healthy survival. Some players became dehydrated all too easily. In extreme cases, these players needed to have fluids pumped into their bodies intravenously in the locker room following workouts, missing valuable practice time as their bodies struggled to recover.

For a player on the edge, this could be devastating. Guys on the bubble needed to be seen by the coaches as much as possible.

Keeping enough fluid in the body was important for everyone, though. Beebe, who usually weighed 183, would lose six to eight pounds per practice. Metzelaars would lose five to seven—but that was less dangerous for him than Beebe's weight loss was for Beebe because Metzelaars weighed about 250 pounds and had more body mass to lose.

"You just have to drink a lot of fluids," Beebe said. "It seems like that's all I'm doing some days. I try to eat a lot, too, to gain back as much weight as I can before going back out there on the practice field again. If you don't, and you're my size, you're going to be in big trouble before you know it."

Added Metzelaars: "I chug two Gatorades after practice in the morning, two more at lunch, and take a couple of bottled waters back with me to my room. Then I try to have a couple more Gatorades before I go back out for the evening practice. You're pumping fluids into your body all the time."

Camp was progressing just fine, McCormack observed one evening after a workout. But one thing was bugging him. Ticket sales for the team's two preseason home games, not to mention all of its eight regular-season home contests, were lagging.

McCormack was perplexed, even to the point of being perturbed. He simply could not understand why folks in South Carolina, in particular, were not flocking to the box office to snatch up tickets. He conceded that some markets in North Carolina, such as the Winston-Salem, Greensboro, Raleigh-Durham areas north of Charlotte, would be slow to buy tickets and drive four hours or more one way to see a game at Clemson the first season; nevertheless, McCormack thought sales would be moving more briskly.

McCormack recounted how he and Jerry Richardson had traveled throughout the Carolinas making promotional appearances prior to the Panthers actually becoming a team. He said they had been overwhelmed by the interest fans had in finding out more about purchasing tickets to games. After each presentation, he said, this would be the number-one concern of most folks who sought him and Richardson out for more information. It led him to believe that the Panthers probably would sell out all home games in their inaugural season, setting the all-time NFL attendance record in the process—even though the games would be played two and a half hours from uptown Charlotte, where they would make their permanent home beginning the following season.

"From the trips we made," said McCormack, "I was really misled."

With only six days remaining before their preseason opener against Jacksonville in the Hall of Fame Game, the Panthers had sold only 45,000 tickets for their preseason home opener against Denver, which was slated for August 12. Clemson Memorial Stadium had seating for 74,300.

"I'm an optimist," McCormack said. "But I'll admit my optimism is fading a little bit."

The optimist in McCormack added that there was a precedent for a late surge in ticket sales. Back in 1991, the promotional group led by McCormack and Richardson that was working to bring the NFL to the Carolinas staged a preseason game between the Redskins and Jets at Williams-Brice Stadium in Columbia, South Carolina. It eventually drew a crowd of 69,117, the largest neutral-site attendance for an NFL exhibition game in 10 years, but not without some anxious moments beforehand.

"The two weeks before the game, we thought we were going to take a [financial] bath," McCormack said. "But we had a tremendous walk-up sale. People were standing in line to buy tickets in a rainstorm during the first half of the game. Everyone said, 'Well, people in South Carolina just tend to do things a little slower.' I hope that is the case here in our situation. I hope this is not all the interest we're going to get."

One man not surprised by the lack of interest was Mike McGee, athletic director at the University of South Carolina and the man who ultimately turned the Panthers away when his school could have hosted their first season's slate of home games. He said the attendance figure for the exhibition game cited by McCormack was misleading—largely because of some creative corporate intervention by Richardson.

McGee examined the tax records of the game between the Redskins and Jets, and he said the records revealed that many of the tickets, possibly 10,000 or more, were given away by Richardson-controlled fast-food outlets.

"Right at the last minute, there was a big buy by Hardee's, which distributed the tickets at outlets in North and South Carolina," McGee said. "When you look at that, you don't know how many were actually bought in the final thrust."

Promising Preseason

T he first preseason opponent for the Panthers was the Jacksonville Jaguars. The setting was perfect, although to outsiders it must have seemed quite ironic—two teams who had never played before meeting in the prestigious Hall of Fame Game in Canton, Ohio, the exhibition that traditionally kicks off the NFL preseason.

The contest was staged at the modest but somehow picturesque Fawcett Stadium, which lurks in the very shadow of the Hall of Fame museum itself, seats only 24,725 on weather-worn wooden bleachers, and was built in a time when luxury suites and club seats were figments of some millionaire's imagination. In the weeks leading up to the July 29 encounter, the Panthers repeatedly stated that the game meant nothing. It was the first of many preseason outings; it would be used as a measuring stick to see how far the team had come since the opening of camp; it was a tool to be used to evaluate talent—and nothing more. That the Jaguars, their expansion brethren, would be the opponent did not add any significance to the outcome, or so the Panthers uniformly insisted. Five days before the game, however, owner Jerry Richardson candidly admitted, "If we play tiddlywinks, we want to win."

The tense faces of Mike McCormack, Bill Polian and assistant general manager Joe Mack in the press box the afternoon of the game confirmed the Richardson-mandated organizational philosophy. For a game that was supposed to mean nothing, as all three had maintained prior to kickoff, they sure were worked up as the Panthers frantically attempted to protect a 20–14 lead in the final minutes. McCormack's hands were balled into tight fists, his face taut and even more beet red than usual, partially because he spent the first half sitting in the sun in the stands with a contingent of Carolina fans. Polian kept stomping his feet and banging his fists on the table in front of him, occasionally adding a loud verbal opinion as to the quality of the latest decision by the officiating crew.

As the Jaguars drove inside the Carolina five-yard line for what they hoped would be a game-winning touchdown in the final seconds, Mack found he no longer could remain seated. He stood and gyrated throughout each play, as if he could somehow alter its outcome. The muscular administrator, a dedicated runner and weight-lifter, seemed dangerously close to tearing off his suit and tie and running onto the field himself to assist in the final goal-line stand.

When Steve Lofton batted away a pass from Jacksonville quarterback Mark Brunnell intended for Mike Williams in the end zone on fourth-and-goal, the front-office triumvirate stood and cheered, thrusting triumphant fists into the air. But by the time reporters approached Polian less than 90 seconds later, he had composed himself. It was nothing, *he claimed with a poker face, but a meaningless preseason game. When one reporter pressed him, offering the personal observation that he obviously was pleased with the victory, Polian jumped him. "Don't tell me how I'm feeling! You have no idea what's going on inside my head!" shouted the GM as he stormed off toward the locker room.*

Later, Mack laughed at the incident and said, "Of course we were happy that we won. Asking someone if he would rather win or lose is like asking someone if he'd rather have some ice cream or take a swift kick in the nuts. We'll take the ice cream every time, thank you very much."

As much as the Panthers tried to slough off comparisons between themselves and the Jaguars, such comparisons were inevitable. They started at the top. Unlike Richardson, a former NFL player who had been the moving force behind the bid for the Carolina franchise from the very beginning, owner Wayne Weaver of the Jags had no NFL background and joined Jacksonville's expansion bid a mere nine months before the city was awarded a team.

In some ways, though, the two owners were not all that different. Richardson made his money in fast food; Weaver in shoes. Both built their multi-million-dollar empires in these retail businesses from modest beginnings over a number of years. Weaver was CEO and majority owner of Shoe Carnival, Inc., a fast-growing shoe retailer based in Evansville, Indiana, that boasted $225 million in annual revenue by 1995. Shoe Carnival grew from a total of four stores in 1985 to a total of 91 by the time Weaver decided to join the Jacksonville bid. Weaver also was majority owner, CEO and chairman of Liz Claiborne footwear, and was previously co-owner and CEO of Nine West Group, Inc., a company widely recognized for revolutionizing the design and marketing of women's shoes. From 1978, when Weaver took over as CEO, Nine West's annual sales mushroomed from $9 million to $550 million by 1993, when the company went public.

How these men chose to have their football franchises run, however, offered a study in contrasts. Richardson leaned heavily on hiring men with years of NFL experience to occupy the upper echelon of his organization, and they, in turn, looked to hire a head coach with plenty of NFL experience. Mike McCormack and Bill Polian shared power at the top in making personnel decisions. Dom Capers, the head coach, was involved to a large extent, as were Joe Mack and Dom Anile. Combined, these men had nearly 70 years of NFL experience between them and, mainly through Polian, appeared to have a strong working knowledge of the salary cap, which in recent years had changed the way the player-acquisition game must be approached.

In Jacksonville, the head coach wielded all the power in football operations. And why not? Tom Coughlin, who had spent seven years earlier in his coaching career as a respected assistant coach with the Eagles, Packers and Giants, had far more experience than anyone else at the top of the organization. Coughlin accepted limited input from others, but essentially made the call on all decisions concerning trades, drafts and hirings. The front office was headed by a pair of 33-year-old NFL novices—president and CEO David Seldin and vice president of football operations Michael Huyghue (pronounced "hewg"). An astute businessman, Seldin nonetheless had no background whatsoever in overseeing the day-to-day operations of a professional football franchise, which he was in charge of doing with the Jaguars. Huyghue at least was a former VP of adminstration and general counsel with the Detroit Lions, where he gained limited experience in negotiating player contracts and developed an understanding of the salary cap.

When it came to building rosters, sharp differences in the philosophies of both teams surfaced immediately. The Panthers were careful not to spend much money in the expansion allocation draft, doling out the relatively reasonable sum of $9 million and saving as much as possible to spend in free agency. They eventually used the money saved to sign several high-profile, high-priced unrestricted free agents like linebacker Sam Mills, defensive end Mike Fox, placekicker John Kasay and quarterback Frank Reich. The Jaguars spent $14 million acquiring players through the allocation draft and signed few high-priced, high-profile players from the unrestricted free-agent pool. In the college draft, the Panthers were much more active, making three trades to wind up with four of the top 36 selections. The Panthers took a quarterback with their first pick; the Jaguars took Tony Boselli, a highly rated offensive lineman.

As the showdown between the two new teams approached, the Panthers steadfastly refused to acknowledge they cast a wary eye toward Jacksonville, almost treating the Jaguars with an arrogant indifference.

A reporter asked Polian how much he monitored the other expansion team.

"Zero," was his terse reply.

McCormack echoed that observation.

"We really don't know what they're doing or what they've done," McCormack insisted. "We haven't studied them because we've been so intent on our own plan."

The Jaguars, meanwhile, readily admitted carefully tracking every move the Panthers made. In an interview two days before the Hall of Fame Game, Huyghue told Charles Chandler of the *Charlotte Observer,* "Sure, we watch them, as we do every other team in the NFL. We put all the teams on a board. But the two at the top, the two we highlight, are ourselves and Carolina.

"We don't watch to see who's ahead. We're watching for ideas. They've got ideas and if we see them doing something we think is smart, we'll steal it. There's no sole ownership of ideas in this league."

McCormack, the man who scoffed at Bill Walsh's prediction that the Panthers could win six games in the regular season, did say he knew enough about the Jaguars to predict they would encounter considerable success. He repeatedly told reporters the Jags had a better chance to win six or seven games than the Panthers because they were in a weaker division, which included Cincinnati and Houston, the two worst teams in the NFL in 1994.

"I think the Jaguars have a darn good chance of winning seven games," McCormack said. "But with the division we're in, it's going to be tough. You've got to play the defending champions [San Francisco] and you've got three other potentially tough opponents in New Orleans, Atlanta and St. Louis. And we have to play each of those teams twice."

But when reporters tried to get McCormack to agree this logic meant the Jaguars should be favored going into the preseason opener, he laughed and began to walk away, adding, "The media is trying to make more out of this game than there is. It's just a preseason game that will have no bearing on how successful these two franchises are this year or in the future."

It was difficult not to make a big deal out of the game against Jacksonville. Despite the preseason tag, it was the first time either team would take a field to see how it stacked up against another NFL opponent in an actual game. It was on national television. It was played in the shadow of the Hall itself.

Hall of Fame officials said they issued 809 working media credentials, nearly double the highest amount previously issued. They obviously had not anticipated the media crush. The press box contained only two working phones.

For Capers, the game carried special meaning. To have his first game as a head coach take place at Fawcett Stadium, which he had driven by countless times going to and from Mount Union as a college student, was hard for him to believe.

"Right at the Hall of Fame, you'll see an intersection that is Interstate-77 and State Route 62. Sixty-two goes east, and if you take that and go about 18 miles, that's where Alliance and Mount Union is," Capers said. "Anytime I would go home or go back to school, I would go right past the Hall of Fame."

It also would be the first time Capers had walked the sidelines in 17 years, dating back to 1979 when he was an assistant coach at California. In 11 years of professional coaching in the USFL and NFL, Capers had never been on the sideline for an entire game, working instead from upstairs in the press box with other defensive coaches.

Jeanette and Julius Capers were among about 70 members of family or friends, many of whom had driven up from the Buffalo area, to attend the game. Dom Capers informed all of them in advance that he would not have time to meet with them, except possibly for a brief moment after the game before boarding the team bus and heading to the airport.

"A lot of people have asked my wife if I'll be available for dinner and that sort of thing," Capers said. "There's just no way. I had to tell them I'll be tied up from the moment we get in until after the game Saturday, and even then I'll only have a couple free moments."

Those who knew Capers best understood. He was pretty much unavailable during football seasons from the time training camp opened until the final game of the season was played. And this, after all, was his first chance as a head coach.

"Dom has waited a long time for this," his wife, Karen, said.

At least Capers didn't have to worry about squeezing in a trip to the Hall of Fame museum. Being so close to it growing up, he had gone through five or six times over the years.

"You just get a feel for the tradition of the game, and how far the game has come, when you first walk in," Capers said. "You see the leather helmets and the old shoes. It's amazing to see how the game has progressed and what it has evolved into.

"The media coverage, how everything is so closely scrutinized . . . I think that has changed tremendously just in the last 10 years. Everything now is highly scrutinized, because there is such high public interest—and that's what has made the game the great game it is today."

Unlike Capers, Richardson made plans to tour the Hall of Fame prior to kickoff. It would be his first time.

"I understand there are some things in there, obviously, about the 1959 championship game," Richardson said. "I wouldn't mind seeing that. Guys that I played with who are in the Hall of Fame, I wouldn't mind seeing that. Mike [McCormack's] display, I want to see that."

McCormack, inducted into the Hall in 1984, was perhaps more emotional about the setting of the game than the game itself. He talked about how inductees inevitably break down during their induction ceremonies—partly because past inductees, sitting near the podium out of the listening range of the audience, but not the new inductee at the podium, talk a little trash.

"You go out there, and it gets to be funny," McCormack said. "At least afterwards, it's funny. But they try to get on you. When past inductees are introduced, they're sitting, in my case, behind the podium where you give your acceptance speech. . . . So as you're speaking, and people watching I guess don't notice it, but you get a lump and they start saying, 'There you go, there you go. Are you going to be able to hold it?' It's an emotional time."

McCormack said he was able to hold it "about halfway. I cracked. Almost all of 'em crack at some point." There is reason to be emotional. There is no higher honor in professional football, according to McCormack.

"I've got World Championship rings, but I wear my Hall of Fame ring more than my championship rings," McCormack said.

It took McCormack a long time to get inducted, which perhaps made him appreciate it all the more. Seven years prior to being voted in, a reporter friend called McCormack to give him some bad news.

"Mike, you missed it by one vote," the friend said. "Next year, you'll get in."

"That was the worst phone call," said McCormack, "because the next year, I was waiting and waiting . . . and I didn't get inducted. The next year, the same thing. And the year after that, and so on.

"Then when I was inducted, I almost had forgotten about it."

It was 6:30 A.M. on a Saturday morning in Seattle when he was reminded of it. McCormack was lying in bed, having a cup of coffee and talking with his wife, Ann. Suddenly the phone rang, jolting them.

"The funny thing was, I hadn't been thinking about it that year—but when that phone rang at that time of day, my wife and I both knew what it was," McCormack said. "Ann just started beating me on the back, saying, 'You made it! You made it!'"

No matter what anyone else was saying, the Carolina players admitted the game against Jacksonville had a historical feel to it.

"I hope we lose the toss," said Paul Butcher, a crooked smile crossing the special-teams maniac's face. "Then maybe I'll get to go out and blow somebody up on the opening kickoff. That would be something—the first blowup in Carolina Panther history."

The players knew it was a day that would be remembered by their fledging fans, for better or for worse. That alone was motivation enough to go out determined to win.

"Whether it's right or wrong," said center Curtis Whitley, "if we win the game people are going to be saying, 'Wow! Look at them. The Carolina franchise really knows how to build a team.'

"But if we lose, they'll be saying, 'Whoa! Look at Jacksonville. They really know how to build a program down there.' And if we look bad and lose, they'll be saying, 'What's going on there with the Carolina franchise?'"

McCormack stated more modest goals for the Panthers as they embarked on their first afternoon of real competition.

"Yeah, we'd like to win it. But I'll take the party line: We've got things we want to do that are more important than winning. I think the thing we want to come out of this with is we don't want to look like an expansion team out there," he said. "We don't want to go in there and have a lot of offsides, have a lot of people jumping, dropped snaps, things like that. We want to look like a professional football team, and I think we've got a chance of doing that."

They did, even though the two teams lined up on the wrong sides of the field before the opening kickoff and then, after switching, the football fell off the tee before Jacksonville's Scott Sisson could strike it.

Jacksonville scored first on an exciting 66-yard punt return by Desmond Howard, a former Heisman Trophy winner and first-round draft pick with a sizeable salary—just the kind of player Polian said the Panthers wanted to steer away from in the allocation draft. The Panthers countered with a 16-yard touchdown pass from Frank Reich, who started at quarterback, to fullback Bob Christian. They then went ahead 14–7 before halftime on an electric 85-yard interception return by rookie cornerback Tyrone Poole.

Reich was efficient as the starting quarterback, playing the entire first half. But Kerry Collins was even better during his stint in the third quarter and the early part of the fourth, completing five of seven passes for 53 yards and inspiring confidence in himself.

"I don't know how good Jacksonville was," Collins later said, "but I felt great. I felt like I was in command. . . . I don't know why I wouldn't be ready [to be a starter] sometime early in the season."

Two field goals by Kasay in the fourth quarter broke a 14–14 tie and set up Lofton's heroics at the goal line. Lofton, it should be noted, was not a starter and normally would not have been in the game in such a situation. The same could be same for Brunell, the Jaguars' second-string quarterback. But as promised beforehand, neither coach pulled reserves for starters with the game on the line, leaving guys like Brunell and Lofton to settle it.

It was the way Capers wanted it, the way he would have scripted it if he could, as he was so fond of saying.

"To me," said Capers, "anytime a team has the ball down there inside your five-yard line and you keep them out, that builds character on your team."

Instead of spending the week following the win over Jacksonville practicing in Spartanburg, the Panthers held a light workout at Wofford Monday morning and then hopped in a plane again for a return trip to Ohio. The plan: to break up the monotony of practicing against the same old teammates in the same old place and try working out against another team instead. The Cleveland Browns, since they were not on Carolina's schedule either in the preseason or the regular season, were happy to oblige.

The Browns appeared to be a formidable practice foe. *Sports Illustrated* had already forecast them as probable AFC representatives for the Super Bowl. They appeared to have the kind of across-the-board depth the Panthers could only hope they would have some year down the line.

"This is a great evaluation process for us," Capers said. "When you're going against the same guys all the time, you start to play to their tendencies. This gives us the chance to evaluate our players in a different setting.

"You don't know how fast or how strong or what the tendencies might be of the player you're going up against."

The Panthers also came to Cleveland hoping to escape the heat a little bit, but it was 95 degrees the first day they staged two workouts against the Browns. Surprisingly, the Panthers initially seemed to hold their own pretty well, causing Rob Burnett, a Pro Bowl defensive end with the Browns, to venture the opinion that the Panthers weren't really an expansion team.

"To me," Burnett said, "an expansion team would be a lot of guys you've never heard of. They've got a lot of guys on their team who have played in this league and made names for themselves in this league. You know who they are."

Asked how far apart the Panthers and Browns appeared to be in terms of talent, Burnett responded with a surprising answer.

"I don't think we're that far apart," Burnett said. "I think they're only a player or two away from being a playoff team."

Polian laughed when informed of Burnett's comments.

"He's just being kind. We've got a long, long way to go at a lot of positions," Polian said. "We're a professional team, but these practices against the Browns really show how far we are from being ready to compete for the playoffs.

"There's a huge gulf between being professional and competitive, and in winning and being in the championship hunt. The Browns have crossed that gulf and are standing on the other side, looking over at us. We're on the other side of it, trying to figure out how to get across."

Polian also took the occasion to defend Barry Foster, who again was sidelined by a sore right ankle but at least surprised a few folks by signing several autographs for fans as he left the practice fields. When reporters nonchalantly asked if it seemed strange signing all these autographs for Cleveland fans after playing for Pittsburgh, the Browns' despised AFC Central rival, Foster simply shrugged, said nothing, and turned to head for the locker room.

"Look," said Polian, "running backs take a terrible beating in this league. I know we said we wanted guys who were going to practice when we started building our roster, but running back might be the one position where you have to make some exceptions.

I guarantee you, you could take a run right down Interstate-90 [which leads from Cleveland to Buffalo] and you wouldn't see number 34 [Thurman Thomas] practicing every day for the Bills, either. And he's headed for the Hall of Fame.

"These guys just take a terrible beating through the course of a season. They've got to save something for the games."

The second day at the Browns' sprawling practice complex in the Cleveland suburb of Berea wasn't much cooler than the first. Capers, in fact, was much hotter after his team got annihilated by the more experienced Browns during a goal-line drill toward the end of the morning practice. Six times during the drill, the Browns took it to the Panthers' defense inside the five-yard line—with much different results than the Panthers enjoyed a few days earlier in a similar situation against Jacksonville. All six times, the Browns scored with ease.

Immediately afterward, Capers gathered his players around him in the middle of one of the practice fields. He was furious.

"That was the worst performance by a goal-line defense that I've witnessed in my 10 years coaching in the NFL," he told his players.

Gerald Williams, a defensive lineman with the Panthers who played the previous three seasons under Capers in Pittsburgh, said Capers' comment wasn't even necessary to put the sorry performance into perspective for the defense.

"We already knew it was bad," Williams said. "But he let us know it was bad anyway. We can't pinpoint exactly what went wrong until we look at the film, but we know there was a lot that went wrong."

A reporter then asked Williams if the outcome would be different if the two teams were to tangle in the same situational drill the following day.

"It definitely would be different," Williams said. "It would be different or some heads would roll."

"It was flat-out embarrassing," cornerback Rod Smith added. "We had some lean years when I played for New England, but we never got handled the way we got handled out there today."

The offense didn't fare much better against the Browns. When they squared off in a goal-line situation, the Panthers scored just once in six attempts—on a fumble recovery in the end zone. Making matters worse, wide receiver Don Beebe, a projected starter, suffered cracked ribs during a passing drill and was declared out for at least the next three preseason games.

That night, the Panthers and Browns met for a final joint workout under the lights and watchful eyes of about 5,000 loyal Browns fans at old Cleveland Stadium. Actually, it was what is called a controlled scrimmage, with each team taking turns with the ball in certain situations that are determined in advance.

Again, the Browns appeared to gain the upper hand rather easily. Veteran wide receiver Andre Rison, for instance, made Poole, one of the Panthers' celebrated rookies, look overmatched more than once. Collins had his moments at quarterback for the Panthers, but that was really about it.

All in all, it was a glorious night for Art Modell, owner of the Browns. In complete contrast to Jerry Richardson, who also was in attendance for the scrimmage, Modell made it a point to be seen—and heard—by many of those who crowded the sidelines. As at each of the Browns-Panthers' earlier practices in Berea, Modell was very visible as he rode around in a golf cart and talked freely with just about anyone who approached him. Richardson even sat with him briefly in the golf cart, but only for a moment before moving on and out of sight. At one point, Modell was surrounded by a total of eight writers from the Carolinas, and he clearly enjoyed sharing his opinions about life in the NFL with them as they laughed and joked and the reporters furiously scribbled notes.

He said cutting Sam Mills from the Browns during training camp in 1981 was "the biggest mistake I ever made," even though the coaches, not Modell, supposedly did the cutting in Cleveland. He said he loved the Browns' plain helmets, and he liked Collins' potential as a quarterback—even though he believed Collins did have a hitch in his throwing motion.

"It's a very, very funny delivery," Modell said. "It's almost as if he had broken his arm as a child. But he gets it done."

Modell said the Panthers would be competitive during their first year, adding the league was probably too generous in letting them and the Jaguars load up their rosters with extra draft picks and then also giving them the opportunity to basically shop as they pleased in the free-agent market.

"I've talked to a lot of owners and none of us know how that happened," Modell said. "We must have all been out to the bathroom."

Modell said the television ratings from the Hall of Fame Game, which included a 43 share in the Charlotte market, were "staggering, absolutely staggering. That was something to behold."

And Modell also talked about leaving Cleveland Stadium, even though there was a planned tax vote in November that city officials hoped would raise some $170 million to renovate the creaking structure on the shore of Lake Erie.

"Look at this place," he told the reporters, gesturing with his hands at the crumbling 72,000-seat mass of concrete and steel beams, some of which blocked views of the playing surface. "It's a dump. This place is coming apart at the seams. We don't have enough luxury suites, and we've got too many bad seats where people can't see what's going on out on the field.

"Parking is bad, too. I want to get out of here. My parking capacity is about eight stalls. Moving to a stadium in the suburbs off the interstate is the only answer for us."

Modell abruptly quit talking to the Carolina reporters as soon as Mary Kay Cabot, a writer who covered the Browns for the *Cleveland Plain Dealer*, approached the scene.

"Oh, look who's coming," he said. "She's a real pain in the ass."

Then, for the first time all night, Modell abruptly quit talking.

Later, though, the Carolina reporters related to Cabot and other Cleveland reporters everything Modell said—since the entire conversation clearly had been on the record.

Modell had observed the reporters taking detailed notes, and never mentioned that any of his comments were not meant for publication. The Cleveland writers were surprised to hear his comments about the stadium, which they suspected to be true all along but had never heard Modell admit publicly. The *Medina County Gazette* ran a story the next morning saying Modell planned to move the Browns to the Cleveland suburbs, and all hell broke loose.

First off, Modell denied everything he said. Unfortunately for him, he had made the comments in front of eight respected newsmen, who had taken careful notes. Nonetheless, Modell told the *Akron Beacon Journal* he never said he wanted out of Cleveland Stadium to build a new stadium in the suburbs.

"I never said that," he told the *Beacon Journal*. "No way I would say that to a strange newspaper. Even if I felt that way, I wouldn't say it."

The goal for the Panthers was to use the lessons learned in Cleveland, and there were quite a few, in the next preseason game at Chicago. As the Panthers took the field at venerable Soldier Field, Dom Anile looked on from the press box and talked about the Cleveland visit. Prior to joining the Panthers, Anile spent eight seasons employed by the Browns, the last three as their director of college scouting.

Anile questioned whether the Browns possessed the goods to get to the Super Bowl, mainly because he didn't think Vinny Testaverde was a consistent enough quarterback to take them there. He also talked about the scary collapse of Rick Venturi, the Browns' defensive coordinator who had been hospitalized for exhaustion right after the Browns scrimmaged the Bears in Platteville, Wisconsin, just prior to the arrival of the Panthers in Cleveland.

The last day Venturi was on the job, he drank five cups of coffee and smoked 12 cigarettes—before 8 A.M.

"Five cups of coffee and 12 butts? Sounds about right to me," the portly Anile said, only half-joking. "I'm telling you, that's about my morning intake, too. You watch so much film and try to squeeze so much into every day that it can really get to you after a while."

The game against the Bears represented a chance for Jack Trudeau to get the coaching staff to think of him as the Panthers' potential starter. When Capers named Reich the starter for the preseason opener, he said Trudeau would have the opportunity to start the second and play an entire half with the first offense.

"I really can't look at this as just another preseason game," Trudeau admitted. "It's not, at least for me. I've played in a lot of big games over the course of my career, including playoff games. This is like another one of those."

Alas, the game was like many others during Trudeau's checkered NFL career. He started off looking like the second coming of Johnny Unitas, completing passes all over the field, but ended up firing more incompletions than anything else. He also miffed Capers by failing to run a play in time on Carolina's very first possession of the night, resulting in a five-yard delay-of-game penalty. His mediocre overall statistics: 9 of 22 for 108 yards and two drives that produced field goals by John Kasay.

On defense, rookie defensive end Shawn King showed flashes of brilliance. He kept invading the Chicago backfield, and ended up with a diving interception, a sack and two passes deflected.

Kasay added three more field goals in the second half, eventually putting the Panthers up 15–7 midway through the fourth quarter. It looked as if they were headed for their second consecutive victory, the only severe blemish on the night being the loss of running back Tony Smith, a promising candidate to back up Foster, to a broken left leg in the third period.

The Bears rallied, however, after getting booed by the home crowd. Third-string quarterback Shane Matthews drove them 79 yards in eight plays before hitting running back Anthony Johnson with a short pass for a touchdown, and then passed to Johnson again for the two-point conversion that tied it. Later, Matthews drove the Bears into position for Kevin Butler's 51-yard field goal with 57 seconds left, giving the Bears an 18–15 win.

Capers was not pleased about the fourth-quarter defensive lapse, nor about the offense's inability to produce a single touchdown.

"We were sitting right there with this team, a good football team, and we had them on the ropes," Capers said. "But you're never happy when you lose a football game, especially in the fourth quarter like that. A week ago we made the plays we needed to win the game. We didn't do that in crucial situations in this one."

Foster, meanwhile, played the first quarter and carried the ball seven times for 31 yards, two more than he produced in the Hall of Fame Game.

The Panthers might have been able to tie the game against the Bears or even win it had Steve Hawkins, then a prospect at wide receiver, not dropped a perfectly thrown bomb from Frank Reich inside the Chicago 20-yard line in the closing seconds. By the following Thursday, Hawkins was no longer a wide receiver. He went to Capers' office and asked to be tried at defensive back, and Capers, weary of all the dropped balls by Hawkins and other receivers, quickly complied.

As the Panthers geared up for their next preseason test, two themes seemed to dominate the scope of organization—one on the football side, one on the administrative side.

On the football side, there was this problem with receivers. One article in the *Winston-Salem Journal* assessing the situation was accompanied by the large hammer headline that stated, "No Hands." Another in the *Spartanburg Herald-Journal* declared, "Receivers Trying to Get a Grip."

Hawkins was an obvious target of criticism because of his late drop against the Bears. But no one in the receiving corps was doing a very good job of catching the ball consistently, except maybe for Mark Carrier and perhaps Willie Green. Don Beebe, the only other wide receiver with much experience at all, was now hurt and out of action for at least a couple of more weeks.

One afternoon in Spartanburg following the loss to the Bears, the Panther receivers dropped so many passes that a fan watching from the hillside instinctively yelled, "Do something exciting, will ya?"

Richard Williamson, the coach of the Panthers' receivers, did not hide his own disgust following that same dismal workout.

"You can't drop balls in games. You just can't," Williamson said. "In the games, you have to produce. If you don't, you won't be here long.

"If we throw it to you deep to win a ball game, you've got to make the catch. The ones that play and win in this league don't drop the ball in that situation. Regardless of how fast you are or how good you look running routes, you've got to produce. None of that other stuff matters if you don't catch the football."

On the administrative side, Panther officials were sheepishly admitting the preseason home opener against Denver August 12 now had no chance of selling out. In fact, it wouldn't be close. They also finally admitted concern over selling out several of their regular-season home games, including the home opener September 17 against St. Louis.

"We've tried everything," McCormack said. "But for whatever reason, we haven't sold out."

McCormack didn't buy into the theory that Clemson Memorial Stadium was just too far for some people to drive. On a good night with light traffic and no construction, it was a two-and-a-half-hour drive from uptown Charlotte. For fans hoping to come from farther north, like Winston-Salem, Greensboro or Raleigh, it was at best an eight-hour round-trip.

"When I was with Seattle, lots of folks drove from Spokane to Seahawks games. That was five hours," McCormack said. "People drove from Portland, too. We even had 300 season-ticket holders in Alaska. The same people didn't come every week, but those tickets were always used by somebody. They shared the tickets, and they would fly in all the way from somewhere in Alaska.

"This is all kind of new to me because I never had a game blacked out in eight years with Seattle."

Worse yet, all games that failed to sell out in both the preseason and the regular season were subject to a television blackout in the crucial market areas of Columbia, Greenville and Spartanburg in South Carolina and in Asheville and even Charlotte itself in North Carolina. This would deprive the Panthers of valuable exposure, which they craved almost as much as victories on the field.

The game against Denver did not sell out. Traffic was a nightmare, both coming and going to the 7:30 P.M. contest for the 57,017 fans who attended. Even the coaches, players and reporters who made the trek, coming early and going late, encountered severe problems. More than two hours after the game's conclusion, cars remained nestled bumper-to-bumper on Interstate-85, traffic backed up for miles.

In some ways, the sleepy town of Clemson did not seem prepared for the invasion of the Panthers, even though they had to know they were coming. A disc jockey at WCCP-FM in Clemson referred to "Coach Tom Capers" of the Panthers on a pregame show, and then promoted an upcoming interview with "Mark Richards," the team's director of business operations who happens to be Jerry Richardson's youngest son.

The news on the field was much better for the Panthers, who won 19–10 behind the strength of their improving defense and four John Kasay field goals.

Reich started at quarterback again and struggled his first three series, failing to complete a single pass. Then, facing third-and-14 from the Carolina 18-yard line on what was to be his last series of the night, Reich made what may have been one of the more important passes of his NFL career, or at least so it seemed at the time. Reich found tight end Lawyer Tillman at the Panther 40, where Tillman caught the pass, bounced off two defenders and rambled another 30 yards downfield for a 70-yard gain.

On the very next play, Reich scooped up his own fumble, recovered and threw to fullback Bob Christian for a 10-yard gain. Then he hit Christian again for a three-yard touchdown pass, the Panthers' first TD since the Hall of Fame Game.

So what if Denver quarterback John Elway spent the last two and a half quarters on the bench, when he might have led a comeback? The Panthers were nonetheless thrilled with their first conquest of an established NFL team.

"They've been in business 35 years or so, they're a team with a Hall of Fame quarterback—and we've only been in business since about June ourselves. And we win!" Jerry Richardson marveled. "It's just incredible, unbelievable."

Randy Baldwin passed Foster as the Panthers' leading rusher, running for 47 yards on seven carries against the Broncos to give him a total of 74 yards and a rushing average of 5.3 yards per carry for the preseason. Foster was stuck at 2.8 yards per carry for the preseason after carrying six times for only nine yards against Denver.

As Frank Reich and Jack Trudeau left the practice fields at Wofford College two days later, the quarterbacks piled into one of the oversize golf carts that transported players up a formidable hill to the locker room. Trudeau rode in the front seat; Reich sat directly behind him.

It should have been the other way around. A few minutes later, Capers emerged to inform the media that he was declaring Reich the winner in the battle for the starting quarterback's job. Reich's completion to Tillman against the Broncos played a huge role in Capers' decision, as did the fact that Reich was able to produce two touchdowns to Trudeau's none during the first three preseason outings.

The second touchdown would not have occurred if not for the completion to Tillman on third-and-14. In fact, had Tillman dropped that pass, Reich would have left the game against Denver with no completions in five pass attempts. According to Capers' script for the game, from which he already had proven he would not deviate, Reich was supposed to play only the first quarter—but he never removed a quarterback in the middle of a possession, letting him finish a series even if the quarter expired, as it did immediately after Reich's pass to Tillman.

Statistically, the drive made possible by the completion to Tillman made the two veteran quarterbacks so close after those three contests that it was uncanny. Reich completed 17 of 37 passes for 198 yards and the two touchdowns. His quarterback rating was 80.7. Trudeau completed 18 of 39 passes for 249 yards and a rating of 70.7. (The touchdowns made the difference.)

"The bottom line is this: Our goal on offense is to score touchdowns," Capers said. "Our offense has scored two touchdowns, and Frank Reich was the quarterback both times."

Capers also felt the time was right to name a starter because the regular-season opener was now less than three weeks away. Instead of splitting the number of repetitions during practices equally among three quarterbacks, Reich now would get roughly three-fifths of all snaps. Trudeau and Kerry Collins were to split whatever was left over, with the idea being to develop more continuity in the offense.

After 10 years as a backup in Buffalo, nine to Jim Kelly, Reich was thrilled to have his first real NFL starting opportunity. Basically, Capers told him it was his job to keep as long as he stayed healthy and produced, and avoided costly mistakes.

"I think the main thing we need on offense is the continuity," Reich said. "There's no doubt that, for any quarterback, it's going to help you the more times you get in there with the same group. You get to know each other more and more. I'm not just talking about the receivers. I'm talking about the running backs, the offensive line, all of it."

Trudeau declined to talk to the media the day Reich was named starter.

"It's Frank's day," he told Charlie Dayton.

The next day, however, Trudeau talked at length about his lost opportunity. He opened by saying to a group of reporters, "The hard part for me is talking to you guys right now—because you're asking me questions I don't want to answer, making me talk about things I don't want to talk about."

Nonetheless, he answered every question amicably. He hinted that the deck might have been stacked against him, considering Reich's close ties with Bill Polian.

"The bottom line is that I think I did all I could do," Trudeau said.

The following Saturday, neither Reich nor Trudeau was the best Carolina quarterback on the field against the defending Super Bowl champion San Francisco 49ers at 3Com Park in San Francisco. It was Collins. Trailing 17–3 late in the fourth quarter, he directed an eight-play, 74-yard touchdown drive while operating out of the Panthers' hurry-up offense. He hit four of six passes for 68 yards, including a 28-yard TD strike to Dwight Stone in the right corner of the end zone with 1:53 left to play.

An onside kick successfully recovered got the ball immediately back into Collins' hands, and he had the Panthers on the move again until, on successive plays, he overthrew an open receiver for an incompletion, failed to detect a blitz and was sacked, and threw an interception over the middle. He played only four minutes and 19 seconds, but the Panthers suddenly got a glimpse of their future.

Foster sat out the entire week of practice with a sore knee and sore ankle, and didn't play against the 49ers. Baldwin started in his place.

Elsewhere, Ki-Jana Carter, the running back the Panthers passed up when they decided to trade the number-one pick in the draft to Cincinnati, suffered a torn anterior cruciate knee ligament and was lost for the season.

As the preseason finale approached toward the end of August—a home date against the New York Giants at Clemson—the Panthers' roster was taking shape. No player's fate seemed more ironic than that of offensive lineman Harry Boatswain, acquired with the team's second pick in the expansion allocation draft off San Francisco's roster.

Four days prior to the Panthers' 17–10 loss at San Francisco, Boatswain was a media darling following a practice. The topic was what made the 49ers so great.

"We wrote history there," said Boatswain, who started the Hall of Fame Game at right guard. "We won five Super Bowls. That's the bottom line. And that's good, but now we're trying to write history here."

Less than 12 hours later, Boatswain himself was history. Predictably, Steve Hawkins, Baron Rollins, Vince Marrow and Richard Buchanan were all gone by the third week of August as well.

A week later, a few more mild surprises were included in the next batch of cuts. Fred Foggie, the defensive back who once proclaimed the Panthers' secondary "the fastest in the league," drawing a howl from veteran safety Bubba McDowell, was one. He was so confident of making the team after being acquired off Pittsburgh's roster in the expansion draft that he was in the process of having a home built in Fort Mill, South Carolina, the day word came that he was no longer employed. Alan Haller, the cornerback who unwisely had his golf clubs delivered to Wofford in full view of Mike McCormack, was waived August 27, just a week before the regular-season opener. Haller would be re-signed 10 days later after Steve Lofton suffered an injury in the game at Atlanta. Upon arriving, he said: "I made sure I didn't bring my golf clubs this time." (It didn't help. He lasted less than three weeks before getting waived for good).

Others, like five-eight Eric Guliford, a wide receiver and punt-return candidate, were beginning to establish themselves as favorites to make the final roster and maybe do even more than that. Guliford caught everyone's attention by catching four passes for 46 yards against the 49ers and also completing a 51-yard pass to Willie Green on "a reverse pass," where Guliford ran an end-around, was handed the ball by Reich and then threw downfield to Green to set up a John Kasay field goal.

Matt Elliott, the former Cablevision guy, had replaced Boatswain as the starter at right guard on the offensive line. Elliott and Brandon Hayes, the rookie discovered almost by accident at Central State by Dom Anile, were performing so well, in fact, that Boatswain was deemed expendable.

Matt Campbell said he wasn't thinking about the possibility of getting cut the day Foggie went down, but he spent the previous day registering for classes at the University of South Carolina just in case. The Panthers kept him because of his blocking ability as a tight end, and school was put on hold.

And Greg Kragen, the grizzled veteran who had to be talked into coming to Spartanburg in the first place after the Panthers selected him in the expansion allocation draft, had decided to hang around after all. After one of the earlier workouts at Wofford, Capers and Kragen knelt down face-to-face in the middle of one of the practice fields.

"Is your heart still in this?" Capers wanted to know.

Kragen hedged, admitting there were times when he wasn't sure.

"If you're with us, you're with us," Capers said. "We want you. But you have to put the possibility of retirement out of your mind and give us everything you've got."

Kragen said he would.

Then, just to make sure Kragen was certain about his decision, Capers made him run extra wind sprints and agility drills with strength and conditioning coach Chip Morton for about 20 minutes, long after the practice fields had been vacated by the other players.

The final preseason game was an ugly, rain-drenched affair played out in front of a disappointing crowd of 49,114—thousands of others scared away no doubt by the terrible weather and all the horror stories of traffic problems that had been circulating since the first home game.

Barry Foster was in attendance, watching the game from the press box. He declined interviews except to admit in one word to Tom Sorenson, a columnist from the *Observer,* that he enjoyed the halftime entertainment, which featured dogs chasing Frisbees all over the field. The day before the game, when it was revealed Foster would sit out yet again, Capers was asked what he expected of Foster once the regular season began.

"That's tough to say," Capers said. "We really haven't seen much of Barry in the preseason."

Foster probably couldn't have made much of a difference against the Giants. There was little scoring and not much excitement, although the defense again excelled. The Panthers won, 6–3.

"You love those baseball scores when you're on defense," Sam Mills said.

The Panther defense also knocked Giants quarterback Dave Brown from the game, a dual hit by Carlton Bailey and Tyrone Poole giving Brown a concussion in the second quarter.

"When I saw his head hit the ground so hard it bounced, I was a little worried that I might have broken his neck," Bailey said.

Once he discovered Brown was OK other than a little headache, Bailey, who played collegiately at North Carolina, was able to take pleasure in the hit on Brown, who played at Duke.

"I didn't even think about it at the time," said Bailey, "but that was Duke versus North Carolina, wasn't it?"

Bailey and the rest of the defenders could afford to gloat a little bit. The Carolina defense had finished the preseason giving up an average of just 12.4 points per game. More than anything else, this is what enabled the Panthers to emerge from the preseason with a winning record of three wins against two losses.

Three and two.

Suddenly, they weren't looking so much like an expansion team.

THE GAMES

Game 1:
Panthers at Atlanta

As the Panthers' regular-season opener approached, Frank Reich, who had been preparing for this day for a very, very long time, admitted he expected to handle it better than Jim Kelly would—at least in the few minutes leading up to the historic 1 P.M. kickoff at the Georgia Dome in Atlanta.

Kelly, the quarterback whom Reich backed up for nearly a decade in Buffalo, used to throw up before almost every game. Reich wasn't planning on establishing the same gruesome ritual.

"That was kind of our signal that everything was going to be all right," Reich said of his days in Buffalo. "He'd do it, and the rest of the team would look at each other and say, 'OK, Jim threw up. We're ready to go.' Usually it was 10 or 15 minutes before we would go out to the field [for kickoff].

"Sometimes, though, he wouldn't make it to the bathroom. That was the problem."

If a Pro Bowl quarterback like the Bills' Kelly is routinely nauseous before games, it seemed reasonable to expect that his longtime former backup would be a bundle of nerves on the eve of starting his first NFL opener for an expansion franchise playing its first game. But Reich prided himself on being Mr. Even-Keel, and he insisted he had a surefire way to calm himself before games and even practices.

He prayed.

Each week, Reich selected a passage from the Bible that he could relate to whatever he was facing. Then he concentrated on it throughout the week, reading it over and over and over again.

The passage for this particular week came from the third chapter of the Book of Daniel. It was the passage in which King Nebuchadnezzar of Babylonia ordered everyone in his kingdom to bow down and pay homage to a golden statue, decreeing that anyone who refused to do so would be thrown into a fiery furnace and left there to perish. Everyone in the kingdom but three friends of Daniel named Shadrach, Mechach and Abednego did as the king ordered. And when they refused to bow down to the false god, Nebuchadnezzar ordered the three young men thrown into the fiery furnace. From there, the passage reads as follows:

> Then the king ordered the furnace heated seven times its ordinary heat. He
> had the young men tied up and thrown into the furnace with their clothes
> on. It was so hot that the men who threw them in were overcome by the

flames and died on the spot. But the young men walked about with an angel in the middle of the flames and sang a song of praise to God's great glory.

Shadrach, Mechach and Abednego eventually emerged from the furnace unscathed. Reich believed he could do the same against the Falcons.

"I guess I've been reading that, thinking that this is like being thrown into a blazing furnace," Reich said of his pending start at quarterback. "I want to have the same attitude as Shadrach, Mechach and Abednego. Whatever happens, I know my God will be able to save me."

He also knew a solid effort by the offensive line wouldn't hurt.

Whatever the offensive line's problems, and there appeared to be quite a few, they had nothing to do with Barry Foster's woes throughout the preseason. Most of Foster's problems were his own doing—and on the Monday prior to the opener, he paid for them when the Panthers unceremoniously announced they were waiving him.

The one time Foster had consented to speak with the media during training camp, he said he hadn't felt so good since 1992, the year he led the AFC in rushing yardage and made the Pro Bowl. But that feeling seemed to slip away as camp progressed. When camp opened, Foster was considered the key to the Carolina running game; but when kickoff came against Atlanta, he wouldn't even be on the sidelines as Randy Baldwin stepped in to start at halfback.

"I wouldn't have expected this in a million years," Baldwin said.

Baldwin was not alone. Foster didn't expect it, either. The enigmatic running back was gone from the Panthers' Winthrop University practice complex by the time reporters began arriving around 11 A.M.—not that he would have had much to say anyway. He had last spoken to the media more than five weeks earlier, just five days into training camp at Wofford College.

Foster struggled through the first three preseason games, rushing for 62 yards on 22 carries for an average of 2.8 yards per rush that was the lowest of any running back remaining on the roster. But he said nothing.

He frequently sat out practices during the week, blaming injuries. But he said nothing.

He even sat out the last two preseason games, citing a swollen right knee. But he said nothing.

Foster was so silent the media often wondered how he communicated his numerous injuries to Carolina management. Some suspected he did it by pointing to the area of the body that was betraying him and maybe grunting—but saying nothing.

By waiving Foster, the Panthers saved themselves the $2.45 million in salary they would have been forced to pay him if he was on the roster opening day. They also hung onto a conditional fourth-round draft pick they would have had to surrender in 1997 if Foster had reached certain levels of production during the 1995 season. The only item nonrefundable from the trade made with the Steelers to acquire Foster at the end of May was a sixth-round selection in the 1996 college draft. That was a price deemed acceptable for taking a gamble on him.

"When we brought Barry in," said Coach Dom Capers, "we felt his upside potential outweighed any possible downside. But as time went on through training camp and the preseason games, we felt the productivity that we saw did not warrant the investment."

General Manager Bill Polian, the man who had staunchly defended Foster's inactivity early in the preseason but had fallen silent on the subject in more recent weeks, insisted that both trading for and subsequently releasing Foster made perfect business sense.

"You can't be afraid to take chances and make moves. You never hit a home run if you don't get to the plate and get some at-bats in," Polian said.

"But a bigger sin than failing to make a move is trying to justify a move when it clearly is not working out the way you thought and hoped it would."

Foster's release sent shockwaves through the Panthers' locker room. Dwight Stone, a former teammate at Pittsburgh and perhaps Foster's only true friend on the Carolina roster, said Foster didn't speak to any of his teammates before leaving abruptly after being waived. Stone had last spoken to him the previous evening, less than 12 hours before the ax came down.

"He was talking about the season. He was talking about playing against Atlanta. This is shocking," Stone said.

Cornerback Tim McKyer and defensive end Gerald Williams, also teammates of Foster's in Pittsburgh, admitted they were caught by surprise when the news reached them. But in retrospect, maybe they shouldn't have been. Capers and Polian had insisted from the start that they wanted players who would practice on a regular basis, and Foster never did fit the bill.

Besides, there are no guaranteed contracts in the NFL unless you are a superstar, such as a John Elway or Troy Aikman or Emmitt Smith. Foster was at one time just a notch below those guys and appeared to perhaps be headed into their stratsophere, but injuries and disagreements with those who signed his paycheck grounded him in a hurry. It didn't help him that the NFL now had a salary cap, either. With a cap of $37 million and roughly 60 players to pay, including those on the practice squad and injured reserve, $2.45 million was a huge chunk to hand over to a player whose productivity and reliability was so questionable.

"Every year, it's the same," McKyer said. "You never know who's going to be here from one day to the next. I might not be here next week. You just don't know."

Foster's stunningly swift departure proved there were no free rides for any Panther who did not practice regularly. That was proven, in fact, less than 24 hours before Foster's release when two other veterans, linebacker Frank Stams and running back Derrick Lassic, two who had frequently missed practices due to injuries, were also waived.

No Panther missed more practice time than Foster, however. He rarely practiced two days in a row after the opening of training camp, citing soreness in his left ankle at first. Later, he missed practice time because of a sore right knee.

Despite some obvious swelling, a magnetic resonance imaging test performed one day before the Panthers' final preseason game revealed no structural damage to Foster's right knee. When Foster met with the coaching staff before the night kickoff against the Giants in the preseason finale, Foster and Capers left the room with differing opinions on the seriousness of the injury, which sounded frighteningly similar to the beginnings of the same scenario that led to Foster's problems in Pittsburgh.

Capers said he thought Foster could have played. Foster told the staff he didn't think he could go.

Nonetheless, it was not an easy decision to let Foster go. He had been acquired to be a focal point of the ground attack on offense. Joe Mack, Mike McCormack, Polian and Capers met for nearly four hours the night after the Giants game, discussing the Foster situation and laying out different scenarios to each other until past midnight. Not the least of concerns was who would carry the mail if Foster was cut loose. But ultimately, of greater concern was the fact that Foster missed too many practices and had trouble making it through the preseason games.

Finally, the others all turned to Capers and agreed it was his call.

"I just don't think it's going to work out. Let him go," Capers said.

Mack later said: "It's a credit to the organization that a person can admit mistakes and not be afraid of the consequences."

Virtually everyone in the front office had begun to question Foster's desire by the middle of training camp. The personnel staff first brought it up to the coaching staff, only to learn the coaching staff had been wondering about many of the same things.

The players may have questioned Foster's dedication, too, but they kept it strictly to themselves.

"The first week or two of training camp, he looked like the old Barry Foster. I don't know what happened," Williams said. "I never question another player's injuries or how bad he's really injured. I know from being hurt myself that it's a tough position to be in."

Having been Pittsburgh's defensive coordinator the previous three seasons, Capers had entered into the Foster Experiment with firsthand knowledge of Foster's reputation, which was that of someone who did not like to play hurt and did not like to talk to the media or even the coaching staff about why he didn't like to play hurt. But Capers insisted Foster's past problems had no bearing on the decision to waive him.

"Everyone has their own personality. I have no problems with that whatsoever," Capers said. "I just think you have to go based off what you see. It's a long season, and durability is a big factor with who makes our team. I also think it's very hard to go out and perform on Sunday if you're not on the field doing the work during the week."

McKyer had the last—and best—word. Noting Foster's frequent trips to the whirlpool in the trainer's room since the very outset of camp, he said simply, "You can't make the club from the tub."

Foster's injuries never seemed to occur while he actually was on the field; they were pains from the past, apparently, that cropped up just when it came time to practice or play in a meaningless preseason game. The rest of the guys weren't so fortunate. Entering the final preseason game against the Giants, Capers and Polian stated the team's main objective for the night was to get through the contest without sustaining any major injuries.

It didn't happen. Matt Elliott, who played so well in the preseason at right guard that the Panthers' second pick in the expansion draft, Harry Boatswain, had been deemed expendable, strained his left calf muscle and was questionable for the Falcons. Brandon Hayes, the promising rookie offensive lineman who was Elliott's immediate backup, tore the anterior cruciate ligament in his right knee; and Dewell Brewer, yet another unknown running back who nonetheless had shown flashes of potential, tore the same ligament in his left knee. Both Hayes and Brewer were lost for the season.

Polian later would term these injuries "catastrophic," displaying his flair for the dramatic more than anything else. But it was true they did affect the Panthers where they least could afford it: in the depth department at two of the weakest position groups on the roster, especially with the double hit at right guard.

Heading into the opener against Atlanta, the offensive line was the biggest question mark for the Panthers, although the running-back situation, what with the sudden releases of Foster and Lassic and the season-ending injuries to Tony Smith and Brewer, was fast becoming a challenger for that dubious honor. The general feeling was that it didn't matter who was back there running the football or throwing it for the Panthers; no matter who it was going to be, they weren't going to have a whole lot of time on their hands for picking out holes to run through or making decisions on where and to whom to throw the ball.

During the two minicamps, offensive line coach Jim McNally attempted to gain the attention of his mostly wide-eyed pupils by bringing in Anthony Munoz, a legendary left tackle who had played under McNally for years in Cincinnati. Munoz spent several days during two separate stretches teaching technique and basically placing a stamp of legitimacy on McNally's methods of coaching. He also took note of the talent the Panthers had on hand, denying there was little with which to work.

"They've got some big guys. Some real big guys. It makes me thankful I'm retired," said Munoz, regarded by many as the finest left tackle in NFL history. "And they've got some guys who are not only big, but have some ability. Of course, the bigger the guys are, you have to work on some technique with them [because they're usually slower than smaller linemen and rely more on technique than athleticism to be effective]. But what better man could they have to teach them technique than Jim McNally? I think his track record shows what he can do.

"He's the type of guy who has all this technique, and he might stay with that technique, but he refines it. He changes with the game. He's constantly studying. I mean, you could probably call him up any time night or day, and he's up studying tape. That's what he does. He watches not only offensive line play, but what the defensive linemen are doing and what other offensive linemen from around the league are doing. Then he incorporates what other guys are doing and comes up with combined techinques. So he's always coming up with new technique for the offensive line as far as how to attack defenses."

In Cincinnati, McNally's involvement in game planning was key. When Buddy Ryan, then a defensive coordinator in Chicago, came out with the famed "46" defense, it was McNally who came up with new blocking schemes to deal with it effectively. This enabled the Bengals to have more success against Ryan's defense than most other teams.

Indeed, Jim "Mouse" McNally was widely regarded as one of the finest offensive line coaches in the NFL. He liked big linemen, believing size and sound technique would always prevail. This was one reason Capers insisted the Panthers snatch him up when he came available, even though it was before the organization had publicly admitted they had hired Capers as head coach. Capers, Polian and McCormack knew all along that hiring a quality offensive line assistant was going to be a key to aiding the team's development.

McNally, 52, did not look much like an offensive line coach. Bespectacled and short at about five feet, nine inches, McNally often wore a rumpled Columbo look, complete with the kinds of bemused facial expressions born of eccentric genius that the television detective would lay on unsuspecting suspects just as he was to leave a room. Whereas the other coaches usually were decked out in Panther gear from head to toe during practices, McNally usually chose to go with the all-gray, nondescript outfit, perhaps befitting the positions he coached, where his players often toiled in anonymity.

Munoz and McNally arrived in Cincinnati the same season, with McNally being hired just four months before Munoz was drafted in 1980. Munoz remembers going to lunch with him shortly after being drafted.

"I was a little stunned by his size," Munoz said. "You think a coach is going to have played his position—and believe it or not, he did. He played offensive line [at the University of Buffalo]. But he was like however tall he is—and I'm not going to guess because I don't want to get into trouble—and went 250 or 260 pounds and that is what he played."

Mike McCormack laughed when he was informed of this story.

"Anthony said Jim played at 250 or 260 pounds?" said the six-three McCormack, who had played at 248 in the NFL. "That just goes to show you how Jim McNally has him completely snowed. Obviously, he's got Anthony believing everything he's telling him, so he must be a great coach.

"Jim McNally has never weighed 250 pounds in his life. At his height, he'd look like a bowling ball if he weighed 250 pounds."

Nonetheless, both McCormack and Munoz agreed on one thing: McNally's height didn't matter; he gained the respect of the players he coached because his methods produced results.

"He's a teacher of technique. That's what Jim McNally is all about," said Munoz. "And it's not like he gives you a technique on the first of May and then you'll come back to it in June. You're going to work on that technique over and over and over again until you get it right.

"One thing I noticed [on the practice field] that is trouble for a lot of guards and tackles working the stunts is if you turn right away, you're going to get picked by the [defensive] tackle coming from the outside, and of course then the [defensive] end working inside is going to be free. So there is a lot of body positioning as far as after your first quick step that you can work on.

"It's difficult, because say there's a guy like Darion Conner coming at you from the outside, a guy who can really move, and your first reaction is to turn and get out there as soon as you can. But you have to realize the angles. In other words, if you do take a deeper drop—wide, but deeper—you're going to be able to cut off the angle for a faster guy. Those are the types of things these guys need to work on."

McNally and his linemen did, throughout May and part of June and part of July and all of August, by which time Munoz was long gone. And still, much of what Munoz and McNally were saying and teaching and preaching seemed like mumbo jumbo to some of the younger guys like big Kevin Farkas.

"When I was in Denver's camp last year, they told us that if you didn't understand what to do on a certain play, just block the end," Farkas said. "Here, it's not that simple. They're throwing a lot of stuff at us, and we go over it again and again and again until we've got it in our heads what we're supposed to do in all kinds of different situations. You walk up to the line of scrimmage with a lot on your mind."

McCormack watched the development of the offensive line with great interest. Times had changed since he established himself, along with Munoz, who played much later, as one of the finest left tackles in NFL history. But the basic philosophy of forming a cohesive offensive line had not.

"I've always made the comparison that a good offensive line is like the five fingers on your hand," McCormack said. "When you make a fist, you don't tell the little finger to roll up first, followed by the ring finger, the middle finger and the index finger, with the thumb on top. It just happens naturally, all together. That's what has to happen with a good offensive line. It has to work together, as a unit.

"It's become a position where you need more strength than when I played. When I was growing up, lifting weights was taboo. They said it would make you too muscle-bound. I got my strength from working during the summers in Kansas in the hay fields and in the lumber yard.

"You had to have foot speed then, too, but you need it even more today. The people offensive linemen have to block these days are bigger and faster than ever. So you've got to have the players to counteract that. Defenses are more sophisticated now, too, so you've got to have players who are able to read stunts and react quickly to them."

McCormack had one more piece of advice for the Panthers' offensive line hopefuls: No one was going to notice them much unless they screwed up. That's just the way it is.

"When you play on the offensive line," said McCormack, "you have to park your ego. There won't be a lot of glory coming your way. Your glory comes from helping other people be successful and helping the team win."

This was reflected even in the way offensive linemen dressed. Kerry Collins or Sam Mills could put on a suit and instantly look pretty sharp. Somehow, suits just didn't hang right on 300-pound offensive linemen. They tried to dress up on game day, but usually ended up looking almost comical.

Starting on the line against the Falcons would be, from left to right, Blake Brockermeyer at left tackle, Andrew Peterson at left guard, Curtis Whitley at center, Elliott at right guard (if his injury didn't keep him out) and Derrick Graham at right tackle. It was an interesting group.

Brockermeyer was the highly touted rookie, who had been switched from right tackle to left early in training camp and still was struggling somewhat to adjust to the most important position on the line, where a good man was needed to protect the quarterback's blind side when he was throwing. But Brock was six-four, 305 pounds and had a Texas-size nasty streak in him that the coaches loved. Munoz, in fact, had been taken with him immediately at one of the minicamps, insisting Brockermeyer could be every bit as outstanding a player as Tony Boselli, who had been chosen by Jacksonville with the number-two overall pick in the college draft, whereas Brockermeyer did not go until late in the first round, 29th overall.

Peterson also was a rookie, though hardly a big name in the draft. When the Panthers selected the six-five, 310-pounder in the fifth round with the 171st overall pick, he wasn't even certain who coached the Panthers. He only knew his good buddy and linemate from the University of Washington, Frank Garcia, had been chosen by the Panthers one round earlier. Pete or Frog, his two nicknames (the latter given because Garcia thought he looked like one in the face), had progressed as quickly as any player during training camp to earn the start at left guard.

The center, Curtis Whitley, was entering his fourth NFL season. A native of Smithfield, North Carolina, who had played at Chowan Junior College in Mufreesboro, North Carolina, before transferring to Clemson, he overcame a drinking problem that had once put his football career in jeopardy. He was squat at six-one and 288 pounds, but also powerfully strong and surprisingly agile and quick on his feet.

Elliott was the starter at right guard. He was the former Mr. Irrelevant, a title imposed on the very last player chosen each year in the NFL draft. In fact, he took pride in calling himself "the last true Mr. Irrelevant" because the year after Washington took him in the 12th round with the 336th overall pick in 1992, the draft was reduced to eight rounds and later to seven. Of the Panthers' Michael Reed, Mr. Irrelevant 1995, and all other Mr. Irrelevants who came after him, Elliott said, "I would have killed to be a seventh-rounder."

If Elliott couldn't go, he would be replaced for opening day by Emerson Martin, who would soon be waived and forgotten.

At right tackle was Derrick Graham, a veteran entering his sixth NFL season who reported to training camp overweight and had been somewhat of a disappointment in the preseason. One of the first unrestricted free agents signed by the team, he was given a signing bonus of $2 million and a first-year salary of $1.5 million on a contract that, although not guaranteed, would pay him $9 million over five years if permitted to run its course. He was given this kind of money because he was supposed to settle in as the line's anchor at left tackle, the line's most critical position, and because he brought needed experience, having started 11 games at right tackle for the Kansas City Chiefs in 1994. But before training camp was two weeks old, Brockermeyer was moved to left tackle and Graham was back at right, where guys often come and go and never make the kind of money in their careers that their counterparts on the other side of the line do.

Total number of NFL games started by the five linemen combined: 22 (18 by Graham, two each by Whitley and Elliott, zero for Brockermeyer and Peterson).

The same day the Panthers released Foster, they announced the signing of running back Derrick Moore, who had been released a few days earlier by San Francisco. Moore was used to following a tougher Barry act on the field, having served as Barry Sanders' backup with the Detroit Lions before attempting to make the 49ers' roster as a restricted free agent.

According to Polian, Moore was going to provide the same sort of hard running the team originally expected but never received from Foster. He also cost quite a bit less. His salary for 1995 was $210,000—or less than 10 percent of what Foster would have been paid.

"Derrick Moore is a hard-driving running back," Polian said. "He is a short-yardage and goal-line specialist, and Lord knows we need one of those. He is a guy who can pack the mail."

With Foster gone, it seemed Moore would not only need to pack the mail, but carry it and deliver it as well. After the failed Foster Experiment, skeptics were beginning to suspect maybe Polian should stick to football and wasn't cut out to make judgments on U.S. Postal personnel.

Moore was thrilled for whatever chance he would receive. But he warned that no one should expect him to run like Barry Foster or Barry Sanders. He would run like Derrick Moore. He also said to attempt to run like Barry Sanders would be physically impossible.

"I learned a lot about how hard you have to work from Barry Sanders," said Moore, who talked in a rapid and exciting manner. "He is an extremely talented player, which everyone knows. What people may not realize is that he works hard every day in practice, that he works hard in the off-season."

That statement distinguished the Barry that Moore backed up in Detroit from the Barry he was signed to replace in Carolina.

"I don't think you can emulate what he does as a runner. That would be stupidity," added the six-one, 227-pound Moore of Sanders. "What you can emulate is his fierceness. You can try to be a back who is going to take the fight to the defense down after down. That's what I try to emulate.

"I'm looking to come in here and take advantage of this opportunity. My style is that I want to bully you. I want to attack, attack, attack."

Meanwhile, in the Panthers' locker room, wide receiver Eric Guliford took a look around at Moore and several other players who had only recently joined the team, including a hard-hitting defensive back named Pat Terrell, who was cut by the Jets.

"It's like we got a whole new team Fed Ex-ed in here overnight," said Guliford, shaking his head.

Told upon his arrival that Rich Kotite, coach of the Jets, had finished second to Dom Capers in Carolina's head-coach search, Terrell said, "Yeah, well, I'm glad he didn't get it—because if he had, I wouldn't be here."

Randy Baldwin, the new starter at running back and a man who had carried the football from the line of scrimmage only 51 times in his entire NFL career, asked a simple question of teammate Howard Griffith.

"What time is it?" Baldwin asked.

"Time for you to shine, baby," Griffith replied, breaking into a grin. "Time for you to carry the ball about 45 times a game, man."

While the Panthers were gearing up for the first real game in their brief history as a franchise, folks down in Atlanta were beginning to get a little nervous. Much was at stake for Coach June Jones' team. If they lost on Sunday, they would become a footnote in NFL history—the first team to lose a game that counts to the Panthers. A loss to a division opponent playing its first game could also dampen hopes for a team that fully expected to make the playoffs.

By their own admission, the Falcons desperately wanted to avoid becoming expansion trivia meat.

"If I said I didn't feel that way, I would be lying," Atlanta wide receiver Terance Mathis said. "We want to win. If we do lose to Carolina, we're going to be the answer to a trivia question from here on out. None of us want that."

The Falcons, coming off a 7–9 season in 1994, were nine-point favorites going into the game. They also were well aware only one other NFL expansion team had won its very first regular-season game—and that was 34 years earlier when Minnesota beat Chicago. Oddly enough, all of this conspired to make the Falcons appear more nervous and uptight going into the Panthers' first game than the Panthers themselves.

"Every time we do something, it's a first," Capers said. "This is our first regular-season game. Five weeks ago, it was our first preseason game. Coming into that Hall of Fame Game, I had no idea how our team would respond. But I knew we had done everything we could to get them prepared for that, and I feel the same way about this game."

The Falcons, on the other hand, were in the classic no-win position. If they beat the Panthers, it was because they were supposed to; if they lost to them, it would be embarrassing and maybe place their entire season in jeopardy.

"They are not a team to be taken lightly," Mathis insisted of the Panthers. "We don't look at them as an expansion team when we're sitting around watching film of them. We look at them as a division opponent.

"Defensively, they can send people [on blitzes] from all over. They've got some solid, veteran players, especially on defense. If we're not tuned in and keyed in on what we're supposed to be doing, we're going to be in trouble."

Jones, the Falcons' coach, was quick to add, "They've invested most of their money in their defense, and it shows. Offensively, they've got some weapons, too, even though they had some trouble getting it into the end zone in the preseason. We respect the skill level of their players on both sides of the ball."

Pregame rhetoric? Or the honest truth?

It probably was a little of both.

There was only one more thing Mathis could not understand. The Falcons had nearly 12,000 tickets remaining for the game with 48 hours left before kickoff.

"We're excited about this game," Mathis said of the Atlanta players. "But we've got 12,000 tickets left, so I don't know how excited our fans are. I'm not that surprised our fans haven't bought them, but what I am surprised about is Carolina fans not coming down.

"This is a big event for them, period. They're about to play for the first time in franchise history. I know if I'm from Carolina, I'd be down there. It's not that far to come."

Mathis had a point. Atlanta was 256 miles from Charlotte. That was roughly 110 miles farther than Carolina fans had to drive to go to "home games" at Clemson.

Jerry Richardson, who spent more than eight years waiting for this particular kickoff, could not sleep as it grew closer.

A tall, graying man of regal bearing, Richardson, at age 58, still moved with the athletic gait of someone who once played the game. And on this day, Richardson nervously moved about his Atlanta hotel room for much of the morning, even though he knew he could have used some rest. Richardson rose for the 1 P.M. kickoff against the Falcons by 6:15 A.M., or, as he put it later, "about 15 minutes after I went to sleep."

Asked if he had butterflies swarming his stomach, Richardson replied, "No, I would say they were more like giant condors."

McCormack and Dom Anile arrived at the Georgia Dome around 11 A.M. and immediately began pacing the press box, or at least Anile did, wearing out the carpet between his designated seat and the coffee urn.

"This is about my fifth cup of the day," Anile said shortly after noon. "Why is it that it seems like one o'clock never gets here on the day of a game? I wish we could just wake up, roll out of bed, and kick it off first thing Sunday morning. All this waiting around is killing me."

McCormack agreed. He kept casting glances at the Rolex watch adorning his left wrist. As kickoff inched closer, he seemingly remained unconvinced that the historic moment would ever arrive.

"Is this thing stuck at 20 minutes to one, or what?" he asked, tapping the wristwatch.

On the field stretched before McCormack and the rest, Darius Rucker, lead singer of Hootie and the Blowfish, tuned up to sing the National Anthem. John Kasay stretched his very valuable left leg. Paul Butcher was jumping up and down, attempting to whip his Carolina teammates into a frenzy.

The Falcons won the coin toss and elected to receive.

The long-awaited moment was finally at hand.

Reich began the game hot, but not like he was operating in the cauldron of a fiery furnace. On the Panthers' very first possession, he marched them down the field on a precise and impressive drive that produced an eight-yard touchdown pass to his old buddy from Buffalo, tight end Pete Metzelaars, for a quick 7–0 lead.

For Metzelaars, catching the first touchdown pass in Panthers' history provided a moment to reflect. He genuflected in the end zone and said a quick prayer, perhaps thanking God for not letting him drop the pass. He mishandled so many during the preseason that one day during a practice, his wife turned to a reporter who had stopped by to say hi and mused, "Pete's not having a very good camp, is he?"

The Panthers eventually moved ahead 13–3 behind the Reich-to-Metzelaars touchdown, two John Kasay field goals and a defense that seemed to confuse the Falcons at first. This was not the 3-4 defense Capers had been talking up since the day he had arrived, but rather, a modified version of it made necessary by the unique run-and-shoot offense Atlanta employed behind their quick-trigger quarterback Jeff George.

Instead, the Panthers opened and played most of the game in their "dime" package, which features six defensive backs. When the Panthers base out of their 3-4, they line up with three down linemen, four linebackers and four defensive backs. Their dime package includes four down linemen (Lamar Lathon and Darion Conner, normally outside linebackers, essentially line up as defensive ends), just one linebacker roaming the middle of the field (Sam Mills, of course), four cornerbacks and two safeties.

George was used to seeing these kinds of defenses. No conventional defense worked against the run-and-shoot, although the reason most teams long ago had abandoned the offense was because it was less effective once you ran out of field to work with. The run-and-shoot was hard for defenses to stop and potentially explosive when its four wide receivers could roam the expanse of the entire field. Inside the red zone, the opponents' 20-yard line, it suddenly lost much of its punch and became much easier to defend because the defense had less ground to cover.

Against the Panthers, George's objective was to take quick three- and five-step drops into the pocket and get rid of the football long before anyone could get in his face. He was good at it.

"You watch Jeff George on tape," said Capers, "and he has as quick a release as there is in the league. He has a gun. He can throw that ball anyplace on the field, and it gets there in a hurry."

The Panthers' early lead evaporated once Atlanta's run-and-shoot offense began firing with accuracy, producing scores on three consecutive possessions to put the Falcons up 20-13. That wasn't the only thing evaporating. After a most impressive first series, the Panthers' offense suddenly began doing the dreaded three-step—three plays and a punt, three plays and a punt. They did this on their first six possessions of the second half. Punter Tommy Barnhardt saw so much action he no doubt would have iced his leg down between kicks if he had the time.

Reich spent much of the second half getting slammed into the hard artificial turf at the Georgia Dome. The offensive line, with Elliott out and speed rushers like Chris Doleman and Chris Smith having their way with tackles Brockermeyer and Graham, was crumbling. Reich had virtually no time to throw, the receivers no time to run their routes.

Doleman, a former NFC Defensive Player of the Year, manhandled Brockermeyer. He came up with 3.5 sacks by himself and infuriated the rookie by later telling reporters of him, "He was a nice young man. He spent a lot of time telling me how great I was."

Smith added 1.5 sacks and had Graham flinching all day, causing the highest-paid and most experienced Panther lineman to commit four false starts—the one penalty Capers cannot stomach because it is the result of a mental error. Graham got little help on the right side of the line from Martin, Elliott's last-minute replacement.

Nonetheless, the Panthers stunned the crowd of 58,808 when Reich connected with Willie Green for a 44-yard touchdown pass to pull within 20-19 with 26 seconds left in regulation. The pass deflected off Green's helmet and neck before he hauled it in.

In the bowels of the stadium, a dejected Falcons mascot who had come off the field and headed for his locker room started for the field again, dragging a Panther stuffed animal behind him.

"You'd think with one minute left, we'd be able to win the damn game," the mascot muttered.

Capers then decided to go for the win himself. He dramatically held up two fingers, signaling the Panthers were not going to settle for—or risk—overtime. They would go for a two-point conversion and the victory right then and there.

The teams approached the line of scrimmage. The coverage Atlanta was in looked good, about what the Panthers were expecting. Capers was confident the play was going to work.

Then Graham moved before the snap.

False start. Five-yard penalty. Forget the try for two.

Kasay's extra-point kick tied it at 20 and sent it into overtime, but what happened next seemed inevitable. Defensive end Lester Archambeau of the Falcons sacked Reich for the ninth time on the day, tying an Atlanta team record set in 1977, and forcing a fumble. The Falcons recovered at the Carolina 31-yard line, setting up Morten Andersen's 35-yard field goal to win it.

In the Carolina locker room afterward, Willie Green entertained in a bright red suit.

"I'll bet I'm not on anyone's fantasy football team," he said. "Maybe now somebody will think about picking me up."

Reich, who had completed 23 of 44 passes for 329 yards, tried to deflect some of the blame from the offensive line.

"Not all of the sacks were their fault," he said. "Some of them were my fault, for not reading the blitz like I should have. Some of them were coverage sacks. I definitely could have done a better job of making my reads."

The loneliest man in the locker room, despite the crowds of reporters who kept gathering around him, was Derrick Graham.

"How did it feel when you committed that false start on the two-point conversion?" asked one unimaginative reporter.

Graham glared at his questioner.

"How the fuck do you think it felt?" he said. "Man, these questions are killing me."

Much the same way his false start had killed Carolina's best chance of winning. No one would ever know what might have happened if the Panthers had been able to run that play.

Final Score

23 Atlanta   **20** Carolina

THE
CAROLINA
PANTHERS

▲ Coach Dom Capers. *John Clark*

1995–1996 SEASON
7 Wins, 9 Losses

◄ Owner Jerry Richardson, shown here celebrating the birth of the team in a parade held in Charlotte. *John Clark*

➤

General Manager, Bill Polian (center), shown here with old friend Marv Levy before the second game of the season, is a firebrand recognized as one of the NFL's shrewdest evaluators of talent. *John Clark*

➤

Team president Mike McCormack, who provided the steadying hand to guide the Panthers through the expansion selection process and beyond. *John Clark*

▲ Safety Bubba McDowell (25) and linebacker Sam Mills (51) crushed Atlanta's Eric Metcalf on this play during the regular-season opener, letting Metcalf and the rest of the world know very early that the Carolina defense would be one that commanded NFL respect.
John Clark

◄ Placekicker John Kasay (4) attempted to console distraught offensive tackle Derrick Graham after Graham jumped off-sides late in the first game against Atlanta, ruining a two-point conversion attempt and costing the Panthers a chance to win in regulation. They eventually lost in overtime, 23–20, and Graham found himself haunted by the play for the remainder of the season. *John Clark*

▼ Defensive back Brett Maxie (39) arrived in Carolina on legs supposedly finished, but they were nimble enough to carry him 49 yards on this interception return of a misguided Jim Kelly aerial during the Panthers' second game, which the Panthers led 9–0 in the third quarter before coming unglued and suffering a 31–9 defeat in Buffalo. Maxie went on to record a career-high six interceptions on the season. *John Clark*

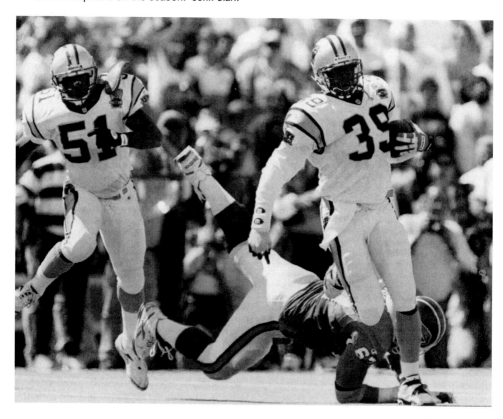

➤

Frank Reich (14) began the season as the Panthers' starting quarterback. But it started unraveling on him in his old home, Buffalo's Rich Stadium. He completed only 6 of 21 pass attempts in the loss to the Bills, struggling to find time to throw behind an offensive line that included the likes of Matt Elliott (52), who spent the previous year out of the NFL and employed as a part-time announcer for a cable television company. *John Clark*

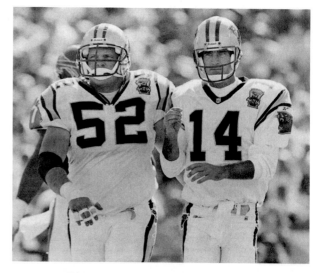

By the third game of the season, an embarrassing 31–10 loss in their home opener at Clemson, the Panthers still hadn't found an adequate starting running back. Randy Baldwin (23) was the first choice after the Barry Foster Experiment failed in training camp, but Baldwin eventually was waived, too. *Craig Bell*

◄ The Panthers lost their fourth in a row to Tampa Bay at Clemson on October 1, but they found a running back when Derrick Moore, shown here spiking the ball after a 53-yard touchdown run, rushed for 123 yards on 21 carries. They also found a quarterback, as rookie Kerry Collins received his first NFL start and played well. *John Clark*

It was already a long season for the Panthers and veteran tight end Pete Metzelaars (88) by the fifth game at Soldier Field in Chicago, which became another loss when the defense failed to protect a lead in the final two minutes. Earlier, though, Metzelaars' season-long struggles continued when he lost the handle on this pass from Kerry Collins, costing the Panthers a potential touchdown. The Panthers lost, 31–27, and Metzelaars, who went in the record books as the recipient of the first TD pass in club history when he caught an 8-yard toss from Frank Reich in the season opener at Atlanta, lost his job after the season. *John Clark*

◄

◄ Victory at last! Linebacker Lamar Lathon, who predicted the Panthers would win "nine or 10 games," finally got to break out the Gatorade bucket and dump some celebratory water on Coach Dom Capers' head after a 26–15 triumph over the New York Jets at Clemson in Game 6. *John Clark*

▼ Some said the Panthers rolled the dice when they lured Sam Mills away from the New Orleans Saints. Mills, shown here after sacking the New York Jets' Bubby Brister, proved them wrong by putting together one of his finest NFL seasons. *John Clark*

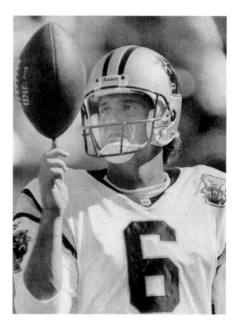

◄ Carlton Bailey, nicknamed Highway 54 because teammates figured opponents traveled a dangerous stretch of road whenever than ran or threw in Bailey's direction, walks off the field after the win over the Jets signaling, "That's one."
John Clark

➤

What do punters do when they're not punting? Tommy Barnhardt of the Panthers frequently passed the time on the sideline by spinning a football on his finger. Not that Barnhardt had much spare time on his hands most Sundays early in the season. Through six games, Barnhardt was on pace to attempt more punts on the season than any player in NFL history.
John Clark

◄ Center Curtis Whitley, who anchored a steadily improving offensive line and didn't miss a snap all season, studies play formations that have been sent down from coaches high above in the press box during the 20–3 win over New Orleans at Clemson on October 22. Linemate Mark Dennis looks over Whitley's shoulder.
John Clark

▲ Derrick Moore was an energetic running back during the Panthers' first season—and one inspired by Julie Andrews in *The Sound of Music*. *John Clark*

➤
Linebacker Darion Conner was a disappointment much of the season for the Panthers. But he had his moments, like this one when he brought down quarterback Jim Everett of the Saints for a sack at Clemson. *John Clark*

◄ Eric Guliford, a wide receiver and punt returner, caught this 24-yard touchdown pass from Kerry Collins during the second quarter of Carolina's 20–17 overtime win at New England. But Guliford later suffered a mild concussion and admitted he had difficulty recalling all the details of the Panthers' third consecutive victory. *Craig Bell*

➤
Lamar Lathon and the rest of the Panthers made it a long day for San Francisco quarterback Elvis Grbac and the defending Super Bowl champions on November 5. The Panthers' 13–7 conquest of the 49ers not only was their fourth win in a row, which had never before been accomplished by an expansion team, but also marked the first time a first-year club had ever beaten a defending champion—and it came on the road. *John Clark*

◄ By the ninth game of the season, Derrick Moore (20) was on pace to rush for well over 1,000 yards. But he suffered a knee injury against the 49ers, the team that cut him in the preseason, and ended up having to settle for 740. No back for an expansion team had ever before rushed for more than 722. *John Clark*

◄ Tim McKyer, the cornerback who was solid on the field with his play and loud with his mouth off it, tries to point the officials in the right direction during the win over San Francisco—toward the Panthers' goal line. McKyer would be the only one to cross it all day, as his 96-yard interception return of a pass by Elvis Grbac was Carolina's sole touchdown. *John Clark*

◄ McKyer, who had three interceptions on the season, steps in front of a Chris Miller aerial intended for All-Pro wide receiver Issac Bruce of the Rams in Game 10 at St. Louis. The Rams eventually prevailed, 28–17, breaking the Panthers' four-game winning streak and spoiling their first bid to reach .500 since the second game. *John Clark*

► Don Beebe is congratulated by fullback Bob Christian and quarterback Kerry Collins after catching a 21-yard touchdown pass from Collins to cut the Rams' lead to 14–7 just before halftime in St. Louis. It briefly gave life to both the Panthers' chances that day and to Beebe's future with Carolina, but only briefly. It would be Beebe's only TD of the season and he would be released shortly after its conclusion. *John Clark*

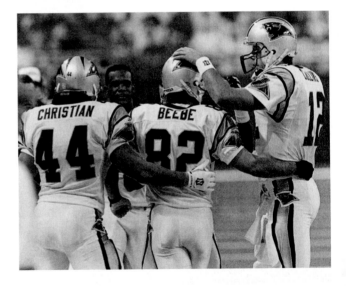

▲ Wide receiver Eric Guliford, who caught four passes for 62 yards, was one of many Panthers who enjoyed a big day at the expense of Buddy Ryan's Arizona Cardinals in Game 10 at Clemson. The Panthers dominated in a 27–7 win, rolling up 362 yards of total offense while holding the Cards to their lowest total—96 yards—in more than 40 years. *John Clark*

◄ In what Coach Capers called one of the most satisfying wins of the season, a 13–10 upset of Indianapolis at Clemson in Game 13, nose tackle Greg Kragen pulled one of the biggest surprises of the season, intercepting a Jim Harbaugh pass and returning it 29 yards to set up a field goal for the Panthers near the end of the first half. Even Kragen couldn't believe it, as he admitted to Sam Mills here. *John Clark*

It was a pain-wracked, sack-filled day for Indianapolis quarterback Jim Harbaugh at Clemson on December 3. Harbaugh, shown here getting trashed by Carlton Bailey, entered the game as the top-rated passer in the NFL but suffered six sacks before leaving with a knee injury that later would require surgery. The Panthers also sacked Harbaugh's backup once, giving them a season-high seven sacks for the afternoon. *John Clark*

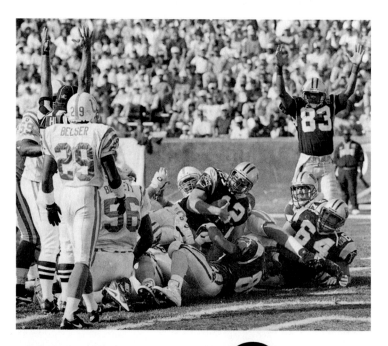

Kerry Collins wasn't certain he got in the end zone for this 2-yard touchdown against the Colts, but wide receiver Mark Carrier (83) was—and more importantly, so was the closest official. It was the only touchdown of the day for the Panthers against Indy's stubborn defense. *John Clark*

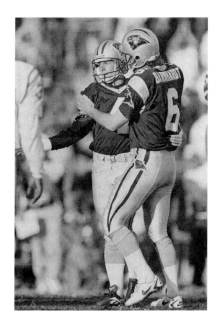

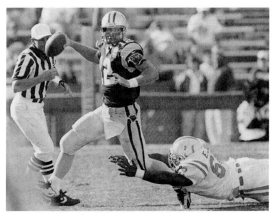

◄ The win over Indianapolis wasn't secure until placekicker John Kasay, being congratulated here after the fact by holder Tommy Barnhardt, booted a 38-yard field goal with eight seconds left.
John Clark

➤

When Collins was flushed out of the pocket, he was athletic enough to create plays while on the run. *John Clark*

◄
It looked as if Carlton Bailey was going to haul down this batted pass for an interception against San Francisco at Clemson on December 10. He didn't, and nothing else went Carolina's way on the day as the 49ers, with Steve Young at quarterback this time, exacted revenge for the earlier defeat suffered on their own soil. Final score: 49ers 31, Panthers 10.
Craig Bell

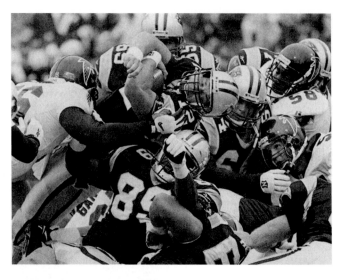

Kerry Collins' size—6-5 and 240 pounds—is an asset when it comes to trying to get into the end zone on quarterback sneaks from close range. He muscled his way through this mass of large bodies to score from the 1-yard line late in the second quarter in the thrilling rematch with Atlanta at Clemson in Game 15.
John Clark

Tyrone Poole was no Joe Best. But he might have been the best rookie cornerback in the NFL.
John Clark

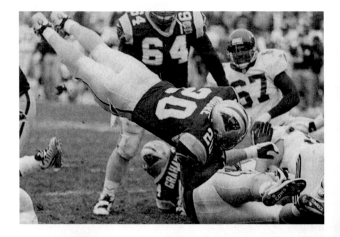

Back from his knee injury, Derrick Moore flashed some of his old form on this 1-yard dive for a touchdown in the third quarter against Atlanta at Clemson. Moore's score pulled the Panthers, who trailed 14–0 after the first quarter, to within 17–14 and they went on to win, 21–17.
John Clark

◄ Blake Brockermeyer, a first-round draft choice from Texas, started training camp at right offensive tackle but was quickly moved to the left side and given the big job of protecting the blind side of Panthers' quarterbacks. He gave up 3.5 sacks to Atlanta's Chris Doleman in his first regular season game, but the likeable rookie played like a seasoned veteran the rest of the year—including an outstanding game against Doleman during a Carolina win over Atlanta in December. He is widely considered a future All-Pro, perhaps as soon as his second NFL season. *John Clark*

➤
Mark Carrier, a wide receiver picked up in the expansion allocation draft, fights for yardage after one of his seven catches for 101 yards in the season finale at Washington. Despite the 20–17 loss, the Panthers remained upbeat afterward because of great accomplishments like Carrier's— 66 catches on the season for 1,002 yards, more than any expansion receiver in NFL history. *John Clark*

◄ Willie Green went from a receiver no one knew to one that teams were routinely double-teaming toward season's end. A pair of Washington defensive backs broke up this pass from Collins, but Green later put the finishing touches on a fine season by hauling in his team-high sixth TD reception of the season.
John Clark

◄ Willie Green was one of the original "street free agents" signed by the Panthers in December 1994. His enthusiasm for the game and his Panthers teammates (he was especially fond of rookie quarterback Kerry Collins' ability to handle a veteran huddle) is matched only by his zest for the lively art of conversation. *John Clark*

▲ A home at last. In the fall of 1996, the Panthers move into the NFL's newest state-of-the-art facility, Ericsson Stadium, in uptown Charlotte (shown here minus the sod). *John Clark*

Game 2:
Panthers at Buffalo

Bill Polian sat mostly in uncharacteristic silence in the press box at Rich Stadium as he watched the Panthers, the team he helped build, forge a 9–0 lead over the Buffalo Bills, the other NFL team he helped construct. He had no illusions.

He thought to himself, "I've seen this movie before."

The difference was, he liked the ending on those previous viewing occasions. This, he feared, was going to be altogether different for him, and all too familiar for the Bills.

Polian served as pro personnel director and general manager for the Bills from 1984 through the 1992 season. He was instrumental in building the Buffalo team that went to an unprecedented four consecutive Super Bowls from 1990 through 1993. But those loyalties had been severed. He was a Carolina Panther now.

"It's always nice to come back to an area where you spent so much time and have so many friends," Polian said before the game. "But once they kick it off, we're the opposition."

Former Bills included not only Polian but a number of others employed in the Panthers' organization: quarterback Frank Reich, wide receiver Don Beebe, tight end Pete Metzelaars, linebacker Carlton Bailey, director of football administration Steve Champlin, director of football security Ed Stillwell and assistant equipment manager Don Toner.

The Panthers had such an ex-Bills presence on their roster that some NFL media had already dubbed them Buffalo South.

It was only the second game of the season, but Buffalo South was colliding with Buffalo North at Rich Stadium in front of nearly 80,000 fans eager to witness the Bills' home opener.

"If I had to characterize the passion of the Buffalo fans," said Metzelaars, "I would say it's more like a college following. Fans are in the parking lots early—picnicking, throwing an old football around. Heck, the Winnebagos start parking in the lots Friday night [for a Sunday afternoon game], staking out the best spots.

"Everyone in the entire city is focused in on the football game that weekend."

During the summer of 1995, Frank Reich stood talking to a group of friends at Jim Kelly's charity golf tournament in Buffalo. Suddenly, Reich felt a large hand rubbing the small of his back.

"I had no idea who it was until I turned around," Reich said.

It was Bruce Smith, his former Bills teammate and certain future Hall of Fame defensive end. Smith was grinning.

"I'm just sizing you up," said Smith, still rubbing Reich's lower back. "I'm just checking you out to see where I'll be hitting you this fall."

Reich's return to Buffalo was triumphant in a way, no matter what happened in the game. He was returning as a starting quarterback. Prior to signing with Carolina as an unrestricted free agent, with the chance to become a full-time starter for the first time in his NFL career, Reich was on the Bills' roster for a full decade, backing up Jim Kelly for the last nine of those years after spending most of his rookie season on injured reserve.

His claim to fame, of course, was that despite spending most of his college career as a backup to Boomer Esiason at Maryland and all that time as Kelly's caddy in Buffalo, Reich somehow had managed to fashion the greatest comebacks in the storied histories of both college football and the NFL.

In 1984, his senior year at Maryland, he entered a game againt the University of the Miami in the second half with the Terrapins trailing, 31–0. He led the Terps on six consecutive touchdown drives to produce a 42–40 victory.

On January 3, 1993, Reich started the Bills' first-round AFC playoff game against Houston in the injured Kelly's place. Buffalo fell behind 35–3 before Reich led them back, throwing four second-half touchdown passes to forge a 41–38 Bills win in overtime. The Bills went on to play in the Super Bowl for the third consecutive year.

The latter comeback spawned the sweatshirts that were all the rage in his hometown of Lebanon, Pennsylvania, as well as Buffalo. T-shirts, hats and sweatshirts, in fact, bearing his mug and such sayings as "Never, Never Give Up" and "The Reich Stuff" helped Reich attain a status with the Buffalo fans that was unequaled for a backup quarterback in any other NFL city.

He even managed to make being religious fashionable, according to those who were around him then. Reich credited a gospel song by Michael English for providing him with the inspiration he needed to stage the comeback against the Oilers, and people loved him for it.

"Frank became almost a religious figure himself in Buffalo, he was so revered," said Jerry Sullivan, a columnist for the *Buffalo News*. "I think by the end of his time with the Bills, he was almost embarrassed by it. People up here really placed him on a pedestal."

It almost didn't happen. Prior to the beginning of his fifth NFL season in 1989, Bills owner Ralph Wilson had come to Polian and told him it was time to cut Reich loose. Reich had thrown a total of only 20 passes his first four seasons and was slated to make a salary of $400,000—as a third-stringer. Gale Gilbert had been signed to be Kelly's backup, and Wilson wanted Polian to keep Stan Gelbaugh, who would make a $150,000 salary, as the number-three QB instead of Reich.

When Polian and Bills coach Marv Levy summoned Reich to Levy's office, Reich thought he was being released. But Polian surprised him.

"You can stay. In fact, we want you to stay. But you'll have to take a $250,000 pay cut to do it. You can't make more than what Gelbaugh was going to make," Polian told him.

If Reich refused the pay cut, he would have been placed on waivers—and if he had been claimed off waivers by another team, he still would have the $400,000. After conferring with his wife, Linda, and praying to God that he would make the right decision, Reich decided to take the pay cut and stay with the Bills.

Six years later, Reich was returning as the starter for the Panthers. He wasn't entirely comfortable with being the starting quarterback, and certainly didn't always act like one. Five days before the regular-season opener at Atlanta, for instance, Reich flew to Pittsburgh to be with his mother, Pat, following the death of her 91-year-old mother. It was an example of the credo by which Reich, a devoutly religious man, lived his life. It was God, family and football—in that order, with no exceptions.

Once on the field, Reich wanted to win. He was a competitor. But football was not, nor would it ever be, the most important thing in his life. That was fine with Polian.

"All I can say is that my sons, all three of them, have grown up around him," said the GM, "and they couldn't have had a better role model anywhere in life."

Smith, Cornelius Bennett, and the rest of the Buffalo defenders respected Reich deeply as well—but they still wanted to flatten him come Sunday.

"It's kind of funny that he'll be going up against all the defensive guys he used to practice against," Kelly said of Reich, who has remained a close friend. "They were never allowed to hit him. Now they can. He's an open target for those guys."

Likewise, the Panthers had a player who was yearning to hit Kelly. Former Bills teammate Carlton Bailey made that very clear.

"For the five years that I was in Buffalo," said Bailey, "Jim Kelly never once invited me to work at his football camp. Now maybe I'm going to get a little hit on him and remind him of that."

If Reich was going to be protected from the likes of Smith, it was going to be left up to the likes of starting offensive tackles Blake Brockermeyer and Derrick Graham. After their disastrous debut the previous week in Atlanta, this did not exactly inject a great deal of confidence into anyone within the Panthers' organization.

Brockermeyer spent much of the week leading up to the Buffalo encounter complaining that he needed more help if he was going to have to play left tackle and block guys like Atlanta's Chris Doleman and Smith—Pro Bowl–caliber players with years of experience, not to mention the requisite skills to go along with them. The Carolina coaching staff, however, did not want to hear it. Starting with line coach Jim McNally, Brockermeyer was receiving very little sympathy.

Asked about his difficulty with Doleman, Brockermeyer got somewhat testy with reporters.

"Most of it was the fact that I had no help there whatsoever," Brockermeyer said. "Doleman is a great rusher. You can't hold him off one-on-one forever. One of his sacks was the result of a missed assignment by the left guard [fellow rookie Andrew Peterson]. For most of the game, I thought I did all right."

All right? Doleman had 3.5 sacks.

When asked whether he expected to receive more help blocking Smith, a seven-time Pro Bowler, Brockermeyer replied, "What do you think?"

Well, the word from McNally was Brockermeyer needed to think again if he was under the impression he would be getting lots of help. McNally said Brockermeyer would receive help on Smith whenever humanly possible—but certainly not every play.

"We're aware of where Bruce Smith is going to be on the field," McNally said. "But sometimes, Blake's just going to have to block him, period. They've also got Cornelius Bennett, Bryce Paup and [Jim] Jeffcoat sitting there, rushing the passer. We can't just run over to give Blake help every down and let those other guys go unblocked."

Everyone seemed to have some advice for Brockermeyer and his pending encounter with Smith.

"Call him Mr. Smith," Polian joked.

Capers smiled and shook his head when the topic of one of his prized rookies being subjected to two of the league's better pass rushers right out of the gate was frequently mentioned.

"Welcome to the NFL, right?" Capers said. "There's no question this is a tough way to go, but the only way a young player is going to get better is to go out there each week and go against the best.

"I've said all along that I fully expect our line, Blake included, to be much better in the seventh or eighth week than it is in the first or second. Blake will be fine. He's made of the right stuff."

Brockermeyer was hardly the only offensive lineman who struggled in Atlanta. The entire unit was disgraced in the 23–20 overtime loss. Three more sacks by the Falcons, in fact, and they would have tied the all-time single-game league record of 12.

McNally was not happy about the state of the offensive line after the season-opening debacle. After years of building a reputation as one of the finest offensive line coaches in the game, he felt embarrassed, almost as if a little of his hard-earned NFL reputation, 15 years in the making, had been stripped from him forever as the result of four hours of botched work in Atlanta. The Graham false-start penalty on the two-point conversion attempt at the end of regulation particularly bothered him—but then, that was to be expected, especially since the normally mild-mannered Capers had jumped in McNally's face on the sideline after the penalty to demand what in the heck was going on with his linemen.

"I think it's been a rude awakening for some of our guys," McNally said. "I hope that in six or seven weeks, it won't be like this. I hope next year it won't be like this. But I don't know how long it will take.

"You're playing big-time opponents and big-time football here. To develop a really good offensive line, you've got to have the same guys playing next to the same guys for a while. But first you've got to find the right guys, and then you've got to have the right guys play next to each other for a couple of years. We're still trying to find the right guys."

McNally said he was certain Brockermeyer was one of the right guys. The Panthers were less sure about Peterson, although they liked his potential. Peterson was out for the Buffalo game, anyway, because of back spasms that became so severe during the

Monday team meeting that he could not sit down. He had to stand for the entire meeting. He was to be replaced at left guard by Frank Garcia, his buddy from the University of Washington and the player who seemed to be involved in the most fights of anyone on the team during practices.

If he had to be replaced in the lineup, Peterson was glad Garcia was his replacement. The two of them were somewhat stunned to be playing on the same NFL team, let alone to be fighting for a starting position.

"Frank and I talk about this all the time," Peterson said. "We never dreamed of coming to the same team. Then, once we did, our main goal was to make the team. We never thought about starting."

Truth be told, on an established team, they wouldn't have had to think about it. But the Panthers, lest anyone forget, were an expansion team. And the offensive line was playing like it. McNally said he had a solution for the line's woes.

"Sometimes you have to just go out and block somebody. It's a very simple rule," he said.

When Polian arrived in Buffalo as pro personnel director in 1984, he did not like what he saw. He wasn't surprised when the Bills went 2–14 that season under Coach Kay Stephenson, who called Polian into his office over the Christmas holidays after its conclusion. To that point, Polian had spent most of his time studying film of opposing teams, so the Bills knew who to go after when someone who might help them got released by another club.

"I want you to take a real hard look at our team," Stephenson told Polian. "Then we'll get together at the Senior Bowl [college all-star game] in a few weeks and see what you think."

Polian's assessment of the Bills' roster was blunt and not very encouraging, but Stephenson expected this.

"Coach," said Polian, "we're 2–14 on merit. We've got the worst personnel in the league, or close to it."

"You're right," agreed Stephenson. "We've got to change that. We've got to make a wholesale change on our side."

As they worked together to develop a plan for doing precisely that, Polian turned to Stephenson one day and said, "Coach, you understand that it's possible someone else might come in behind us and reap the rewards of this."

Stephenson simply nodded.

Less than a year later, in the midst of another 2–14 disaster, Stephenson was fired and replaced by Hank Bullough. Polian thought he would be fired, too, at the season's end. He got called to a meeting in Detroit, thinking that that was exactly what he was going to be told.

Instead, the Bills told Polian they were firing Terry Bledsoe as general manager and promoting him to GM in Bledsoe's place.

"I was stunned," Polian said. "I had little or no inkling of it. . . . In my mind, I was going to take another job. I presumed I was out."

What happened next would formulate much of the philosophy Polian would later use to build the Panthers from the ground up. First, though, he had to reverse the public's image of the woebegone Bills, whose season-ticket base had shrunk to 18,000 and whose home crowds rarely exceeded 40,000 in a stadium that seated twice as many.

Metzelaars remembered the final home game in 1984, when there weren't many fans and the ones who were there weren't being too polite to the players who were putting the finishing touches on another 2–14 season.

"The crowd couldn't have been much more than 20,000 to begin with, and by the fourth quarter most of those had gone home," Metzelaars said. "The few thousand who were left seemed to mass behind our bench, and they started pelting us with snowballs. They just kept throwing the snowballs and yelling at us, telling us how sorry they thought we were. It was definitely a low point."

"Many people were saying that maybe the team should leave, that it was an embarrassment," Polian said. "People had this perception that there was a black cloud over the team, a black cloud over the city, and that things could never work out."

Polian started changing that by signing Kelly, who had earlier spurned the Bills to play in the USFL and then tried to force Polian to trade his NFL rights to a team whose home was in a warmer climate.

"We had to sign him," Polian said. "Otherwise, I think the team was headed for the sewer and might not be there today."

Polian called Kelly's agent and asked what it would take to get the quarterback to come to Buffalo.

"You've got to come and recruit him," the agent said.

"Come and recruit him?" Polian asked. "Hey, this is pro ball. We've got his rights. I'm not sure I need to recruit him."

"No, you must," the agent insisted. "You need to recruit him."

So they met in New York, and Kelly told Polian right off that he wanted to play somewhere on the West Coast. He didn't want to play in a cold-weather city like Buffalo because he thought it might shorten his career. Plus, he didn't have to say, the Bills were a lousy football team, coming off consecutive 2–14 seasons.

"Well," said Polian, "you may not sign with the Bills, but you're not going to the West Coast. I'll trade your rights to Green Bay or someplace like that."

Kelly left the room with his agent. A few minutes later, Kelly returned and said, "We'd better talk."

The week Kelly agreed to a long-term contract, the Bills' season-ticket base jumped from 18,000 to 28,000 "and it would have been more if we would have had the manpower to handle all the calls," according to Polian.

Polian was a hands-on GM for the Bills in every sense of the word. He literally directed traffic in the Rich Stadium parking lots early during his days as GM, occasionally launching into obscenity-laced tirades at drivers, who also happened to be paying fans, when they ignored his directions. A local television station caught him doing just that once. He also struck a deal with Marine Midland Bank, giving Bills' fans the opportunity to buy tickets at the bank's branches the same day they cashed their paychecks, assuring they would have money in hand.

Kelly's signing was the beginning of a new era for the Bills, over which Polian and his good friend Marv Levy, hired when Bullough was fired in the midst of a 4–12 season Kelly's first year, would preside. They eventually built a team that won four consecutive AFC championships, though they never won the Super Bowl, and Polian was told he was history before they made it to the third one.

Owner Ralph Wilson told Polian he would not be back for another season prior to the start of the 1992 campaign, after Polian unwisely engaged in a dispute with Wilson's daughter, Christy Wilson Hofmann, the team's director of merchandising.

"It was tough," Polian said. "I had roots there. My kids had roots there. My wife had roots there. It's still hard for her. . . . You expect to get fired when you lose. You don't expect to get fired when you win. That's what made it difficult for me, professionally."

Personally, though, Polian later said it might have been best that he was the first one from the Super Bowl era ushered out the door. He remembered the day linebacker Ray Bentley retired, and remembered how tough that was for him to handle. He and Bentley sat in Polian's office for hours, talking and even shedding a few tears.

Polian still gets misty-eyed talking about the Bills he helped build.

"We were like a family in every sense of the word," said Polian, his voice cracking. "To go through what we went through, with all the bumps and bruises and heartache, who would have thought the Bills would go to four straight Super Bowls? Even the people in Buffalo didn't think it was possible.

"I've said before, and I'll say it again: that history will treat those guys as the Boys of Autumn. . . . I think they will go down as one of the greatest teams of all time, just as the Purple People Eaters [from Minnesota's losing Super Bowl days] will. History is always best served by stepping back and allowing the facts to be filtered by time, to filter the emotions out. And when you stack the Buffalo Bills up against the greatest teams of all time, they're going to be right there.

"Their heart, if you want to use that term, their collective heart was as big as any team that's ever played."

Yet the one blemish on their legacy is that they never won the Super Bowl. Polian found taking the three Super Bowl losses while he was there particularly difficult to accept—for a limited time.

"For 30 days, it's the end of the world," Polian said. "Except for losing a child, a wife or a close loved one, it's the worst thing that can happen to you—for 30 days. And then you put it behind you and you realize that there are a lot tougher things that happen to people. There are kids in hospitals dying every day. During those 30 days when you're mourning and moping, kids who are eight- and nine-year-olds are dying of leukemia, and 30-year-olds are having heart attacks. You realize there are a lot worse things in life than losing in a Super Bowl."

Regardless of whether the Panthers were able to pull an upset against the Bills, this was no Super Bowl. It was a game Marv Levy, Polian's old friend, desperately wanted to win because the Bills had looked awful in a season-opening 22–7 defeat at Denver the previous week. But it was not the Super Bowl.

Kelly may have been the key to the Bills' resurgence under Polian, but against the Panthers in the second game of the 1995 season, he looked terrible. For one half and one series, in fact, Kelly had the type of game against the Panthers' defense that would have, in the past, had the Rich Stadium crowd calling for Frank Reich to replace him.

Since Reich was playing for the Panthers, the crowd had no recourse but to implore Kelly to start hitting his own receivers instead of Carolina's defensive backs, and finally, the game turned in Buffalo's favor on one play. Kelly was having a miserable time until finding wide receiver Russell Copeland with a 77-yard touchdown pass early in the third quarter, cutting what had been a 9–0 lead for the Panthers to 9–7 and shifting the momentum into Buffalo's favor, where it would remain the rest of the afternoon.

Prior to the Copeland TD reception, Kelly was embarrassing himself. In the first half, he completed twice as many passes to Panther defenders than he did to his own. His first-half statistics: 1 for 11 for four yards, with two interceptions. Every time he looked to find a receiver, the receiver seemed to be covered. Eventually, he started trying to force passes when he should have thrown them away.

As Kelly left the field with his teammates at halftime, the crowd of 79,190 booed lustily, picking on him in particular.

"It was very frustrating," Kelly said. "I would drop back, and I couldn't find anybody open. There were some plays we were calling that were 15-yard routes, and their DBs were coming up about 12 yards, like they knew exactly what the route was. They were reading things perfectly. They were covering our guys like blankets.

"So I started pressing. I wasn't getting anyone open, so I figured I had to try something to make something happen."

This is exactly the state of mind the Panthers wanted to get quarterbacks in every Sunday. The problem was, the Panthers' own quarterback was looking quite confused himself.

The game plan called for Reich to abandon many of the usual five- and seven-step drops back into the pocket on pass plays, so he was attempting to take quick three- or five-step drops, with the five-step drops coming at an accelerated pace to avoid the Bills' fearsome pass rush. The result was that everything seemed rushed, and most pass plays failed to develop in time for Reich to throw with any kind of accuracy.

Reich wasn't getting sacked as often as during the Atlanta loss, but he wasn't completing many passes, either. His totals for the day would be meager: 6 completions in 21 attempts for only 44 yards, a far cry from the NFL-leading total of 329 he had thrown for one week earlier.

Once Kelly hit Copeland for the 77-yard touchdown, the Bills' offensive fortunes improved in a hurry. The Panthers were forced to punt from their own end zone on their next series when the Bills sacked Reich for an 18-yard loss, backing the Panthers up to their own five-yard line. That essentially set up the next Buffalo touchdown after a mere 41-yard drive, Thurman Thomas capping it on a four-yard run. The next time the Bills had the ball, Thomas scampered 60 yards after taking in a screen pass from Kelly to set up yet another touchdown. And three plays after that, a Reich pass intended for Beebe, one of the ex-Bills boys, landed in the hands of one of the current Bills, free safety Kurt Shulz. He returned it 32 yards for the fourth Buffalo touchdown in less than 10 minutes, and the possible upset for the Panthers was suddenly the Bills' rout it was supposed to be.

Final score: 31–9 Buffalo.

Reich had received a standing ovation from the fans during pregame introductions, but his homecoming rapidly dissolved into a nightmare shortly after halftime.

"I was hoping to turn those cheers into boos by the end of the game," Reich said. "But it just didn't happen."

Capers said the 77-yard Kelly pass to Copeland, on which the zone coverage in the secondary broke down, was clearly the difference in the game.

"Really, that one play threw the whole tempo of the game around," Capers said. "We did not respond very well after the big touchdown pass. Things kind of went south on us in a hurry from that point on."

About the only bright spot on offense for the Panthers was the hard running of Derrick Moore, who hadn't gotten to carry the ball the previous week in Atlanta. With Randy Baldwin struggling as the starter at halfback for the second consecutive outing, managing just 11 yards on five carries, Moore stepped in as the game against the Bills progressed and stepped up. He finished with a team-high 53 yards on 14 carries.

"It's been a while since I've run the ball that much," said Moore, who carried the ball only 27 times for 52 yards while working as Barry Sanders' backup in Detroit the previous season.

Interestingly, Kerry Collins also received some work at quarterback. Even though he was listed as the number-three "emergency" quarterback behind Reich and Trudeau, new NFL rules permitted the emergency QB to play in the fourth quarter of games. And since the game was out of reach, he played. Trudeau didn't. Collins played only one series, Carolina's last of the game. He threw two incomplete passes.

"It was just an opportunity for me to get a little experience," Collins said. "The game was already decided, so it was a chance for them to get the rookie in. But I don't see it changing anything at all. This wasn't a case of me playing over Jack. It was just a thing where the game was decided and so they put me in."

Polian was a popular interview with the press from both Carolina and Buffalo following the game. He did not seem particularly upset. And he certainly did not seem surprised. In a strange sort of way, he almost seemed as if he was proud of the Bills for teaching his new team what he considered a valuable lesson.

Even when the Panthers were clinging to their 9–0 lead early in the second half, even after the Bills had managed only 46 total yards of offense in the first two quarters, Polian said he knew what was coming. He said the Bills played "15 or 20 games like these" when he was their GM.

"You've got to put them away," Polian said. "The reason they've been to four Super Bowls is because they're great players with great courage, great heart and a great winning attitude. They don't beat themselves.

"That's been the story of the Buffalo Bills in Rich Stadium during this modern era. They get the momentum going, they get the crowd going, they get the tempo going their way—and they're tough to stop. A lot of other people have gotten stomped on here, too."

Although he obviously still harbored some deep affection for the Bills, Polian wanted to make it clear that he did not enjoy losing to them. But he felt it could be useful down the road to the fledging Panthers.

"It hurts like the devil to get pummeled, but we've got to take something positive from this," Polian said. "That positive is that we hung in against a great team for a half. Now we've got to learn how to hang in with great teams for four quarters. It's all part of the growth process.

"I knew [the Bills] weren't going to lose on a TKO. They weren't going to lose on points. It was going to have to be a knockout."

It could have been argued that the Panthers had the Bills on the ropes with a 9–0 lead and should have delivered the knockout blow, but Polian knew that a nine-point lead wasn't enough. He also sensed the Panthers didn't yet know how to deliver the punch that could take the other team out.

"Everyone likes to tell jokes about the Buffalo Bills because they lost four Super Bowls," Polian said. "Unless you've sat there and watched them annihilate teams like we were annihilated today in the second half, it's very easy to tell jokes about them on *The Tonight Show* or in a newspaper column or when you're sitting 3,000 miles away.

"You don't realize how tough they are until you see a game like this. Try being across the line of scrimmage from them. You'll see how tough they are in a hurry."

Because of this deep respect for the Bills, Polian was not the least bit discouraged by the Panthers' second-half collapse.

"We didn't build this thing here in three months, either," Polian said, waving his hand toward the home locker room across the hall from where he stood talking with reporters in a crowded but quiet visitors' locker room. "What's in my head is that we've got to get better. I'm not fooling myself. In a lot of cases, we've got to get better players. But nothing happens overnight."

Final Score

31 Buffalo   **9** Carolina

He didn't look too worried about the first-ever home game of the Carolina Panthers, due to kick off in about 16 hours—even though he had been hearing about it for years.

Instead, University of South Carolina athletic director Mike McGee was smiling ear to ear in his spanking-new executive suite at Williams-Brice Stadium in Columbia. The Gamecocks had rolled up 34 points against Louisiana Tech by halftime on the strength of four touchdown passes by senior quarterback Steve Taneyhill. The stands were filled with 70,411 fans—about 20,000 more than would show Sunday afternoon to watch the Panthers in Clemson—including 18 groups partying in new luxury boxes and another 750 fans paying $300 to $400 per game to sit in cushy wide seats and munch on goodies in a special club seating area, formerly the press box.

Perhaps best of all, Hootie and the Blowfish, a wildly popular rock band whose members are South Carolina alums, were watching the game from McGee's booth, cheering and propping their feet up on the front window ledge. All to the palpable delight of McGee's 30-year-old daughter Kathy.

"Our four children have grown up around athletics," McGee said. "It's fun to share these experiences with them."

For his part, McGee was simply relieved to have the stadium ready for this Saturday night home opener. Workers were welding right up until the gates opened, and a final construction punch list would not be completed for another few weeks.

The $9 million stadium renovation project was originally intended to be part of the package for luring the Panthers to play their first NFL season here, about an hour's drive from Charlotte. But the deal went sour after four negotiating sessions—along with the promise of millions of dollars pumped into the regional economy during the fall of 1995. Columbia business owners looking for a scapegoat settled on McGee.

"There was some negative reaction in the local community," said McGee. "But I don't think those people understood the potential [negative] long-term impact on USC athletics and our season-ticket sales. We needed to look down the road when considering the short-term income."

Some experts estimated a $30 million to $60 million windfall for whatever South Carolina college town hosted the Panthers during their first NFL season.

"Even $30 million was extremely optimistic," said McGee late in 1995. "Our information shows it turned out to be a lot less."

The punchline to a running joke in the Carolina front office all season was that the visiting team might make it back home on Sunday nights sooner than the Panthers when games were played at Clemson Memorial Stadium. Later in the season, that's exactly what the Atlanta Falcons did. But nobody was laughing at the disappointing turnout for the home opener—announced at 54,000 based by turnstile count and appearing to be even less than that in a facility that can hold more than 81,000 for a football game. Not one section was entirely filled and there was a gaping emptiness in end-zone seating.

Many Panthers officials were privately disappointed but pointed out the logical reasons—drive time, overhyped traffic problems, not making 1996 season ticket holders ante up for 1995, overestimated walk-up sales—to any media member who asked why so many Carolina fans didn't make the trip for a historic home opener.

NFL commissioner Paul Tagliabue, guest of Carolina owner Jerry Richardson, said he was "not unhappy" about the attendance and expressed confidence the Panthers would start selling out every game in 1996. He offered no qualifying apology to the visiting St. Louis Rams, whose fans had been rejected by the league expansion committee but were now comprising overflow home crowds in answer to the franchise's move from Los Angeles.

At the Clemson United Methodist Church, attendance among worshipers was also down—about 150 for the usual Sunday services. Just three days earlier its leader, Rev. David Nichols, lost his fight to prevent beer to be sold at Panthers games (four dollars per cup) when the South Carolina Supreme Court granted the team its alcohol permit.

That was just the pregame disappointment.

The Rams were off to a 2–0 start, including the previous Sunday's win over Green Bay, who would eventually play in the NFC championship game. Many people around the league were surprised by the quick start for St. Louis, but not Dom Capers. He figured the Panthers' new division rival looked about ready to bust through years of mediocrity and no playoff games. He sees St. Louis as a serious playoff contender during the next few seasons.

For one thing, they had 14 players selected in the first, second and third rounds during the last five drafts. Most all were fairly high choices in the round due to the Rams' 23–57 record during the same stretch.

"I look at the Rams and I see a team that is coming," said Capers during the week. "They've added [defensive tackle] Sean Gilbert, who was the best pass rusher coming out of the 1992 draft. They've added [defensive end] Kevin Carter, who was the best pass rusher who came out this year.

"Offensively, they've added guys like Jerome Bettis at running back, Isaac Bruce at wide receiver, and Troy Drayton at tight end during the last few drafts. In the defensive secondary, [cornerback] Todd Lyght is a former number-one pick and I also like the safety they drafted last year, Keith Lyle. These guys are all over their roster."

The Panthers proceeded to play what would be their worst game of the 1995 season. The Rams' 31–10 rout included more touchdowns for the St. Louis defense (two) than the Carolina offense. The offense had seven turnovers. The game prompted more than one newspaper columnist and TV sportscaster to ponder the dreadful possibility of a 0–16 season. Clemson's famed Death Valley was nothing but a graveyard of Panther dreams on September 17, especially for the expansion team's quarterbacks.

In what would be his last start, quarterback Frank Reich continued to struggle. The sputtering offense had only converted 17 percent of its third downs into first downs during the opening two weeks of the season. The week of practice focused squarely on ways to boost third-down efficiency. Yet Reich made good on only two of six third-down situations against the Rams, stalling the first five drives of the game without reaching the St. Louis half of the field. The offense was worse than simply inept; it had become boring. Not a good concept for a team struggling to draw fans and at least keep games close.

When Reich threw an interception directly into the arms of Pineville, North Carolina, native and St. Louis linebacker Roman Phifer (named after former Rams quarterback and current Panthers broadcaster Roman Gabriel), Capers proved he was nobody's fool if not his own. During his usual Monday press conference earlier in the week, he said it would be "foolish" to change quarterbacks in the middle of a game. Capers said he disapproved of giving a "quick hook."

Yet when the Panthers offense trotted on the field with 6:40 remaining in the first half, Jack Trudeau was the quarterback. The crowd cheered noisily for the first time since player introductions, figuring the veteran Trudeau, who unlike Reich had started regularly for other NFL teams, might infuse some excitement into the passing game. He promptly fumbled on his first regular-season play when sacked by the Rams' Carlos Jenkins.

"I felt putting Jack in there might give us a little spark," said Capers after the game.

Trudeau did catch fire a bit when he completed his next five passes and set up John Kasay's 45-yard field goal to cut the lead to 14–3 at halftime. Then Trudeau's fleeting hold on the quarterback job went up in smoke when he threw three interceptions. Kerry Collins relieved him in the fourth quarter.

The prized rookie Collins scored his first pro touchdown on a quarterback sneak late in the game. He finished 7 of 11 for 45 passing yards after throwing a gift interception on his first play in front of a Panthers home crowd. Torin Dorn, who played his college ball at North Carolina and never emerged a victor against Clemson (a fact of which he is constantly reminded by fellow Rams defensive back and former Clemson star Dexter Davis), returned the errant sideline pass for 24 yards and his first touchdown at Death Valley.

"It was fun getting in that Tiger end zone," Dorn told reporters after the game.

Back in St. Louis, everyone was celebrating the Rams' 3–0 record. Local TV sportscasters, like Mike Bush of NBC-affiliate KSDK, on his popular Sunday night show, were practically gleeful about the surprising Rams—and the empty seats at Clemson. Bernie Miklasz, a columnist for the *St. Louis Post-Dispatch,* wrote some stinging words in the next day's newspaper.

Don't ask us why so many supposedly rabid fans stayed away from the epic, history-making first game of the Carolina Panthers. Maybe this was oil-change day or something (here in NASCAR country). . . . On this sunny Sunday, the Rams reminded us of the most significant revelation to be culled from this victory: How fortunate we are to have the Rams in St. Louis instead of some drooling, expansion-team carcass. . . . Memo to [Paul] Tagliabue: Thanks. After watching yet another inept, poorly-dressed expansion goober self-destruct in hideous teal-colored clothing, I'm prepared to admit the NFL did [St. Louis] an expensive favor. Upon further review, we'll keep the Rams.

Sentiments likely changed as both teams eventually finished with 7–9 records for the season—with the Panthers finishing strong and Rams falling apart amid a quarterback crisis. But on this day, there was plenty of disappointment in the Carolina locker room.

Though five interceptions and two fumbles netted 14 points and favorable field position all day for their opponents, the Panthers defensive players were making no excuses. The stat sheet showed St. Louis rushed for 116 yards and gained 222 in the air, for a total of four touchdowns. What's more, St. Louis kicker Steve McLaughlin missed three make-able field goals, sparing further embarrassment for the home team. After one touchdown, head coach Capers waved away the defensive coaches and took an extended moment to make his feelings known to this veteran unit.

Cornerback Tim McKyer wasn't afraid to speak his mind when the first of many reporters reached his locker after the game.

"You can't play like the JV in the NFL," said McKyer. "I was always taught you play this game with your heart, but today we go out like we're not even there. We can't accept it. I won't personally accept it and I won't accept any guy around me who does.

"We need to do some deep soul-searching. Are we going to accept the same old rhetoric—You win as a team, you lose as a team, blah, blah, blah and all that garbage—or are we going to have heart? It's frustrating and I'm challenging every guy on this team. This crap is just not acceptable."

Not far away, linebacker Lamar Lathon said, "I'm embarrassed to pick up my check tomorrow."

In the winning locker room, St. Louis coach Rich Brooks was either feeling charitable after his team's 3–0 start or seeing the Panthers' defensive prowess sooner than most—including the Carolina players themselves. "You've got to understand, Carolina has a very good defense. They do things to make you look bad," said Brooks, who knew a little something about Panthers' offense, too, after watching Kerry Collins and Penn State soundly beat his University of Oregon team nine months earlier in the Rose Bowl.

Dom Capers was a realist during his postgame press conference: "We played our sloppiest football game today. You can't go out and turn over the football seven times and have any opportunity whatsoever to win the game or even to be close.

"We have to come back and take a look at what caused those turnovers."

The coach was referring to a review of the game film, which video technicians and assistant coaches would start segmenting into offense, defense and special-teams reels as early as Sunday night. Though you wouldn't think players would want to see a replay of this loss, it was quite the contrary in the Panthers locker room.

"Until we look at film," said fullback Bob Christian, "you don't know exactly what's happening. Your nose is in it, you can't hardly see anybody but the guy you're blocking. When a play doesn't go right, you don't know why."

Christian was in the middle of a plot twist concerning the Panthers offense. Derrick Moore had been announced as the starter at halfback, but when Carolina started its first offensive series, only Christian trotted out as the coaching staff opted for a one-back, three-receiver set.

Moore carried the ball only five times for 11 yards all afternoon. He was close to hostile after the game.

"My expectations were to carry the ball until the wheels fall off. I wanted them to wear me down to the rims," he said. "I never got a chance to do anything."

Sam Mills, the veteran linebacker who by this game was clearly the respected leader on defense, stood calmly answering every last media question put his way. As usual, he was impeccably and completely dressed after a quick shower and change.

"We have to concentrate on our side," said Mills with fistfuls of tape recorders thrust toward his face. "How many turnovers did we cause? We can't focus on offense. Every player has to break down his game and learn from the film.

Mills said the upcoming bye week would help. The Panthers would not play again until hosting Tampa Bay at Clemson on October 1.

"This team hasn't been together long. I want to make sure the guys aren't down. It's not the end of the season. We want to win football games, not just be close. The two weeks will give us chance to correct our mistakes."

A bye week in the NFL is usually a time best used to regroup and maybe rest up some injured players. For Carolina's coaching staff, three weeks into the team's history, it was time for major reform. The coaching staff planned to take a long look at naming Collins the starter at quarterback. Capers admitted "the original plan" was to give Collins a fair amount of practice snaps from training camp through the home opener, then increase his workload during two weeks of workouts before the Tampa Bay game.

One reason the front office staff preferred Collins to the other star quarterback in the 1995 draft, Steve McNair, was because they figured a small-school player like McNair needed more seasoning before adjusting to the complex pro game.

"All along, I've felt Kerry has the talent that made us want to draft him with our first pick," said Capers. "It's just a matter of him getting a good feel of what we're doing—and more importantly, having a feel of all the things he's going to see from the other side. That's where, to me, a quarterback faces the biggest change from college.

"In college, you might work against three or four different coverages. In the pros, every play you're seeing them change up something."

Capers and Pendry figured the upside potential was great for Collins, even during his rookie season.

"Now you have evaluate the downside risks," noted Capers. "I look back and the Dallas Cowboys went 1–15 with Troy Aikman as a rookie quarterback."

Of course, winning any of the first three games might have delayed the plan. But Reich and Trudeau did nothing to change the coaches' minds.

Willie Green was moved to do more than apologize for fumbling a pass from Trudeau.

"I've got to take this team on my back and make the big play," he said as several reporters exchanged he's-got-to-be-kidding looks.

Green, prone to exaggeration at times, was nonetheless quickly becoming a candid team philosopher of sorts. He told one reporter he could easily see why fans might have "some skepticism about whether we can win a game at all after the way we played today."

Earlier in the week, before practice on Wednesday at Winthrop College, Green revealed his thoughts on an even more lasting subject in the Carolinas.

Just days after an article was published in the *Charlotte Observer* describing Green as a "devout Muslim" and generally portraying him as deeply religious, he was cursing at length in the locker room. Even Green himself didn't seem to quite know why he was swearing.

Sitting a few locker stalls to his left was Dwight Stone, the soft-spoken ninth-year receiver and special-teams player who hopes to pursue a career with the FBI after his playing days.

"Come on now. We don't need all that profane language in here," said Stone, gently chiding his fellow receiver.

Green was indignant, and not about to hush up.

"Well, who in the hell decides what is profane anyway?" asked Green. "Who decides what is a curse word and what isn't?"

"Society does," replied Stone, quietly.

"Society? Fuck society!" said Green.

Green then started searching for his football helmet before taking the field for what is typically the most intense day of practice each week.

"Where's my goddamn helmet, people?" Green shouted at no one in particular. "Where's my goddamn helmet. I'm getting tired of this bullshit, y'all!"

Final Score

31 St. Louis   **10** Carolina

Game 4:
Tampa Bay at Panthers

The night before Kerry Collins was to make his first NFL start, he sat in his hotel room at the Ramada Inn in Clemson and watched his alma mater lose to Wisconsin, 17–9, on ESPN. The previous year, with Collins as Penn State's starting quarterback, the Nittany Lions did not lose in 12 starts.

In a strange sort of way, Collins gained confidence from reminding himself of this fact.

That Collins was going to start against the Tampa Bay Buccaneers had to be the worst-kept secret in the Carolinas since television evangelist Jim Bakker first denied there was anything untoward going on in his troubled PTL ministry. Collins knew he was going to start as soon as five days earlier, and he intended to use this start to help begin building a winning football empire that would be greater and last longer than anything Bakker had ever dreamed of.

"I'm going to be jacked up for this game," Collins told reporters, even though the reporters weren't supposed to know the rookie was starting until the day of the game. "I enjoy being in that competitive environment so much. I've missed it."

Watching Penn State lose to Wisconsin without him refreshed his memory. It also reminded Collins of the time he won the starting job at Penn State under similar circumstances. Much like the Panthers, who had lost their first three games, the Nittany Lions were coming off consecutive losses to Miami and Boston College when Coach Joe Paterno decided to turn to Collins for a game at West Virginia on October 24, 1992.

"I was a 19-year-old quarterback, a sophomore, going into a hostile situation on the road," Collins said. "It certainly was kind of a gut check. We had already lost two games in a row, and whoever heard of Penn State losing three straight? There was some serious pressure on me not to let that happen."

He didn't. Collins led an 89-yard touchdown drive in the final six minutes to break a 26–26 tie, and the Nittany Lions eventually went on to win, 40–26. It was a day worth remembering as the NFL rookie contemplated making his first start as a pro.

To outsiders, Collins was a 22-year-old kid living the Perfect Life. And in many ways, he was. But there was a flip side to this life-style.

Two months after receiving the first of two hefty installments on his $7 million signing bonus, Collins still struggled to receive more than a few channels on his television set (and even those were fuzzy) because he hadn't bothered to have the cable connected yet. He and a recent visitor, older brother Patrick, described to reporters an empty, lonely apartment (his best friend on the team and former roommate, Brian O'Neal, had been cut by the Panthers) that was both a bachelor's dream and a bachelor's worst nightmare, complete with dirty socks on the floor, T-shirts and jeans thrown over chairs, mountains of unpacked boxes and, on most nights when he returned home from practice, no one at all with whom to talk.

"In a lot of ways," Patrick Collins told one reporter, "he's living the same way he did when he was 15, waking up every day and playing sports."

People tended to forget Collins was only seven years removed from that existence. Like most young adults who were beginning a new job in a new city, far away from old friends and family, he was finding it to be quite an adjustment.

"I don't care how much money you make or what position you're in, that's hard to go through," Collins said as the Buccaneers game approached. "I'm trying not to let it affect what's going on out there on the football field. I don't think it has been. For the most part, I've been happy with the way practice has been going for me.

"But I have to admit, when I go home after practice, I go home to an empty apartment. It's like, What do I do now? Who am I going to call first? "

Collins's phone bills were huge. He spent much of his evenings talking with college buddies or pals from his high-school days, biding time until the next practice at Winthrop University.

It was there, on the practice fields behind Winthrop Coliseum, where Collins felt most comfortable. He had come a long way from those first few days during the Panthers' minicamps, when offensive coordinator Joe Pendry referred to him as "a time bomb." He also knew he still had a long way to go to become a top-flight NFL quarterback, but this Sunday would be a start.

Collins wasn't always a quarterback, and he didn't always love football. When he was a kid, in fact, he gave up the sport for two years and wasn't sure if he would ever go back to it.

"I was 10 and they had me playing fullback and tight end," Collins said. "I hurt my knee a little and didn't care for that, so I quit."

Collins also remembered what happened when he went deep as a tight end one game and dropped a perfectly thrown pass from Patrick, who was the quarterback at the time.

"He yelled at me—a lot. I didn't care for that, either," Kerry Collins said.

The younger Collins re-emerged as a quarterback for the freshman team at his junior high school in Lebanon, Pennsylvania, and quickly discovered he had a much better knack for throwing the football than catching it. A star was born.

"We had a great team," Collins said. "One game, against our archrival, I threw for something like 330 yards. It was ridiculous. We just kept airing it out, and I said to myself, Hey, I think I found something I'm pretty good at."

Unfortunately for the Collins household at the time, Patrick thought he was pretty good at it, too. The next year, the two brothers competed against each other for the starting quarterback's job on the Lebanon High varsity squad. The two Collins brothers were no stranger to this type of fierce competition, having frequently played one-on-one basketball games at the playground across the street from the house where they grew up. Those matchups often ended with them taking swings at each other, or with the younger Collins running home, tears streaming down his face.

"He knew how to push my buttons to make me mad," Kerry Collins said of Patrick.

So when Kerry won the starting job at Lebanon High over Patrick, the older Collins did not take it lightly. Kerry later joked that Patrick didn't speak to him for about six months.

The next season was easier from their standpoint, but not so easy on the family as a whole, because the brothers' parents split up. Kerry stayed with his father and transferred to West Lawn High in nearby Wilson, Pennsylvania, while his brother stayed with his mother in Lebanon.

Collins was being called upon to perform CPR on the Carolina offense. It was that simple. Three touchdowns in the first three games—none that really mattered since the season opener in Atlanta, with Collins scoring the third in the closing minutes of the 31–10 loss to the Rams—made it clear to Dom Capers that something drastic needed to be done.

Although Capers reiterated at the beginning of the week leading up to the Tampa Bay contest he felt it would be best not to publicly name a starter until game day, his players kept giving away the secret. Collins was getting the reps in practice, they said. Collins looked good, they said. This is just what we need, they said.

"I didn't place a gag order on the players," Capers said. "I realize they have a feel for what I am going to do. I would be foolish to think otherwise."

Nonetheless, he stuck to his plan not to publicly name a starter until Sunday.

The Buccaneers were not fooled by this ridiculously thin attempt at sleight of hand. Then again, this should have been no surprise. Their coach, Sam Wyche, was an accomplished magician, even though he hadn't yet discovered the magic required to turn the traditionally moribund Tampa Bay franchise into a winner.

Mike McCormack, the Panthers' team president, remembered Wyche from the days when McCormack served as an assistant coach with the Washington Redskins and Wyche was a backup quarterback.

"Sam was always cutting up and doing magic tricks," McCormack said. "We'd be flying to or from a game, and Sam would walk up and down the aisles of the plane performing magic tricks with a deck of cards. But when he wasn't doing that, he was always talking football. You knew he understood the game and might just become a coach himself one day."

It was Wyche, as a former quarterback himself and the coach who only a year earlier had thrown his own rookie QB into the heat of the battle, who understood exactly what Collins might be going through on this week. The same could be said of Trent Dilfer, the quarterback who made his first pro start in 1994 against none other than the San Francisco 49ers, who went on to win the Super Bowl. The 49ers trashed Dilfer and the Bucs, 41–16.

"It was a tough deal," Dilfer said. "I thought I was really ready to play. Kerry will think he's ready to play, too, and that he has all the right answers.

"But [the 49ers] did some things to me early and I made some bad throws early. We got down, and it's tough to come back against the 49ers when they've got Deion Sanders sitting there in one corner. You couldn't do a lot of the things you wanted to do. I think I was 7 for 22 for 46 yards, or something like that. It wasn't exactly a stellar performance."

Actually, Dilfer was 7 of 23 for 45 yards against San Francisco that afternoon. For his entire rookie season, Dilfer completed just 38 of 82 pass attempts for 46.6 percent and 433 yards. His quarterback rating was a dismal 36.3.

Tampa Bay made Dilfer, who missed the last seven weeks of his rookie year because of an injury to his rib cage, the sixth overall pick in the 1994 draft. He admitted he was only now beginning to feel comfortable on most snaps, after starting in each of the Bucs' first four regular-season contests in 1995. Even so, there were times when he felt lost.

"There are still times when it seems like everything is going 100 miles per hour out there. I would be lying if I said otherwise," he said.

So what advice would Dilfer, the sixth overall pick in the 1994 draft, give to Collins, the fifth overall pick in the 1995 draft, on the eve of Collins's first start?

"If I was going to talk to Kerry, I would tell him to enjoy it," Dilfer said. "It's going to be a thrilling time for him. I mean, it's his first NFL start if it happens. There will be a lot of hype surrounding it.

"You have to try to kind of put that on the back burner and just go out and try to do the things you do best. He needs to have the confidence that he can do the same things in this league that he did in college, where he was very successful."

Not that college and the pros are the same, warned Dilfer.

"I think if I could do it all over again," said Dilfer, "maybe the one thing I would change would be to put a little more pressure on myself in practice to try to make my reads quicker. The one thing that his coaches will tell him, that you guys in the media will tell him, that he will hear all week long leading up to the game, is that the game is going to be a lot quicker. And he really needs to be ready for that.

"But there's no way to prepare for it. It's a totally different situation when you step out on the field on Sunday in this league. It's faster, it's more intense, the hits are harder, the coverages are tighter, the throwing lanes are a lot tighter."

Collins was not the only one who needed to realize that. Dilfer said bad afternoons are inevitable for young quarterbacks, sounding much like Capers when he first acknowledged that Collins might be named the starter. That was one thing Collins seemed to have going for him: The Panthers understood his plight; they did not expect him to take them to the Super Bowl this year, next year or even the year after that. They, in fact, expected him to struggle at first, just like the team. But they also expected Collins and the team to grow hand in hand, little by little, improving gradually but in a way that offered staying power.

Dilfer pointed out that all teams say they are going to be patient with young quarterbacks, but often are not. Changes in the coaching staff or ownership or injuries are factors. So is confidence. A young quarterback was bound to have his tough days along with the good ones. How the young quarterback handled the down days would go a long way toward determining the quality of NFL career he was going to have.

"What happens sometimes is that fans and the media are beating you up because of false expectations," Dilfer said.

"That's when you really need your coaches and teammates behind you, saying, 'Hey, we understand this is going to take some time. We know you're going to be a great player.' The more he hears that, the more comfortable he'll become and the more confident he'll become."

Collins already was receiving endorsements from his teammates.

"If we execute around him, he'll be successful," running back Derrick Moore said. "He has confidence in himself; you can see that. I think it's good to have that swagger.

Willie Green described Collins as "perky" and said it was obvious the rookie did not lack confidence. But Green liked something else about Collins.

"The worst thing a young quarterback can do, and I like Kerry because he hasn't done this, is come in and start criticizing players," Green said. "If he goes in there pointing fingers and cussing people out, that won't work. Let me tell you something: I'm a veteran and us veterans don't want to hear that.

"He's confident. He's understood in the huddle. But he's smart enough not to do things like that, because I think he knows it would turn a lot of us off."

One week removed from his assessment that the Panthers were playing like the junior varsity, outspoken cornerback Tim McKyer was feeling a little better. But only a little. In fact, he wouldn't say whether he was still upset with his teammates until he saw the results of the game against the Bucs.

"We'll see after the game," McKyer said. "Yeah, we've had a couple of great weeks of practice since playing the Rams. We had a great week of practice before we played the Rams, too. None of that means anything until you see how it relates to what you do on Sunday.

"The bottom line is what you do on Sunday. Nothing else matters. I've been taught to play the game with a passion, to leave your heart out on the field. Let's face it: Everything is on the line for 16 weeks—and if you don't let it all hang out for each one of those 16 Sundays, you won't be around this game very long. I've stayed around for 10 years because that's my attitude."

Unfortunately for McKyer and the rest of the Panthers, the Bucs no longer resembled the pushover opponent they had been for more than a decade. Among the high-profile free agents who had been signed to bolster the Bucs was wide receiver Alvin Harper, the former Dallas Cowboy.

"Alvin Harper is just another wide receiver who is going to come in here and try to embarrass me," McKyer said. "I have to get up for that."

It was time, McKyer said, for the entire team to get up for a run at victory. After all, they didn't want to keep this losing up for so long people started comparing them to the 1976 expansion Buccaneers, who lost 26 consecutive games before winning the last two of their second season.

After one of the losses, Tampa Bay coach John McKay was asked what he thought of his team's execution.

"I'm in favor of it," McKay replied.

Capers said he had been hearing several McKay-isms from those years during the week, but he warned writers covering the Panthers not to expect those kinds of colorful quotes from him.

"If I start ripping off one-liners like that," said a smiling Capers, "you'll know something is wrong."

Something *was* wrong. The Panthers hadn't yet won a game. But Capers continued to tell his players and anyone else who would listen that they were doing some things right. They were getting better. He could see it on the practice field, especially during the bye week following the embarrassing loss to the Rams.

Capers only hoped his players would believe him when he kept saying they were doing the right things. He knew that after a while, if victories didn't follow, this would begin sounding like empty rhetoric to them no matter how hard they tried to believe.

"I don't like being 0–3," said McKyer, who played on winning teams that made the playoffs in eight of nine seasons before coming to the Panthers in the expansion draft. "When you've been accustomed to winning, losing is not part of you.

"But at the same time, no one wants to lose to an expansion team. Guys are getting up to play us because no one wants to be the first to have that expansion black eye, so to speak. That's why we have to play extra hard to get that first win."

The Panthers did play hard. They even made Tim McKyer proud.

"We were elevated to varsity status this week," McKyer said.

But they did not beat the Buccaneers.

It was an afternoon in which the Panthers lost the game but felt they found an offense. In the process, they validated their belief that Collins was a quarterback of the future bearing down on an impressive present and discovered that Derrick Moore was a running back of rare determination.

The Panthers, in fact, thoroughly outplayed the Bucs, piling up 393 yards of total offense and holding the Bucs to just 61 yards rushing on 28 attempts. They lost because they could not hold on to the football.

Collins completed 18 of 32 passes for 234 yards. He led several long drives, two of which produced touchdowns. Three others might have done the same if not for untimely fumbles, two by Moore, including one at the Tampa Bay one-yard line. Since the Bucs escaped with a mere 20–13 victory, they ended up feeling very fortunate indeed.

"I'm glad we're heading out of town," Wyche said. "We want to get on the bus and get out before they have any reviews."

The Panther defense made Trent Dilfer look confused and then knocked him silly, forcing him to leave the game late in the first half with a concussion. His backup, Casey Weldon, completed just 8 of 20 passes but was poised just enough to spoil Collins's debut.

Then again, the Panthers themselves spoiled it by turning the ball over so much. Collins threw one interception, but the two fumbles lost by Moore and one lost by fullback Bob Christian were too much to overcome. Moore first fumbled on third-and-goal from the 1 on the third play of the second quarter; he fumbled away another potential scoring opportunity on third-and-one at the Tampa 32 with just under nine minutes left in the game. Christian lost his fumble at the Tampa 14 on the Panthers' second possession of the day.

Otherwise, Moore was exceptional in his first starting opportunity, although it came a week later than he expected. He rumbled for 123 yards on 21 carries to become the first Panther back to rush for 100 or more in a game. Through the first three games, Moore was the team's leading rusher with the modest total of 64 yards; he nearly doubled that on one exciting touchdown run of 53 yards against the Bucs, tying the score at 7–7 in the second quarter.

After the game, Moore remembered the fumbles more than anything else. He sat dejectedly at his locker and sobbed so fiercely his body shook. But then he gathered himself, stood up and answered every question from reporters about what happened.

"I have a bittersweet taste in my mouth," Moore said. "The 100 yards are great, but we didn't win. We can't win when we turn the ball over the way we did today."

For that, he knew he had no one to blame more than himself.

"As a man and as a pro football player, I accept my role in the loss," Moore said. "I have to get my act together. I have no excuses."

Blake Brockermeyer paved the way for Moore on the long touchdown run with a crushing block to spring the running back into the open field. The offensive line played well overall against the Bucs, with Collins making it through without suffering a single sack.

Collins was impressive. He threw touch passes and he threw some bullets. He connected on long passes and short ones. He stood tall in the pocket to make throws and proved difficult to bring down when defenders converged on him. He was mobile enough when he had to be, helping circumvent possible sacks. He even called an audible on one play when he approached the line and saw the Buccaneers were stacked to play the run, dropping back quickly, pump-faking to freeze a defensive back and hitting Mark Carrier for a 41-yard gain that led to the Panthers' second touchdown.

"It's still football. It's just a different level," Collins said. "It's a game I've been playing for a long time. I was nervous out there, there was no doubt about it. But it wasn't like I was jittery or wasn't confident."

Willie Green paid Collins the ultimate compliment.

"He ran the offense like a veteran," Green said. "He earned a lot of respect today from the veterans on this team. One game doesn't make you a Pro Bowl player, but he earned our respect."

And that of the Buccaneers.

"I think they found a quarterback," Wyche said.

As a matter of fact, Wyche was impressed with the Panthers as a whole.

"The Panthers are formidable," Wyche said. "This is a competitive football team right now. This is a team that does not make strategic mistakes. They don't make fundamental mistakes in terms of being sound on offense and defense.

"This football team is going to knock some people off very soon. They're right at the edge."

Capers and Bill Polian were inclined to agree.

"I'm disappointed but not discouraged by our performance," Capers said. "Kerry Collins did an admirable job in his first start. We had more big plays today [on offense] than we had all season. We had a better rhythm offensively. We were able to run the ball and throw the ball better than we have all year."

Polian added, "Every time you compete, you try to take something positive from it. What we got out of this game is that our quarterback of the future is now our quarterback of the present. And he's going to get better."

Final Score

20 Tampa Bay   **13** Carolina

Game 5:
Panthers at Chicago

For the Panthers, the play's effect was temporary euphoria. For the Chicago Bears and the crowd of 59,668 watching at historic Soldier Field, it was nearly total silence.

Eric Guliford, an NFL journeyman who only now was beginning to find a home, had just returned a punt 62 yards for a touchdown, giving the Panthers a 27–24 lead over the Bears. His run set off a wild if slightly premature Carolina celebration in the end zone. It spilled over to the Panthers' sideline before the celebrators sobered up to the realization that this game was not over.

Yet only 2 minutes, 37 seconds remained. All the Panthers had to do was hold the Bears with their veteran-laden defense, the self-declared backbone of the team.

The Panthers seemed on the verge of their first regular-season victory—and it would be against an original franchise in the league, one that was more than 75 seasons old. They were just about to thumb their noses at Chicago's hard-boiled fans, including the local radio station that had rented a plane to fly overhead trailing a sign that read PANTHERS-R-PUSSIES, which flew proudly next to the plane pulling an advertisement for Ramses condoms that read ROLL ON ONE.

But first, it was up to the defense to stop Erik Kramer, one of the hottest quarterbacks in the league. No problem. There wasn't one of the Carolina defenders taking the field who didn't relish the challenge to play hero.

"Hey, if we stop them, we win," linebacker Sam Mills told his defensive comrades on the sideline. "Now let's go out there and get it done."

Upstairs in the press box, Mike McCormack and Bill Polian glanced around and tried to look confident. After all, they built this team from the defense up. These were precisely the moments when that strategy was supposed to pay off.

Each Monday, Capers and his staff and the players convened at Winthrop Coliseum to dissect videotape of the previous day's game. The regular players would arrive by 10 A.M. for a weight-lifting session. Meanwhile, Capers had a 7 A.M. defense meeting to pick apart the previous day's game. That would last two hours, then it was the offensive coaches' turn to explain what went right and wrong. Capers finished off his Monday mornings with a half-hour review session with the special-teams coach, Brad Seely. After that, Capers made it a point to lock his door and collect his thoughts for the team meeting.

Lunch was served at 11:30 A.M. and the team meeting was at 12:15 P.M.. The entire team watched the special-teams films before splitting up into offense and defense units.

The afternoon film sesson might go three hours. The coaches, of course, arrived long before the players, and in some cases were even in the offices doing film work by late Sunday evening. They also stayed late on Monday nights to start working on next week's game plan.

Tuesday was the players' day off, although a few—Sam Mills being one of the regulars—came in to look at more film. This generally was the day when the coaches met to make decisions on possible personnel moves and begin game planning for the following Sunday's opponent. In the morning, coaches watch film individually to develop their own ideas and opinons about how to succeed against this week's opponents.

Next, the coaches watch "cut-ups" in the afternoon in groups by defense and offense. This helps pin down what the Panthers should do on any particular down or situation. For example, the defensive cut-up for the coming week showed all the Bears' recent run plays during games in one segment, followed by first- and second-down pass plays, play-action plays, screen plays, third-down passes, red-zone runs and passes (played inside the opponents' 20-yard-line) and two-minute drills.

The coaches then devise a first- and second-down game plan before dinner at 5:30 or 6 P.M. After the meal, it's time to arrive at critical third-down strategy for the week.

Practices resumed on Wednesdays, with the hardest workouts usually coming that day and Thursday before a scaled-back practice on Friday. Saturdays were used for meetings and walkthroughs before either boarding a bus to go to Clemson for the night before a "home" game or flying to an away site.

The Tuesday before playing in Chicago, Capers arrived, as usual, a few minutes early in the same room where he had been meeting with his defensive coaches every Tuesday at precisely 1 P.M. since the season began. Capers was a stickler for being on time. He didn't like anyone being late, especially for meetings. Players, in fact, were fined $50 per minute for each minute they were late getting on the practice field or attending a meeting.

So Capers was rather annoyed when 1 P.M. passed on this particular Tuesday and his entire defensive coaching staff was nowhere in sight. Of course, Capers may have been the only person in America who did not remember the O.J. Simpson verdict was being announced live on television at that very moment.

"At one o'clock I was sitting in the defensive room wondering where in the hell everyone else was," Capers said. "I thought maybe the assistant coaches had quit on me."

"Then I come to realize they're all in the video room, watching the O.J. thing. It was kind of comical. I thought maybe my watch was wrong."

There were times during the season when he would ask reporters what was going on in the sporting world outside the NFL. He read newspapers religiously, but only to scour them for what was being written about his team or his team's opponent for the week. He didn't have time to read the rest of the sports section, let alone the paper's other sections. Not during the season, anyway.

The O.J. Simpson saga was a hot topic in the locker room. Like many Americans, there was much debate over Simpson's guilt or innocence.

One lively discussion involved Willie Green, who is from Athens, Georgia, and Jack Trudeau, from Livermore, California. They were talking the day after the innocent verdict was revealed.

Green was complaining about how some Californians obviously were closet members of the Ku Klux Klan, given some reactions to the news.

"At least down South here, you know who's in the Klan," he told Trudeau. "They still wear sheets on their head and shit. Out where you're from, I could be riding in a car with a guy in a suit-and-tie and never know it, but he could be in the Klan."

"Ah, Willie," said Trudeau, "we don't have the Klan out where I'm from. We're not like that out there."

"Oh, that's right. I forgot," Green said, laughing. "Everyone knows who's in the Klan out there, too. They even wear uniforms. They just don't call it the Ku Klux Klan. They call it the LAPD."

The dog days of training camp, when rookie Kerry Collins was required to deliver newspapers to the doors of the veteran quarterbacks each morning, seemed long past to the Panthers by this time.

As did Reich's rookie season, which occurred more than a decade earlier. Reich was now 33—and if Collins was the player everyone hoped, Reich's starting days were over. After just three weeks, he had been relegated to the role of backup quarterback again.

Collins' hazing didn't stop once the regular season arrived. He began spending hours watching videotape with Reich and Trudeau at the team's Winthrop practice facility. When the veterans got thirsty during these sessions, they would dispatch the rookie into the nearby office of Coach Capers.

"He had a refrigerator of Cokes and Diet Cokes that are supposed to be for his own personal use," Collins said. "They would send me in there in case Coach Capers happened to drop by."

By the week of the Tampa Bay game, Collins was no longer retrieving newspapers or drinks for the others. "I guess all that stuff stops when you get your first NFL start," said Collins, smiling.

The quarterbacks finally had their own small refrigerator in the room where they watched film. No one said so for certain, but they suspected it was because Capers had grown weary of his personal supply being raided.

Reich took his loss of the starting job to Collins as well or better than could be expected. This was supposed to have been Reich's coming-out season after 10 years as a backup in Buffalo. But after just three games, Reich found himself where he had been most of his career—back on the sideline, watching someone else play. No one could have blamed him for being bitter and upset.

"My main concern is helping the team win," Reich said. "That takes precedent over any personal feelings I might have.

"You could be in the game in one play [if the starter gets hurt]. You just never know. So you have to stay tuned in to what they're doing on defense. That's the mental approach you have to take."

That seems easier said than done.

"I'll be very honest with you," Reich said. "I know, looking at the circumstances, it should have been difficult for me. But it really wasn't that difficult."

Reich's role on Sundays now was to man the headset on the sideline and feed plays and bits of information relayed to him from Joe Pendry, the offensive coordinator who watches the game from the press box, to the new quarterback playing on the field. Collins, like all NFL quarterbacks, wore a helmet with a tiny microphone in it, through which he could hear Reich.

"You don't want to clutter Kerry's mind too much when he's out there playing," Reich said. "I try to limit how much I say."

Collins said he appreciated the way Reich was helping him.

"Frank has been great," Collins said. "I'm sure he's disappointed. I don't think there's any doubt about that. But he's been very professional about trying to do whatever he can to help me and the team. It's never easy for anyone when they get benched."

Collins, Trudeau and Reich still met every Wednesday and Thursday at 7:45 A.M. to watch videotape together before meeting with Pendry. They also watched film together extensively at other times during the week.

"The fact that Kerry is a rookie, I think people put too much into that," Reich said. "We've all got to learn, there's no doubt. But I think Kerry's got a real good grasp of what's going on. Jack and I treat Kerry more as an equal than as an understudy."

They had no choice.

Their 0–4 record notwithstanding, the Panthers went into the week of preparation for the Bears with some obvious positives developing within the framework of the team. Collins looked good at quarterback. The offensive line was improving. Derrick Moore, despite losing the two costly fumbles against the Bucs, looked to be a keeper at running back.

And Tyrone Poole, another of the Panthers' first-round draft picks, was beginning to shine at cornerback. So much so that Capers named him a starter for the first time at left cornerback for the game in Chicago, announcing that Tim McKyer, who had been starting there, would move to right cornerback, and Rod Smith, who had been starting on the right side, would be coming off the bench to assist in nickel and dime coverages only.

McKyer had some advice for Poole going into the contest against the Bears, whose quarterback was Erik Kramer, the former North Carolina State star who was enjoying his finest pro season.

"When you're playing cornerback and you're a rookie," said McKyer, "you might as well go out there with an *X* marked on your back—because they're gonna come after you and they're gonna be coming hard."

The cocksure Poole didn't mind.

"I'm pretty sure they're going to come at me, and that's what I want," Poole said. "To be considered one of the best, you have to be tried. Once you establish yourself, that's when the other teams will start saying, 'This guy's a good corner. You'd better look out for him. There are certain routes we can't run on him.'

"I'll be looking forward to it. I hope I get a lot of balls thrown my way."

Kramer no doubt would be willing to oblige. He entered the game with a quarterback rating of 97.9, which ranked fourth in the NFL behind only Steve Young, Dan Marino and Troy Aikman. He had three capable receivers to throw to in Jeff Graham, Curtis Conway and Michael Timpson. Poole knew that, at times, he could be matched up against any one of the three.

Poole played quite a bit in the Panthers' first four games, even though he didn't start. Against the Bucs, for instance, he was on the field for 37 of the 59 plays Tampa Bay ran from scrimmage. He played in all the nickel and dime coverages, when five and six defensive backs were required on the field, and had subbed some for Smith as well when the Panthers operated out of their base 3-4 defense.

"All along I had it in my mind that left corner or right corner, whichever it may have been, it was mine," Poole said. "That's the attitude I have. Anything I do, I don't want to be second to anyone. I want to be the leader."

McKyer had predicted early in minicamp that Poole had the right mentality to become a successful cornerback in the NFL. After Poole intercepted a pass and ran it back 85 yards for a touchdown in his first pro outing—Carolina's 20–14 preseason victory over Jacksonville—McKyer said simply, "You know, he reminds me of me."

It took a special kind of player to excel at cornerback, according to both McKyer and Coach Capers. For one thing, the player had to be able to shake off the bad plays, which are inevitable in the pass-happy NFL.

"You have to have a short memory to play cornerback," Capers said. "You could play great for 50 plays in a row, but then get burned for a touchdown on the next play—and that's the play everyone will remember. It won't be easy to forget about it, either, because every day you go down to the corner store to buy a newspaper, the guy behind the counter is likely to remind you of it for at least a year."

McKyer and Capers would know. They were together in Pittsburgh the previous year when McKyer got burned in the AFC championship game by San Diego receiver Tony Martin for a 43-yard touchdown with 5:13 left to play. It proved to be the difference in a 17–13 loss that kept McKyer, Capers and the Steelers out of the Super Bowl.

McKyer often referred to the play, which continued to haunt him. Usually, he was the one who brought it up. Reporters would be talking about an entirely different subject, and McKyer would suddenly say something like, "I've been playing the game at this level for 10 years, but all you reporters ever remember is Tony Martin. Y'all keep reminding me of Tony Martin. You won't let me forget that one play, will you? It's like it's the only play I've ever been involved in in my whole career."

One time, a reporter from a small town who was not a regular visitor to Panthers' practices learned firsthand about McKyer's Tony Martin complex. The reporter was visiting to write a story about the team in general and was not yet all that familiar with pro football. Someone told him McKyer was a good talker, so he went to the cornerback to solicit some general comments.

"You're not going to bring up Tony Martin, are you?" McKyer said when approached by the reporter. "All you guys ever want to talk about is Tony Martin. Tony Martin. I'm sick of talking about Tony Martin."

The reporter seemed stunned by this outburst.

"Who's Tony Martin?" he asked innocently.

Of course, McKyer had a habit of wanting to forget the past, even if he sometimes couldn't escape it. When another reporter during one of the minicamps had referred to him in an article as the Mouth of the South, a nickname he earned by popping off while playing one season for Miami and two opposite Deion Sanders in Atlanta, McKyer was furious.

"Why do you want to bring up all that old bullshit?" he demanded upon confronting the reporter. "Why write that old bullshit? Don't you know I'm gonna give you plenty of new bullshit to write about this year?"

This was one of Poole's mentors. There were times McKyer made sense, of course, and it was true he was a decent cornerback. It's just there was also a reason the Panthers were the sixth team he had played for in the last seven seasons after beginning his career playing four years for the 49ers. He didn't know when to keep his mouth shut—or at least he refused to—often making comments that caused friction in the locker room.

"One thing about playing cornerback is on one play you can look like a hero, and on the next you can look like you've never played the position before in your life," McKyer said. "I've played it 10 years in this league. I think that's why I'm half crazy."

Half crazy or not, the 23-year-old Poole said he was ready to meet the challenge that awaited him in his first NFL start. But he planned to handle it in his own personal manner.

"With me, I go out thinking I'm the best on the field, that no one can beat me. I feel that with that attitude you can go a long way," said Poole.

For the first time all season, perhaps, the Panthers entered the game against the Bears feeling certain they were going to score some points. Both the offensive line, on which Curtis Whitley and Blake Brockermeyer were emerging as leaders, and Moore at running back were literally bursting with confidence based on their success against Tampa Bay.

"I had 21 knockdowns," Brockermeyer boasted of his performance against the Buccaneers. "It's going to be hard to get more knockdowns than that the rest of the year."

When he played for the Texas Longhorns in college, knockdowns were measured differently and the big tackle never managed to register more than "13 or 14." He had to go all the way back to his high-school glory days in Arlington Heights, Texas, to remember a game in which he was so dominant.

"I had a lot of good games in high school. Our team sucked, but I had a lot of good games," Brockermeyer said. "I probably had 50 knockdowns in some of those."

It appears Brockermeyer had his own system for judging his ability to knock over an opposing player. When Capers was asked about the 21 knockdowns, he smiled and said, "If that's what Blake said he had, more power to him."

Despite the Panther line's rapid improvement, Brockermeyer and line coach Jim McNally both warned not to be to hasty in passing out criticism or praise. A line is judged by its level of effectiveness over time, they said.

"We're still not where we want to be," Brockermeyer said. "It takes years for an offensive line to learn to play well together. People who expect us to dominate every play and every team we play, well, it's just not going to happen.

"They've got to realize it's a process that takes a while. But if everyone stays here for several years, it could happen for us."

McNally was more blunt.

"When I think we're good," he said, "I'll say we're going to the playoffs or the Super Bowl. Right now, we're just trying to get through this day and eliminate mental errors. I'm serious. It's get through this game, go to the next game, then the next game, and keep improving.

"Everything is about improvement. As soon as you get cocky about something . . . well, I don't even want to talk about that."

Moore, meanwhile, was willing to talk about anything, anytime, anywhere. He was still regarded somewhat as a newcomer, having only been around in the locker room for about five weeks, but reporters were already making a habit of crowding his locker space.

Moore talked in a rapid, excited manner, frequently punctuating his comments with gap-toothed smiles and sudden, loud bursts of laughter, which were usually followed by comments made in ultra-serious, low tones that offered a remarkable contrast. Listening to him talk was like attending some kind of concert, and he usually had something of substance to say that held reporters and sometimes teammates alike in rapt attention. Some teammates, however, tended to wonder aloud on occasion if he wasn't laying it on a little too thick.

Moore proclaimed he had put the costly fumbles against Tampa Bay behind him and boldly predicted another big game for himself against the Bears.

"I'm a confident, upbeat guy," he said. "I may make some mistakes, but I don't dwell on them. I'm totally at peace with myself and my teammates. The best is yet to come with me. I'm just getting started. I'm just getting it cranked up.

"I'm not a fumbler. That's probably the first time I've fumbled since I've been playing pro football. . . . Fumbling is not something that I do.

"Sunday was not a shock to me. It's the kind of thing I thought I could do if I was given the opportunity. I'm still working out some kinks, though. You've got to realize that I haven't really run the ball in two years. I'm still getting used to this thing. If I can keep working hard and stay healthy, it's going to be scary come four or five weeks from now."

Tyrone Poole got his wish early against the Bears. The game was only seven minutes old when Bears wide receiver Curtis Conway turned Poole around and gained inside position to catch a 41-yard touchdown pass from Erik Kramer, giving the Bears a 7–0 lead.

Capers later would defend Poole, saying he had good position on Conway, but adding that Conway made a great catch of a perfect throw by Kramer. The play was a stinging lesson nonetheless for the rookie cornerback who was not easily humbled.

It was the beginning of a wild game in which the two teams traded dramatic blows. The Panthers scored on a 66-yard touchdown pass from Collins to Mark Carrier, and took a 20–17 lead early in the fourth quarter when Greg Kragen sacked Kramer at the Chicago one-yard line and forced a fumble that he recovered and rolled into the end zone with for a touchdown.

"I knew I was right there by the end zone, so I just kind of crawled in," Kragen said. "I've seen it happen before. It's ugly, but it works."

It was the second touchdown of the 33-year-old Kragen's 11-year NFL careeer, with the other coming on a fumble recovery he returned 17 yards for a TD against Kansas City while playing for Denver in 1989.

"I guess I'm glad I didn't have to try and pick this one up and run," Kragen said.

The Panthers' lead did not hold up for long after Kragen's trashing of Kramer. A short, low kickoff by John Kasay, who was having problems all day, gave the Bears great field position at their own 49-yard line. Kramer drove them right down the field for another touchdown and a 24–20 lead with 9:22 left.

Then came Guliford's punt return of 62 yards. The Bears had their own struggling kicker in Todd Sauerbrun, a rookie punter. He booted one that Guliford had a good chance to return, and Guliford obliged, juking defender James Burton early and then streaking down the right sideline untouched behind a wall of blockers.

Only 2:37 remained on the clock. Surely the Panthers' proud defense could protect a 27–24 lead for that long.

But they didn't. Kramer, who threw for 259 yards, alternated between picking apart the Carolina secondary and handing off to rookie Rashaan Salaam, and the Bears marched right down the field. Again, it hurt when Kasay kicked low and short, resulting in a return from the 21-yard line to the 40 by Robert Green. The Bears eventually scored the game-winning touchdown on a somewhat controversial third-and-goal play from the 1 with 38 seconds left, when Green at the last instant stretched the ball out before going down and, at least in the opinion of the officials, broke the plane of the goal line.

McKyer stormed off the field afterward, kicking a water bucket on his way out and shouting to no one in particular, "Y'all are a bunch of piss ants!"

The Panthers, far more than after any of their previous losses, painted a locker-room picture of dejection and frustration that bordered on despair in some cases.

"This one bothers me more than any of the others," Sam Mills said. "It hurts the most because any time you can go on the field as a defense and say, 'Hey, if we stop them, we win,' that's what you want. We just didn't get it done."

Defensive lineman Mark Thomas added: "We had the game in our hands twice. As a defense, that's what you live for. If we did everything we were supposed to do, we would be sitting here happy right now."

It should have been a happy day for Guliford, who not only had scored his first NFL touchdown but also caught three passes for 63 yards, including one that went for a 49-yard gain. But it wasn't.

"I was hoping my punt return would give us the momentum we needed to nail the coffin shut. But it didn't," he said gloomily.

McKyer was furious and again questioned the desire of his defensive teammates, which drew glares from the nearby locker stalls of fellow veterans Brett Maxie and Bubba McDowell.

"Obviously," said McKyer, "keeping people out of the end zone doesn't mean a whole lot to us. That's something we've got to start doing. Otherwise, we'll never win. We'll go 0–16.

"You've got to play this game with your heart. That's something that can't be coached. It has to come from within. We just didn't get it done. We didn't want it. We didn't make the plays and we lost the game. I feel terrible. This was awful."

McDowell obviously did not appreciate McKyer's lecture.

"I don't know what he's talking about," McDowell said. "But Tim's his own man. I'm not going to get into a discussion with him about this because Tim can argue you down all day long. But one thing I know is I believe everybody out there was playing with heart. I believe everybody was giving their all. Everybody was playing to win.

"We just weren't good enough in the last two minutes to get it done."

Asked about McKyer's outburst, Maxie just shook his head and said, "Consider the source."

While McKyer's speech was not appreciated, Kerry Collins was in the next room leaning against a wall, asserting himself as one of the team's leaders after only his second week as starting quarterback. He had played well again, completing 14 of 28 passes for 228 yards with one interception and the long touchdown pass to Carrier.

"This is a tough one to take, a real tough one to take," he said, his voice shaking a bit with emotion. "What can you do in a situation like this? You can get mad. You can get angry. We just need to regroup and focus all that anger and frustration on the practice field this week. We have to focus on every play in every practice between now and next Sunday when we tee it up again.

"I don't think there's a guy in that locker room right now who's not angry and frustrated and fed up with losing. But how do you respond to that? If you let it go in a negative way, it just hurts the ballclub. What we have to do is hopefully channel all that energy into what we're doing this week. That's the only thing we can do. There's not one other thing we can do."

Capers tried to be as positive as he could, but it was difficult.

"We know now we can play with teams," the coach said. "We just have to start finding ways to make the big plays at the end of them that will turn the losses into victories. There's no consolation in this league for coming close."

The Panthers had come close two weeks in a row and in three out of five on the season. The headlines in the following morning's *Chicago Sun-Times* blared of the Bears: "Stretched to the Limit." And in the *Chicago Tribune:* "Barely finer than Carolina." Back home in the *Winston-Salem Journal,* the headline was "Defense deserts Panthers." And in the *Charlotte Observer:* "UNBEARABLE."

There was no way to hide the truth. The Panthers' record was now 0–5.

"You could say this should have happened or that should have happened," Collins said. "But that just doesn't do it. I don't care how close we came or how many great plays we made. There's just no excuse for losing. We have to find ways to win.

"I believe that you can will things to happen, that you can will things to go well. I think we have that on this team. I think the players that we have possess the will to win. For some reason, it hasn't happened yet. But it will. It's up to every person on this team to refocus and regroup and come back next week prepared to win.

"There's nothing else we can do. We could sit around and feel sorry for ourselves, and just take the wrong attitude about it. But I don't think we'll let that happen."

Final Score

31 Chicago   **27** Carolina

Game 6:
New York Jets at Panthers

As if the anticipation of finally facing a team they knew they should—not could, but should—beat was not wearisome enough, the Panthers were forced to wait until 4 P.M. to play the Jets at Clemson Memorial Stadium the week after losing at Chicago. It was the only late-afternoon start of the season at Clemson.

Players began filtering onto the field shortly after 2 P.M. At 2:08, Willie Green emerged with Eric Guliford, the wide receiver who had just replaced him in the starting lineup. Apparently, no hard feelings lingered over the role reversal. Green and Guliford laughed and threw a football back and forth for more than 10 minutes, Green winding up and hurling like a baseball pitcher much of the time. Green, a wild left-hander, proved no threat to switch careers. In contrast, the ambidextrous Guliford soon began effortlessly throwing left-handed as well as right-handed, his spirals tighter than Green's every time.

At 2:20, Guliford broke off as he spotted his family arriving, including a special guest: his estranged father. Guliford lifted daughter Breanna, age five, out of the south stands and onto the field, where they began doing stretching exercises together. Green continued to toss poorly thrown passes with ballboys who obviously were overjoyed to have been blessed with the duty of catching them and throwing them back.

At 2:30, Bill Polian wandered onto the field. He conferred nervously with defensive coordinator Vic Fangio and defensive secondary coach George Catavolos in the west end zone, gesturing vigorously with his hands as Fangio and Catavolos nodded intently.

By 3:10, all the players were on the field in full uniform. As is the custom, Coach Capers began striding from player to player as they did stretching exercises, pumping hands, slapping backs and offering brief nuggets of encouragement. Polian did the same.

At 3:20, Jerry and Mark Richardson met Rich Kotite near midfield and engaged in an animated conversation with the coach they almost hired but didn't. Kotite had since gone on to be named head coach of the Jets, but again, there appeared to be no hard feelings.

The marching band of the University of North Carolina began its pregame revelry at precisely 3:45.

The coin toss followed at 3:55.

A feeling of confidence permeated the air near the Carolina bench. This was it. This was the day they felt certain they would win their first real game.

The week of preparation for the game against the Jets began with Capers playing psychologist on Monday. His goal was to make the players feel good about themselves despite the 0–5 record and the late defensive collapse in the loss to the Bears. There was no question that the Jets, at 1–5, represented the best chance yet for Carolina to break into the victory column. Capers just wanted to be sure that the players realized this, and therefore recognized that now was not the time to doubt the system.

To get his point across, Capers displayed on an overhead projector in a Monday afternoon meeting the fact that the five teams who had beaten the Panthers to that point owned a combined record of 19–7. Beginning with the Jets, the next three teams they were to face had the combined record of 2–14.

When the players convened for the meeting at 12:45 P.M., the mood in the room was decidedly somber. As Capers began talking and jabbing at the facts illustrated on the overhead projector, the mood gradually transformed into one of optimism.

"Guys were feeling pretty down when we got here today, especially myself," said Brett Maxie, the veteran defensive back who took the Chicago defeat personally. "We've been so close [to winning], and that was the closest yet. . . . But Dom helped put it in perspective by telling us that he's impressed by the fact that we're not pointing fingers, and we're not jumping on each other.

"We're staying with it. He said we just need to keep practicing the way we have been and things are bound to get better. He said some things that I think we needed to hear."

Capers downplayed the effect of his speech and visual aids. But as with everything he does, it was no doubt carefully planned.

"There are different approaches you can take," Capers said. "But number one, I think our team has played hard. I would be far more upset if I thought we were playing with a lack of effort—but I certainly don't think that has been the case. One thing we as coaches look very hard for is that we're getting the type of effort that it takes to win.

"We're making some mistakes and they've been costly at times. But that's part of growing as a team."

It was not Capers' style to go into team meetings and start ripping his players. He felt that would be counterproductive. According to Maxie and others, the coach was more likely to calmly explain why things happened and what must be done to correct errors, rather than railing at the players who made them. He also was fond of finding one or two motivational themes for a week, and this week's theme was that the Jets were a very beatable opponent. Play like they did against the Bears, for example, and the Panthers were sure to overcome the woeful Jets.

"You could go into a meeting and yell and scream, but that accomplishes nothing," Capers said. "They players want to know the how-to. They want to know what they have to do to win.

"The first thing you can't do is lose confidence in yourself or lose confidence in your teammates or lose confidence in what you're doing. We've got to circle the wagons and pull closer together and continue to go out and work the same way as if we were 5–0. That's the only way you get better in this league."

Another angle Capers tried to work with his players was to point out that even established teams often endure extended losing streaks. He used the 1994 New York

Giants and New England Patriots as examples of good teams gone bad that eventually turned their seasons around.

He did not use the Jets as one of these examples, seeing as they had managed only two winning seasons in the last 10 and none since 1988. He tapped at the facts displayed on the overhead projector again.

"We've played five good opponents," Capers told his players. "They've all got winning records. Now we've got a chance to do something against some teams that maybe aren't quite as good. We can beat these teams."

While the Panthers remained winless, there was joy down in Jacksonville, where the Jaguars were still celebrating their second consecutive win, 20–16 over Pittsburgh in Jacksonville. Capers wouldn't say so publicly, but this one stung him. It bothered him doubly because the other expansion team not only was succeeding at a pace far superior to his own, but also because the Jaguars had taken their latest leap ahead at the expense of the Steelers, the team for which Capers had served as defensive coordinator the previous three seasons.

When asked about it by reporters, Capers tried to show respect. He said the right things.

"Hey, it's obviously a big win for Jacksonville over a divisional opponent," Capers said. "Jacksonville obviously did a good job. They beat the team that had the home-field advantage in the AFC in last year's playoffs. That's a tremendous win for them, a tremendous win."

Capers then insisted that it didn't bother him that the Jaguars had already won twice.

"That really doesn't concern me," he said. "We aren't playing Jacksonville. They aren't in our division. It's a totally different set of circumstances. We've got enough to concern ourselves with here with our team."

Tuesday marked the trade deadline, and it passed quietly for the Panthers. Polian, the man responsible for making trades for the team, said that this should not have surprised anyone. Despite their record, Polian remained convinced that Capers had the Panthers pointed down the right path. It was only a matter of time until that was going to start translating into victories on the field. Furthermore, it was no easy matter to negotiate trades that made sense in today's NFL marketplace.

"It's getting harder and harder to make trades in this league," Polian said. "The free-agency era has changed all that. As an example, why would you give up anything for a guy entering the last year of his contract? That's number one.

"Number two, if you're a growing team, you want to husband your picks. Why would you want to give picks up that in all likelihood are going to be relatively high for a player that might not help you in the long run?

"So there are all those considerations, plus there's a scarcity of players. Expansion has dried up the talent pool, as I'm sure you've heard others say around the league."

Polian made the last statement with a bemused grin. He knew it to be true. He also knew that many of the established franchises—in fact, practically all of them—were upset by the fact that the Panthers and Jaguars had been permitted so many advantages in stocking their original rosters. Extra picks in the college draft; essentially as many picks as they wanted in the expansion allocation draft, although the talent available there was marginal at best, either high-risk and expensive or cheap and unproven; and the biggie—money to spend freely in the free-agent market—Polian and Mike McCormack had used them all to stock a roster that was, at least defensively, the envy of many a team.

But on this day, as the trade deadline passed, the Panthers found no ways to improve their winless team partly because of the rules that helped them become more competitive than past expansion teams in the first place. Despite their record, no one considered the Panthers to be a typical expansion team because of the way they had constructed their roster around high-priced, veteran free agents and some high, quality draft picks. Kotite, the man who would have coached them, said he had as much respect for the Panthers as any opponent the Jets would face.

"All 30 teams in the NFL are capable of winning," Kotite said. "Jacksonville and Carolina are no exceptions. They aren't expansion teams in the true sense of the word."

In the Panthers' case, then, they appeared to be an expansion team only in record. Despite being 0–5, Polian said he was encouraged by much of what he had seen on the field. He pointed out that, except for a total of three and a half quarters against Buffalo and St. Louis, the Panthers had been able to remain highly competitive for most of their five games. For this achievement, he paid tribute to the man he ultimately decided to hire over Kotite, and to the rest of the staff operating under Coach Capers.

"I felt pretty early in training camp that we would be competitive basically two-thirds of the time," Polian said. "I mean, there are some games where things just go wrong for you like the Ram game. You're going to have games like that. But we're so well-coached that they're getting as much as there is to get out of what's here."

What impressed Polian so much was the way Capers and his staff coached individual players on every single play of every practice. They stressed fundamentals. They repeatedly decried the sins of mental errors. They stressed consistency in carrying out assignments and cooperation with teammates. They paid attention to all the little details.

Then they saw to it that every single play of every practice was videotaped and later the same day picked apart by position coaches, offensive and defensive coordinators and, finally, Capers himself. As Capers liked to say, "You can't hide on our practice field. If we miss something during the actual practice that needs [to be] addressed and corrected, one of the coaches is going to catch it during the film work and bring it to [our] attention."

"As long as our guys keep believing what the coaches tell them and keep doing what the coaches tell them and keep staying with the program," said Polian, "they'll continue to improve and they'll be competitive every week. And we'll win a few."

Polian stopped short of predicting the first win would come against Kotite's Jets. When someone mentioned the fact that Carolina's next three opponents had a combined record of 2–14, Polian positively bristled.

"Every week is critical in the National Football League," Polian said. "You can't think any more than from week to week. You have to concentrate on the opponent ahead and don't worry about what lies beyond that.

"If you look beyond this week's opponent, you're going to get an anvil dropped on your head. It's a guarantee."

Kotite found himself in an unusual position as kickoff approached. Some observers of the NFL said that Kotite lost twice when Capers beat him out for the Carolina job. Kotite not only didn't get to coach the Panthers, the cynics said, but he also ended up having to coach the Jets. And now he found himself in the unenviable position of possibly becoming the first coaching victim of the expansion team he ultimately was deemed unworthy of coaching.

Kotite didn't look at his situation that way. He was, after all, happy to be a head coach in the league at all after being fired the day after Christmas by Philadelphia owner Jeffrey Lurie. He felt fortunate in that respect. He also held Jerry Richardson, Bill Polian and Mike McCormack—the triumvirate brain trust that powered the Panthers' organization—in the highest regard, despite their joint decision to go in another direction after he interviewed for the team's head-coaching position just three days following his firing in Philly.

"They're great people . . . Bill Polian and Mike and Mr. Richardson. But they got the man they wanted. I think he's done a very solid job," Kotite said.

"They're great people with solid football backgrounds. I think they're approaching things the right way from the expansion standpoint. I think they're getting better each week. It's kind of a growing thing for them."

The Jets seemed to be experiencing growing pains as well, even though they had been in business since 1960. Their only win on the season came at the expense of Jacksonville, the other expansion team. They had lost two of their other games by the embarrassing scores of 52–14 and 47–10. Kotite was relying on a number of young players, and, like the Panthers, they were making mistakes. The Panthers ranked last in the NFC in takeaway-giveaway ratio at minus 7; the Jets were next-to-last in the AFC, also at minus 7.

The difference for Kotite was that he didn't have the same latitude as Capers when it came to enduring growing pains. In fact, Jets owner Leon Hess didn't want to hear anything about growing pains. He already had experienced too much of the pain accompanied by chronic losing.

Hess had been part-owner of the team since 1963, so he had witnessed the glory years of Joe Namath at quarterback. But since becoming the sole owner of the team in 1984 at age 69, Hess had witnessed mostly mediocrity—three winning seasons in 11, with the last coming at 8–7–1 under Coach Joe Walton in 1988. You could see his patience with head coaches was lessening as Hess aged, as Walton lasted seven years; his successor, Bruce Coslet, four years; and the latest coach, Pete Carroll, only one. Kotite was Hess' fourth coach since becoming sole owner of the Jets, and Hess laid down the parameters of what was expected at a news conference the day Kotite's hiring was announced.

"I'm 80 years old," Hess said. "I want results now."

The game itself against the Jets began brilliantly for the Panthers, with Bubba McDowell blocking Brian Hansen's first punt of the game to give the Panthers the ball at the New York seven-yard line on their very first possession. From there, though, the Panthers' fortunes fizzled quickly. Kerry Collins threw two incompletions, Derrick Moore ran for two yards, and the Panthers had to settle for a 23-yard John Kasay field goal.

The remainder of the first half proceeded about as badly as it could have for the Panthers. During back-to-back possessions in the second quarter, Collins, still the novice rookie quarterback, was sacked in his own end zone for a safety and threw a pass that was intercepted by Vance Joseph of the Jets and returned to the Carolina 20-yard line. Bubby Brister, subbing for the injured Boomer Esiason at quarterback for New York, could not get the Jets in the end zone from there—in fact, they went backward, losing eight yards in three plays—but a 50-yard field goal ensued by Nick Lowery for a 5–3 Jets lead.

Earlier, after the safety, the score had been stuck on 3–2. "It looks like both teams are getting pretty good pitching today," someone quipped in the press box. "This is the worst game I've ever seen," complained another.

But after a first half of bungling that included another interception thrown by Collins that was returned 13 yards by linebacker Mo Lewis for a touchdown and a 12–6 New York lead with 3:17 left before intermission, the game turned on a bizarre play near the end of the half.

Kotite would be second-guessed for permitting the play call. Sam Mills, the veteran linebacker whom Capers loved to call "the quarterback of our defense," would make the Jets pay for it.

It was a shovel pass. Yes, a shovel pass. Or a shuffle pass. Or an utterly stupid pass. Whatever you want to call it, Brister attempted to throw it on second-and-10 from the New York 40-yard line with 22 seconds left in the half. And he tossed it right to Mills, who had broken through the line undetected on a blitz.

Once Mills got his paws on it, the fun really started. At 36 years of age, Mills wasn't quite Leon Hess; but in the relative terms of being a pro football player, he was no Kerry Collins or Tyrone Poole, either. Mills nonetheless grasped the football and began lumbering toward the end zone, with fellow linebacker Darion Conner serving as his lead blocker. Mills had to cut back twice to avoid tacklers, but he eventually rumbled 36 yards for a touchdown, the third of his 10-year NFL career.

"I was really surprised when the ball came at me," Mills said. "The first thing I thought was to catch it and then start moving. Thank God I was able to hold onto the ball and head down the field.

"I give a lot of credit to Darion Conner on that play, too. He did a good job of blocking for me because there was a guy who could have caught me. But with Darion out there, I was able to zigzag a little bit and make it to the end zone."

His zigs and zags took quite some time to develop, cynical teammates later noted.

"I was trying to catch up to him," said safety Bubba McDowell, "and he was kind of bobbing and weaving in front of me. It was a very good run. I was very surprised."

Added defensive lineman Gerald Williams: "I've never seen a 35-year-old make a run like that. Or is he 36? I think I'm being too kind.

"I saw what was in front of him and what was behind him, though, and I thought he could make it. He had Darion in front blocking for him, and all he had chasing him were offensive linemen. I didn't think he would let them catch him, even at his age."

Even Capers was amused, although he cautioned not to be too critical on the old guy.

"Sam doesn't get to practice his open-field running too much," Capers said. "I told him he looked like he was 25 again out there on that run."

Brister was stunned, as were the rest of the Jets. They never fully recovered.

"I was supposed to go to the left like a rollout and turn to flick it underneath," Brister said. "I saw him coming, but I thought someone was going to block him. . . . I just went ahead and flicked it, and it went right to him. I've never seen anything like that before."

Mills' touchdown and Kasay's subsequent extra-point kick gave the Panthers a 13–12 lead and a whole new outlook on their season as they headed into the locker room for halftime. The Panthers were euphoric in the locker room, one player after another slapping Mills on the back or exchanging five with him as he sat, grinning, at his locker. The warm feeling carried over to the second half, while the Jets, who slinked away to the visitors locker room at halftime wondering how in the heck this could be happening to them, never quite recovered.

Collins took the team 56 yards in seven plays for a touchdown on their second possession of the third quarter, increasing the lead to 20–12. Kasay later added two more field goals, the defense held this time when it had to, and the Panthers had the first regular-season victory in their brief history.

As the game came to its inevitable conclusion, Lamar Lathon and Pat Terrell grabbed a bucket of water and conspired to dump it on the head of their coach.

"I wanted to be the first," Lathon said. "It's a good thing he wasn't wearing a toupee. It would have washed to midfield."

For Mills, the victory was especially sweet. For Capers, too. The two men sometimes seemed to be one and the same, perhaps because their histories on the professional level were so intertwined, almost codependent to a degree on one another's.

Capers' fondest memory of Mills was forged in 1986, when the New Orleans Saints were about to embark on the Jim Mora coaching era. It was a time of uncertainty for the NFL franchise, and skeptics abounded. Mora had spent the previous two seasons as head coach of the Philadelphia/Baltimore Stars in the USFL, where Capers served as his defensive secondary coach and Mills his unlikely defensive star.

Sure, the Stars won back-to-back championships, but exactly what did that prove? Wasn't the league disbanded after their 1985 run to the title?

The late Jim Finks, then general manager of the Saints and a future Hall of Fame inductee, thought enough of Mora's accomplishments to not only hire him but also

Mora's entire USFL coaching staff, which included a young Dom Capers, then 34. One of the players both Mora and Capers admired and trusted most was an even younger Sam Mills, an undersized but tenacious 25-year-old linebacker who stood but five-nine and weighed 217 pounds. Mora and Capers insisted that they be permitted to bring Mills along with them for a tryout with the Saints as well.

"I had been with Sam for two years, so I knew all about Sam," Capers said. "But when we first went to New Orleans, it was a whole USFL staff coming into an NFL situation. So I think there were some questions about bringing the whole staff and not hiring guys with NFL experience.

"The first day Sam walked on the practice field, we really wondered, too, how he would stack up under NFL competition. He walked out on the field with [linebacker] Vaughan Johnson, who is 250 pounds and looks like a stud. And here's Sam, this short guy, walking alongside him.

"I know exactly what everyone thought. They thought, 'Well, this is a favor because of the USFL staff. They had Sam there, so they're just bringing him in as a favor.'"

It didn't take Mills long to change that opinion.

"I'll never forget the first time that we had contact," said Capers, smiling. "Sam did just like he always does. The guard fired out, and Sam would stick his pad out underneath him. Anytime you'd hear a big hit out there, you'd look around and number 51 would be there.

"The offensive linemen hated to go against Sam in any of the drill work, because Sam only knew one speed. So it took him probably about three days to gain everyone's respect."

Capers considered Mills the rudder that guided and steadied the 3-4 Carolina defense from his position at left inside linebacker. Mills made all the defensive calls and kept the other defenders focused on where they needed to be and what they were supposed to do on each snap of the ball.

The victory over the Jets would not have been possible without Mills' interception, and everyone knew it. Reporters crowded around his locker afterward.

Jerry Richardson arrived and sought Mills out, parting the sea of reporters. Later the euphoric owner surprised everyone, especially the players, who looked at each other with arched eyebrows when their esteemed owner let out a loud Panther "Grrrrrrrowwwl!" in the middle of the locker room.

Curtis Whitley, who had become a father just two days earlier when his wife, Tracy, bore daughter Hannah Jane, passed out large cigars and then sat smoking one in the corner of the room. To hell with the stadium's no-smoking policy.

"Is that a victory cigar or a cigar to celebrate the birth of your daughter?" a reporter asked.

"Both," Whitley answered, grinning widely.

To Whitley's left, a couple of other offensive linemen were talking about statements made earlier in the week by Johnny Mitchell, the Jets' tight end who had guaranteed victory in a New York newspaper. Capers had gotten wind of the prediction, made copies of the article and passed them out to the players.

"We'll win. Write it down," Mitchell had mistakenly informed a New York reporter, who simply did as he was told.

"Johnny Mitchell? Who's he?" Whitley asked in a mocking voice. "Did he play today? I don't recall seeing him catch any passes, do you?"

Actually, Mitchell caught one for seven yards. But that was it. And the Jets didn't win.

"All we wanted on defense was for him to catch one pass across the middle and run into Highway 54," McDowell added. "He would have been road kill."

On Highway 54?

"Oh, yeah, that's our nickname for Carlton Bailey [who wears number 54]," McDowell said. "He really wanted a shot at Mitchell. Frankly, I would have liked to have seen it myself."

Mark Rodenhauser, the Panthers' long-snapper, was asked about Mitchell's statement. He said that, yes, Coach Capers had made the team aware of it, and that, yes, he, Mark Rodenhauser, had found an appropriate place for the article.

"We hung it over one of the urinals in there," he said, pointing to the bathroom.

Richardson was so pumped up after the victory that he seemed determined to shake every hand in the place. He even tapped Tim McKyer on the back as McKyer stood at one of those urinals, relieving himself. The surprised cornerback turned, shrugged and stuck out a hand, which Richardson grasped and shook vigorously before quickly moving on.

"I think we all feel pretty terrific here today," Richardson admitted.

"This is a special day for us," Capers said. "It feels awful good to get this first win and see the guys rewarded for their efforts."

"We finally grabbed the chicken by the jugular," Derrick Moore added, almost shouting.

It was a joyous locker room. As the hero of the day stood at his locker describing for the umpteenth time his interception and return for a touchdown, the 17-year-old son of Sam Mills, Sam III, stood dutifully nearby, shaking his head.

"I didn't know Dad could run that fast," he said.

Final Score

26 Carolina   **15** New York

Game 7:
New Orleans at Panthers

As the Panthers trudged to their Clemson Memorial Stadium locker room at the end of the half of their game against the New Orleans Saints, the score tied 3–3, some of them were feeling pretty good about the way they had held their own against their vastly more experienced opponent.

The feeling did not last very much longer.

Coach Dom Capers was not pleased. The Saints had held the ball for more than 18 minutes, while the Panthers had controlled it for less than 12. This enabled the Saints to run 10 more offensive plays and outgain the Panthers 141 yards to 50. Another half like that, and surely the Saints would emerge easy victors.

"You've got to play better in the second half," Capers told his players in the locker room. "If we don't turn the ball over and come up with a few big plays, we'll win this game. But another half like that won't be good enough. They'll bury us."

He challenged his defensive players in particular to turn the balance of the game in the Panthers' favor.

"Make some big plays out there," Capers said. "Create some turnovers. Make something happen."

Four minutes into the third quarter, safety Brett Maxie obliged. He intercepted quarterback Jim Everett of the Saints and gave the Panthers the ball at the New Orleans 49-yard line.

But the Panthers' offense sputtered and did not take advantage of the ensuing possession, mainly because Kerry Collins fumbled the snap and took a five-yard loss on second down.

Maxie was not fazed. When the Saints took the field again and Everett faded back to pass on first-and-10 from his own 20-yard line, Maxie read the play perfectly and so did linebacker Sam Mills, two players who, ironically, had spent most of their lengthy and distinguished careers in Saints uniforms. Mills cut in front of tight end Wesley Walls to deflect the ball, which then bounced off Mills' back before landing in Maxie's hands. He returned it eight yards to the New Orleans 23.

As Maxie trotted triumphantly to the sideline, a smile lit up his face underneath the silver-blue-and-black Panthers helmet. This was sweet, he thought. He had answered Capers' challenge. But this was especially sweet coming against the team that basically told him his career was over two years earlier.

For the first time all season, the Panthers' players looked forward to talking with the media on Monday, after their match-up with the Jets. The locker room was closed but a few players, upon request, dropped by the press room at Winthrop Coliseum to talk with reporters. They finally had a victory to chat about. For once, they didn't have to talk about how close they had come or how disappointed they were or how frustrating it was all becoming.

The Jets, back in New York, were feeling no such joy or relief. The heat was on. The New York newspaper headline writers were having some fun with this one. The *New York Post* screamed, "THE WORST: Lowly Panthers get first win vs. awful Jets." The *New York Daily News* proclaimed, "Jets hit rock bottom." And in *Newsday:* "J-E-S-T-S . . . This is no joke: Jets are laughing stock of NFL after becoming Panthers' first victim."

So they had only beaten the Jets, an admittedly lousy football team. The Panthers didn't care. They were in the victory column. The locker room was loose and carefree all week as a result.

Bubba McDowell, who had lost his starting job less than three weeks earlier to Pat Terrell and admitted he wasn't happy about it, sure seemed happy now. His blocked punt early in the game against the Jets set up the Panthers' first field goal. He claimed this made him the first recipient of a nice little pile of cash in a little-known incentives program established by Sam Mills. The program was established to reward special-teams players by asking each of the 22 starters to pay a special-teamer $100 if he blocks a kick. Special-teams coach Brad Seely also was required to kick in $100, according to McDowell.

"That means I get $2,300—if everyone pays up," McDowell said.

He went on to complain that the starters were being a little slow in coming up with the cash owed. Only Derrick Graham had forked over his $100 as of late Monday afternoon.

McDowell was furious when Capers benched him during the bye week because, according to Capers, McDowell's left knee was limiting his mobility on the field. McDowell shortly thereafter became the first Panther player to publicly voice criticism of the coaching staff.

McDowell claimed Capers did not directly inform him of the lineup change, in which Terrell moved in as the starter at free safety and Maxie, who had been starting there, moved over to start at strong safety in McDowell's place. Capers denied this, saying he did inform McDowell—but whoever was correct, there obviously had been some miscommunication somewhere.

"Just be truthful about it and tell me what's going on," McDowell complained at the time. "That's all I ask. Don't use my knee as an excuse for sitting me down. I feel fine."

By the Jets game, McDowell was keeping himself satisfied by playing in nickel and dime coverages in the secondary and by busting his tail on special teams—and earning extra money by doing it.

McDowell still said what was on his mind. He usually was brutally honest, and in his opinion, the win over the Jets came at just the right time to prevent the Panthers from possibly become a divisive, self-destructive group. While other players and the coaches routinely talked about a team that showed heroic resolve in pulling together during the adversity of the 0–5 start, McDowell described a team that appeared to have been moving closer to splintering apart.

"It was hard, very hard," said McDowell, signed as a free agent two days after the previous April's college draft. "It was like we started separating from each other. Guys started arguing among one another.

"The defense [was] blaming the offense for not getting the job done. There were a lot of times when we were in position to score, inside the 20 in the red zone, but they could never get the ball in there. Guys were like, 'Come on, man. If you're down there, you've got to get the ball in the end zone.' I mean, there were times when we were down there and didn't get it in, and the defense had to go right back out there. Or they would turn the ball over, and we would have to get right back out there on the field again."

This was precisely one of the sins Capers would not tolerate. He constantly preached the offense didn't need to worry about what was going on with the defense, and vice versa. All they needed to do was cheer each other on.

But it rarely is that simple in the NFL. As losses pile up, the tendency for individual players or units to tear each other down and shift blame is often all too tempting.

McDowell compared the Panthers' situation to the 1993 season he spent in Houston, when the Oilers lost four of their first five games before regrouping. The Oilers then ripped off 11 wins in a row to finish 12–4, winning the AFC Central Division.

"It was like the offense and the defense were two separate units," McDowell said. "The offense was doing their thing, and the defense was doing their thing."

McDowell wasn't suggesting the Panthers were good enough to reel off 11 wins in a row. But he did think the win over the Jets served as a bonding agent in the locker room, which would make several more victories possible when otherwise the season might have gone the other way.

"It's a lot happier atmosphere around here this week," he said. "Guys are joking around with each other. It's always more fun when you're winning."

Well, they had one win. Whether that classified as "winning" was debatable. Regardless, Capers said he was never worried about his players starting to point fingers at each other—even during the season-opening five-game losing streak.

"Winners win, and losers make excuses," Capers said. "Show me an excuse-maker and a finger-pointer, and I'll show you a loser. I didn't think we had a group of losers on this team."

Neither did McDowell, despite observing some warning signs.

"There is a different attitude around here than when I was in Houston," said McDowell, who spent the first six seasons of his NFL career with the Oilers. "I don't know if it's because this is a new franchise and all that, or what. [But] there was not a lot of pressure on us to win games this year, because we are a new team.

"Realistically, I think we can get quite a few more now. If we go out and play like we did last week—actually, I should say better than we did last week because we made some errors the Jets just didn't take advantage of—who knows? If that had been a good team we were playing out there, one that executed real well, they probably would have seen those mistakes and taken advantage of them."

Running back Derrick Moore, in fact, said the Panthers' offense was inspired by the defense in the victory.

"All the guys were together," Moore said. "No one was separated. It encouraged me to run a little tougher. I would have hated to be a running back on the other football team. I was compelled by our defense to play even harder and tougher. Those guys were out there playing their butts off."

Capers was still beaming about the victory over the Jets when he met with the media on Monday. He was proudest of the fact that the Panthers held the Jets to 138 total yards—their lowest offensive output in the 1990s. Asked if he had ever coached a team that held an opponent to fewer total yards, Capers answered yes.

"With the Steelers last season, we held one team to 105 total yards," he said.

"Who was it?" a reporter inquired.

Capers paused, grinned and said, "The Eagles."

He didn't say anything else, but the irony was obvious. The head coach of the Eagles in 1994 was Rich Kotite, the head coach of the Jets in 1995 and the guy who had finished second to Capers in the Panthers' head-coaching selection process in between.

Capers said he was most pleased about the win over the Jets because it finally rewarded the players for all their hard work. He insisted he could see improvement week to week all along, which was in his own mind more important for the time being than how many victories were accumulating. But he also admitted, "Until you start winning games, there is always going to be a perception out there that you are a bad football team."

There wasn't much time for Capers to enjoy the victory over the Jets, however. Another game loomed, and it was one that held special implications for a number of Panthers, Capers included.

Though the Panthers had gained the nickname Buffalo South because of their connections with former Buffalo Bills, the nickname New Orleans North might have been more appropriate.

Capers began and nutured his pro coaching career under Jim Mora, head coach of the Saints. Mora hired him off the staff of Ohio State University to coach his defensive secondary with the old Philadelphia Stars in the USFL back in 1984, and then took Capers with him to New Orleans, where Capers served in the same capacity on Mora's staff for six seasons before moving on to Pittsburgh.

Capers had the utmost respect for Mora. Likewise, Mora felt the same way about not only Capers, but Panthers defensive coordinator Vic Fangio, Sam Mills and Brett Maxie (who he figured was washed up physically). He often referred to Mills as "the best player I ever coached." Other ex-Saints on the Panthers' roster included punter Tommy Barnhardt and linebacker Darion Conner.

"I worked with Jim for eight years," Capers said. "In this business, you really get to know people because you spend so much time together, first of all, and secondly because it's such an up-and-down business. You go from tremendous highs to tremendous lows. You see how people handle those situations, so you get to know what a person is really like.

"One of the qualities Jim has always had that I admire is during times when things are tough, that's when he's the strongest. He's an honest, straightforward person and a tremendous competitor. He has strong beliefs and the things he believes in, that's what he's going to stick with. He's mentally tough and he's very consistent."

Fangio was another fan of Jim Mora. When Fangio left the University of North Carolina coaching staff in 1984 to work as an unpaid assistant on Mora's staff with the USFL Stars, he expected to return to Chapel Hill and resume coaching the Tar Heels' defensive line a few months later.

Instead, the position with the Stars shaped the rest of his life as a football coach.

Mora hired him full-time and kept him around as a paid assistant for the next 11 years—until Capers lured him away to become defensive coordinator of the Panthers. Mora offered Fangio the same position in New Orleans, matching the Carolina offer much the same way the Saints had eventually matched the Panthers' free-agent offer for Sam Mills. But after some agonizing moments coming to a decision, Fangio left Mora's side and joined Capers.

"It wasn't easy," Fangio said. "Besides working well together, we're friends. He's been a big part of my coaching career. I wouldn't be here without him. He gave me a chance way back when I was 26 years old or whatever the heck it was. You don't ever forget about things like that, so it was hard to leave."

While Capers and Mora both downplayed the fact that it probably would seem a little strange to be going against one another, Fangio said he couldn't help contemplating it as kickoff moved closer.

"I was with those guys a long time, so it is a little unusual," Fangio said. "The day-to-day stuff isn't unusual because I'm just working to prepare for another game. But I'm sure when I see them on Sunday, when I look over on the opposite sideline, it'll be funny. I've been their biggest fan these first six games. I'd like to see them win every game—but not this game."

Mora needed to win this game. The Saints were entering it, in fact, with the same 1–5 record as the Panthers. The difference was that the Saints entered the season with an offense they advertised as their best in 10 years, with high hopes of competing with the San Francisco 49ers for the NFC West title. The Panthers were expected to be about 1–5 after six games.

"At least your buddy is keeping you out of last place," a reporter joked with Capers one day.

Capers did not smile at the joke, and the next day the reporter apologized for the remark.

"Hey, if the truth kills a man, let him die," was Capers' response.

The truth was, the Saints' defense missed Sam Mills. The inside linebacker was named NFC Defensive Player of the Week for his heroics against the Jets for the first time in his 10-year NFL career, and it was as if the award was being flaunted in the faces of the Saints, with whom he spent the first nine of those years. In addition to his momentum-swinging interception of the Bubby Brister shovel pass and its return for a touchdown, Mills also had six tackles, one sack and one quarterback pressure against the Jets.

"What Sam has been doing is probably amazing to people here in Charlotte," said Fangio, "but it's not amazing to me because I've been around him so long. He's a guy who has always had more ability than people gave him credit for. He's just a little short."

The Saints defense, long considered the foundation on which the team was built, was in the process of being reconstructed after the loss of Mills. They had a new defensive coordinator and had switched from the 3-4 alignment favored by the Panthers to the more mainstream 4-3 base alignment, amid much confusion. Fangio said Mills could have helped make the transition go more smoothly for them had he stayed in New Orleans instead of signing with the Panthers.

"I think losing Sam hurt them," Fangio said. "When you have a new system like that, you need leadership. You need guys who will take a quick grasp of the defense, and he would have done that. . . . Sam was a special part of that football team."

At one time, so was Maxie. But by late in the 1992 season, when he tore the anterior cruciate ligament in his left knee, and certainly by early in the 1993 campaign, when he tore the same ligament in his right knee only nine days after coming back from the first injury, the Saints suspected Brett Maxie was finished as a player.

No one could really blame Jim Mora for letting Maxie go when he elected not to re-sign the unrestricted free agent after the 1993 season, saying he felt the need to go with younger players who did not have a history of recent injuries. But Maxie blamed him and the entire Saints organization at first.

"I was a little bitter for awhile, I admit," Maxie said. "But that was when I learned first-hand that the NFL is just a big business. I had to let it go and get on with my life."

Maxie signed with Atlanta, but appeared in just four games in 1994. The whispers that he could no longer run well enough to play safety effectively began to grow louder. When the Panthers signed him, it wasn't like they had to beat off interest from 10 other teams. A few, including the defending AFC champion San Diego Chargers, had offered him a look, but nothing more. He signed a one-year deal that would pay him a base salary of $350,000 and took a modest $50,000 signing bonus without working out for any other teams, saying he liked what Capers, who had coached him six seasons in New Orleans, had to promise in the way of a real opportunity to play again.

As for his supposed lack of speed, Maxie was quick to laugh.

"That's something I'm still working on," Maxie said. "I've never had any speed."

By the time the Panthers were preparing to confront his longtime former employer, Maxie already had made three interceptions, using his suspect speed to return one theft 49 yards against Buffalo. He also ranked among the team leaders in tackles and had established himself as the leader on the field in the secondary, even though he said far less in the locker room than Tim McKyer, didn't hit quite as hard as Bubba McDowell or Pat Terrell, and wasn't as outwardly confident or nearly as young as the brash rookie, Tyrone Poole.

Maxie's natural position was free safety, where he could roam the field. But with the lineup switch designed to move the promising Terrell into a starting role, Maxie was asked to move over to the more structured position of strong safety and did so without a complaint. He even played some cornerback in a pinch, because of injuries to others or because the Panthers were in a rare dime situation all afternoon against teams like Atlanta, who ran the run-and-shoot offense.

Respect for Maxie among teammates was geniune and widespread. This was one reason he quickly had been named the club's player representative to the Players Association, a position he took seriously. He was intelligent and classy, and was able to project this image in a quiet, dignified manner in the locker room.

On the field, he seemed to be everywhere on some days. He was one of those guys who always seemed to be in the right place at precisely the right time.

"He's instinctive," Capers said. "Brett makes plays. He's 33, and I wish he were 23. I'd like to have a number of Brett Maxies on this team.

"I personally coached Brett for six years in New Orleans. There was never a time I didn't have a lot of confidence on Sunday that Brett was going to be ready to play. I never feared he was not going to know what to do. When it comes to communicating in the secondary, Brett gives you the same thing Sam Mills gives you in the linebacker corp."

Mills greatly admired Maxie's skills, and vice versa. The two were close friends.

"He's not the fastest safety in the world," Mills said. "But the fastest and strongest guy is not always the best guy.

"It's just like racquetball. You can be a great athlete, but go out there with a guy who is 70 years old and he'll kill you on the racquetball court because he knows where the ball is coming. Meanwhile, you're a quick guy and you're running all over the place, and he's standing there on the court just whacking away at the ball. Brett is like that."

Except he wasn't quite a senior citizen. Maxie did understand, however, that 33 is pretty old for any NFL player—especially so for one who was twice before declared finished and played a position where healthy legs were needed to cover a lot of ground in a hurry.

"I'm very appreciative of the interest the Panthers showed in me," Maxie said. "Because of my age and past history with injuries, no one else wanted to take a chance on me. You expect that in this era of the salary cap. But I always thought I could still play at this level. What it takes to be successful in this league is to play well every week—not play well one week and play like crap the next week. You want to maintain a nice equilibrium. For most of my career, I think I've been able to do that."

Kerry Collins geared up for the outing against the Saints by attending the second NBA game of his life. But he didn't get to watch much of the Charlotte Hornets–Denver Nuggets exhibition at Charlotte Coliseum because he was so busy signing autographs before, during and long after the game was over.

Apparently, fans had already forgiven his first somewhat forgettable performance, which came a week earlier against the Jets when he was guilty of throwing two interceptions deep in Carolina territory, including one that was returned for a touchdown. Three starts into his NFL career, Collins already appeared to be the most popular Panther in town with the fans, and he always tried to accommodate by signing as many autographs as humanly possible when out in public.

The first NBA game Collins attended was at Madison Square Garden a year earlier, when Michael Jordan, recently returned to basketball after a failed attempt to make it in baseball, scored 55 points against the New York Knicks.

"He hit his first four shots and I said, 'Uh-oh. Look out,' " Collins said.

Basketball was "a close second" to football as Collins' favorite sport, and he played it reasonably well in high school. He was a second-team all-state selection as a senior in Pennsylvania, although he vehemently denied playing center at six-foot-five and 230 pounds, as advertised in the Panthers' media guide.

"I was more of a 'three man,' a swing guy," Collins said. "I could post up inside and did it a lot because I was the tallest player on our team. But I could shoot threes, too."

Unfortunately for Collins, his basketball-playing days appeared to be behind him, a fact that "kind of bums me out," he said. It wasn't specifically forbidden in his contract with the Panthers, but he said he thought it was covered in a clause that prohibited him from doing anything that might cause physical harm.

At least he still had his hoops memories. He recalled the time he once guarded Billy Owens in high school, noting that Owens now plays in the NBA for the Miami Heat.

"I was a freshman. I was about 13," Collins said. "He was a junior. He was about 19. He scored about 28 points on me."

Collins played about as well against the Saints as he did against Owens in high school. He completed only 8 of 21 passes for 48 yards, meaning the offense had to rely on the defense to bail them out.

Thanks to all the ex-Saints and Bubba McDowell, they did. After Maxie came away with his second interception of the day, giving him a career-high five for the season before this seventh game of the season was through, Collins finally got the Panthers into the end zone to break the 3–3 tie. They scored on a two-yard run by Howard Griffith to take a 10–3 lead.

On the Saints' next possession, McDowell remarkably made it three consecutive Everett pass attempts picked off when he came up with his first interception of the season and returned it 33 yards to the New Orleans 19. Griffith capped the short drive that followed by catching a one-yard pass from Collins, giving Griffith, the former college touchdown machine, his first two TDs as a Panther in a span of just over three minutes.

It also gave the Panthers a 17–3 lead, which was more than they would need on an afternoon when the defense was smothering, especially after Capers' halftime encouragement.

As a senior at Illinois in 1990, Griffith scored eight touchdowns against Southern Illinois and broke the NCAA single-game record of 43 points set by Jim Brown of Syracuse in 1956. He scored 33 touchdowns during his career at Illinois to break the school record of 31 set by Red Grange, whom many considered the best running back in college history.

Prior to playing his final collegiate game in the Citrus Bowl in Tampa, Florida, Griffith had been surprised to learn that Grange, who lived about two hours away in a small Florida town, had asked to meet the young man who broke his record. Griffith drove over with Coach John Mackovic and the school's sports information director, where he became one of the last people to see Red Grange alive. Grange died a short time later.

"It's something I'll always cherish," Griffith said. "He would have been proud of me today. Anytime someone from Illinois does well, I know he's happy."

Grange also would have been proud of the economic manner in which Griffith scored his two touchdowns. While Derrick Moore was the workhorse in the backfield, carrying 21 times for 88 yards, he did not get to grace the end zone with his presence. Griffith, meanwhile, ran three times for three yards and caught one pass for one yard—and accounted for 12 of the Panthers' points in a 20–3 victory.

Someone reminded Moore it was sort of how Barry Sanders must have felt all those times he made long runs and fell just short of the end zone, only to then have Moore give him a breather and then score the touchdown. It happened often during Moore's three seasons as Sanders' backup and a short-yardage specialist in Detroit.

"Now I know how Barry feels," Moore joked.

The ex-Saints on the Panthers' roster seemed to be feeling the best of all in the home locker room after the game.

Mills and Maxie had been superb. But Tommy Barnhardt also had his best punting afternoon of the season, averaging 44.6 yards on 10 kicks; and Darion Conner, slowed the first five games by a sprained knee, came up with his first sack of the season.

"It's a turn of fate," Maxie said. "Every guy from the Saints did something today to help us win. It was real special. Any time you beat your old team, you're overjoyed. It was very sweet. . . . This year is like a rebirth year for me. This is something really special."

"It's strange playing your old team. Real strange," Mills added. "But without a doubt, it's a great feeling to beat them."

For many Panthers, meanwhile, this was not a special occasion as much as an expected outcome.

"There wasn't quite as much celebration in the locker room this week," Griffith said. "It was more like, 'Hey, we're supposed to win some games. We're just getting down to business here.' "

Owner Jerry Richardson showed up in the locker room wearing a gray suit, black sweater vest, black tie, white shirt and black shoes—the same exact outfit he had worn the previous week when the Panthers beat the Jets. He even had his hair slicked back like Pat Riley for the second week in a row, which somehow skewed his otherwise regal appearance and made him look more like an oversize door-to-door salesman.

"Yes, you've seen this all before," Richardson shouted to reporters. "Same sweater, same shoes, same belt—even the same mousse!"

Final Score

20 Carolina   **3** New Orleans

Game 8:
Panthers at New England

Surely two consecutive wins would go a long way toward convincing the rest of the NFL the Panthers deserved some hard-earned respect. They felt that way about themselves, anyway, and pretended not to care what anyone else thought.

When the Sunday morning editions of the Boston Globe hit the team hotel the day of their game against the New England Patriots in Foxboro, Massachusetts, the ruse was up. The Panthers did care what others thought about them, and they couldn't hide the fact when Patriots beat writer Ron Borges of the Globe predicted right there in black-and-white print a 56–7 victory for the home team.

Fifty-six to seven!

What would Borges' prediction have been if the Panthers weren't on a two-game winning streak?

Ed Stillwell, director of football security for the Panthers, grabbed a copy of the Globe and flashed it to everybody he could find. He was the one who brought it to Kerry Collins, who shook his head in disbelief.

"This just shows these people here have no respect at all for us. This really makes me mad," Collins said.

Stillwell also made certain Dom Capers received a copy, although there were plenty of people seeing to that.

"How could I not take notice of it?" Capers later said. "I must have had it brought to me by about 20 different people."

Outwardly, Capers feigned outrage and laughed off the ridiculous prediction. Inwardly, he was thrilled. This was just the type of hook he needed to get his players worked into just the right mental frenzy, not that he believed in all that fire-and-brimstone stuff, or so he would always tell the media.

"Come over here for a minute," Capers implored linebackers Lamar Lathon and Darion Conner when they arrived at the team breakfast.

Capers had the Boston Globe in his hand, turned and folded to page 75. He held it up to Lathon and Conner and pointed to the prediction.

"If that doesn't get you guys fired up," said Capers, "nothing will."

The Panthers' franchise was still a babe in the NFL woods, but at least it was starting to talk and walk like an adult. Two victories in a row and a defense that hadn't allowed a touchdown in eight quarters had a way of bringing on maturity at an accelerated pace.

But both victories came at home, or at least what passed for a home in this inaugural season. Now came the next test: taking the winning show on the road. Beginning with the game against the Patriots, the next three games for the Panthers would be played on enemy turf.

After the Patriots, the Panthers were slated to play at San Francisco and at St. Louis—two teams with a combined record of 10–4—before returning home to Clemson Memorial Stadium to face the Arizona Cardinals on November 19.

"This week is a brand-new challenge for us," Capers said on Monday. "I didn't have any illusions of coming in here and having everything fall right into place where we'd be 6–0 or 7–0 right off the bat. To me, it was the challenge of starting from scratch and trying to build something where the team would come together that was appealing.

"I've seen some of those things happen, where we're maturing and coming together as a team. I felt I was seeing some of those things when we were 0–5. That's why I was probably not as discouraged as most people might think when we were 0–5 because, number one, I knew we were a better football team than we were showing, and number two, I knew we were playing a lot of rookies."

By now the Panthers' rookie starters included not only Collins at quarterback, but Blake Brockermeyer and Frank Garcia on the offensive line, and Tyrone Poole at cornerback. Defensive end Shawn King was another rookie who was beginning to see increased action, emerging as one of the team's best pass rushers in their nickel packages. And Chad Cota, a backup defensive back, was proving to be one of the team's top special-teams coverage men. Earlier, Andrew Peterson had started on the offensive line, making it a total of seven rookies who saw significant time during the Panthers' first seven games.

"To me," continued Capers, "it's just common sense. When you're playing the young guys, you're only going to get better. But you're going to experience some growing pains, especially when you're playing a rookie quarterback."

The Panthers won against the Saints despite Collins, not because of him. But at least the offense did not turn the ball over for the first time all season, and for that Capers credited Collins for not making any foolish decisions. On days when the completions are rare and each yard gained is difficult, many quarterbacks have a tendency to start forcing things—much like Jim Kelly admitted he did against the Panthers in their earlier meeting. Collins resisted that urge against the Saints, which was another sign of his growing maturity, according to his head coach.

The coaching staff was helping Collins along, of course, by keeping the game plans simple. As he gained experience, they would add plays and variations of plays already installed bit by bit, but for now the game plans were relatively simplistic in terms of what was expected of the rookie quarterback. For this, Capers already was catching some mild criticism for being "too conservative," a criticism he found ludicrous.

"When you look at us offensively, you're looking at a lot of young, inexperienced players," Capers said. "We could go out there with an expansive game plan, but the more we expand that game plan, the more errors you're probably going to see, the more turnovers you're probably going to see. You're probably going to see more things come into play that decrease your chance of winning the football game.

"The ideal situation would be to be like the Dallas Cowboys or somebody like that, where you've got a veteran quarterback, a veteran running back and a veteran offensive line—where you're running up about 400 yards of offense per game and putting it in the end zone for about 30 points a game. That's ideal. Hopefully, we'll reach that at some point in time."

But the Panthers would try to reach that point gradually, not all at once. The offensive game plan would be expanded slowly, only as the coaching staff felt the younger players, not only Collins, but all the others, could handle it. In the meantime, the Panthers would continue to rely heavily on a veteran-laden defense and a special-teams unit that, except for a few minor breakdowns, had been consistently solid.

"I think when you're starting out, defense and special teams are extremely important," Capers said. "If you don't give up many points and you play solid on special teams, you give yourself a chance to be in most games."

Now all they had to do was prove they not only could stay in a game on the road, but win one.

———————

There wasn't much doubt about which was, on a daily basis, the most interesting player to visit in the Panthers' locker room at Winthrop Coliseum. There was always something going on around Willie Green's locker stall.

One day, Green talked about Dennis Rodman, the enigmatic NBA player.

"I saw how he said he wanted to play the last game of his career butt naked," Green said, laughing. "Butt naked. Can you believe that? I would love to see that."

Then, after a pause, he shook his head and said, "No, I guess I wouldn't want to see that.

"But maybe I should go out that way, too. Could you see me running out of the tunnel in some place like Soldier Field with no clothes on in the dead of December? I tell you what: You wouldn't need to worry about getting tackled. Guys would be running from you."

Green talked about how he recently had looked into buying Larry Johnson's old house on Lake Wylie. Johnson, the star forward of the Hornets, was building a newer, bigger place right down the road.

"It's a nice place, but I ain't paying no $550,000. That's outrageous," Green said.

Green was always joking with teammates or reporters who happened to stop by his stall. But he had a serious side, too. What he was most serious about was being a visible and positive role model for kids, and also giving underpriviledged children the opportunity to do some things they otherwise would never have a chance to do, like attend a pro football game.

It was in that spirit that he had agreed to donate tickets for 22 schoolchildren to attend each of the Panthers' remaining four home games. Green planned to either charter a bus to transport the kids to the games at Clemson, or arrange for them to ride the Panther Prowler, the special Amtrak train that ran from Charlotte to Clemson on game days. But he emphasized that the children had to first earn their way there by entering an essay contest, which was going to be run by Mecklenburg County's 11 recreation centers.

The first topic: "How can I make a difference?" Children in the fourth through eighth grades were eligible to write a 250-word essay on a weekly topic to enter the contest.

Said Green: "The chances for these kids to make it in professional sports are slim to none, but that's what many of them dream about anyway. I want them to see and understand they have to be able to read and write and think in the real world. That's what is going to get them through life."

Green blamed the media somewhat for giving professional athletes a bad name, and lectured that more should be written about the many positive things pro athletes try to do for their communities.

"There are a lot of players here in Charlotte and elsewhere who are doing things, but it's not publicized much," Green said. "You only hear about the bad things players are doing. You get tired reading and hearing about Mr. NFL drinking and driving or beatin' his wife or something like that. . . . If you're going to recognize the bad, recognize the good, too."

Green felt certain his gesture of bringing those 22 kids to Clemson would have a long-lasting positive effect on the children. He compared it to when he was growing up in Athens, Georgia, and his mother, Corene, got tickets for him and some of his friends to go to a Braves game at Atlanta Fulton County Stadium through the local recreation department where she worked. He still remembers fondly the day he got Hank Aaron's autograph.

"This is something those kids will always remember," he said. "I can vividly remember the thrill of going to that Braves game, and the Braves were losing then. But that field was the greenest field I had ever seen. I remember that stadium that day better than any stadium I've played in since.

"It's the same thing with these kids. They're going to remember this day and this stadium for the rest of their lives, until the day they die."

Green said he planned to continue working with kids even after he retired from professional football. In addition to setting up the essay program, he tried to speak once a week to one group or another ("they don't have to be kids") about being a positive role model and trying to improve the society in which everyone has to live. He had been doing this kind of stuff for quite some time, having helped found a Big Brothers/Big Sisters program while in college at the University of Mississippi and being active with the Police Athletic League and the D.A.R.E and Just Say No drug programs while playing professionally in Tampa Bay and Detroit.

So Green does have his serious side. And he saves it for discussions about things that matter to him—and should matter to everyone else as well, according to Green. He calls it a lifetime commitment.

"Football will end for me," he said. "If God blesses me with a couple of more years, I'll be happy. But when my career is over with, kids will still look up to me as a professional athlete or at least someone who was a professional athlete.

"You can make a difference for some kids. You can make a hell of a difference. . . . The problem with society today is we don't get involved with kids the way we should.

I mean as parents, as people, as anything. Little kids are our future. But no one is putting emphasis on it. No one is giving them direction.

"Why do you think kids go to gangs? Because gangs show they care about them and tell them they love them. They're not getting it anywhere else, so they join up. If you give your kids love and direction at home, they've got no reason to go to gangs. You've got more control over them as parents and role models than any gang would."

Green would know. He was an out-of-control student in junior high school. But when he entered Clarke Central High in Athens, three teachers and the school principal cornered him almost as soon as he walked in the door.

"Listen," they said, "we know you're a hell of a person because we know your mother. We all go to church together.

"We're gonna straighten you out. You're not gonna get anywhere being the class clown. Look at all the class clowns who were here before you, and look where they are. Straighten yourself out."

He did. Now he figured it was his duty to try to help some others do the same.

You couldn't tell Bill Parcells, coach of the Patriots, that the Panthers were an expansion team. He wasn't buying it.

Like many coaches and front-office people around the NFL, Parcells was beginning to wonder if the league hadn't been a little too generous in awarding competitive advantages to the new teams in Carolina and Jacksonville. It only took two wins apiece by the new clubs to bring about this mock outrage.

"I guess everyone is a little surprised at the success the two expansion teams are having so quickly," Parcells said. "But they have twice the resources to work with [compared to earlier expansion teams]. They had more draft picks than the other teams had, and they had the free-agent market to go to.

"I mean, you take a look at their defense and put their years of experience together, you've got one of the most experienced defenses in the league playing there. That is a veteran defense. There isn't any question about it. And it plays like a good, veteran defense. That's where the advantage is for these two new teams."

Parcells denied he was complaining about this, even though it sure seemed like he was.

"Hey, the league wanted it that way. I'm not complaining about it," he said. "The league wanted these teams to be more competitive, and they are. And that's good. That's good for football."

Parcells had his own problems. The 2–5 Patriots were struggling in general, even though they were coming off their best game of the season—a 27–14 win over Buffalo on the stage of Monday Night Football. Young quarterback Drew Bledsoe was struggling in particular, and both he and his coach were wary of a veteran Carolina defense.

"They present you with a lot of different looks," Bledsoe said. "They do a good job of putting pressure on the passer. It's hard for quarterbacks to set up good when they have to throw off their back foot, which they've made quarterbacks do, especially in the last two games. It hurts your accuracy.

"Then they do a very good job with their coverage. Every time you watch the films of them, there's nobody running around wide open in their secondary. So if you're going to complete a pass against this defense, you'd better be accurate with it."

There was one more thing that impressed Bledsoe about the Panthers.

"They just play hard on every play, and that's probably the one thing that separates this defense from other defenses we play," he said. "Everybody is going 110 percent on every play, so if you're going to beat them, you've got to be ready to play some physical football and give it your best effort on every play, too. You've got to be ready to get hit in the mouth and still be ready to come back and give it your best on the very next play."

These were the kinds of comments that quickly brought gratifying smiles to the faces of Dom Capers, Bill Polian and Mike McCormack.

Barry Foster was back in the news, albeit briefly, and that also brought a few smiles and chuckles from those who ran the Panthers' organization. On the Tuesday prior to the Panthers' game at New England, Foster signed a one-year contract with the Cincinnati Bengals worth $1 million, including a hefty $300,000 signing bonus.

Two days later, Foster marched into Coach Dave Shula's office in Cincinnati and quit. He even handed back the signing bonus check, telling both the Bengals and his agent, Jordan Woy, "his heart wasn't into it."

The news of Foster's abrupt and self-imposed retirement hit the Panthers' locker room shortly before noon, during an open session with the media. A couple of reporters brought with them copies of the Associated Press article detailing Foster's amazing saga. Players were unable to mask their shock.

Dwight Stone grabbed a copy of the AP story and read every word at his locker.

"This is stunning," he said when he was done. "I'm speechless."

Gerald Williams and Tim McKyer, who, like Stone, were Foster's teammates previously in Pittsburgh as well as with the Panthers, were surprised but hardly speechless.

"At least he returned the check," Williams said. "I respect him for being a man and saying his heart's not in it. Nothing that guy does surprises me anymore."

"I guess he just got tired of the rigors of football," McKyer added. "It can happen, man. This life can get to you."

Asked if he had spoken to Foster since the Panthers waived the running back, Williams seemed surprised by the question.

"Are you kidding? I never talked to him when he was here," Williams said. "He was pretty much alone all the time."

Indeed, Foster had once described himself as "the lone wolf" when asked who he hung out with on the Panthers.

Capers, meanwhile, just shook his head when asked about Foster one last time.

"Nothing in this business surprises me anymore," Capers said.

The *Boston Globe* prediction was considered an outrage by the entire team. It inspired frowns, grunts of disbelief and, finally, full-fledged anger.

Earlier, a reporter mentioned to Capers how Rod Smith, the former New England cornerback who was chosen number one by the Panthers in the expansion allocation draft as much for his affordability ($714,000 salary) as his potential, thought Parcells turned the Patriots' previous season around with an inspiring halftime speech made in the midst of a four-game losing streak. The Pats finished the season out by winning their next seven contests.

Capers listened to the story, a smile crossing his face. Then he insisted he didn't believe in such speeches.

"Whatever emotions you stir up with something like that is gone two minutes into the next half, and your preparation and execution has to kick in," Capers said. "I believe in preparation and execution, not speeches. If your players need a last-minute speech to get them jump-started before a game or a half, something is wrong anyway."

Yet he did not hesitate to use Borges' prediction to pump up his team. In fact, he mentioned it at breakfast, on the bus on the way to the game and even in the pregame speech. It was the very last thing, in fact, he mentioned to his players before they headed out of the locker room to the field.

"It was our last battle cry before we went out," Blake Brockermeyer said.

"It fired us up," Derrick Moore said. "I don't think you make those kinds of statements. That shows no respect at all for this football team. Yes, we are an expansion team. But we aren't your typical expansion team, and we've been playing well for the last few weeks.

"To make comments and write it in the paper that we're going to get beat 56–7, it's an insult. It's just downright disgusting. We're professionals just like they're professionals. But the only way to get respect in this league is to go out there and knock some heads around."

The Panthers proceeded to do just that, winning in overtime, 20–17, for their first road victory. Collins, who had berated himself during the week for his lousy performances against New Orleans and even the Jets, went from his worst pro outing to his best in one week. He completed 25 of 45 passes for 309 yards and two touchdowns.

With Collins throwing, receivers such as Green, Carrier and Eric Guliford taking turns making clutch catches and Moore running hard behind an offensive line that continued to show improvement despite—or perhaps because—aging veteran Mark Dennis had replaced the injured Derrick Graham at right tackle, the Panthers piled up a season-high 434 yards of total offense.

They led 17–3 at one point after Collins' touchdown throws of 24 yards to Guliford and 33 to Green in the third quarter.

The defense added three more quarters to its streak of not allowing a touchdown, bringing it to 11, and then had to hold on. It almost didn't. The Patriots eventually tied the score at 17 with 52 seconds left in regulation, but Collins then displayed the calmness and craftiness of a veteran, using completions of 16 yards to tight end Pete Metzelaars and 31 yards to a sliding Green to move into position for a 39-yard field-goal attempt by

John Kasay with eight seconds left. Green was alert enough to call timeout even as he was still sliding along the turf after his acrobatic catch.

Kasay's kick, however, hit the left upright and fell back toward the field, sending the game into overtime.

The Panthers won the toss and elected to receive, despite tinkering with the idea of taking the 20-mile-per-hour wind at their back. Collins moved them to the New England 37-yard line before stalling, and Tommy Barnhardt got off a great punt to pin the Patriots on their nine-yard line.

This time, the Carolina defense held magnificently on three consecutive plays. Pat O'Neill, New England's struggling punter, booted a line drive that traveled a mere 32 yards from his own end zone—with the wind at his back, no less. Guliford returned it to the Pats' 32. Four consecutive thrusts up the middle by Moore, and the ball rested on the 12.

Capers called on Kasay once again, and this time his kick was true from 29 yards out, giving the Panthers their first road victory, their third victory in a row, and ammunition with which to blast Ron Borges and the *Globe*.

"No one beats anyone 56–7 in this league," Sam Mills said. "I hope that was a misprint."

It wasn't. Borges admitted up in the press box that he didn't make the prediction in jest. He really thought the Patriots would manhandle the Panthers.

"Sometimes that's a facetious pick," he said. "But this time I honestly thought the style of defense the Panthers play would play right into the Patriots' style of offense. I figured Bledsoe would get a few guys behind those blitzes and hit some long ones."

Bledsoe completed 22 of 44 pass attempts for 228 yards, but did not connect for a touchdown.

"This was a get-down-and-dirty, come-off-the-ball, old Texas-style win," said the proud Texan, Brockermeyer.

No NFL expansion team had ever won more than three games in a season. No NFL expansion team had ever won more than two in a row. The Panthers now had three wins, all neatly in a row, with half their schedule left to play.

The win left them with a 3–5 record and had some of them pondering the impossible. Moore said it was time to start thinking about the playoffs.

"We're relishing this win," said Moore, who rushed for 119 yards on 28 carries and continued on pace to rush for well over 1,000 for the season. "It's the first time an expansion team has won three ball games in a row. We have the potential to win more games and have a shot for what some people think is not a reality, and that's the playoffs.

"We haven't talked about it much, but this football team is getting better. That's what we're so excited about. We're getting better every week.

"I'm reminded of the saying of the little kid in the [Disney movie] *Angels in the Outfield:* 'Hey, it could happen.' We're little kids dreaming, man. And you've got to be able to dream and think big. That's what we're doing."

The Panthers clamied that even when they started the season 0–5, they were convinced they could play with virtually anybody.

"In this league," said Brockermeyer, "you've got two or three great teams. But the rest of them, you can throw into a pile. Whoever is not making turnovers and is executing is going to win. That's just the way it is."

One of those great teams awaited the Panthers the following Sunday in San Francisco. Mills, ever the veteran, said that was all the Panthers should be thinking about.

When told Moore uttered 'the *p* word,' Mills smiled broadly and cautioned, "What he should have uttered was 'the *n* word'—for 'next week's opponent.' That's what we need to do: focus on next week. If we can continue to play better, there's no telling what might happen.

"We're very excited about what's happening, about what's going on right now. But we've just got to take it in stride. The playoffs would be great. That's not out of the picture, but that's not in focus right now. San Francisco is all that should be in focus for us right now."

Moore was asked if the win over New England finally meant some respect for the Panthers. He wasn't sure, pointing to the game Mills said he should be focused on.

"We're playing at San Francisco next week," he said. "The prediction there will probably be 72–0."

Final Score

20 Carolina   **17** New England

Game 9:
Panthers at San Francisco

When Kerry Collins led his teammates into San Francisco to play the defending Super Bowl champion 49ers, November 5, he figured to see at least one familiar face in what promised to be an intimidating situation.

"I know Kerry pretty well. We're pretty good friends," said quarterback and Super Bowl XXIX Most Valuable Player Steve Young.

"How's that? How did you two become friends?" a reporter inquired.

"Well, you know, he was there with [agent] Leigh Steinberg in the limo after the Super Bowl, when I threw up on both of them," Young said. "I kind of got a little drained and drank too much Gatorade and all that other stuff. Then I got in the limo afterward. Leigh was with Kerry, and I just turned and, well, Kerry can tell you the rest."

Collins did.

"Steve was kind of dehydrated from the game," Collins said. "Then he got in the limo with us and he was sitting backward, facing us. I think that, combined with the fact that he was dehydrated, gave him motion sickness. All of a sudden he turns and says, 'Man, I don't feel too good.'

"Then he grabbed a towel and started puking. I kind of turned and tried to move my feet so it wouldn't get all over my shoes."

The driver abuptly stopped the limousine just a short distance from the hotel where Young and the 49ers were staying. Young staggered out and kept right on throwing up.

"Actually," said Collins, "Steve couldn't ride anymore. He was violently ill. We were about 200 yards from the hotel, on the side of the road with all these people milling around, and Steve is there doubled over.

"All any of those people had to do was look over there to see the quarterback who just had the best performance in the history of the Super Bowl puking his lungs out."

Luckily, Collins's quick feet saved his shoes from devastation.

"It wasn't too bad. I didn't see any chunks or anything," he said.

Asked if he figured this was the beginning of a beautiful friendship, Young brought up a good point.

"How can you get any closer?" he asked.

Steinberg, the man who represented both men, surveyed the chaotic scene and finally turned to Collins.

"Welcome to the NFL, Kerry," he said.

Teams were losing to the Panthers. With amazing frequency.

Carolina was playing well defensively, moving steadily up the charts that monitored NFL defensive proficiency. Collins was inconsistent, but showing signs of brilliance at quarterback. Derrick Moore was running hard behind a remarkably stable offensive line.

They were forcing opposing players and coaches to respect them, even if the general public lagged behind. There is an old joke in professional athletics that fans tended to be about two years behind the times; using that barometer, the Panthers could expect their due respect by about 1997.

By then, Collins hoped to have the Panthers making some noise in the playoffs. If he continued to play like he did at New England, it was very possible.

"I went into that game with a new attitude," Collins said. "I was going to be relaxed about it. I was not going to put how the whole offense was going entirely on my shoulders."

Collins then went out and set career highs in completions, pass attempts and yardage. He threw for two touchdowns without an interception, although he did lose one fumble. On each of his touchdown passes, Collins had to make quick adjustments he might not have correctly made a week or two earlier.

On the first, he checked off on a New England blitz—calling an audible at the line that resulted in a 24-yard score to Eric Guliford. On the second, a 33-yard strike to Willie Green, Collins had to read a blitz adjustment that Green actually made in altering his route. On both occasions, Collins passed the Panthers out of a hole. They were facing third-and-10 on the pass to Guliford and a third-and-20 on the one to Green.

"Our offense really came of age," Capers said. "One of Kerry's strengths is that he's big and strong. He doesn't react to players flying around him in the pocket."

Derrick Moore said none of Collins' teammates were surprised the rookie bounced back so strongly from the previous week's horrendous performance.

"I think it's just ongoing skill development for Kerry," Moore said. "The guy went back to practice this week and said, 'All this rookie stuff is over.' He's got four or five ball games under his belt. He's a veteran now.

"Kerry went out and proved once again that he's worth what his position is on this football team. I'll be in my wheelchair and be an old man, and he'll still be here slinging that football around."

Moore admired the rookie's stability.

"It's unusual for a rookie to stand in there and throw it like he does," Moore said. "I mean, they're all around him back there, and he just stands in and throws. A lot of guys will start chucking it or running away. He doesn't. He makes good decisions in the pocket. I think that's rare for a rookie quarterback."

Moore was a rare find himself for assistant general manager Joe Mack, who was familiar with every rush the running back had made since being drafted by Atlanta. Moore stepped in the very day the Panthers released Barry Foster and immediately began providing the type of hard-driving, inside running that Capers felt was vital to the success of the offense.

No one knew much about Moore the day he was signed, which was only four days after San Francisco released him. Perhaps 49ers coach George Seifert knew less than he should.

Though he had carried the football in only seven of the Panthers' eight games, Moore already had rushed for 534 yards. He entered the season with 457 for his career—but now was on pace to smash all records for expansion running backs. Only one other, Paul Robinson of the Cincinnati Bengals, had ever cracked the 1,000-yard barrier, rushing for 1,023 in 1968. But the Bengals were an expansion club in the old AFL. They didn't join the NFL until the two leagues merged two years later. The actual rushing record for an NFL expansion back was a mere 722 yards by Junior Coffey with Atlanta in 1966.

"I'm not really surprised by what Derrick has done," Seifert told the Carolina media prior to the 49ers' game at San Francisco. "Then when I say that, I'm sure you're thinking, 'Well, why in the hell didn't you keep him then?' I think you watch his style of running, the way he ran at Detroit and the types of runs they used him in there and the types of runs and the way he's being handled now, and no, I'm not surprised by it. He's a great kid. Just a hard-working, tough guy."

This was followed by a discernible pause in the interview.

Then one of the writers who cover the Panthers cracked, "Well, why in the hell didn't you keep him then?"

Seifert laughed heartily at the jab.

Then he said, "Believe me, at this moment, my wife even asks 'Why in the hell didn't you keep him then?' And my brother-in-law and my uncle. So I hear it all the time myself.

"I give them some philosophical answer about having all the knowns and unknowns you have at the time of making a decision like that. I go on and on, babbling. They look at me inquisitively and just kind of shake their heads."

At 28 years old, Moore was past the prime age for most NFL running backs, yet he was only beginning to discover the prime time. And he was, well, a little different.

When Moore felt the need for inspiration, he would head for the VCR in the living room of his modest one-bedroom Rock Hill apartment, which he shared with his wife of 18 months, Stephanie. But he wouldn't pop in a videotape titled *The Greatest Running Backs of the NFL* or some other similar choice. Instead, he would opt for *The Sound of Music,* the old classic musical starring Julie Andrews.

"Julie Andrews doesn't know how much of an impact she's had on me!" he once shouted enthusiastically at Scott Fowler of the *Charlotte Observer.* "Those other nuns in *The Sound of Music,* they think Julie is being ornery. But she's just following her dreams. Like me."

Moore even admitted to wandering about his apartment, singing along with Julie Andrews as she belted out verses like:

When the dog bites
When the bee stings
When I'm feeling sad
I simply remember

My favorite things
And then I don't feel so bad.
—"My Favorite Things." © 1959 Richard Rodgers and Oscar Hammerstein 2nd.

He said he especially liked that song and that particular verse when he was feeling down. To an outsider, this seemed comical because Moore was such an upbeat person that he never seemed to be down. But he insisted there were plenty of times in his life when he needed Julie Andrews's musical inspiration to lift his sagging spirits.

Moore took a circuitous route to the NFL. He didn't play football at all in high school until his junior year, and then did not play running back until he was a senior. Despite rushing for more than 700 yards, he didn't even get a scholarship sniff from any big schools. He dreamed of playing someplace like Auburn or Clemson, but his only offers came from smaller schools like Troy State in Alabama. So he decided to give up conventional football and attend Albany Junior College in his hometown of Albany, Georgia.

There was no football team at Albany Junior College, so Moore displayed his skills in flag football games.

"I was a superstar in flag football," he said. "I'm serious! I was the stud of the city!"

No doubt. By this time, Moore weighed 220 pounds and could run a 40-yard dash in 4.4 seconds. He also decided he didn't want to make a career out of flag football, so he called Troy State's coach to ask for another chance.

He sat out a year, played two and then discovered, because of some red tape involving Troy State's move to Division I-AA status, that he was no longer eligible for a senior season unless he transferred down to an NAIA school. So he transferred to Northeastern Oklahoma State, gained 1,500 yards and then wowed the NFL scouts by being named Most Valuable Player at the Blue-Gray college all-star game that year in Montgomery, Alabama.

He was sure he would be chosen in the first three or four rounds of the draft. So sure that he flew Stephanie, then his girlfriend, to Oklahoma and invited a bunch of friends over to watch the draft unfold on ESPN.

But Moore wasn't chosen that day. He almost wasn't chosen at all—finally going to Atlanta in the eighth round of a draft that only lasts seven rounds today.

"I was embarrassed," Moore said.

Still, he arrived in Detroit after being waived by Atlanta during the 1992 preseason with his jaw set square. He quickly established himself as Barry Sanders's capable backup and a hard runner who could gain the tough yards inside. Three years later, he was a restricted free agent and felt he could do more somewhere else.

The Lions called him in and told him the 49ers were interested. They would match the offer if Moore wanted, but he would still be a backup. If he wanted to go to San Francisco, though, they would let him go.

Moore felt he could replace the departed Ricky Watters in the 49ers' backfield, so away he went. Instead, the 49ers cut him in favor of Derek Loville, a runner they thought was more versatile than Moore.

Four days later, the Panthers came calling with what developed into the opportunity he thought he was going to receive in San Francisco.

"I've always done well just about anyplace I've gone," Moore said. "The one thing that separates me from just about any other running back in the National Football League is opportunity. I haven't had the chance to go in and run the ball 20 times on a consistent basis until this season. I've always played behind a great running back.

"I've had to come in the back door, and it's tough in the National Football League to get that opportunity if you come in through the back door. So my thing is that I've lacked the opportunity. I've never lacked the skills or the ability. I've never questioned that it was nothing more than a matter of getting the opportunity."

George Seifert, no doubt, was wishing now he had granted Moore a better one.

Rock Hill was alive with the sound of Moore singing about the possibility of the Panthers making the playoffs after his comments in New England, but it was a tune with which Dom Capers did not yet care to hum along. The head coach did not hear of Moore's proclamation that the playoffs were a possibility until one day after the game, and he wasn't particularly thrilled when he did.

"Aw, geez, I don't even want to hear that," Capers said with a laugh.

Capers claimed to be more of a realist.

"That story in the paper I saw about Derrick, where he talked about singing that song where you 'Climb every mountain and ford every stream,' I'm sure he probably had been listening to that before he mentioned the playoffs," Capers said.

"Believe me, it's like us against the world when we're facing a team like San Francisco. We've got a long way to go."

All Capers wanted was for his team not to get ahead of itself. Start thinking too much about the future, in his opinion, and the present could quickly become a muddled mess of missed assignments, sloppy execution and unforced mental errors.

In many ways, he welcomed the lack of public respect from which his team still suffered. He liked being the underdog.

"It's human nature to sometimes relax when people start saying good things about you," said Capers. "But if you relax in this business, you're asking for big trouble. You better feel a sense of urgency every week. You better take care of details and go about business exactly the same way."

Capers's message to his team was clear: Forget about playoffs and focus on 49ers.

The Panthers' locker room was overflowing with loose and confident players during the week leading up to the encounter in San Francisco.

One topic being discussed was punting. Eric Guliford, the team's punt returner, mentioned he had voted to award a game ball to Tommy Barnhardt after the win at New England, citing the difficulties Barnhardt overcame to punt in a 20-mile-per-hour wind.

"That wind was doing funny things to the ball," Guliford said. "It wasn't always going where you thought it was going to go."

Pat O'Neill was aware of the situation. He was New England's punter—with "was" being the key word. He had such a horrible day against the Panthers, Bill Parcells waived him two days later.

Barnhardt, 32, was playing in his ninth NFL season and, in truth, was having a somewhat mediocre season. Through eight games, he ranked 18th in the NFL in punt average and 16th in the more important category of net yards gained per punt. But at least he had been relatively consistent all year and hadn't cost the Panthers any games, as O'Neill arguably did with a terrible kick out of his own end zone in overtime the previous Sunday.

Barnhardt was a proven pro, which is why the Panthers went out and signed him the previous March to a two-year contract worth $900,000. Unproven punters like O'Neill had a nasty habit of costing teams valuable field position until they either became proven or found another line of work. This was a fact Capers kept in mind when he began to construct the first roster in Panthers history.

"A good part of our philosophy was that we wanted to develop a strong kicking game early," Capers said. "We thought the kicking game might be even more important early on—because of the type of team we might have. And it has been.

"For us to be competitive, we have to be good in the kicking game. It can be the type of thing where, if you're playing in a windy stadium, it can totally affect the outcome of the game."

Guliford added: "That's why I voted for Tommy to get a game ball. Their kicker had the wind with him and couldn't get off a decent punt when he needed to most. On the other hand, when we needed Tommy to really pin them down back there in overtime, he came through for us. The field position he helped create then and all day long really is what helped us win the game."

So did Guliford, who caught his first NFL touchdown pass and piled up 159 yards in receiving (career-high 94) and on punt returns (65). He paid a price for this, suffering a mild concussion after being laid out by New England free safety Myron Guyton in the fourth quarter. Guliford returned to the game, but maybe he shouldn't have.

"I went through a series of tests with them [team physicians] on the sideline," said Guliford, "and I answered most of the questions clearly and as accurately as a I could. So I went back in the game. But after the game, I had trouble recollecting exactly what happened.

"They asked me when I caught my touchdown pass, and I said the second quarter. They asked me what the score was at halftime, and I said 3–3."

He was wrong on both counts. He caught his 24-yard touchdown pass from Collins with 4:21 left in the third quarter, and the score was 3–0 in favor of New England at halftime. Of course, had Guliford actually scored a touchdown in the second quarter, there was no way the halftime score could have been 3–3 anyway.

Guliford still hoped to play against San Francisco, but he didn't want to be hit like that again, and doctors wouldn't even risk letting him participate in practice early in the week.

"Everything got real blurry when I took that hit—like it looks when the tracking on your VCR is off," Guliford said.

Sitting a few stalls away from Guliford, Willie Green discussed Alonzo Mourning's situation with the Hornets, who were in the process of attempting to trade him.

"How can they afford to let that guy go?" Green wanted to know.

And just across the way in the locker room, Tim McKyer also was entertaining some reporters. The subject was Jerry Rice and how difficult it was to defend the great San Francisco receiver.

"I remember when you were in Atlanta, Rice beat you for a long touchdown early in a game, but you came back to make an interception that you returned for a touchdown, too. Right?" Willie Smith of the *Greenville News* said to McKyer.

"It was two interceptions!" McKyer snapped back. "I had two interceptions that game! Two! But you guys never remember stuff like that. All you ever remember is how I got beat by Tony Martin! [in the 1994 AFC Championship game]."

Then McKyer stormed off.

Smith walked away, muttering: "Geez, I tried to pay the guy a compliment."

Earlier in the week, it looked as if Steve Young would return from a shoulder injury to quarterback the 49ers against the Panthers. But after Young attempted to practice in the middle of the week, it looked more and more like he would have to sit this one out.

This, on the surface, at least appeared to give the Panthers a chance. But they remained 15-point underdogs, according to the oddsmakers out in Las Vegas who had yet to favor the Panthers in any game.

Young didn't play in the end. Elvis Grbac started at quarterback and Cary Conklin finished, which is probably all anyone would have needed to know to realize the Panthers became the first expansion team to upset a defending Super Bowl champion. Not only that, but they did it on the road in front of 61,722 disbelieving fans at the place that claimed it was 3Com Park but would forever be Candlestick to hard-core football fans everywhere.

"This is just superb, just superb," said McCormack after the 13–7 victory. "To fly out here five and a half hours, to play them on their soil, their turf, and beat them . . . that's just superb."

"This is a very special day for us," Capers said.

"This is huge," added Sam Mills.

The victory was the fourth in a row for the Panthers after their 0–5 start, giving them more wins after nine games than six previous NFL expansion teams had been able to manage over 14-game seasons. Remarkably, it moved them to within one game of the 5–4 49ers in the NFC West standings, and only two games behind first-place Atlanta (6–3).

The 49ers entered the afternoon with the NFL's top-ranked defense, and played like it. But it was the Carolina defense that stole the show, despite surrendering 404 yards of total offense while the Carolina offense struggled to manage 204.

The difference came in the takeaway-giveaway battle Capers constantly stressed as crucial. The Panthers forced five turnovers—one that resulted in a 96-yard interception return by McKyer for their only touchdown—and held the potent San Francisco offense scoreless for more than three quarters. McKyer took advantage of a terrible decision made by Grbac on a ball that should have been thrown away, picking it off at the Carolina four-yard line and racing down the left sideline, avoiding Harris Barton, a diving offensive lineman, and outrunning Ted Popson, a 49ers tight end.

"My eyes got so large when I saw that ball coming to me," McKyer said. "The ball just kept getting bigger and bigger. When I caught it, I said to myself, 'Man, I'm gonna take this one to the house.'

"It was so sweet. People have been pointing fingers at Tim McKyer his whole career, trying to sweep him under the rug. Well, you can point your finger at Tim McKyer today. You can say he made the play that was the difference in the game and nobody can deny it."

So much for Tony Martin.

Two of the other costly San Francisco turnovers were created by Tyrone Poole, McKyer's cornerback counterpart. Though he got beat often by the 49ers' gifted receivers, Poole made up for it by forcing a pair of fumbles inside the Carolina five-yard line—including one where Poole, having been beaten badly to the outside by Jerry Rice, ran the receiver down and poked the ball free at the one-yard line. The ball shot out of Rice's arm and through the end zone, giving the Panthers possesson on an automatic touchback.

"The Lord blessed me," Poole said. "I got there in time."

"I don't know where the guy came from," Rice said. "He must have been really hustling to get back into that play. I thought I was going to score."

Later, Poole stripped the 49ers' other star receiver, John Taylor, as he darted inside the five-yard line and appeared to be heading for a touchdown with the Panthers clinging to a 13–0 lead early in the fourth quarter. Sam Mills recovered the loose ball at the 1.

"Those are big-time plays right there," said Fox television announcer John Madden, who called the game. "I don't know if Tyrone Poole knew what he was doing or not, but those are big-time plays anyway."

Unfortunately for the Panthers, the victory did not come without exacting a price. Derrick Moore suffered an injury to his right knee midway through the fourth quarter and had to be carried from the field by teammates Andrew Peterson and backup guard Sean Love. Polian said he feared it was a serious injury—although the true extent of it would not be known until Moore could undergo X-rays and an MRI examination upon the team's return to Charlotte.

After the game, Moore first attempted to limp out of the locker room, in full uniform, with a teammate offering support on each arm. But when he accidentally placed the tiniest bit of pressure on the knee, Moore screamed out loudly as pain shot through his body.

A few minutes later, Moore was wheeled back into the locker room on a stretcher. As he passed Jerry Richardson, the running back smiled weakly, shook his head and said simply, "Sorry."

Richardson then leaned over and whispered something consoling in Moore's ear.

Otherwise, it was a fine afternoon for Richardson and his beloved Panthers.

"I'm real proud of our team," Richardson said. "To come out here and beat the defending world champions on their field in a game they needed to win, it's just extraordinary. I mean, there was pressure on them to win this game.

"We've got guys with a lot of pride. They came in here and made the plays they needed to beat them on a day when they needed to win. This was a big game. This was not just another Sunday afternoon at the 'Stick'."

"It hasn't completely sunk in yet," defensive lineman Gerald Williams said. "I'm sure it will on the airplane ride home, when we start asking for Tylenol because our bones hurt, and we're feeling all the aches and pains we earned in this game. That's when it probably will hit us.

"We beat the world champions."

"It's indescribable how it feels," added Brett Maxie. "We beat the team that is the defending champion and takes a lot of pride in winning."

And from center Curtis Whitley: "It's a beautiful damn thang."

Kerry Collins, who played just well enough to win against a tough, veteran defense, completing 17 of 30 passes for 150 yards with one interception, said he could not have envisioned coming into the 49ers' home and beating them during his first NFL season. He was proud that the offense was able to piece together several long drives, even though none produced a touchdown.

"When I first got drafted," said Collins, "I wasn't too sure how much success we would have the first year. You look at what happened to all the other expansion teams, and you almost shudder.

"But I think we've proven we can play with anybody. Hopefully, we can continue this momentum and give ourselves a chance to win every week from here on out."

Over in the other locker room, the NFL's defending champions were not taking the loss well at all.

"This is a low point for us," Seifert said. "But congratulate them. They did a hell of a job."

"This is agonizing," 49ers center Jesse Sapolu added. "This is about as low as we can get."

"To the very end," said 49ers safety Tim McDonald, "I thought we could pull it out. Even walking off the field and seeing '0:00' on the clock, I still felt like it must be the end of the third quarter or something—until I saw guys shaking hands.

"They made the plays to beat us. There's nothing more to say."

Final Score

13 Carolina   **7** San Francisco

Game 10:
Panthers at St. Louis

T he giant peach was the tipoff. That's when Fox Network's Terry Bradshaw, the Super Bowl hero, knew someone had fumbled the ball.

"Are you sure this is where we're supposed to be?" Bradshaw asked the limousine driver who picked him up at Charlotte-Douglas International Airport on the Wednesday before the Rams game and had just passed the Gaffney, South Carolina, water tower on I-85 painted to advertise the region's most plentiful fruit. "I just can't imagine why the Panthers would practice way out here."

He was right. The driver, not much of a football fan, was taking Bradshaw an hour out of his way to the team's summer camp facility at Wofford College (which Bradshaw kept incorrectly calling "Woooooford" to the amusement of sportswriters) in Spartanburg, rather than to the 1995 in-season practice site at Winthrop University in Rock Hill.

Only a call from his Fox producer on the car phone turned the limo in the right direction. But not before "I got me a peach," said Bradshaw.

Things remained equally goofy when the former Steelers quarterback performed a skit with coach Dom Capers and QB Kerry Collins to be aired on that Sunday's Fox pregame show (which eventually included lead-in promos such as Dom Capers with Vulcan ears and Collins being beamed up to the USS Enterprise, as Carolina had "gone where no expansion team has gone before").

The television segment started with Bradshaw locked in the basement of the Panthers practice facility at Winthrop, pounding on a door.

"Hey! Help me! Help me! Somebody! Anybody out there!" yelled Bradshaw.

A few more seconds passed before Capers opened the door. The camera cut to the coach talking about his team's newfound success and celebrity. Bradshaw speculated that a veteran defense and four straight wins had the Panthers fans conjuring heady thoughts. Just then a voice announced the Panthers as the NFC representative at January's Super Bowl XXX in Phoenix, while a film showed Carolina taking the field before a game.

Sam Mills could only laugh on camera when asked about the possibility (maybe Fox should have asked Lamar Lathon instead). "I'll tell you where our Super Bowl is being played, Sunday at St. Louis."

Next, Collins walked into a room to visit with Bradshaw.

"Collins was so thrilled to meet me," said Bradshaw as part of the script. "In fact, he grabbed me so hard it knocked out my contact lenses.

"Collins really admires me, so I wasn't going to let him know I can't see a thing without contacts."

Then Collins addressed Bradshaw's surprise about the four-game winning streak.

"I don't think you ever want to be surprised when you're successful. Maybe—"

"But you're a rookie, man. You're not eight, nine years in the league," said Bradshaw, who also started in his first year as a pro quarterback.

Collins laughed. *"But I don't want to take that approach, 'I'm a rookie so I'm going to screw up.'"*

The two men stood facing each other on camera. Collins was clearly four to six inches taller than Bradshaw, who took the Steelers to four Super Bowl titles as one of the first of today's prototypical big, rugged quarterbacks.

"You want to know the secret to being successful?"

Collins nodded.

"When they're open—"

"Throw 'em the ball," said Collins, finishing the sentence and chuckling.

Then Bradshaw said his good-byes (on camera) and headed the wrong way one more time for the day.

"Kerry Collins already knows how to pick up the blitz," said Bradshaw, thinking to himself. *"But no way did he pick up on the fact that without my contacts I can't see a thing."*

Bradshaw then exited through the basement, destined to lock himself out again.

"Why did Terry exit into the basement?" said Collins, musing to himself as Bradshaw is heard off-camera yelling for help. *"I'm just a raw rookie so I won't say anything. As a quarterback I have a lot to learn. But I do know this, Terry Bradshaw may be in the basement, but in the NFC West the Carolina Panthers are no longer the cellar dwellers."*

When aired, the pregame show was a howling hit at the Collins family home in Pennsylvania. Even Kerry seemed to enjoy himself, and Bradshaw never seems not to have fun.

"Kerry had a sense of humor about it," Bradshaw said a few weeks later. *"We always ask players if they are willing to cooperate with a skit idea, and he was all for it. Not all players are such good sports.*

"What I saw was a kid. He is a really nice person unspoiled by his success. It's a pleasure to be around people before they turn into big stars, although I think Capers will keep a finger on Kerry."

Bradshaw addressed the issue of being too nice. He compared Collins favorably to Vinny Testeverde, the former Heisman Trophy winner and can't-miss University of Miami quarterback who has struggled as a pro, first at Tampa Bay and then the ill-fated Cleveland Browns.

"Vinny is one of the nicest people I will ever meet," explained Bradshaw. *"But I have told him he has to get nasty in the huddle. I didn't become a good quarterback until I got a chip on my shoulder.*

"Kerry is not naive like Vinny was. He takes charge out there, but is smart enough to know you only yell at guys who are your age. He is a confident player and will only get better. If he has panicked—and believe me he has felt panicked—he hasn't showed it."

The first person you see when entering the Panthers locker room is the late Vince Lombardi. At least on a plaque—with Dom Capers' favorite quote from the Green Bay Packers longtime coach: "I firmly believe that any man's finest hour—his greatest fulfillment to all he holds dear—is that moment when he has worked his heart out in a good cause and lies exhausted on the field of battle, victorious."

The quote seems more appropriate as game day approaches, but on Wednesdays, the locker room is at its most relaxed state. Last week's game is a few days gone, and next week's game is still a few days away.

Turn left from Lombardi and you see Howard Griffith, one of the more personable players on the team who always offers a friendly hello to passing reporters. Next you see— actually you hear him first—running back Derrick Moore. He is constantly in motion.

Veer right from there and that's where the offensive lineman hang out. They don't seem to mind that the media often passes them by on the way to players at more glamorous positions. In fact, guys like Mark Rodenhauser and Matt Elliott seem to take special pleasure in shouting good-natured insults at reporters and players conducting interviews.

Rodenhauser's locker was a famed spot during the first year in Pantherdom. Each week, he produced a new computer-generated graphic that poked fun at someone in the organization. One week he spoofed the eating habits and extra pounds carried by 60-year-old security director Ed Stillwell. A rendered cereal box showed "Ed Stillwell's Cholesterol Crunch—1,000 percent of the minimum daily allowance of fat, sugar and cholesterol."

Another week he portrayed a picture of Moore's head on the skirted body of Julie Andrews in *The Sound of Music* to honor the running back's infatuation with the inspirational message of the movie.

But Rodenhauser's gallery hours were about to stop. The next week, he posted a mock *National Enquirer* tabloid front page claiming exclusive evidence of a "Fifth Beatle found!" The subtitle read, "John, Paul, George, Ringo and . . . Dom?" The Carolina coach, who is balding, was presented in cute mop-top haircut thanks to the latest advancements in computer digitization. While Capers laughed when he first saw the photo illustration, he later told reporters it was an "in-house thing," and a team official asked members of the media to not mention the practical joke. But Capers himself never asked to keep it out of the paper, so some reporters used the item in their newspaper notes packages. The next Wednesday, Rodenhauser's weekly poster was missing.

This was the week owner Art Modell announced he was moving the Browns from Cleveland to Baltimore. All of football was affected by the once-proud franchise falling on hard times, especially some Panthers officials with special connections.

Dom Anile, the former college scouting director at Cleveland, said he felt bad for his friends with the team. "I say a novena to Bill Polian every night for bringing me here," said Anile. "Otherwise, I'd just be calling him now for a job."

"There was a time when I wanted to be head coach of the Cleveland Browns more than anything else," said Capers, who grew up in Ohio. "I hate to see it happen. When I think of Cleveland, I think Browns."

"I feel almost like we should be wearing black arm bands," said team president Mike McCormack, who played most of his illustrious career in Cleveland, blocking for the likes of Jim Brown and helping the team win championships.

A starting quarterback takes more than a thousand snaps from center during a regular NFL season, and thousands more in practice. It is routine, a forgotten thread in the tapestry of the game. But with 3:12 remaining in the third quarter of a close game at the brand-new Trans World Dome in St. Louis, Kerry Collins snagged. He pulled out too early from a surprised Curtis Whitley, who was waiting for the second half of a "hut-hut" snap count that never came. Whitley hurriedly adjusted by snapping the ball once Collins was moving, but the young quarterback never got a clean grip. Rams linebacker Carlos Jenkins pounced on the loose football, ending a Carolina drive at the St. Louis 42-yard line. Eight plays later, the Rams took a commanding 21–10 lead.

Collins took full blame for the fumble. He said he looked to the left slot and saw no defensive player was covering Eric Guliford, the wide receiver who was open on two previous plays that would have been big gainers if Collins hadn't overthrown his target. This time, Collins planned to remedy his mistakes.

"I tried to get the snap as quick as I could so I could get the ball out to Gully so he could run with it," said the Panthers quarterback after the game. "In my haste, I forgot the snap count. Whit knew it was on two."

In another part of the locker room, Whitley was having no part of pointing fingers. Like every game of his stellar season, the expansion draft lineman was working hard to protect his leader and quarterback.

"The snap was on two, somebody went on one," Whitley explained amid unusual media attention. "It seems like there was offsides on the play. We'll have to check the films."

Dom Capers called it the key play to swing momentum. He was calling it a little something different during the heat of the game when two penalty flags had actually been dropped on the play.

"Bullshit!" he yelled, popping the veins in his neck as he screamed at the line judge and back judge a full minute after the play was ruled a fumble and no penalty charged. "That's bullshit! . . . Bullshit! "

Capers was slicing his arms in a motion similar to a baseball umpire calling someone safe. He was vehemently arguing that St. Louis nose tackle Jimmie Jones was lined up in the neutral zone and a penalty should have nullified the play. Defensive end Mark Thomas, who played at North Carolina State, lent his moral support on the sidelines by vigorously nodding and pointing himself as he stood by the coach. The film did indeed make a possible case for the neutral-zone infraction.

Things would get worse for Collins and the Panthers offense. On the next drive, Collins was sacked on two straight plays. On the second sack, Rams star D'Marco Farr slapped the ball from the quarterback's right hand. The safe move would have been falling on the ball and then letting Tommy Barnhardt come in to punt. But Collins, as was his nature all season, had eyes on making a big play.

The ball bounced twice as Collins attempted to scoop it on the run. He kicked it accidentally. Then Rams safety Toby Wright bumped Collins out of the way and cornerback Torin Dorn fell on the ball and then got up to run 26 yards for the touchdown. Dorn, a tailback during his college days at North Carolina, scored his second touchdown of the season—both off Collins miscues. It turned out to be a birthday gift for Dorn's first child, Torin Jr., who wife Rhonda gave birth to at 7 A.M. that morning back home in Charlotte.

A four-point game was now a rout. "Obviously I should have put a fork in it," said Collins. "I should have just fallen on it." In all, Collins provided St. Louis with five turnovers in the second half (three interceptions, two fumbles).

"I get mad when things don't go my way," said Collins, doing some self-analysis in the locker room and freely discussing the game as usual. "When I'm not doing well, it makes me very angry. I think that's when I'm at my best, when I'm an angry person. I've always been that way since I was a little kid."

Collins said he was so mad he even started yelling at the big St. Louis linemen who were rushing his passes all day. It was an atypical display for the cool QB.

"But, hey, they yell at me all the time," said Collins, grinning.

The young quarterback had gained plenty of supporters as Collins improved and the Panthers went a solid 4–4 in his the first eight pro starts.

"I was impressed today,' said the Rams' Farr, comparing the Kerry of the home opener at Clemson to the Kerry in the rematch at St. Louis. "He wasn't visibly rattled. It was like the bull and sword. We kept sticking in the sword, but he wouldn't go down."

"Collins is a star of the future," said St. Louis coach Rich Brooks earlier in the week. "He is a guy who with a little more experience will be headed for the Pro Bowl."

Joe Theismann, the ESPN commentator and former Super Bowl quarterback for the Washington Redskins, said the Panthers were actually smart to give the starting job to veteran Frank Reich in training camp.

"It gave [Collins] time to learn," said Theismann, who got some seasoning as a Canadian Football League quarterback before trying the NFL. "He wasn't thrown in there and asked to carry the team like Jim Plunkett in New England [who eventually righted himself, but by winning a Super Bowl for the Oakland Raiders rather than the Patriots]. Kerry told me he wasn't ready to start the first games of the season. The coaching staff has also helped his progress by deciding three- and five-step drops for him so he can quicken his release."

"He is just so doggone big and strong," said John Madden, the wildly popular Fox analyst, who along with partner Pat Summerall, called the previous week's big win at San Francisco. "No matter what is going on all around him, it doesn't bother him."

"He's huge," said former all-pro defensive end and Fox studio analyst Howie Long, who met Collins at the ESPY awards earlier in 1995. "Kerry could eat a sandwich off the top of my head. He makes Terry Bradshaw look like Doug Flutie [the former Boston College star who is 5–9 and winning Grey Cups in Canada because he was deemed too short for the NFL]."

Madden said recent rule changes make it even more important to have quarterbacks with strong arms and the capacity to endure a physical beating. He said the Panthers have a rare find in Collins.

"Every down is a passing down," he noted. "NFL quarterbacks have to be able to drop back and pass on every down and take all those hits. Colleges just aren't developing quarterbacks like that."

"Kerry will grow in leaps and bounds," said Terry Bradshaw when asked if fans can expect even bigger things from Collins in 1996. "Your first year in the NFL is kind of like cutting a path through the underbrush of thick jungle. There's so many vines and branches and all that stuff at your feet you never look up to see the big trees and the magnificence of it all. You reach the other side exhausted and just sort of happy to get there.

"In the off-season you realize it really wasn't that bad. You look back and the path you cut is fairly straight. You realize you swerved a little here and a little there, and if you knew about that ditch, you could have avoided it. But overall it wasn't as bad as you thought.

"Then you come back through the jungle. You know those ditches and when the hills get steep. You know where to spend the night. You know about the lions den. You don't have to cut through nearly as much underbrush. You start to look at the big trees and enjoy yourself.

"Once you get to know that jungle, you don't worry about it so much. You take off and just play. You're not as anxious or fretful. You have fun; you just blast through there."

Bradshaw said Collins and his Carolina teammates, especially the younger players, will feel the effects of the first-year success.

"The expectations will be greater than a team like Tampa Bay, which has been in the league 20 years," said Bradshaw. "They set a standard and they will be measured by it. Fans will say, 'Hey, they beat this team last year, why can't they do it now?'

"The kids will feel some pressure. I want to see Kerry's response after a bad game or bad half or negative reactions from the fans. Then we see the stuff he's made of."

Collins has said playing for Joe Paterno at Penn State has helped him stay on an even keel. "Coach Paterno always said, 'You're never as good as they say you are, and you're never as bad, either,' " he explained.

"This [St. Louis] game won't bother him too much," said Bill Polian to a *Sports Illustrated* reporter who was on hand to see the new dome in St. Louis and catch up with the streaking Panthers. "You don't fold your tent because you had a tough loss. You have to look back at his college career. Kerry had a very rough start at Penn State. He was booed off the field and came back to have great career there. He has been through some hard times before, and he has been able to handle it."

Mike McCormack, a Hall of Fame lineman who played in such defunct places as Polo Grounds, was in the upper row of the two-tiered open-air press box at the new Trans World Dome. There were no higher seats in the house. He sat calmly elbow-to-elbow with Bill Polian, who was in full screaming voice when he thought Collins was wrongly called for intentional grounding in the third quarter. The Panthers general manager really doesn't worry much about pregame announcements over the press box loudspeaker that "this is a working area for the media" and no cheering or referee-baiting is allowed, especially since no NFL official could hear anyone so high up. Leave the hooting to those guys down in a section near the end zone who painted their faces Ram blue and yellow, please and thank you.

Chris Polian, a pro scout for the team who clearly has inherited his father's emotional palate, was the first to loudly protest the call.

"No!" pleaded the younger Polian, raising his fists to his ears.

"He had a screen!" Bill bellowed through clenched teeth trying to restrain his delivery just a bit. He clearly believed running back Howard Griffith was close enough to the incomplete pass.

The Polians watched the replay on one of the dozens of TV monitors in the press box.

"He . . . had . . . the . . . screen!" lamented Polian, biting off each word and getting louder on each.

During all the outburst, McCormack simply folded his arms across his chest. He later worried that the two St. Louis games, in which the Rams scored a cumulative 59 points, would give away some family secrets.

"I expect those tapes will travel a lot to our opponents in the off-season," said McCormack.

Maybe so, but 13 turnovers in the two losses—equal to half of the team's 26 in the first 10 games—certainly played a role in the outcomes. The Rams scored three defensive touchdowns off the mistakes, and 14 more points came on drives starting in good field position after a fumble or interception. That's 35 points.

In the locker room, Panthers defensive players were adamant the Rams had nobody's number.

"We had sloppy tackling all day," said Tim McKyer, twirling a lollipop in his mouth. "We would have a guy wrapped up and then just come off him."

"Lots of guys are hurt by this loss," said Sam Mills. "We have grown accustomed to that feeling of expecting to win."

"It's frustrating because we know this is a team we can beat," said Greg Kragen.

Linebacker Darion Conner was the most frustrated member of the defense. He dropped a sure interception and touchdown return which would have produced a 17–14 Panthers lead in the third quarter. It was about three minutes before the wheels came off the victory express.

Conner was running a stunt at the line with rookie Shawn King. He was double-teamed by King who penetrated and pressured Rams quarterback Chris Miller into rushing his pass. Conner leaped high into the air like Larry Johnson pulling down a rebound for the Charlotte Hornets. He actually batted the ball on his way down from the top of the jump and the ball fluttered straight up in the air.

All Conner needed to do was wait on the ball, then run a clear path to the end zone. But he started moving to his right before catching it. It slipped through his hands and he ended up facedown on the dome carpet, pounding his fist on the artificial turf. Bubba McDowell came by to tap him on the helmet, but Conner was not consoled.

"Jesus, Mary and Joseph!" yelled Polian in the press box. "It was right in his hands! How could he drop it?"

"It couldn't have been any better," said Conner in the locker room. "It was a sure interception. It was a free touchdown. There was nobody there to stop me."

Miller was grateful. "I'm going to send Darion a thank-you note and a pair of gloves," he told reporters after the game.

The St. Louis quarterback, like many players, was not overly impressed with the Trans World Dome's new playing surface. Players don't generally like artificial turf and especially don't like new turf. It causes all sorts of burns and rashes.

"That stuff out there is like sandpaper," said Miller. "We may have to hire a crew to go out there with fingernail files."

The St. Louis stadium makes the third dome in the five-team NFC West. It generally received favorable reviews for its sight lines, scoreboard replay screens and other fan amenities. There was a sellout crowd of 65,598 and only 45 no-shows. The location is convenient to downtown St. Louis. It was slated to open a few weeks earlier but construction delays made the Panthers the first guest.

Sunday morning, when Panthers officials took a tour, there were kudos all around for St. Louis. But privately, the feeling was "we'll keep our open-air, state-of-the-art stadium that cost more than a $100 million less to build."

Final Score

28 St. Louis   **17** Carolina

Game 11:
Arizona at Panthers

In Buddy Ryan's warped mind, there was no doubt about who deserved much of the credit for the defensive success of the Carolina Panthers. He felt he did.

This was only one of the claims Ryan made during a brief but typically feisty teleconference call with writers prior to bringing his struggling team, the Arizona Cardinals, into Clemson Memorial Stadium to face the Panthers. The call lasted only 12 minutes, but that was all Ryan needed to take credit for inventing the best parts of Dom Capers' defensive scheme, which Capers obviously copied, in Ryan's opinion, by watching film of the 1993 Houston Oilers' defense. Ryan was defensive coordinator for the Oilers that season.

"Their defense is a takeoff on what we do," Ryan said.

What exactly would those things be, he was asked.

"Oh, everything they do," Ryan insisted.

Ryan was pressed on the matter. And when it was pointed out that most coaches around the NFL were crediting Capers with perfecting the zone-blitz strategy that so many were now beginning to copy, he exploded and caught himself in a contradiction.

"I don't understand the zone blitz," Ryan said. "They blitz and give up a zone. I don't give up anything when I blitz. I believe in man-to-man coverage."

Who knew what to believe when it came to the boastful, blustery Ryan? Who could understand him?

Later, during the same teleconference call, Ryan said he had been coaching for 50 years. Assuming the Cardinals' media guide was correct, this meant Ryan had been coaching since age 11. He had been around the NFL for a long time, but not quite that long.

When Capers was informed of Ryan's comment later that same afternoon, the usually composed coach burst into an uncontrollable spell of laughter that lasted 28 seconds and left his face red, his eyes watery.

"Awwww. . . . well, he's correct in one statement," Capers said. "I did watch a lot of Houston film in 1993 when I was defensive coordinator of the Steelers. But I was watching their offense."

To know Buddy Ryan is to love him—or hate him. Few people who crossed Ryan's path had an opinion of the man that fell anywhere in between. Even his age was a source of controversy. The Cards' media guide said he was 61. A Sports Illustrated article written about him in 1994 reported that his real date of birth was actually three years earlier than Ryan admitted in his biography, which would have made him 64 at the start of the 1995 NFL season. The SI story said Ryan altered his age when he decided a younger man would have a better shot at landing an NFL head-coaching position.

Ryan once punched a fellow assistant coach on national television, or at least tried to. In Buddy lore, he probably knocked Kevin Gilbride cold that day when Ryan, then Houston's defensive coordinator, stalked Gilbride, then Houston's offensive coordinator, on the Oilers' sideline. In reality, Ryan's weak left-handed punch didn't even connect.

This was the essence of Buddy Ryan. What you saw and what you heard wasn't always what it seemed. In fact, it rarely was. Lamar Lathon and Bubba McDowell, two Panthers who played for Ryan during the 1993 season in Houston, were well aware of this.

"I hated the man at first," Lathon said. "But I ended up loving him."

Lathon said the turnaround came after Ryan played some mind games with him.

After Lathon broke an arm in training camp, a reporter asked Ryan what Lathon's role would be once he returned. Ryan's response was, "Lamar who?"

But when Lathon returned and went through a series of practices with the arm still in a cast, he felt he earned Ryan's respect.

"That's one of the toughest SOBs I've ever coached," Ryan then told reporters of Lathon.

McDowell said Ryan never liked players who were injured. Often, he wouldn't even talk to them, treating them with an air of disgust.

"I was hurt a lot the one year he was in Houston, and I still feel bad about it," McDowell said. "I'm sure I didn't live up to his expectations."

Once, when McDowell tore a pectoral muscle during a game, Ryan was waiting for him when he staggered off the field.

"You're hurt again?" Ryan asked. Then Ryan turned and stomped away.

"If we lost, it was because the players didn't execute and lost the game," McDowell said. "If we won, it was because of the great defensive game plan he structured. That's the way it always was with him."

Despite these kinds of antics, Ryan's players—especially those on defense—routinely seemed to stick up for him. Even McDowell said he would play for Ryan again, adding, "I sort of miss him for some reason." One of Ryan's Arizona players, defensive tackle Eric Swann, said it was because Ryan's honesty, though sometimes delivered in a brutal manner, was usually appreciated by most of the players on his team.

"Buddy is very personable outside of football," Swann said. "He isn't always harsh. But as far as football goes, it's always cut-and-dried. If you're playing well, you're playing well. If you suck, you suck. He'll tell you exactly how it is."

Lathon said it just took time for players to understand that much of what Ryan says and does is done purely for shock value, intended to motivate.

"When Buddy came to Houston," said Lathon, "he was looking for a couple of guys to step up and be leaders on defense—myself and Al Smith [a fellow linebacker]. Al Smith was just coming off a Pro Bowl year.

"He said Al Smith was too fat and couldn't play for him. He told me that I wasn't going to have my way, that I was going to have to listen to him and do what he said.

"I remember I missed a couple of meetings and he demoted me to fourth string. So we kind of started off on a bad note. But I think he really brings out the best in people. He's probably the best defensive coordinator I've been around. He's very aggressive, very straightforward."

Indeed, Ryan was brash and would say exactly what was on his mind.

When he was head coach of the Philadelphia Eagles from 1986 through 1990, he feuded with Dallas coaches Tom Landry and Jimmy Johnson. He was accused of placing "bounties" on the heads of certain Dallas players he hated, an accusation he denied by saying there weren't any Dallas players good enough to be worth a bounty.

And Buddy Ryan was coming to Clemson, if only for a day. The place might never be the same.

Nonetheless, Ryan had lost just a little of his swagger on the way to the meeting with the Panthers. As of Monday morning, for the first time in their history, the Panthers were favored to win a game. They rated as a one-point favorite over Buddy's Boys in Las Vegas.

Ryan built his NFL reputation on his defensive genius. He was the architect of the famed "46" defense that helped the Chicago Bears win a Super Bowl in 1986, when the Bears led the league in nine defensive categories. The same defense—based on stuffing the run and gambling with a wide variety of blitzes and man-to-man coverage against the pass—set an NFL record for sacks with 72 a year earlier.

Offense was sometimes an afterthought for Ryan, especially when he wasn't burdened with being head coach.

"In Houston," said Lathon, "if you didn't play defense, you were nobody as far as Buddy was concerned."

But in his second season with the Cards, Ryan's defense was crumbling around him and threatening to take him down as well. The Cardinals ranked dead last in the 30-team NFL in defending the run, and 28th overall defensively.

It seemed amazing to Ryan that the 4–6 Panthers, in their first year of existence, actually had one more victory at this point in the season than his 3–7 Cardinals. After all, Ryan had declared when he accepted the job, "Y'all got a winner in town now." And after an 8–8 first season, Ryan had gone public with his prediction that the Cardinals should make the playoffs in this, his second season.

Ryan denied that a loss to the expansion Panthers would place his job in further jeopardy. He claimed owner Bill Bidwill understood that much of the Cards' plight had been brought about by injuries, something over which no coach, even Ryan, had control.

"He's as disappointed in the year as I am," Ryan said of Bidwill. "But he's a guy who's been in the league for 50 years [actually, since 1960] and he knows what it's like when you end up losing an Eric Swann for five or six games [actually, it was only four] and [linebacker] Eric Hill for two or three games [two was correct]. He's a football man, and he understands that. Anybody who knows anything about football understands."

Ryan must not have heard the old story about how some in the NFL suspected Bidwill's secret goal in life was to have fired every single person to have ever worked in the league.

Joe Gibbs, who later would go on to gain fame as head coach of the Washington Redskins, said he was told early in his tenure as an assistant coach with the old St. Louis Cardinals (whom Bidwill eventually moved to Arizona) that he would know he was fired the day he saw the van from a local locksmith out in front of the Cardinals' team offices.

"I thought that was a joke," Gibbs said. "Then one day I saw the locksmith's van out front when I was driving by. I went home and told my wife that I'd better get down there and clean out my office, just in case. But by the time I got down there, it was too late.

"Bidwill had already changed the locks. None of the coaches could get in their offices to get their stuff out. That was how we found out the coaching staff had been fired."

Ryan insisted he wasn't worried about an appearance by the grim locksmith. He insisted this game against the Panthers could be just what his struggling team needed to turn its season around.

———————————

As he took a late-afternoon stroll across the field at 3Com Park in San Francisco two Sundays earlier following the Panthers' 13–7 win over the 49ers, Mike McCormack was wearing a smile of pure joy on his rugged, handsome Irish face.

"If this doesn't get the people back home to load up their Winnebagos and drive to Clemson, I don't know what will," the beaming McCormack said of the Panthers' upset of the defending Super Bowl champions.

In the locker room at San Francisco, Jerry Richardson was asked if he thought four wins in a row, including one over the defending champions, would be enough to send more fans flocking to Clemson.

"You certainly would think that more people would want to come out and watch a team that fights as hard as this one does," he answered.

Yet by the time Arizona was coming in, it seemed nothing would get those people to load the Winnebagos and drive all the way to Clemson. By the Thursday prior to kickoff against the Cards the Panthers had sold only 49,000 tickets to the game, which was the first one at home since the historic victory over the 49ers. That was about 4,000 fewer than the advance sale the Panthers had managed for their previous home game against New Orleans, when their record was 1–5.

When McCormack heard those numbers, he was no longer smiling. Nor was he optimistic.

The Panthers' president admitted the organization had finally become resigned to the fact that there was a strong corp of about 50,000 fans who were willing to make the long drive to and from Clemson for the first season's home games. And that was as good as it was going to get. There would be no attendance records, after all.

"I think we're become sort of resigned to the fact that we've done about all we can do at Clemson this season," McCormack said. "The first Denver game [in the preseason on August 12], with all the traffic snarls and all the resulting publicity, had a tremendous negative effect on what we were trying to do."

Average attendance after four regular-season home games was 53,058 in a stadium that seated 76,000. Counting the preseason, the Panthers had played seven games at Clemson; the crowd of 57,017 at the Denver game was by far the largest. But McCormack said that was about to change. Though he was disappointed in the advance sales for the Cardinals game, he said the rematch against the 49ers, set for December 10 at Clemson, was shaping up as a possible sellout. The advance sales for that game, three weeks away, was already 68,000.

Buddy Ryan would have been amazed to discover there was a better draw out there.

While many players were beginning to grumble about the two-and-a-half-hour bus ride to Clemson for "home" games, Kerry Collins and his ears were ecstatic about the return to Clemson Memorial Stadium for the game against the Cards.

No, the unflappable rookie wasn't worrying about the debacle in St. Louis. He said he was happy to come home because it meant going through a week of practices without the distraction of a jet engine whining in his helmet at a decibel level high enough to hurt the eardrum. The previous week, as during all weeks when the Panthers were preparing to play on the road in a dome, practice sessions at Winthrop involved the offense running plays while an elaborate speaker system simulated the crowd noise they would encounter in the hostile, potentially deafening dome environment.

Capers said he wasn't sure what the noise being piped in was, but he thought it sounded like a jet airplane engine. The first time this soundtrack was used was the last time most of the assistant coaches arrived for a practice during a dome week without a pair of earplugs.

"Yeah, it sounds like a bunch of jet engines out there," Collins said. "Then we go to the games and it's not even half as loud as it is during our own practices.

"Going into last week, we were all worried that we weren't going to be able to hear a thing [at the Trans World Dome in St. Louis]. Brockermeyer was saying to me, 'Man, I'm not gonna be able to hear the snap count. What am I gonna do?' Then we started thinking about it, and we realized there was no way it was going to be any louder than at practice, so why worry about it?

"They had something like this to prepare us for dome games at Penn State, but it wasn't nearly as loud. I wish I had that kind of power in my own stereo system at home."

So on this week, the Panthers prepared for their encounter with Buddy Ball in relative silence.

But when the game arrived, this is not what they faced in the Arizona Cardinals. As one fan noted on a well-placed sign in the stands, they encountered "Cruddy Ball."

The Panthers took advantage, too, dominating the Cardinals on a sun-filled afternoon when Arizona's best play came on a field-goal attempt by the opposition. Unfortunately for the Panthers, their end-to-end domination was witnessed by a crowd of just 49,582, the smallest home gathering of the season.

The 27–7 victory lifed the Panthers' record to 5–6 and rekindled hopes of the playoffs.

Throughout the week leading up to the game against the Cards, who fell to 3–8, the Panthers insisted the Cardinals were not as bad as their record or their woeful defensive statistics indicated.

They were right. The Cardinals were even worse.

But as bad as Arizona was, Carolina was that good.

"I believe this is our most complete game," Capers said. "Our offense moved the ball, and our defense had an outstanding day."

Indeed, the defense did. They held the Cardinals to no first downs for more than one and a half quarters at the outset and held them to a mere 96 total yards—their lowest yardage total in more than 40 years.

All season long, Capers kept saying sacks were overrated, that players had to be careful "not to bow down to the Sack God." As long as the Panthers were applying pressure on opposing quarterbacks and forcing them to throw the ball before they wanted to, that was enough. But on this day, the sacks did come. In bunches.

The Panthers sacked Arizona quarterback Dave Krieg a season-high six times in all, including two apiece by linebacker Lamar Lathon and defensive end Mark Thomas. During one vindictive stretch in the second half, Krieg went down behind the line of scrimmage on three consecutive plays—pulled down by Lathon, fellow outside linebacker Darion Conner and blitzing cornerback Tyrone Poole. This was the kind of havoc Capers dreamed of creating in opposing backfields when he convinced Mike McCormack, Bill Polian and Joe Mack to acquire players who could excel out of the 3-4 defensive alignment.

Sacks might be overrated in the opinion of most coaches. But Capers would be the first to admit they also motivated many defenders in a positive way on some occasions, including this one. Telling an outside linebacker or defensive end not to worry about getting sacks is sort of like telling David Letterman to lay off the Top 10 lists–it's just not going to happen.

"As a defensive lineman," said Mark Thomas, "you don't get the chance to score touchdowns—at least not that often, and maybe never. So a sack for us is kind of like scoring a touchdown would be for a receiver or running back. That's what we're out there to do."

Added Lathon: "Today we got second effort from everyone. No one tried to do more than what the defensive scheme asked them to do, and everything fell right into place for us. It felt great."

And from the veteran Sam Mills: "We had been getting pressure on the quarterback all year, but a lot of times we would come close to sacking him and not make the plays. Today, we got pressure from a lot of people, not just one or two guys. And when we got to the quarterback, we usually finished the play."

Getting sacked was nothing new to Krieg, of course. The six sacks at the hands of Carolina defenders meant he had now been sacked 456 times over a 16-year NFL career.

"It's amazing he's still alive," Panthers cornerback Rod Smith said.

The Panthers' offense, led by a resurgent Collins, was as crisp and as efficient as it had been all season, rolling up 362 total yards to Arizona's meager total of 96. The Cards hadn't been held to less than 100 total yards in a game since a September 26, 1955, game against Pittsburgh—and that was two franchise moves earlier, when they were known as the Chicago Cardinals. The franchise moved to St. Louis in 1960 and to Phoenix in 1988.

On this afternoon, they weren't the Chicago Cardinals, the St. Louis Cardinals or the Arizona Cardinals. They were simply Buddy's Cruddy Cardinals. They stunk, and Buddy knew it.

Ryan was a bowed and humbled man reduced to mumbling almost inaudibly to a crowd of reporters afterward.

"I feel sorry for our players and coaches," he said. "It's a tough situation. . . . We made mistakes. Everyone did."

He did credit the Panthers' defense, whose scheme he earlier claimed Capers had copied from him.

"They've got a veteran defensive unit that shut down the great 49er offense a couple weeks ago," Ryan said. "They've got people here with 10, 11 years experience in the NFL. It's not like they're a rookie team."

No, that was the Cardinals.

Despite playing again without leading rusher Derrick Moore, out with the bum knee, the Panthers racked up a season-high 180 yards rushing. Howard Griffith gained 88 yards on 25 carries, while newcomers Blair Thomas (12 carries, 59 yards) and Anthony Johnson (five carries for 33 yards, including a 23-yard touchdown run) also contributed. The Cardinals had to respect the Panthers' ability to run, and therefore bit more often than not when Collins faked a handoff and threw. This enabled Collins to complete 15 of 23 passes for 201 yards—with no interceptions.

"When you've got it going like that," said Collins, "it makes your offense very tough to defend. I felt like we kept them on their heels pretty much all day."

One unlikely recipient of a Collins pass was offensive lineman Mark Dennis, who pulled down a ball tipped at the line of scrimmage by an Arizona defender and actually turned the botched play into a three-yard gain for the Panthers. Collins, however, was not impressed.

"He'll have to gain more than that if he expects me to throw to him again," Collins joked. "He should have gotten the first down."

The only whimper heard from the Cards came on the very last play of the first half, when placekicker John Kasay lined up for a 42-yard field goal that would have given the Panthers a 17–0 lead. But Arizona linebacker Seth Joyner broke through the middle of the Carolina line and blocked it. Cards teammate Aeneas Williams scooped up the loose ball and returned it 72 yards for a touchdown, meaning the Panthers, who seconds earlier thought they were going to be headed to the locker room with a 17-point halftime lead, now only led by 14–7 despite totally dominating the Cardinals.

It was the kind of momentum-swinging play that could turn a ball game in the other direction. Capers was furious. He sprinted off the field, clenching his teeth.

As they came off the field and into the locker room, it was procedure to have the coaching staff convene in a room by themselves, where Capers would exchange thoughts and comments about the first half with all the coaches. Then the offensive staff would break off with the offensive team and the defensive staff would break off with the defensive players. Capers would use this time to stay in a room by himself "to collect my thoughts before I speak to the team as a group."

From experience, Capers felt this was a foolproof method against saying something stupid he might come to regret later. It's an emotional game, he admitted, but he was determined not to let his emotions get the better of him after Aeneas Williams almost ruined what had been a perfect first half.

"For me to go in there and react emotionally to that one play would have sent the wrong message to the team," Capers said. "I think it would have sent a message of panic, as opposed to one of confidence."

Instead, Capers addressed the team by saying, "Let's forget about that play and move on. We've done everything right. Our game plan is working.

"We made one mistake; it's a great example of why we've got to take care and play every play in the second half the same way we did in the first half, except for that one play. We don't want to take the chance of going out and playing a great football game, and letting one or two plays beat us."

Later, Capers told reporters, "We knew that to beat this team, it was going to be a physical football game. It was going to be like a 15-round fight. And both teams were going to stay in there slugging, so we had to find a way to get in there and deliver the knockout punch in the second half."

They did, playing Muhammed Ali to Buddy Ryan's Jerry Quarry for two more lopsided quarters.

Afterward, Capers raced to midfield to shake the opposing coach's hand, as is his custom, win or lose. For the first time all season, the opposing coach did not show up. Buddy Ryan was nowhere to be found.

Final Score

27 Carolina   **7** Arizona

Game 12:
Panthers at New Orleans

When the players and coaching staff convened for their weekly Monday meeting at Winthrop Coliseum, the prevailing mood was one of jubilation. Even so, Coach Capers discovered a way to send spirits soaring even higher.

Capers told the players their weekly weigh-in, which usually took place on Friday mornings, would be held Thursday morning instead—before the players were to partake in their Thanksgiving dinners. For a guy like defensive lineman Gerald Williams, who is six-foot-three and weighed anywhere from 290 to 296 pounds depending on what his wife, Suzie, had been feeding him, this was welcome news indeed.

Williams was fined twice earlier in the season for being over his prescribed weight of 293 pounds. Each player had a prescribed weight to meet on a weekly basis. The fine was $50 per pound for each pound the player was over, and Williams said he had to fork over $150 for being three pounds over on both occasions. Had Capers not switched the Thanksgiving week weigh-in, Williams admitted he probably would have had to arrive at the scales on Friday with his checkbook in hand.

"I guess I usually gain two or three pounds during a Thanksgiving meal—give or take a drumstick or two," he said.

Most of the Panthers said they intended to spend the holiday in the same manner as most football-loving Americans. They planned to stuff themselves full of turkey and then hit their respective couches to watch some football on television.

But Williams claimed that would not be possible at his house this year.

"Normally I would eat quite a bit on Thanksgiving Day, I must admit," Williams said. "My wife makes wonderful pies. But I doubt if I'll be able to do it up that much this year. We just moved into a new house about a month ago, and my wife has a honey-do list for me that's about a mile long. I've still got so many things to do, she'll probably have me running around all day."

Then Williams spotted wide receiver Dwight Stone, a former teammate in Pittsburgh, sitting at a nearby locker stall, going through some mail.

"Ask Dwight about my wife's pies. He's tasted all kinds of 'em," Williams said. "Hopefully, maybe we'll get Dwight to drop by this Thanksgiving."

Stone looked up just long enough to shake his head.

"No way, man," said Stone, who earlier admitted his plan for the afternoon was to "grab the remote and do nothing. Absolutely nothing."

Returning his attention to the mail in his lap, Stone added to Williams, "No way I'm coming over to help you with that honey-do stuff. I ain't coming over to help you with your yard work."

Teamwork, after all, had its limits. Even on the surging Carolina Panthers.

Gerald Williams wasn't the only Panther looking forward to Thanksgiving. In addition to moving up the weekly weigh-in, Capers also gave the players reason to be thankful by moving up the time of the Thursday workout and canceling the usual lunch. Practice was to end at about 1:10 P.M. instead of around 3:45—and most of the players expected to be showered and gone by about 1:20.

"I guess I wanted to show the players I had a heart," Capers said. "Thanksgiving is one of those holidays when everyone wants to be around family."

If family was around, that is. Otherwise, they planned to gather around each other.

Kerry Collins said he planned to eat dinner at the home of Jack Trudeau, the team's number-three quarterback. Then Collins intended to go over to the home of fellow rookie Blake Brockermeyer to watch Baylor play Texas, Brockermeyer's alma mater.

"Somebody's got to go over there and give him shit," Collins said. "I'm going to root for Baylor."

"Do that," warned Brockermeyer, "and I might just have to throw you out of the house."

Several players, including Collins, cornerback Tim McKyer and wide receiver Willie Green, spent some time delivering turkeys or Thanksgiving meals to needy people in the Rock Hill/Charlotte area. Donnie Shell, the former Pittsburgh defensive back who now was employed as the Panthers' director of player and community relations, said some players themselves came up with ideas to assist folks in need.

"Kerry came to me about wanting to do something," Shell said. "And Willie told the woman who runs the soup kitchen [for the homeless] in Rock Hill to call and tell him whatever they want him to bring, and he'll bring it."

Some of the Panthers appeared to be in serious trouble for Thanksgiving dinner.

"Can you buy a microwaveable turkey?" linebacker Carlton Bailey asked.

Another NFL tradition on Thanksgiving Day involved veterans dispatching unsuspecting rookies to collect "free" turkeys, usually at some remote outpost that either didn't exist or had no plans to give away any poultry. The Panthers claimed their rookies were too smart for this stunt, and there were no reports of it. But it reminded Frank Reich of the time in Buffalo when a group of Bills veterans went one step further with a rookie whose name he could no longer recall.

This particular rookie was told to go to a local grocery to pick up his turkey. But when he got there, he was met not by a real grocer, but by a comedian hired by the veterans to play a grocer.

The fake grocer told the rookie that, yes, he had a free turkey for him. Then he took him into a back room, where, with video cameras rolling, the comedian showed the rookie a live turkey and handed him a small ax.

"What's this?" the rookie asked.

"An ax. You have to chop the bird's head off," he replied.

Reich said the rookie's response was hysterical, especially when videotape of the event was played back during a Bills' film session the next day.

"He just kept backing off, saying, 'No way, no way I'm chopping that thing's head off,'" Reich said. "The look on his face was priceless."

The holiday mood permeating the Panthers' locker room and practice fields was so overwhelming, it even engulfed Capers. A reporter asked Capers how much he thought he would have had to fine Carlson Leomiti, the 400-pound, piano-playing offensive lineman who was one of the Original 10, if Leomiti hadn't been waived at the beginning of training camp.

"Carlson might have had to pay us to play," Capers said, laughing.

Naturally, Brett Maxie was looking forward to playing his former teammates again, this time in the very building where he wore a Saints uniform with pride for nine seasons. But he had other, more important matters on his mind as Sunday's game approached.

Like geography.

Maxie was regarded as one of the most intelligent, articulate Panthers. But his knowledge of Carolinas geography was a little weak—and his wife, Angelia, was thankful for that the Tuesday before Thanksgiving.

Maxie was at Charlotte-Douglas International Airport preparing to board an 8:45 A.M. flight for Greenville when an airline representative called his name and informed him he was supposed to have boarded a plane bound for Greenville, South Carolina, that had departed five minutes earlier. Maxie was about to step onto a plane headed for Greenville, North Carolina.

"I had no idea there were two Greenvilles," Maxie said.

Ten minutes before he was to board the next flight out to the correct Greenville, where he had scheduled a speaking engagement, Angelia reached him via the pager he was carrying. When he called her, she said she was in labor.

So Maxie skipped the flight and rushed home. Shortly thereafter, he took his wife to Carolinas Medical Center in Charlotte, where their first daughter, Maya, was born shortly before midnight.

"Had I gotten on that first plane," said Maxie, "I might have missed all the fun."

As it was, all Maxie missed was one day of practice for the Panthers. Angelia and Maya Maxie were doing fine and returned home in time for Thanksgiving dinner.

"My wife is a tough woman," Maxie said. "Here she was [Wednesday morning], having just gone through labor, and she's calling around to find out where we can get turkey, dressing, vegetables, all the trimmings. She was going to cook, but under the circumstances she just couldn't. She still wanted us all to have a nice family Thanksgiving, though."

It was a special week for Maxie and his family, which also included Brett II, three, and Adam Kennedy, two. Not only were they sharing Thanksgiving with a new addition, but Dad was going back to New Orleans to prove once again to the Saints that he could still play.

Capers still marveled at Maxie's resolve in returning from not one but two serious knee injuries to excel at the age of 33.

"When there has been something that you've done your whole life and suddenly it's taken away from you—and then you get a second chance to get it back, I think you want to make the most of the opportunity," Capers said. "I think we have some players on this team who fall into that category. Brett is one of them."

Mora admitted regret at letting Maxie go two years earlier.

"Brett Maxie, back when we were really good on defense, he was one of our best players," the Saints' coach said. "We just felt, at the time when we elected not to re-sign him, that from an injury-risk standpoint and from a financial standpoint, we had to look in another direction.

"I guess I'm not surprised Brett has come back the way he has. Brett's got a lot of heart and desire, plus a great work ethic."

As great as Maxie was with the Saints, he never had more than four interceptions in a season and he never made a Pro Bowl. Upon this return to New Orleans, Maxie was tied for first in the NFC with a career-high five interceptions—and along with another ex-Saint, the ageless Sam Mills, was being mentioned as a possibility for the Pro Bowl.

"This week will be special," Maxie said. "It will be the first time I've gone back there where I'll actually be playing for another team.

"As for going to the Pro Bowl, that would be nice if it happens. It would be something that I felt I deserved a couple of years ago and it didn't happen. It would be the icing on the cake for me this season."

Life had changed dramatically for Capers since 1991, the last year he served as an assistant coach on the Mora's staff in New Orleans.

For one thing, Capers no longer had time to work on his lawn.

While he was coaching the defensive secondary for the Saints, Capers prided himself on taking care of his own yard. Although he claimed the enormous time commitment of an NFL coach is "about the same" whether you are an assistant or a head coach, he also admitted that the mind worked a little differently when you oversaw the entire operation.

"When I have a couple of free hours now, my idea of a good time isn't to crank up the lawnmower and go out to trim the yard," Capers said. "We had the nicest yard in our neighborhood in New Orleans for a while. That came to a screeching halt when I realized it was starting to control me instead of me controlling it."

As a coach in the NFL, you must always be in control. Especially of your time.

Now Capers was returning to the Superdome in New Orleans, another of his old neighborhoods. It wasn't the first time Capers had returned to his old home since he and Mora parted ways at the end of the 1991 season, when Capers left to become defensive coordinator in Pittsburgh. The next season, the Steelers played their second preseason game in the Superdome.

Asked what he remembered most about that game, Capers smiled and replied, "Well, they kicked our tail. You tend to remember when that happens."

Capers said he also remembered meeting Mora at midfield after that game and having Mora tell him what a wonderful job he was doing. Though Mora, who remained a close friend, obviously meant well, the comment struck Capers in an unappealing way.

"I remember Mora coming over and saying, 'Don't worry things will get better,'" Capers said. "It was kind of like the first five opponents we faced this year. It's kind of funny when someone comes out, shakes your hand and says, 'Hey, you're doing a good job' when they just got finished kicking your tail."

Of course, things did get better for Capers after that midfield meeting with Mora. He built the Pittsburgh defense into one of the most feared in the NFL, and then parlayed that success into his position as the first head coach in the history of the Panthers.

And when Capers met Mora at midfield after their teams played the first time in 1995, it was under circumstances Capers enjoyed quite a bit more. His Panthers had pummeled Mora's Saints 20–3 at Clemson Memorial Stadium.

For the six years he was employed in New Orleans, Capers had a routine for those Sunday afternoons when the Saints played at home. The Saints would spend Saturday night at a hotel near the Superdome, and Capers would rise early Sunday morning and jog five miles up St. Charles Avenue. Then he would return to the team hotel to leisurely read the newspaper and shower before attending a pregame meeting and chapel.

Finally, Capers would head over to the Superdome, where he entered the home team's locker room a good three hours before kickoff.

Capers expected to find this latest Superdome experience "totally different"—and not only because it was an 8 P.M. kickoff.

"You're staying at a different hotel," he said. "And once you get there, now you're the enemy."

Maybe Lamar Lathon wasn't so crazy, after all.

The Panthers entered the game at New Orleans with a record of 5–6, with five games remaining in the regular season. They had won three in a row at home and proven they could win on the road, too.

All anyone had to do was a little math to realize Lathon's dream season was still alive.

Way back during one of the minicamps, Lathon predicted the Panthers would win "nine or 10 games" in their first season. Reporters chuckled. Teammates grimaced. Capers groaned. Charlie Dayton, director of media communications, pointed out once again that no NFL expansion team had ever won more than three contests.

When the Panthers lost their first five games and Lathon struggled to excel in the defense that was supposed to feature him at left outside linebacker, suffice it to say that Lathon wasn't looking at an alternative career as a psychic. He even pleaded compassion with the media after one of the early losses, warning not to expect too much too fast. But he never said he regretted making his well-publicized prediction, and he surely had no intention of saying it now.

"That was a prediction, my prediction," Lathon said. "We've got guys here who believe in one another. When that happens, anything is possible.

"I knew a lot of guys felt that way when I said we could win 9 or 10 games. I might have been the only one willing to say it in public, but it was being said in our locker room. The way I'm looking at our season now is that we still have the opportunity to win 10 games."

To do so, the Panthers not only had to win at New Orleans, but also would have to defeat Indianapolis, San Francisco and Atlanta—three playoff contenders—on consecutive Sundays at home, and then close out the season on Christmas Eve with a win at Washington.

If that was going to happen, or even if the Panthers were to win four of those five games to finish 9–7 and challenge for the playoffs, the Panthers would need more big plays from Lathon. There were moments when Lathon looked like he was worth every penny the Panthers were paying him, and there were moments when he looked frustrated and confused and hardly worth a salary of $3.1 million. Prior to the Cardinals game, he had even hinted that maybe this wasn't the defensive scheme for him after all.

"Buddy Ryan played me the way I wanted to be played in Houston. He told me, 'Just go get the football,' " Lathon said. "He turned me loose. That's what it's all about. I'm not the type of player you give a million assignments to and expect to be very productive. . . . I think those are some of the things that are happening to me now."

But Lathon's moods fluctuated wildly. One day he was the friendliest guy in the locker room; the next, he wouldn't talk and wasn't all that polite about it. He also seemed to forget that he willingly came to Carolina as a free agent with the prior knowledge that he was going to have to learn a new position; the Oilers had played him at defensive end, not outside linebacker. Regardless, after coming up with only three sacks in the first 10 games, Lathon came up with two in the second half against the Cardinals—and all was well in his world once again, at least for the time being.

He admitted that he had been struggling early on to adapt to Capers' complex defensive system.

"I'm feeling a little more comfortable with it every week," he said. "But initially I was like a fish out of water."

Lathon was not alone. It took many of the Panthers some time to feel at home with Capers's unique concept of blitzing often, but leaving each individual player responsible for plugging certain gaps on the line or patrolling definitive zones in the secondary. Sometimes, for instance, a defensive lineman or linebacker was supposed to feign like he would be rushing the passer and then drop back into coverage. No matter what position a player occupied, he always had to be thinking on his feet. There were times when Lathon longed to pin his ears back and rush the passer with raw emotion and power, which he possessed in great abundance, on every play.

As the weeks passed and roles became more defined, however, the Panthers developed into a formidable defensive unit. They entered the game at New Orleans ranked third in the NFC in total defense behind only San Francisco and Philadelphia.

"I guess we're not doing what we're supposed to do," Brett Maxie said. "We've surprised a lot of people. I don't know why we've surprised so many people, though. When you look at the talent we've got here, you knew it was just going to take some time to put it all together."

Well, not everyone knew—but Lamar Lathon claimed he did.

———————————

Capers loved to use statistics to prove points to his players. When they were 0–5, he attempted to prop up their sagging spirits by pointing out they were ranked among the NFL leaders in kick-return yards allowed. An obscure stat? Maybe. But Capers felt it would allow the Panthers to at least feel good about something. One week later, the Panthers won their first game, beating the Jets. A week after that, they won again—defeating the Saints at Clemson.

But now, heading into the rematch with the Saints at the Superdome, Capers was taking a different approach. He recycled the statistics from the two teams' first meeting to make certain the Panthers weren't feeling too good about themselves.

"We may have won the last game," Capers told his players, "but they won every statistical battle but three: the score, which was 20–3 in our favor; turnovers, which were 5–0 in our favor; and rushing yards, which was 126–64 in our favor.

"To me this just shows what a great equalizer turnovers are. It also shows that the Saints are a good football team that outplayed us for much of the afternoon the last time we met."

Capers insisted there was no way Jim Everett, the Saints' quarterback, was going to make the same kinds of mistakes he made in the previous encounter, when Everett was guilty of throwing four interceptions, including three on consecutive passes during one awful stretch. Everett insisted it wasn't going to happen, either.

"My performance against Carolina last time was probably the worst one of my pro career," Everett said.

Everett had been criticized earlier in his career for having "happy feet"—suggesting he danced around in the pocket under pressure and often unloaded the ball before his feet were set underneath him. He admitted that against the Panthers in their first meeting, he often was forced to throw the ball in a hurry off his back foot.

"It's kind of like physics," Everett said. "Usually there was someone in my face, and I had to hurry up and get rid of the ball to avoid taking a sack. That causes you to sometimes throw off your back foot, which sometimes causes the ball to sail on you and not go where you want it to go.

"Hey, the key for any defense is to try and get pressure on the quarterback. They're very good at it. That's their MO. They were kicking our butts all over the place."

Capers was right. Everett did not make the kinds of mistakes he made the first time the teams met.

Playing for the first time on prime time, in front of a Sunday night ESPN national television audience, the Panthers were the ones who got their butts kicked all over the place. The final score of 34–26 in the Saints' favor was deceptive; it wasn't that close.

Kerry Collins turned into the Turnover Kid again, as he was apt to do about every third game. This time he lost one fumble and threw four interceptions, accounting for five of Carolina's six turnovers. He also threw a pair of 60-yard touchdown passes, one to Mark Carrier and one to Willie Green. But the one to Carrier came with just 23 seconds left and was rather meaningless.

"It was feast or famine for me tonight," Collins said.

It was mostly famine, and he knew it. Collins threw for 335 yards, but completed only 17 of 46 passes and had all the turnovers.

"This game actually was the toughest for me to take, tougher than even the St. Louis game [when he had six turnovers]," said Collins, who seemed more dejected than after any other loss all season. "Every time we got something going, it seemed like I'd throw another interception.

"You have to be real decisive about making throws. On a couple of throws, I wasn't real decisive. I hesitated a little bit and wasn't sure. You can't do that on this level or you'll pay for it."

Even when Collins connected with a teammate, it was a night when all didn't go smoothly for the Panthers. On his long touchdown reception, Green started dancing before he was in the end zone, causing near panic among the Panthers' hierarchy watching from the press box.

"Get in the end zone!" Mike McCormack implored.

"Get in the goddamn end zone!" Bill Polian added, pounding the table in front of him for more emphasis.

Green did, but it didn't matter in the end.

The Carolina defense could not stop Everett or a New Orleans rushing attack that had entered the game ranked 29th out of 30 NFL teams. The Saints amassed more than 100 yards rushing by the third quarter, whereas only one of the Panthers' previous six opponents had been able to manage 100 yards for an entire game. The Saints rushed for only 64 themselves in the first meeting.

It wasn't the kind of impression the Panthers wanted to leave with their first national television prime-time audience. But at least they made it close at the end and never quit, even when the Saints were threatening to blow the game wide open.

"It was a chance for us to show the country the Panthers are for real," wide receiver Eric Guliford said. "I think for the most part, we did. We didn't play as well as we wanted to and we didn't win, but I thought we showed a lot of heart. We didn't quit."

Final Score

34 New Orleans   **26** Carolina

Game 13:
Indianapolis at Panthers

Yes, *these were the same Colts who last made the playoffs in a nonstrike season in 1977, long before they moved out of Baltimore in the middle of the night and took up residence in Indianapolis.*

Dom Capers was perhaps most proud of beating Indianapolis late in the season because he figured them to do well in the AFC playoffs. It was hard to argue, since in 1994 he was acting as Pittsburgh's defensive coordinator in the AFC championship game.

Capers worried all week about Jim Harbaugh, the NFL's hottest quarterback, whose rating entering the December 3 game against the Panthers was the best in the league. He thought they possessed one of the most versatile offensive weapons in the league in running back Marshall Faulk, who also lined up at wide receiver on certain plays.

And he was certain the Colts had a solid, stingy defense.

"I knew going in we weren't going to score a lot of points on that defense," Capers said. "So the only way we were going to win was to stop Harbaugh and contain Faulk. I knew that wasn't going to be easy, either."

Jim Harbaugh was a reborn football player. He entered the week of the game at Clemson on a roll, as he continued to prove to the rest of the NFL that he had come a long way since engaging in a shouting match on the sidelines with ex-Bears coach Mike Ditka, when Harbaugh was Chicago's much-maligned quarterback. You might say both Ditka and Harbaugh emerged losers in that well-publicized dispute in front of a national television audience on Monday Night Football.

"There were times earlier in my career when I wanted to be like Joe Montana," said Harbaugh, who was less than one month shy of his 32nd birthday. "But I've just come to realize that I'm not going to the Hall of Fame, and I'm never going to be compared with any of the great quarterbacks in the league.

"So I don't fight it anymore. I'm happy with who I am and what my game is, as ugly as that might be."

As a starter with the Bears, Harbaugh never completed more than 62.4 percent of his passes or had a quarterback rating higher than 81.9. He never threw for more than 15 touchdowns in season, and only twice in seven seasons finished the year with more touchdown passes than interceptions.

Much of the credit for his success, according to Harbaugh, had to go to Faulk, who burst onto the NFL scene a year earlier when he rushed for 1,282 yards and caught 52 passes for another 522 yards en route to being named Rookie of the Year. Faulk was in the process of proving his first pro season was no fluke. He entered the game against the Panthers as the Colts' leading rusher (904 yards) and leading receiver (48 catches, 415 yards).

The reason Capers feared Faulk was because of his speed.

"He has as much speed as any player we'll face this season," Capers told his players. "If you get an angle on him, wrap him up. If you don't, he'll be long gone."

Faulk presented defenses some unique problems because he alternately lined up in the backfield, in the slot or wide to the outside. He had already matched his rookie total of 12 touchdowns, with four of them coming through the air. As a rookie, he had only one touchdown catch.

"We've got a superstar in the backfield," Harbaugh said. "I'm just trying to ride his coattails to glory."

Capers didn't quite see it that way. He admitted the balance the Colts had on offense, with Faulk operating as a dual threat on the ground and through the air, was critical to their success and kept opposing defenses guessing a great deal of the time. But he was quick to add that it wouldn't be nearly as effective if the quarterback wasn't delivering the ball on target with consistency. Harbaugh was.

"The key is the quarterback," Capers said. "Harbaugh has found a rhythm. He's playing well, and they've got a difference-maker in Faulk who's touching the ball more because they've developed more ways to get it into his hands.

"You look at Harbaugh's completion percentage, plus the fact that he's got 14 touchdowns and thrown only three interceptions. That's the dream mix for your quarterback, if you're a head coach."

The Colts, in fact, had exactly the kind of balanced offensive attack coveted by Capers. They struck often with the pass and possessed big-play potential, but they never forgot the run. They mixed things up as well as just about any team in the league.

Oddly enough, Harbaugh was not the Colts' projected starter when he arrived at training camp the previous July. The Colts had traded for Craig Erickson, who was with Tampa Bay, with every intention of having Erickson quarterback the team. By the second game of the season, though, the job was Harbaugh's after he led the Colts back from a 24–3 deficit to beat the New York Jets 27–24 in overtime.

"They told me [before the season] that I was going to be the backup," Harbaugh said. "After all the moves they made in the off-season, getting rid of people, I was just happy to have a uniform."

The Panthers were determined to make sure that pristine white uniform got plenty dirty come Sunday.

Blake Brockermeyer was pretty much miserable. It was never like this at the University of Texas. Name any college or university in the country, and playing football there for a season cannot compare to surviving a full schedule in the NFL.

This was something every rookie learned eventually. Brockermeyer was learning it now.

Shortly after sunrise each day, during which he often had to battle some very large defensive linemen later on, Brockermeyer attempted a painstaking task. He attempted to lift his six-four, 315-pound frame out of bed.

It seemed every joint ached these days. Every movement off the field was cautious.

Brockermeyer was a youngster in terms of age, not yet 22. But with the Panthers preparing to play their 13th regular-season game against the Colts, on top of five presesason games and six weeks of training camp, Brockermeyer admitted he felt more like a grumpy old man.

Twice a week, Brockermeyer visited a chiropractor to have the kinks worked out of his throbbing back. He had recently moved into a new home in the prestigious Dilworth section of Charlotte but hadn't had much time to check out the neighborhood because when he was home, he was almost always in one of three places in the house—the sauna, whirlpool or steam room.

He said he had developed a routine for every Wednesday, Thursday and Friday. It began when he awoke about 7:30 A.M. and headed to Rock Hill for practice. Brockermeyer tried to arrive early enough to squeeze in the first whirlpool treatment of the day before player meetings began.

After meetings, a two-hour practice, more meetings and film-watching sessions, it was usually well after 5 P.M. when Brockermeyer returned home. He would walk his dog, True Grit, eat dinner and jump in the hot tub. Then he would move on to a cold tub and top it off with a steam bath.

By the time he was done with all that, it was just about bedtime.

"I'm usually in bed by 10 P.M. and asleep by 11," Brockermeyer said.

Overhearing Brockermeyer tell reporters this from his nearby locker stall, Kerry Collins, who had been pretending to play a violin in mock sympathy, looked up and cracked, "Tell us, Brock, what do you do from 10 to 11 before you fall asleep?"

Asked if he had a similar routine to battle the aches and pains that accompanied the job, Collins laughed and feigned a limp wrist.

"Nah," he said. "That stuff is for pussies."

Collins then insisted he was fine. Brockermeyer pointed out that the quarterback simply didn't play as manly a position, or else he wasn't quite telling the truth.

"I'm not hitting a rookie wall or anything—like some people," Collins said.

"Yeah, you're fine. Tell them about that one hit you took last Sunday," a smiling Brockermeyer said. "You didn't know where you were."

"I was a little shaken up," Collins admitted. "But only for a second or two. Seriously, I feel fine. No problems."

But he did have one serious complaint. He claimed the officials were not protecting him from cheap shots when he ran with the football and attempted to slide feet first. Under NFL rules, quarterbacks who slide are supposed to be off-limits to defensive players. Quarterbacks who don't—or quarterbacks who slide late—are considered fair game.

Collins was particularly upset about a play during Carolina's 34–26 loss the previous week at New Orleans, when he felt three Saints converged on him, one coming in to hit him with his helmet, after he tried to slide.

"If I slide, I'm supposed to be protected," Collins said. "The guy came in with his head and speared me, plain and simple. What's the story? Am I protected or not?"

Collins was so upset about that play and others like it, he admitted he was thinking about abandoning the slide. At six-five and 240 pounds, he said he might feel better going in body first.

"I'm thinking about starting to go in there and deliver the blow, instead of taking one," Collins said. "That's what it's coming to. I'm going to go in there and try to protect myself as best I can. If I slide, I'm totally exposed in the open. And if the officials aren't going to do anything about guys hitting me when I slide, why do it? If I'm going to get killed, why not go for it?"

Told later of Collins' comments, Capers grinned and said, "That's not what I want to hear. Tell him if he's going to start doing that, we'll just stick him at fullback."

Meanwhile, Brockermeyer listened to Collins' little outburst and could not help chuckling.

"Yeah, you're fine. No problems," he joked.

Brockermeyer made no such claims. He said he had expected his rookie season to be a grinder, and it was one.

"I knew it was going to be bad," he said. "Every single person I talked to said this was going to happen."

What had happened was Brockermeyer's large body was taking a severe beating from similarly large bodies in opposing uniforms each Sunday. To a lesser extent, he even absorbed punishment from defensive teammates while practicing against them during the week. And he was feeling it with every breath he took, every step he attempted to negotiate.

"I feel pretty bad," Brockermeyer said. "In fact, I feel terrible."

The problem was there were still four games remaining on the Panthers' schedule. To listen to Brockermeyer moan the rookie blues, one could not help but wonder if he would even show up for them.

But then he explained how he does it after dragging his weary body out of bed on a Sunday morning and attempting to block some of the most powerful human beings on this planet.

"Adrenaline," he said. "That's what gets you through the games. I've never had to worry about being ready to play a game or about being out there and thinking, 'Man, I'm hurting. How will I be able to make it through this?' Once you step on that field for a game, that adrenaline is pumping and that's what pulls you through. I've never had it fail me yet. When that stops, that's when I'm in trouble."

Carlton Bailey knew all about what Brockermeyer was going through as the season entered its home stretch. Playing in his eighth NFL season, less than two weeks from his 31st birthday, Bailey remembered his Friday-night routine as a rookie with the Buffalo

Bills back in 1988. Bailey used to take Bruce Smith, the Bills' perrenial All-Pro defensive end, out to dinner.

"My feeling was then, and always has been, to surround yourself with greatness whenever possible," Bailey said. "You surround yourself with the best and try to pick their brains; find out what makes them the best. That can only help you.

"That's why we all listen to Sam Mills so much around here. That can only help you. If you're a young linebacker like an Andre Royal, you'd better be following guys like Sam Mills around and asking all the questions you can think of. Soak up as much knowledge as you can. It can only help you."

That's why Bailey, who said he was making "about $50,000" at the time, would not flinch at taking Smith, who was making "$700,000 or $800,000," to dinner every Friday night.

"Bruce would take it easy on me, though," Bailey said. "We wouldn't go to a real fancy place. Usually it would only cost me about $40.

"It was kind of a tradition for rookies to do that back then, and I got a lot out of it, so I didn't mind."

Was it a tradition he was carrying on with the Panthers, having rookies take him out?

"I wish, but it doesn't work that way today," Bailey said, "Most of the time, the rookies say they don't have enough money. They're making more than we ever did when we were rookies, but they say they don't have enough money to take the veterans to dinner."

As a rookie with the Bills, Bailey figured taking a guy like Smith out to dinner could have a lasting effect on his career.

"It seems like you've played forever and you're still going strong," Bailey remembers telling Smith. "What can I do to last a long time in this league?"

Smith replied: "Carlton, the most important thing I can tell you is to take care of your body—during the season and the off-season. Take a month or five weeks off when the season ends and do nothing but let your body heal and rest. Then start getting it into shape for the next season, because it will be here before you know it."

Bailey intended to play against the Colts with a fractured right thumb. He broke it during the Arizona game, but had not missed any time because of it. You played hurt during the season, let the body heal in the off-season.

"At this point in time during a season," said Bailey, "it's all about the mental aspect. Everyone is dealing with some nagging injuries. Everyone is hurting. When you've been through it, you know it's coming, and it's easier to fight through it.

"Your first year in the league, it's kind of tough. Everyone wants to play professional football, but a lot of the younger guys just don't realize how long the season is. You're used to playing 12, maybe 13 games in college. Here, counting the preseason and if you go to the playoffs, you're talking more like 23, 24 games every year."

As the season progressed, Capers was widely being credited throughout the NFL (Buddy Ryan being the lone exception) for popularizing the zone blitz. The Colts were one of the many teams who sort of copied what Capers did in Pittsburgh with the Steelers and was doing even more of as head coach of the Panthers.

The zone blitz had been around for years but used by teams only occasionally, like in special third-down situations. No one seemed certain of its origin, although it can be traced back to the Philadelphia and Baltimore Stars of the USFL. Capers was coach of the Stars' defensive secondary in 1984 and 1985; Vince Tobin, the defensive coordinator for the Colts in 1995, who over the winter replaced Buddy Ryan as head coach of the Arizona Cardinals, was defensive coordinator of the Stars from 1983 through 1985.

Some claimed the zone blitz was born under the direction of Tobin and Capers. The Stars won USFL championships in 1984 and 1985, and in three years under Tobin ranked first in total defense twice and second once.

Capers laughed at the suggestion he invented the zone blitz, however.

"Here's my feeling on that, all right. And a lot of different things: Sometimes people are ready to step up and take the credit for things, OK? And they had to get their ideas from somewhere else. Everyone knows the 46 defense is Buddy Ryan's defense, right?" he said.

"Well, there were people who worked with him back then who said there were a lot of ideas they incorporated that came from other places, all right? People said he didn't really invent it. As you go along, the thing you have to understand is when you work on different staffs, everyone has input. And when you put everything together, sometimes you come up with variations.

"I couldn't tell you who invented the zone blitz. I know we did a little bit of it in Philadelphia. But we didn't invent the zone blitz. Systems come together and are influenced by a lot of different things. To me, it's really irrelevant who invented the zone blitz. It would be interesting to me to see who would step up and take credit for it.

"Coaches are copycats. We all copy off each other other. The important thing is we all want the same thing. We all want to be as successful as we can."

Maybe Capers didn't invent the zone blitz, but he did not deny he had a large hand in increasing its popularity. Until recent seasons, most coaches did not believe in its widespread use. But more converts were coming over every day.

The concept is built on disguising various blitzes so the offense has no idea who is coming or from where. Then, instead of protecting behind the blitz with more conventional man-to-man coverage on receivers, defenders are responsible for protecting certain areas of the field. Capers believed that by assigning coverage zones to his defensive backs, they gained better vision of the ball as a play developed. He argued that made them less susceptible to giving up the big play when a blitz was on.

Critics of the zone blitz—such as Ryan—argued that it gave up too many medium-range passes. Ryan would rather gamble on giving up the occasional big play by pressuring the opposing quarterback with all-out blitzes and relying on solid man-to-man coverage in the secondary.

"I can tell you my background with the zone blitz," Capers said. "We did a little bit of it in Philadelphia, not a lot. . . . We did a little bit of it in New Orleans, more on third down than anything else. We did a little bit of it the first year in Pittsburgh. Now there are guys on those staffs—Vince Tobin, Steve Sidwell, Vic Fangio—they all have ideas. And when we first came to Pittsburgh, Dick LeBeau had probably done more of it than anybody at Cincinnati. They weren't very big and physical at Cincinnati, so they felt they had to play that way. They had probably dabbled in more of it than anybody else on first and second down.

"The first year in Pittsburgh, we didn't do that much of it. But the first year in Pittsburgh, we were awful at rushing the passer. We were just awful. . . . If you would have looked at our team, we had good coverage people. We could cover them forever—but we had to cover them forever because the quarterback could sit back there all day. So what do you do? You come back [in the off-season] and everybody's crying about how you can't rush the passer, so from the coaching standpoint you have to try to find ways to rush the passer. So we emphasized [the zone blitz]. We worked on it in the off-season, we worked at it in training camp and we went into the next season feeling much more comfortable about being able to bring pressure on the quarterback."

It helped that the Steelers also signed Kevin Greene as an unrestricted free agent that year, pairing him at outside linebacker with the relentless Greg Lloyd. They also brought in as inside linebackers LeVon Kirkland, who had been an oustide linebacker at Clemson before playing only special teams as a rookie with the Steelers the previous year, and Chad Brown, a second-round draft choice in 1993, who had been an outside linebacker at Colorado.

"So now you're essentially playing with four outside linebackers. Your two inside linbackers can rush the passer," Capers said. "We're sitting there playing the 3-4, and we've got four guys who can rush the passer. So we started thinking about how we can bring those four guys in different combinations.

"And it's like anything. As you go along, certain things you have success with, you're going to start doing them more and more. We went from 19th in the league in sacks to 12th. . . . But we still weren't in that upper echelon, so we continued to work on it. And then we went from 12th to first. We did far more of it [zone blitzing] my last year, and that's when all the Blitzburgh stuff started."

As in Pittsburgh, Capers had tailored his Carolina defensive roster to the 3-4 base defense and the zone blitz, although the Panthers obviously could slip into a 4-3 alignment and often did, or even man-to-man coverage in the secondary, which they occasionally did.

To beat the Colts, they would have to beat them at their own game. The Colts liked to do many of the same things defensively.

"We were successful at the end of last year going with the zone blitz, so we decided to expand on it this year," Colts coach Ted Marchibroda said. "It's become more dominant throughout the league this year. I think it's becoming more prevalent every year in the National Football League. More teams are having success with it. It's certainly a tremendous scheme.

"There's no question Coach Capers did a tremendous job with it in Pittsburgh, and is continuing to do a tremendous job with it now."

So the outcome of this game could depend on how well the two quarterbacks, Collins and Harbaugh, reacted to defenses that probably would resemble the ones they faced every day in practice. Capers said he was confident Collins would be able to read some of the zone blitzes sure to come his way.

"A lot of their zone blitzes are very similar to the ones we run," Capers said.

Pausing, Capers then smiled and added, "A couple of them, in fact, are exactly the same."

The Panthers were pleased to get their two Derricks back for the Indianapolis game, with both running back Derrick Moore and offensive lineman Derrick Graham returning from their knee injuries.

OK, so they were more pleased to get Moore back. Capers said he intended to start Moore but did not know how much he would be able to play.

"I'm like a volcano waiting to erupt," Moore said.

Graham, meanwhile, returned to find he no longer had a starting job at right tackle. Mark Dennis, who had been selling commercial real estate in Chicago when Graham signed his whopping contract with the Panthers the previous spring, had played well enough while Graham was out that the coaching staff did not want to make a change.

"I'm not going to lie to you: Not starting is a disappointment," Graham said. "I would like to start."

The running joke around the locker room was that he probably would false-start. No matter how many decent plays or even decent games Graham could string together, no one would ever completely forget or forgive his false start on the two-point conversion attempt in the regular-season opener at Atlanta, when he cost the Panthers a chance at victory.

"It has haunted me," he admitted. "We had a chance to win the game. Was it my fault we lost? Maybe, maybe not. All I know is that we kicked the extra point and went to overtime, so we still had a chance to win."

Against the Colts, the Panthers' key to having a chance of winning rested on their ability to pressure Harbaugh.

It did not look good when Indianapolis started its first drive of the game at the Carolina 33-yard line after a personal-foul penalty on Dwight Stone forced Tommy Barnhardt to punt out of his own end zone. On the Colts' second play from scrimmage, Harbaugh lofted a beautifully thrown pass to wide receiver Sean Dawkins for a 31-yard touchdown.

Surprisingly, the Panthers used a four-man rush and man-to-man coverage on the play, hoping to throw the Colts, who surely would be expecting zone blitzes from the 3-4 package, out of their rhythm at the start. It didn't work, and the Panthers quickly abandoned this rather absurd reverse-psychology strategy.

"It was going to be a long day if we didn't change our scheme back to what we do best," Capers said. "Harbaugh had time to sit in the pocket and let the route develop on his touchdown throw. That play looked exactly like a lot of the film we had been watching of Harbaugh all week long."

The rest of the afternoon, however, the Panthers unleashed a variety of fierce zone blitzes, which had become their trademark, usually out of a 3-4 alignment. The Colts scored again on their second possession of the game for a 10–0 lead but had to settle for a field goal when Harbaugh was sacked twice.

From there, Harbaugh became harrassed relentlessly. He was confused, frustrated and, finally, injured and unable to continue. The Panthers sacked him a total of six times and drummed him from the game with a knee injury that would require arthroscopic surgery two days later. After their first two possessions, the Colts never again penetrated past the Carolina 46-yard line.

Even when the Panthers weren't sacking Harbaugh, they were forcing him to make costly mistakes. On one play late in the first half, linebacker Darion Conner bore down on Harbaugh and forced a hurried throw in the direction of Marshall Faulk, who never turned to see the ball. Instead, Greg Kragen of the Panthers grabbed the second interception of his 11-year career and began lumbering downfield on a 29-yard interception return that stunned his teammates and foes alike.

"I thought he might even make it all the way to the end zone," Sam Mills said of Kragen. "But then I looked at his number and saw who it was, and I knew he wasn't going to score. He did get a lot farther than I thought he would, though. And the important thing was, he didn't drop the ball."

"I'm not very fast," Kragen admitted. "And I showed it, too. I haven't been timed in the 40 in years. They'll be able to figure it out, though, by watching the film. And that's what's bad."

Cornerback Tim McKyer came over to help block on Kragen's return, and appeared to be begging for the nose tackle to lateral the ball to him toward the end of the play. Kragen ignored him.

"I'm sure he wanted the ball, knowing Tim," Kragen said. "But I was going to enjoy my 15 yards of fame."

Kragen's surprisingly nimble return helped set up a 34-yard John Kasay field goal that tied it at 10–10 just before halftime.

On the Colts' first possession of the third quarter, Conner sacked Harbaugh on consecutive plays, giving him three sacks for the day in by far his most productive game as a Panther. Harbaugh left the game soon thereafter, leaving it to his inexperienced backup, Paul Justin, to finish up.

The Panthers sacked Justin once over the last one and a half quarters, giving them a season-high seven sacks for the day.

Though the Panthers struggled offensively as well, their receivers dropping at least six passes, they played well enough to win. Kasay added a 38-yard field goal with 12 seconds left after a controversial facemask penalty on Colts defender Derwin Gray gave the Panthers the ball at the Indianapolis 23-yard line.

It wasn't a routine field goal.

"When I planted to kick it, I slipped," Kasay said. "The whole ground just gave way. I just thank God I was able to get enough foot on it to get it through."

Capers was ecstatic, clearly as happy as he had been after any previous victory.

"I'm happy because we beat a darn good football team out there today," he said.

Carlton Bailey was happy, too.

"Yeah, Harbaugh was the number-one quarterback in the league as far as efficiency and everything," Bailey said. "But nobody had put heat on him like we thought we could. It was definitely a challenge to go out there and get in his face and knock him around a little bit.

"I was praying to God on the sidelines [for Kasay's winning kick]. I was saying, 'Listen, I'm a little bit banged up. My thumb hurts. Please let him put it through so I can rest a little bit.'"

In the losing locker room, Marshall Faulk mumbled answers to a few cursory questions and then rudely brushed reporters aside. Harbaugh talked freely, but kept one eye on the door for a quick exit and a date with the X-ray machine, which he feared would reveal torn cartilage in his right knee, courtesy of the Panthers.

Final Score

13 Carolina   **10** Indianapolis

Game 14:
San Francisco at Panthers

Finally, in the 15th week of their inaugural season, the Panthers had a sellout at Clemson Memorial Stadium. But were the fans coming to see the Panthers or the San Francisco 49ers?

Even some of the Panthers weren't so sure. Derrick Moore, the Panthers' best running back and surely a player Carolina fans should flock to see in person, said he could fully understand why folks would rather spend their hard-earned dollars to watch such NFL standouts as Steve Young and Jerry Rice and some of the other 49ers instead.

"Those guys are legends, true Hall of Famers," Moore said. "If I was a father and I had a son, I would take my son to see those guys play if I could. It's a thrill to watch them play."

So maybe the Panthers would have sold out their home game against the 49ers all along, no matter how the Panthers themselves had been playing.

And maybe not.

As it was, the sellout was assured because the game offered a delightful matchup packed with intrigue and riveting subplots that no one could have imagined possible prior to the season—or even five games into it. The Panthers were 6–7 and clinging to slim hopes of becoming the first expansion team in NFL history to make the playoffs. The 49ers were still smarting from a 13–7 defeat at the hands of the Panthers in San Francisco a month earlier, and hellbent on avenging the embarrassing loss.

The Panthers were thrilled to be staging this contest of large possibilities in front of their first full house at home. They realized the 49ers would look to bury them and their crowd early in a rush of raw revenge—but the Panthers were determined not to be put to shame too quickly in front of so many home fans.

Or at least what they hoped would be fans rooting for Carolina. They privately feared there might be more Young and Rice supporters than their own in the 76,000-plus throng.

"If we win this one, I think the entire season turns. I mean, everything changes for this organization," Moore said. "I didn't think I would be saying this our first season, but this is a huge football game."

It was huge because with victories came expectations. And the expectations for the Panthers, even in terms of what they had come to expect from themselves each Sunday, had risen with each win—especially so after the earlier win in San Francisco.

In a way, it was flattering to have so many people asking about the playoffs. But Dom Capers still didn't want to talk about it heading into the week of preparation for the second encounter with the defending NFL champions.

"I'm going to be very honest with you," he told reporters at his Monday news conference. "I don't have any idea about the standings right now. When we beat San Francisco, then I'll get real interested in it—*real* interested."

Capers obviously meant to say "if we beat San Francisco," but it was an interesting slip of the tongue. The Panthers, with only three weeks left in their inaugural season, still had an outside shot at one of the three NFC wild-card playoff berths. But Capers was right. They needed to beat San Francisco for a second time to make it happen, and then they would have to beat Atlanta at home and Washington on the road in their final two games, too.

The 49ers were determined to put an end to Panthers' playoff talk. Since losing to the expansion club a month earlier in San Francisco, they had been playing like the Super Bowl champions they were last season—winning four in a row, including one very impressive victory at Dallas the week after losing to Carolina.

"There's no question about it," said 49ers linebacker Ken Norton, Jr. "The Carolina game was our wake-up call."

The loss to the Panthers had dropped the 49ers' record to 5–4 and started talk that they might struggle to make the playoffs. But now the 49ers were 9–4 and again sitting in control in the NFC West.

Moore, who as usual, was in the mood to talk as the week progressed, said this should have surprised no one.

"Just being out there in training camp with them," said Moore, "I got a taste of what the standard is for the 49ers. They don't come to training camp with a goal of getting to the Super Bowl. They come to training camp with a goal of winning the Super Bowl. Every year. The goal never changes."

Moore said he did not expect to hear much pregame bravado from the 49er camp. That just wasn't their style. But he suspected they were pumped up to avoid being swept by the upstarts from Carolina.

"They won't say a lot. You won't hear a lot of quotes from their guys. That's not the way they do things. But you'll see it in how they play Sunday. I've been around the 49ers and I understand how they feel when they lose. . . . They're committed to winning. They take all the little things very seriously."

One factor that was going to be profoundly different from their first meeting was the fellow who would be standing under center from the start for the 49ers. Out with an injured shoulder during the earlier game, Steve Young was back.

"They're a well-oiled machine when he's in there," cornerback Rod Smith said of the 49ers and Young.

Added Capers: "He will challenge us. No one can scramble around and make plays like Steve Young."

Moore said Young was such a unique player that he had the ability to lift the performances of others. Mere mortal quarterbacks could not possibly have such a positive impact.

"When that number 8 is in the lineup, he has a way of creating an atmosphere of confidence, not only on offense, but also on defense and special teams," Moore warned. "The old saying is that as long as Steve Young is on the field, they have hope, man. His presence is impressive."

The best way to counteract Young's presence was to put together some long drives on offense and keep him in a ballcap on the far sideline as much as possible. On this, Moore and Capers and all of the Panthers agreed.

"The thing we're going to have to do is not turn the ball over and control the clock some," Moore said. "I think we need to keep Steve Young off the football field. I mean, he's a dynamic player. So is Rice. But if Steve Young is on the football field a long time, there isn't a defense in the world that can stop him. He's going to find a way to beat you.

"So the thing I've got to do is get my butt in gear and pound the ball between those tackles. And then Kerry has to hit them for some big plays, and our receivers have to come through with the catches. That's what we have to do to keep Steve Young on the sideline as much as possible."

Moore paused, as if he suddenly realized he had been talking a long time.

Then he looked around his own locker room and wondered aloud what future lay in store for the Carolina teammates he had grown to cherish. Moore knew he would become a free agent at season's end. So would several other starters. Would they ever have a chance to stay together and develop the kind of camaraderie that seemed to drive the 49ers year after year?

Moore asked the question, but he couldn't quite answer it. No matter how long he talked, he always seemed to come back around to Sunday's game and what a challenge it was for such a fledgling team. If the Panthers beat the 49ers a second time and bore down on the playoffs, surely management would find a way to keep all of them together, wouldn't they? Or maybe it was impossible to keep any team together in this day and age of the salary cap and wide-open free agency.

Moore's mind was spinning with all these possibilities as he gazed around the room one last time before heading off to a meeting for the running backs. He knew he was right about one thing—this was a huge game. Were the Panthers ready for it?

"We have some fine football players in this locker room," he said. "That's a real credit to the organization, to go out and get the players. I hope we can stay together. We've gone out and we've demonstrated that we can win. I don't think anyone thought that, as a first-year team, we could be in a situation against the San Francisco 49ers this late in the season to possibly be in the playoff hunt. I mean, nobody would have thought that.

"Sometimes you don't prepare for these things, and then suddenly they're right in your face.

Paul Butcher, the Panthers' leading tackler on special teams, had spent all season waiting to play a game like the one against Indianapolis the previous week. Dr. Psycho was playing against some ex-teammates again, and he obviously was pumped. He even went so far as to bump one of the Colts aggressively during the coin toss.

"I played there the last two years and we're good buddies," Butcher said. "But when I went out there to shake hands, [Colts linebacker Jeff] Herrod drilled me. I didn't appreciate it. I thought, 'So here we go.' I told him we're not going to have any of that stuff."

Later, Butcher leveled various Colts on several special-teams plays. He labeled two of them "nice blowups" and said he had a total of four knockdowns, "although I think I clipped a guy on one of them. Even though the officials didn't call it, I guess I shouldn't count that one."

Butcher said slipping a clip by the officials wasn't all that unusual.

"A lot of times, those guys are so worried about getting out of the way and not getting hurt that they don't have time to watch what we're doing. Or else everything is happening so fast and so many bodies are flying around, they can't see it. It happens all the time," he said.

Of the blowups, Butcher said, "That's what I play for. I love those."

Blake Brockermeyer, the aching rookie, wasn't so pleased about all that had transpired on the field during the win over the Colts. He had to sit out one play after getting kicked in the groin, which was only the second play he sat out all season.

"That was a true test, that game," Brockermeyer said. "It's a tough thing to keep playing with after you get hit there, but I just hate missing plays. It sucks. My goal was to play every single play of the season."

Brockermeyer pointed out this was the goal of all starting offensive linemen on the Panthers, but it wasn't easily achieved. First, you had to stay healthy all the time. Secondly, you had to play so well and so hard on every single play that the coaches never thought about taking you out for even a one-play breather. The only Carolina offensive lineman to achieve this goal thus far was center Curtis Whitley, and Brockermeyer did not hide the fact that he was a little jealous.

"I need him to miss two now, so I can get the team lead," Brockermeyer said.

Then Brockermeyer yelled across the locker room to fellow rookie Andrew Peterson, also an offensive lineman.

"Hey, Pete! Maybe you could help me. Why don't you hide Whitley's helmet for a couple of plays this week?"

Joe Gibbs, the man who could have been coach of the Panthers but turned them down, visited Winthrop Coliseum to interview Capers, the man who became coach of the Panthers, for a pregame show that would air on NBC-TV prior to Sunday's game against the 49ers.

Gibbs insisted if he had taken the job, there was no way he could have produced more positive results than Capers had.

"My thought, first of all, is that they can't do any better than they're doing," Gibbs said. "They got the right guy, I tell you. As a matter of fact, I would have to say this has been phenomenal."

When he interviewed Capers, Gibbs playfully told Capers so.

"You'd better back off a little," Gibbs jokingly said to Capers. "They're going to expect you to win the Super Bowl next year. You're going to get yourself in a mess."

Capers smiled and replied: "Well, that's easy for you to say. From where I'm standing, you want to win every one that you can win."

Gibbs later recalled his first year as head coach of the Redskins in 1981, saying he found similarities between it and the Panthers' first season. At the same time, he admitted what the Panthers faced in their inaugural season was far more awesome a task than what he had faced in Washington.

"When I came to the Washington Redskins, I started out 0–5," he said. "I didn't think I was ever going to win a game. That first year was a nightmare. You're trying to get used to everybody for the first time, all the personalities that are involved, you're trying to change the offense and everything. You're seeing all these players for the first time. You don't have anything to base things on. You don't know how they fit into your offense at all.

"It's difficult enough if you're going from one year to the next. But when you start from scratch, you've got nothing. You've got nothing to go on—defensively, offensively, special teams, all that. Man, I tell you, it's a nightmare. You watch most coaches that go through it, and it's a killer.

"But these guys, shoot, they went through it like it was nothing. It was like they breezed through it. Bill Polian did a great job of getting the players and Dom, I think, has just done a phenomenal job of coaching."

Someone mentioned to Gibbs that his team that started out 0–5 finished 8–8. One year later, the Redskins captured the first of three Super Bowls they would win during Gibbs' tenure, winning 12 of 13 games in the regular season and playoffs during a strike-shortened season. Gibbs laughed at the memory of the sudden turnaround.

"I said I thought that 0–5 [start] drove us to the Super Bowl," he said. "The players didn't want to go back to that. We were called every name in the book. We would all look for different ways to get home at night. In Washington, believe me, it was serious at 0–5."

The Panthers already had far exceeded everyone's expectations, Gibbs said. But another win over the 49ers, while highly unlikely, was not out of the question.

"I don't care what anyone says—[Fellow NBC analyst and former Bears coach Mike] Ditka might say he thought the expansion teams would win this much, but I think he said it after they already had won five. I don't remember him saying it earlier, but he says he said it.

"Truthfully, I would have thought they'd win three or four. Who would have thought you'd even be thinking at this point in the year that they could maybe win half their games? I just didn't think that would be possible."

His reasons for that, Gibbs said, were based largely on all the logistical problems the Panthers faced at the start in finding and then working out of a temporary practice facility, and then playing their first season's worth of home games two and a half hours from where the team was supposed to be based. Having to worry about all that stuff on top of trying to build a roster from scratch made the job being done by Capers all the more impressive.

"I think this has been harder [than what he faced in Washington]. You've got to go to a place like this [Winthrop], which is a backup facility," Gibbs said. "What I found as a coach and a general manager is that stuff like this eats up all your time.

You spend all your time running around trying to get everything together. Are the fields right? Are the facilities OK? You worry about things like that instead of worrying exclusively about coaching the offense and the defense, which is what you should be worrying about.

"All first years are difficult for coaches, but I would have to say this one is a lot harder than anything I ever went through."

Like many other close observers of the NFL, Gibbs was beginning to figure any team with a coach like Capers calling the shots was going to have a chance to win most Sundays, no matter who the opponent. Gibbs was asked how much of the Panthers' remarkable first-year success could be attributed to Capers.

"A lot. I would say it takes everybody. Obviously, it takes everything. You can't win in the NFL if you're weak anyplace. And it's like any other professional sport. I say it in auto racing, too. If you're weak anywhere, you're not going to the top," Gibbs said.

"You have to have somebody to pick the players. You've got to have the front-office management to get 'em signed. And you've got to have somebody to coach 'em. And that coach, now that I'm out of it I think I can say, he influences which players are picked . . . he's gonna have the biggest influence on that coaching staff, and that coaching staff is gonna have a huge influence on everything that goes on around here for a long time. Then he's gonna have that direction on the field. So you're talking about somebody who is extremely important. That's a key guy. It's like picking the CEO. You're picking somebody there who's going to have a big influence.

"That's one of the things I admire about Jerry and Bill and Mike. I think they knew that from the beginning. Mike had been a head coach. And I think Bill is a little different than most general managers. He's a head coach's general manager. He'll fight for you. I think all of those guys realized that this was a very big decision. If you're going to pick somebody who has never been a head coach, you'd better pick one that's been great at what he does. Dom has been great at what he does. Certainly he's been one of the top defensive coaches the last few years. He's also been in the eye of the hurricane calling plays. If you're going to be a head coach, you'd better make good game-day decisions. And then, the thing that you're not going to know about because you haven't really seen it, is handling people. You can be great at the X's and O's, but not be able to handle people. This guy can handle people, too.

"I think he's just doing a fantastic job and he was a great pick. I think you've got a guy who's going to be a coaching star."

Gibbs was not the only one convinced Capers was going to be a NFL coaching star, or even already was one. George Seifert, coach of the 49ers, was another fan.

Asked during the Wednesday conference call with writers who covered the Panthers if he thought Capers was a legitimate candidate for the NFL Coach of the Year award, Seifert responded: "I don't think he's a candidate. I think he's the guy.

"It goes beyond being a candidate when you take a brand-new franchise and have them playing like a seasoned group of veterans. There aren't many teams who have been around for a long time and have a winning tradition, like we do, that are playing any more efficiently than the way they're playing."

There were, in fact, teams that had been around a long time who were playing a whole lot less efficiently than the Panthers had been playing over the previous eight weeks, a span over which they owned a 6–2 record.

Capers visibly squirmed in his seat when told Seifert had endorsed him as NFL Coach of the Year.

"I don't want to hear that," Capers said. "I know Coach Seifert. I've got a tremendous amount of respect for him. I think he's an outstanding coach. But I think he's a very good tactician, too. He's trying to soften up the troops before he brings the hammer in here."

Maybe so, but Gibbs revealed Capers was his preliminary choice for Coach of the Year as well.

"I was going to make that [prediction] on TV," Gibbs said. "I can't picture anybody doing any better than this in coaching this season. What they're doing here is phenomenal."

He may have been a potential Coach of the Year candidate, but Capers still had those moments when he seemed all too human and down to earth, which was part of his appeal to the masses. Friday night, roughly 42 hours before his Panthers were to meet the 49ers in front of the first NFL sellout crowd at Clemson Memorial Stadium, Capers was at Belk's department store in Southpark Mall, fulfilling a commitment to sign autographs for fans that had been made against his knowledge long before anyone realized how ridiculous the timing of such a session would be. Yet Capers not only showed up for what was supposed to be a 45-minute session, but stayed for two hours.

"I finally had to leave, and there were still some people left in line," he said. "It wasn't my idea of a good time the Friday night before such a big game, but I said I would do it, or at least someone said I would do it, so I did it."

The key to the Panthers' surprising success, according to Seifert, was they weren't playing like an expansion team. They were playing more like a team that had been together for years, like Moore hoped they would continue to be.

"I look at their talent and look at the talent of some established teams, and they're right there," Seifert said

Yet many of the Panthers arrived from places like Buffalo, Detroit, Pittsburgh and Kansas City, where they were no longer wanted. They called themselves grunts, castoffs and misfits.

And they did not care in the least that the 49ers were listed as 15-point favorites for Sunday's encounter.

"I'm glad. I wish they were 30-point favorites," cornerback Tim McKyer said. "That takes all the pressure off us and puts all of it on them."

The Carolina roster was littered with guys like McKyer, who was left exposed in the expansion draft by Pittsburgh and chosen by the Panthers in the 12th round. The underdog makeup of the Carolina roster was illustrated when compared to that of the 49ers. Thirteen of the 49ers' 22 starters had been to the Pro Bowl; twelve of the Panthers' 22 starters basically were rejects from other teams.

Mark Carrier and Eric Guliford, the starters at wide receiver, were obtained in the expansion draft, as was Whitley, the starting center who never missed a play, and starting fullback Bob Christian. Two more starting offensive linemen, right tackle Mark Dennis and left guard Matt Elliott, were free-agent pickups off the street, while Derrick Moore, the team's leading rusher, was signed as a free agent after being waived in the preseason by San Francisco.

On defense, McKyer and starting nose tackle Greg Kragen were by-products of the expansion draft. Linebacker Carlton Bailey and defensive backs Pat Terrell and Brett Maxie were all signed as free agents after being cut loose by teams who no longer wanted them.

There were some key reserves, like wide receiver Willie Green, special-teams madman Butcher, and long-snapper Mark Rodenhauser, who also were unwanted until the Panthers came calling. All of these guys were beginning to feel somewhat vindicated by the success the Panthers had been having on the field.

"I'm not surprised by where we're at," Green said. "Everyone is playing as a team. Everyone is playing as a unit. Even when we started out 0–5, no one was pointing fingers.

"I call us grunts because no one else wanted us. Not too many guys came here by choice or because they wanted to. They came because they had no other options."

Kragen, a hero during the previous week's win over Indianapolis, had to be talked out of retirement twice by Capers after being selected off Kansas City's roster in the 18th round of the expansion draft. First Kragen almost didn't come to Carolina at all; then he nearly quit early in training camp.

"It's been fun," Kragen said. "I don't know about the rest of the guys, but I did not think I would be having this much fun playing this year. If I had decided to sit this one out, I would be at home kicking myself right now."

Kragen had promised his wife Cindy he would retire following the previous season in Kansas City, when Kragen made a career-low eight tackles and played sparingly. The only reason he didn't announce it was at the request of the Chiefs, so they could put him in the expansion draft pool.

The Panthers were aware of Kragen's plans to retire, but took him anyway. They hoped to talk him out of retirement and did eventually, but Kragen was still wary of the season that lay ahead.

"My honest opinion of what I expected on an expansion team?" Kragen asked, repeating a reporter's question. "I thought there would be a lot of guys high-fiving over the top of my body on the ground as they were scoring another touchdown on us. I thought it would be a long, frustrating year."

Despite playing with what Kragen called "a bunch of misfits and castoffs," that hadn't been the case at all.

"This year has been full of surprises," he said. "This team is as competitive as any team I've ever played on. I wouldn't have believed it, but it's true."

The Panthers hoped to pull yet another wonderful surprise out of the helmet when Sunday dawned, a crystal blue sky and beaming sunlight failing to block out the numbness of a surprisingly cold day in Clemson. It was 34 degrees at kickoff, with a wind-chill factor of 12 degrees. It also grew considerably colder as the game progressed.

Especially on the Panthers' sideline.

The objective entering the game was to keep Steve Young off the field as much as possible. By early in the fourth quarter, Young was wearing a parka and a ballcap on the sideline—but he was not there because the Panthers were hogging the ball or because their defense had knocked him silly. Young also was wearing a wide smile after picking apart the highly rated Carolina defense in what became a 31–10 rout for the defending Super Bowl champions.

In the process, the Panthers had their hopes of becoming the first expansion team in NFL history to make the playoffs squashed. Their record slipped to 6–8, and the league reported they were officially eliminated from the race for an NFC wild-card berth.

Young was magnificent, as Derrick Moore had feared he would be. The San Francisco quarterback completed 31 of 45 passes for 336 yards, throwing for two touchdowns and running for another. He showed the sellout crowd of 76,136 exactly what Moore had been talking about when the Carolina running back said the 49ers are a completely different team with Young at the helm.

In the first meeting between the teams, when Young watched from the sideline while nursing an injured shoulder, the Panthers' defense forced five turnovers and held the 49ers to one touchdown. In this second meeting, the Young-directed offense matched that scoring total before the game was five minutes old.

The only chance the Panthers seemed to have of keeping the game close was snuffed out on a controversial play call and bonehead decision by Kerry Collins toward the end of the first quarter. After a great defensive play by Sam Mills produced a sack and fumble by Young that Mills himself recovered, the Panthers seized the opportunity and promptly drove to the 49ers' one-yard line.

But instead of running the ball on first-and-goal, as expected, Collins faked a handoff and rolled out to the right, fooling no one—least of all Bryant Young, a 49ers' defensive tackle who immediately was in hot pursuit. Under pressure from Young, Collins panicked and fired the ball directly to Tim McDonald, the 49ers' strong safety. No Panther receiver was visible in the immediate vicinity.

"It was a poor decision on our part," Capers said. "We should have thrown the ball away there."

Well, Collins knew the "we" was he. Though the play call would be questioned, and Young would later claim he was tipped off on what it was going to be by the stances taken by the Panthers' offensive linemen, the truth of the matter was it wouldn't have been such a disaster if Collins had only exercised good judgment and chucked the ball into the fifth row of the stands.

Capers said the play call, made by offensive coordinator Joe Pendry from the press box, was considered a safe one because that is exactly what Collins had been instructed to do. Then the Panthers would still have two downs, and maybe even three, to attempt to run the ball into the end zone.

"It was a bad decision," Collins admitted. "There was nothing wrong with the call. . . .If you throw it out of bounds, you can still come back on second down and try to get it in."

Moore was upset the Panthers didn't simply hand him the ball on first down.

"That was the beginning of the end to the day for our football team," Moore said. "It was first-and-goal, so you figure you've got four shots at it. I guess that's why coaches coach and players play. But you know what was in the back of my mind. . . . When we got down there, I'm smelling paydirt, man."

Capers said the decision to go with a play-action pass on first down was made in part because of a fumble 49ers linebacker Gary Plummer caused at the goal line the previous week against Buffalo, producing a 96-yard return for a touchdown by teammate Lee Woodall. The Panthers' coaching staff had taken a good look at the play on videotape and had determined in advance during the week that they would try a play-action pass instead if they got into a similar situation on the goal line against the 49ers.

When told of this explanation, Moore still wasn't satisfied.

"Hindsight is 20-20," he said. "I'm not the offensive coordinator or the head coach—but you know, I thought we ran well with the opportunties we had. . . . Whether or not lightning can strike twice on the same play, I don't know. That was the kind of play in the Buffalo game where they made a play that you might make once or twice in a career."

After the botched scoring chance, the 49ers quickly moved to put the Panthers away and did. They led 21–3 by halftime, as Jerry Rice went on to have a great day receiving: six catches for 121 yards, including two long ones brilliantly hauled in to set up 49er touchdowns. That meant one thing: Tim McKyer had a lousy day defending him.

Although McKyer wasn't always the one on Rice, he did seem to be the one who was on him just about every time he caught a pass.

"I'm extremely disapppointed in how I played," McKyer said. "I feel I let the team down. I was out there and I was fighting to make plays, but I couldn't. I don't even want to know [Rice's] numbers. He made some incredible plays."

McKyer felt the 49ers picked on him a little bit, but he wasn't complaining about it. When you get picked on, he said, you have to rise to the occasion and make plays. He didn't get it done.

"If you consider our last game against them," said McKyer, "I made the play that beat them [on a 96-yard interception return]. I gave them 96 reasons to want to come in here and make me look bad. I think that left a bad taste in their mouths, and a lot of those guys said, 'Let's go make Tim look bad.'"

They succeeded. But McKyer was not alone. Collins was terrible, completing only 12 of 27 passes for 127 yards. Derrick Moore went nowhere on the ground, gaining just 28 yards on nine rush attempts. The defense, other than perhaps the irrepressible Sam Mills, spent too much of the chilly afternoon attempting in vain to slow a San Francisco offense that piled up 398 yards and churned out 26 first downs to Carolina's 12.

"We got a taste of what a championship team looks like today," Moore said.

Final Score

31 San Francisco   **10** Carolina

Game 15:
Atlanta at Panthers

T he loss to San Francisco ended the Panthers' hopes for the playoffs, but the playoffs were very much on their minds as they prepared to host the Atlanta Falcons. The Panthers knew a Falcons' victory would secure a playoff berth for the NFC West foe they had fallen victim to in their regular-season opener. The Carolina players still felt they would have won had offensive tackle Derrick Graham not been guilty of a false start on a two-point conversion attempt late in regulation of the 23–20 overtime defeat.

Avenging that bitter setback wasn't the only reason the Panthers were pumped for their final "home game" at Clemson. At long last, this was going to be it for the bus rides.

Playing at Clemson meant enduring long bus rides going to and returning from each home game. It seemed appropriate, in fact, that Carolina's final opponent at Clemson actually had a shorter drive—100 miles from its training facility in Suwanee, Georgia, to Death Valley—than the home team itself. The Panthers' training facility in Rock Hill was 140 miles away.

Asked a one-word description for the bus rides to and from Clemson, Panthers rookie Blake Brockermeyer responded: "Torture." Asked to expand it to two words, Brockermeyer would say, "It sucks."

"It's like every game we've played has been an away game this year," added Paul Butcher.

"You lose out on 12 hours of your weekend," Brockermeyer explained further. "And that long bus ride back after a game is the last thing you want to do when you're sore and tired. You don't have any room at all to stretch out. Those trips back seem like they last forever, especially if you lose the game."

Brockermeyer usually passed the time by playing cards on Bus No. 3, one of the four buses the Panthers piled into at precisely 3 P.M. the Saturday before each home game after holding a brief walkthrough at Winthrop University. The walkthrough normally was held in the gym at Winthrop Coliseum, but one time it took place on the asphalt in the parking lot, next to the buses. The women's volleyball team from Winthrop had dibs on the gym that day.

"You don't mess with Title IX these days," Coach Dom Capers said.

Capers was determined from the beginning not to let the long bus trips become a serious issue with the players. Sure, they complained about them—with increasing frequency and intensity as the season wore on—but Capers tried to keep the complaints to a minimum by running a rather loose bus.

Each bus showed a movie, usually provided for by the players. The head coach always rode shotgun up front in Bus No. 1, sitting to the right of the driver. Most trips on the way to Clemson, he slept. But sometimes he watched the movie.

"I watched Cool Hand Luke, *the one starring Paul Newman," Capers said. "That's an old classic. I've always liked that movie."*

Others rode Bus No. 1 for different reasons.

"That's where the Kentucky Fried Chicken is," running back Derrick Moore said. "I really don't know what's happening on the other buses. I just make sure I get to where the chicken is."

Capers, of course, was a health-conscious eater who abstained from that kind of food, which was provided on a rotating basis by one of the starting linebackers. Capers would bring along a tunafish sub instead, although he later admitted, "I won't say I haven't had any of the chicken."

Most of the defensive backs rode on Bus No. 2, where the featured food was pizza purchased by the rookies. A local pizzeria in Rock Hill always gave the Panther rookies a huge discount, as if they needed it.

Bus No. 3 was regarded by some veterans as "the scavenger bus" because there rarely was any organized plan to bring food and they scavenged off the other buses just before departure to make certain they didn't go hungry. It also was the bus where Brockermeyer and Bubba McDowell and others engaged in spirited card games.

Bus No. 4 was reserved for players and staff who preferred to keep kind of quiet, content to watch whichever movie was on. Oftentimes, players rode different buses based on what was playing at the movies.

"They just go up to the bus, look on the window to see what's playing and go to whatever bus has the right movie to suit their tastes," Capers said. "But it's first-come, first-served—just like going to the theater. If one show is sold out, you've got to move on to another one."

Other pregame movie favorites, appropriately enough, were The Longest Yard *and* Young Guns. *The linebackers particularly enjoyed* The Longest Yard, *starring Burt Reynolds as a former pro football star who gets jailed and puts together a formidable prison team of inmates who beat up on a team comprised of overbearing guards.*

"Look at Mike Fox there," said Carlton Bailey, pointing to the towering defensive end. "He looks exactly like the guy in that movie who tackles a guard and then stands over him and says, 'I think I broke his friggin' neck. I think I broke his friggin' neck.'"

The first time the Panthers played the Falcons, Chris Doleman ran through and around Brockermeyer for three and a half sacks. Afterward, Doleman told reporters Brockermeyer was a nice enough young man.

"He gave me a lot of compliments out there on the field today," Doleman claimed. "He kept telling me how good I was."

These comments infuriated Brockermeyer.

"I never said any of that stuff. It really pissed me off that he said I did," Brockermeyer said. "He said I was telling him how good he was and stuff like that. I don't know where he came up with all that. I didn't say a word to him the whole game."

It wasn't like Brockermeyer was the only one abused on the Carolina offensive line that afternoon. The Panthers surrendered nine sacks, permitting the Falcons to tie a club record set nearly 20 years earlier. It was an afternoon the Panthers' offensive linemen hadn't forgotten.

"That was probably the offensive line's worst game of the year," Brockermeyer said. "I know it was my worst game of the year. I know that this week I have to go out and play better than I did a couple of months ago. A lot better."

He knew because he realized Doleman was waiting again. Even though he planned to treat Doleman with a whole lot more disrespect this time, he also was intelligent enough to know it wasn't going to be easy. A six-time Pro Bowler and former NFC Defensive Player of the Year in his 11th NFL season, the 34-year-old Doleman was making offensive tackles look bad when Brockermeyer, 22, was playing youth football.

"He has a pretty good shake to him," Brockermeyer explained. "He can go either way on you. He has a lot of moves. He's not like one of those guys with only one move. Blocking guys like that is never easy. He's got six or seven moves. It's guys like that who are the toughest to block."

In the 13 games since the season-opening loss at Atlanta, Brockermeyer had successfully blocked just about everyone who had charged his way. After the disastrous day against Doleman, Brockermeyer had surrendered only one sack since—to Sean Gilbert of the Rams late in the 28–17 loss at St. Louis on November 12.

Quarterback Kerry Collins said he had no doubt Brockermeyer would protect his blind side against Doleman this time around.

"Like a lot of us, Blake has more experience now," Collins said. "He's got some games under his belt. That was the first game of the year. Doleman isn't going to get that many sacks again. There's no way."

Capers pointed out that for many rookies, a Doleman-type introduction into the NFL might have done long-term damage to the psyche. But he never worried about adverse results with Brockermeyer.

"That was a tough indoctrination for a rookie left tackle," Capers said. "That's not an easy position to play against all those speed rushers over there. . . . But if there's anybody I wouldn't be worried about, it's Blake—because he's made of the right stuff."

The coaching staff, meanwhile, had long ago begun to question whether Graham, the goat of the first Atlanta game, was made of the right stuff. Graham had played very little since returning from his knee injury, and he wasn't likely to play many downs in the rematch against the Falcons.

Still, he was the highest-paid lineman. And still, he defended his season—perhaps because he was the only one about to do so.

"Even the first game against Atlanta, other than the [false-start] penalities [he had three others besides the gaffe at the end of regulation], I thought I played well," Graham insisted. "How I view it, that was one of the best games I played—even though I jumped offsides the four times. I personally grade myself out, and of the six games I played [as a starter before getting injured and being replaced by Mark Dennis at right tackle], I graded myself a winner every game except the Buffalo game."

Reporters listening to Graham were dumbfounded. One was instantly reminded of an episode of the situation-comedy "Cheers," in which Norm Peterson, the beer-guzzling sage who sits night after night at the end of the bar, listens to one of Cliff Clavin's endless stories and finally says, "Cliffie, tell us, what color is the sky in that little world of yours?" Graham did not seem to be operating in a world of reality.

Capers was, as usual, reserved and cautious about every sentence he uttered during his daily briefings to the press. One afternoon, he talked about knowing firsthand the value of having a placekicker like Morten Andersen on your roster, having coached in New Orleans when Andersen played there.

"If you have a kicker like Morten Andersen and a good defense, you have a chance to win every game," Capers said.

"Well," joked a reporter, "at least the Falcons have one of the two, right?"

Capers did not respond. He only leaned back in his chair and smiled, apparently at a loss for words.

That the Falcons were a disaster defensively, despite their early sack success against the Panthers, was no secret. They were ranked 29th in the 30-team NFL in overall defense, and had long since abandoned the reckless blitzing style they flaunted in the first meeting against the Panthers, finding that it was, in the long run, much too vulnerable to giving up the big play.

So the reporter was right. And Capers no doubt agreed with him. But the Carolina head coach wasn't going to go on record saying so four days before his team had to face the Falcons.

Another reporter who witnessed this nonexchange was Andy Friedlander of the *Spartanburg Herald-Journal*. Friedlander once covered the Falcons for the now-defunct *Gwinett Daily News* and remained friendly with Len Pasquarelli of the *Atlanta Journal-Constitution*. In a subsequent phone conversation he described to the Atlanta writer Capers' reaction to the other reporter's comment.

Friedlander also relayed to Pasquarelli a quote from Brockermeyer about Doleman: "When he plays, he's as tough as they come."

Pasquarelli ran with this information, and kept on running with it. He used it to fuel his stories for three consecutive days, including one on the Saturday before the game in which he wrote, "When the teams meet Sunday, the Falcons figure to bring a healthier respect for Carolina than the Panthers possess toward Atlanta."

Of Brockermeyer, Pasquarelli wrote, "Brockermeyer, beaten for $3\frac{1}{2}$ sacks in the opener by Chris Doleman, began a reply to a question about the Atlanta defensive end by noting: '*When he plays . . .*' Brockermeyer, who has allowed just one sack since the first game, was implying that Doleman doesn't go hard every down."

Of Capers, Pasquarelli implied the Carolina head coach had no respect whatsoever for the Atlanta defense, based solely on his "leaning back and smiling" during the exchange described to him by Friedlander. The article concluded with a quote from Doleman, who said he wasn't disturbed by the Panthers' apparent lack of respect.

"After all," said Doleman, "they can't go anywhere, and we still have a chance to go everywhere."

Capers was furious about the series of articles that stemmed largely from Len Pasquarelli's liberal interpretation of the coach's body language when Pasquarelli wasn't even in the room to witness it. At first, he couldn't figure out how Pasquarelli obtained this information. Then someone in the public relations department told him Pasquarelli and Friedlander were friendly. He called Friedlander into his office.

"Do you know what I had to do first thing this morning? I had to call June Jones on the phone and apologize," Capers said. "June Jones is a good friend of mine. And apologize for what? I never even said anything.

"How could you do something like this? Do you think this isn't going to have an effect on the outcome of the game?"

"Do you think this isn't going to end up on the bulletin board in their locker room?" Capers asked, his voice rising. A copy of one of the Pasquarelli articles, the headline of which read "Falcons not focusing on Panthers' smug shots," sat on his desk.

"Coach, I didn't write those articles," Friedlander said. "I only relayed the information. If you've got a problem with what was written, I suggest you call Len Pasquarelli."

"It's just like I tell my players: You must be held accountable for your actions. You're not being accountable," Capers said..

"Coach, I would be accountable if I wrote that stuff. I stand by whatever I write. But I didn't write that. I just relayed the information," the reporter said.

"Well, we're through then," Capers said. "You can sit in on group interviews if you want, but I'm not going to answer any more of your questions. And I'll never give you any more of my time one-on-one.

"You guys in the media think I'm boring and never say anything? Well, I'm really going to start watching what I'm saying now. If you think I'm boring now, just wait."

It was a side of Capers seldom seen. He also was too nice of a guy to completely follow through on his threat. A few days later, Friedlander fired off one of the first questions in the daily news briefing. Capers answered it.

Did the Panthers lack respect for the Falcons?

Perhaps. Some of them, outspoken cornerback Tim McKyer included, did not hide the fact. McKyer had made the playoffs in eight of the nine seasons he had played in the NFL for five different teams; the only time he had missed out was in 1992 when he played for the Falcons. This was nothing new for the Falcons, who had missed the playoffs in all but one of their previous 13 seasons.

"One thing is the way they handle talent and the way they evaluate talent," McKyer said. "It seems like every talented player that left there went somewhere else and became All-Pro—Brett Favre, Deion Sanders, Brian Jordan. It seems like everyone leaves there and goes on to make a name for himself.

"If you're not good at evaluating talent and keeping talent, you won't win. You just can't win without talent in this league. I don't care what kind of scheme you have; you have to have good players.

"Look at the two expansion teams. The Panthers went after guys who could play. The Jaguars just went for youth or whatever and it cost them. With free agency, the future is now. You can't depend on building a team because by the time you build it, the free agents are gone."

The Jaguars were entering the home stretch of their inaugural season in a terrible tailspin. After winning three of their first five games, the Jags had dropped nine in a row to fall to 3–11 with two games remaining.

The budding Interstate-85 intrastate rivalry picked up even more intensity when, three days before kickoff, it was learned Sam Mills was not selected for what would have been his fifth Pro Bowl. Among the three inside linebackers selected ahead of him: Jessie Tuggle of the Falcons' 29th-ranked defense.

Mills was informed as he left Winthrop Coliseum to head home after practice on Thursday. He ran into Lamar Lathon on the way out to the parking lot and told him the bad news.

"You didn't make it? You're kidding me, right?" Lathon said.

"No, man, I didn't make it," Mills said.

"No way. This is a joke. You're just joking, right?" Lathon pressed.

"No, I really didn't make it," Mills repeated.

Finally, Lathon relented and shuffled off to his car, still shaking his head in disbelief.

Mills was named second alternate at inside linebacker, and Brett Maxie, who had held out hope of being named to his first Pro Bowl and was at the time tied for second in the NFL in interceptions with six, was named third alternate on the NFC team at safety.

Fans were involved in the voting process for the third consecutive season, with their votes, cast up until December 3, counting as one-third of the total vote. Ballots submitted by the coaches and players accounted for the rest, one-third each. No player or coach could vote for someone on his own team.

Capers was downcast after the announcement that Mills fell short in the voting. In fact, he looked more downhearted about this than he did after some of the earlier losses during the season.

"In terms of a guy like Sam Mills, I don't think there is a linebacker in the league who has had a better year," he said. "I think Sam's statistics would bear that out. I wouldn't trade Sam Mills for anybody else in the league this year.

"I also believe Brett Maxie had a very good year statistically. . . . From that standpoint, we're disappointed—because we would like to see the guys who have played well for us be rewarded."

Mills said, "It is disappointing. I do feel like I'm deserving. . . . I've been in the league long enough to know what is a Pro Bowl year and what isn't."

Maxie added, "A lot of guys feel like they deserve to go every year. I'm not the only guy on this team who thinks he should go."

Capers and Mills said the leading Panther candidates might have had a better chance if fan balloting was not part of the process.

"With the fan vote, teams that play on television a lot and have more exposure are obviously going to have a tremendous advantage in that area," Capers said.

It was pointed out that Mills had a total of 17.5 impact-type plays—sacks, forced fumbles, fumble recoveries and interceptions. Tuggle and the other Pro Bowl starter, Ken Norton Jr. of the 49ers, had the combined total of 10.

"If you just took our numbers for the season and put them up and didn't put a name next to them, I think people would probably pick my number," Mills said. "But fans probably would be more likely to vote for people they saw the most on TV—and that sure wasn't the Carolina Panthers."

In the locker room earlier in the day, before Mills knew his Pro Bowl fate, he looked around and said he was more worried about how his teammates would react if he didn't make it than he was about how he would handle the disappointment himself. This kind of selfless attitude was typical of Mills.

"I think a lot of guys in this locker room will be more upset than I am if I don't make it," Mills said then. "They seem to have their hearts set on it. I've been around long enough to know anything can happen. You don't always make the Pro Bowl when you think you deserve it."

During practice the next day on the fields behind Winthrop Coliseum, Mills made a routine interception. A chant went up immediately among his teammates. Undaunted by the official vote, they shouted: "Pro Bowl! Pro Bowl! Pro Bowl!"

Kerry Collins usually kept to himself on the long bus rides to Clemson, preferring to strap on the headphones to his portable CD player and listen to some rock and roll. His favorites: Pearl Jam and Bob Marley.

Collins was about to start his 12th consecutive game. The last three, during which he completed only 39 percent of his passes, had been forgettable. But he knew a victory against the Falcons would carry some historical significance, making his first NFL season something to remember for a lifetime.

Collins carried into the game a 6–5 record as a starter. One more win in the final two games, and he would become the first NFL quarterback since Miami's Dan Marino in 1983 to fashion a winning record as a starter during his rookie season. Collins could forever link himself in the history books with Marino, one of the greatest pro quarterbacks of all time.

"This year has already exceeded my expectations," Collins said. "I didn't think I would have a winning record going into my 12th start—because I'm a rookie and this is an expansion team. But still, I'm not satisfied.

"We're sitting here at 6–8 and I look back and see that we could easily be 8–6 and still be in the hunt for the playoffs. That's disappointing. But one thing I've learned is that you can't get too caught up in what might have been. You have to have a short memory and keep pushing ahead."

That was one of the traits Collins possessed that pleased Capers most: his ability to forget and move on. Yes, you learned from mistakes. You had to dissect them and figure out why they occurred. But then you filed away that information and moved on. To dwell on mistakes could kill the confidence of a young quarterback.

Collins had been way up and way down throughout his first season. He had the six-turnover game in St. Louis, suffered through a five-turnover debacle at New Orleans and was still lamenting the poor decision on first-and-goal the previous week against San Francisco at Clemson.

He even admitted he was too inexperienced to understand exactly what caused his good days and his bad ones.

"I don't think I've been around long enough to know what's affecting me, what makes me play well and what doesn't," Collins said. "Some teams change coverages a lot, and I guess that's one factor because it's something I'm not used to seeing so much. But it's hard for me to pinpoint exactly the reason why I play well one week and not so well the next. I wish I could."

Against the Falcons, it was time for Collins to play well again.

But the game did not start out too promising for the rookie or any other Panthers. The Falcons surged to a 14–0 lead before the first quarter was over. The vaunted Carolina defense was reeling, on its heels from the precision run-and-shoot passing of Atlanta quarterback Jeff George. Slowly, though, the game turned—and over the last three quarters, George was not the best quarterback on the field.

When Sam Mills came up with a huge interception of a George pass intended for Falcons running back Craig Heyward at the Carolina five-yard line early in the fourth quarter, killing another probable Atlanta scoring drive, it set up the play of the day. Collins was the quarterback who made it.

With the Panthers trailing 17–14 midway through the fourth quarter, a play call from backup quarterback Frank Reich, who was relaying orders from offensive coordinator Joe Pendry, buzzed into the radio receiver in Collins' helmet as "Turn 200-Winston-X-Denver," a routine slant pass to a wide receiver. The Panthers had run it several times already against the Falcons, with moderate success.

Collins decided in the huddle to change the call to "Turn-200-Winston-X-Slug." This was not an audible at the line. This was open defiance of a call being sent down from Pendry up in the press box. It was something Collins had not risked doing before, even when he thought he might know more than the man upstairs.

By substituting the word "Slug" for "Denver," Collins turned the play into a slant-and-go for Willie Green, the wide receiver for whom the play was originally designed any-way. (The first part of the call is to set the blocking scheme, the middle part identifies the hot receiver and the latter part tells that receiver which route to run.)

Green executed the play perfectly, sucking in Falcons cornerback Ron Davis, who bit hard on the slant fake and watched in horror as Green broke right past him into the great green expanse beyond. Collins helped the cause by pump-faking once to freeze Davis momentarily. Green caught the pass in stride from Collins, pulling it in a full 10 yards ahead of the exasperated Davis. Green then kept on running until he was in the end zone, the recipient of a 89-yard touchdown pass for a 21–17 Panthers' lead.

Collins was so excited he sprinted the length of the field, looking to embrace anyone in a Panthers' uniform who crossed his path. Finally, he found Green near the end zone and gave him a bear hug, lifting Green off the ground.

"I knew if I got caught from behind and didn't get in, I was going to get ragged on by some of the guys on the sideline," Green said later in a boisterous Carolina locker room. "It was really a gutsy call on Kerry's part. I've got to give him a lot of credit."

As he went to the sidelines, Collins was greeted by an euphoric Trudeau, who slapped him on the back as if to say, "I remember the first time I did something like that, too! Isn't it great?" Reich walked over to offer congratulations as well, but looked more somber—as if he realized with some finality that his career was slipping away and Collins had the whole world at his feet, stretched ahead of him in what was shaping up as a very bright NFL future.

Collins later said of switching the play call, "It entered my mind that maybe I shouldn't be doing this, but I'm going to do it anyway."

In the end, Pendry didn't mind. He hugged Collins after the game and told him it was OK to occasionally change a call; just don't get too carried away with it. Pendry wouldn't have had much ammunition to argue anything else after Collins' decision resulted in the longest play in the team's brief history.

The lead it created looked shaky when the Falcons drove right down the field again on their next possession. But true to form, when the run-and-shoot offense ran out of field, it became much easier to defend.

On first-and-goal from the Carolina seven-yard line, Sam Mills stuffed Heyward on a run up the middle. Gain of one.

On second-and-goal from the six, Lamar Lathon flushed George from the pocket and nearly sacked him, prompting an incompletion that might have been called intentional grounding.

On third-and-goal, George tried to get a pass to wide receiver Tyrone Brown in the end zone. Steve Lofton, the cornerback who saved the day with a similar play five months earlier against Jacksonville in the Hall of Fame game, broke the pass up even as Brown tried to pull him down on what the Panthers argued could have been offensive interference.

Finally, on fourth-and-goal, the crowd of 53,833 at Clemson stood and stomped their feet and cheered loudly. George crouched behind center and cupped a hand to the left side of his helmet to try and shut out the noise. Then the ball was snapped and two Panthers—Lathon and Darion Conner—were upon him, chasing the quarterback out of the pocket. George was forced to throw on the run for Bert Emanuel, a wide receiver in the back of the end zone.

The lead created by the Collins-to-Green touchdown pass stood up when strong safety Pat Terrell of the Panthers broke up the pass with 1:07 left to play. Emanuel argued that Terrell had interfered on the play, and the replay did show that Terrell had sort of draped his right hand over Emanuel's shoulder before the ball arrived. But it was too close for the officials to make the call.

Terrell said later the play was eerily similar to one he made for Notre Dame in 1988. With that game on the line against number-one-ranked Miami, Terrell batted away a two-point conversion pass by quarterback Steve Walsh, sending Miami to its first defeat in 37 games.

"Why do they always pick on me?" Terrell joked.

In the losing locker room, the Falcons were devastated.

George sat with his head in his hands, playing his final pass to Emanuel over and over again in his head. He was not alone in figuring the loss, which dropped their record to 8–7 with a home game against San Francisco looming in their season finale the following Sunday, probably was going to keep them out of the playoffs. (It didn't when the Falcons pulled an upset the following Sunday.)

"That was the season right there," George said. "It didn't work out for us. We had a chance to control our own destiny—but the last three or four weeks, we blew it.

"We don't deserve to go anywhere. The bottom line is we don't deserve it. . . . We'll be home for Christmas."

Kevin Ross, Atlanta's strong safety, added, "I have no intentions of quitting at all. But being realistic, if we can't stop [the Panthers], do you think we're going to stop the world champions? I don't know. You talk about a difficult task . . . When we see 'SF' on a helmet, we usually roll over and die."

The Falcons simply could not believe they had put themselves in a position where they had to beat the 49ers to get into the playoffs. They had arrived at Death Valley full of confidence. They believed they would dispatch the Panthers much more easily than they had in the first game of the season.

They were wrong.

Collins, who also scored on a one-yard quarterback sneak, completed 18 of 28 passes for 283 yards on the afternoon. His only interception came on a ball the usually sure-handed Mark Carrier let slip through his hands.

The offensive line, disgraced in the earlier meeting between the teams, gave him time to throw when he needed it. He wasn't sacked once.

Brockermeyer tangled with Doleman again, but with vastly different results. The Falcons did not blitz as much, deciding instead to lay back and provide more secure coverage in the defensive secondary. So that helped, but Doleman charged hard much of the afternoon nonetheless.

"Believe me," said Brockermeyer, "I had my hands full out there on the corner again today. They could have blitzed 15 guys up the middle and I would never have known it. I really didn't block [Doleman] a whole lot better this time than the first time. A little better, but not much."

Even so, Collins was more mobile than Reich. And Brockermeyer had developed enough trust in his offensive linemates to be confident that while he was handling Doleman one-on-one on the outside corner, no one was going to blitz up the middle without someone at least getting a piece of him and giving Collins the extra split second he needed to get rid of the football.

It wasn't the same line that took the field in Atlanta. Matt Elliott was at right guard instead of the long-forgotten Emerson Martin; Frank Garcia was at left guard instead of fellow rookie Andrew Peterson, who was declared inactive for the rematch and didn't dress; and the cursed Derrick Graham had been replaced at right tackle by Mark Dennis.

"The fact that we went from nine sacks to no sacks in these games against Atlanta says something about our offensive line," Dennis said. "I think all of us kind of took it upon ourselves individually to not let that happen again."

As well as the line played, Collins' daring play-call change was the talk of the locker room afterward. He said it was something he wouldn't have chanced a week or two earlier. Or for that matter, a year or two earlier.

"I wouldn't have done that at Penn State, that's for sure," a grinning Collins said. "Coach [Joe] Paterno runs a pretty tight ship there. You get in the pros and I guess you have a little more freedom to do some things."

The long bus ride back to Rock Hill from Clemson was a joyful one. Capers sat in his seat and, as was his postgame custom, reviewed the game on a small portable videotape machine he balanced in his lap.

As he watched the Collins-to-Green 89-yard touchdown, Capers smiled to himself.

His quarterback had come of age. And maybe, just maybe, so had his entire team.

Final Score

21 Carolina   **17** Atlanta

Game 16:
Panthers at Washington

Game-time temperature for the season finale against the Washington Redskins at RFK Stadium was 35 degrees and dropping rapidly. That was a problem for some Panthers. It didn't seem to faze others.

Frank Garcia, the hard-nosed rookie offensive lineman, and Anthony Johnson, the running back who played for Chicago earlier during the season, went through early warm-ups wearing sleeveless T-shirts. But Willie Green, a native of Athens, Georgia, emerged from the locker room wearing two pairs of tights, plus long johns on his lower half, and a sweatshirt, heavy jacket and wool hat covering his upper body.

Asked about Garcia and Johnson, Green shook his head and said, "They're sick. Everything I have in my locker, I'm putting on."

Including the wool hat?

"If it fits, I'm wearing it underneath my helmet," he said.

Mark Rodenhauser said he was indifferent to the cold.

"It's an extension of the machoism of football," Rodenhauser said. "Besides, nobody ever died from frostbite of the arms.

"They have had to have skin grafts, however."

Many people who visited RFK thought it was a dismal, miserable place. But when Joe Gibbs coached the Redskins, he absolutely loved it.

"Most of the stadiums today are pretty, with nice locker rooms and everything," Gibbs said. "But you go to a place like RFK that is just a dump, with crud hanging from the ceiling, that's real football.

"Everyone always asked me, 'Boy, wouldn't it be great to get a new stadium?' And I would always say, 'Man, I love this one.' I thought we had a real advantage."

While most visitors to RFK weren't quite as sentimental as Gibbs, Mike McCormack was one who enjoyed the football ambience. He also liked the cold.

"This is the kind of weather football was meant to be played in," McCormack said just before kickoff. "And this is the kind of stadium it was meant to be played in. Outdoors, on grass, in cold weather. This is great."

McCormack made these comments in the press box—the only open-air press box in the NFL. He was wearing an oversize Panthers' parka and a hat, which he claimed were merely concessions to age.

"I never used to wear this stuff," he said, tugging at the sleeve of his thick coat. "Back when I played, the only thing I'd wear on a day like this was an extra T-shirt."

Just as it seemed fitting that the Panthers started their inaugural preseason by playing Jacksonville, it seemed appropriate to end matters with a game against the Redskins in Washington. Long before the Panthers were born, Carolina was Redskins country.

For some extreme loyalists, that would never change. Redskins fans, in fact, were the only local NFL fans pleased about the Panthers failing to sell out all but one of their home games at Clemson. Carolina's nonsellouts were blacked out on television from Clemson to Greenville to Columbia in South Carolina and from Asheville to Charlotte in North Carolina. Usually, Redskins games were televised in their place.

Joe Gibbs grew up in the North Carolina mountains in a tiny town named Enka, where he figures he adopted the Redskins at about age six. His Uncle Walter lived nearby and was the first person in Enka to own a television set, which he hooked up to a 125-foot antenna so he could assure quality reception on Redskins games and other major sporting events. Then Uncle Walter would place the television in a window and seemingly everyone in Enka would come over to his place and crowd around it to watch the biggest games.

But Gibbs, who now lives in Charlotte, admitted the Panthers already were his second-favorite team behind the Redskins. He and his Winston Cup race team owned a total of 18 permanent seat licenses at Carolinas Stadium.

"We got 12 for the race team, and I bought six for myself. So man, I'm all set. But I'm not making the drive over to Clemson. I'm waiting for them to come here," Gibbs said.

"As a matter of fact, I didn't think they'd be winning that many games or maybe I would have gone. But I'm a fan. I'm still wondering why nobody gave me a deal on those tickets."

Gibbs was laughing as he delivered the last sentence.

"The first thing I learned coming from college coaching to the NFL, when our owner in St. Louis was Billy Bidwill, was that the NFL never gives away free tickets," Gibbs said. "Bidwill called us all together and said there are only two firing offenses, and I thought to myself, 'Geez, I wonder what they are. They must be pretty important, like losing too many games or something.'

"Then Bidwill pointed to a door that led to the breakfast area where all the cooking was done. He said, 'Anyone leaving that door open, I'll fire you.' So I said to myself, 'Well, I guess I can handle that.' Then he said the second thing was, 'If you let anybody in here with a free ticket, I'll fire you.' That set me straight right there. That's when I knew there were no free tickets in the NFL."

For Redskins fans in North Carolina and South Carolina, there were no assurances their team wouldn't eventually be blotted out entirely in their communities by the upstart Panthers. The Panthers' radio network had 94 affiliates, second only to the Dallas Cowboys in the NFL. Their games could be picked up virtually anywhere in the two-state area. But the Redskins' radio network dropped from 93 in 1995 to 79 in 1996, largely because of switches made to the Panthers by affiliates in the Carolinas.

Sonny Jurgensen, the former great Redskins quarterback and now a broadcaster of the team's games, grew up in Wilmington, North Carolina.

"The Redskins were the team we saw. All we knew anything about was the Washington Redskins," he told the *Charlotte Observer* in an article devoted to the divided loyalties of NFL fans in the area.

Dee Blackwell, a fan from Hickory, told the *Observer* he was disappointed he hadn't been able to follow the Redskins as closely as in years past. It had been his habit to tune the television set into their game and turn the sound down, so he could turn the radio up and listen to Jurgensen, Sam Huff and Frank Herzog call the game on the Redskins radio network. Now he was having trouble tuning them in.

"I got real used to this being part of the country where we saw the Redskins—and to heck with everybody else," Blackwell said. "I could count on the Washington Redskins. That seems to be out the window now."

Nonetheless, Blackwell admitted that he too had purchased PSLs for the following season at Carolinas Stadium, going in with three friends. But he still considered himself a die-hard Redskins fan.

"If it's a choice between going to a Panthers' game and watching the Redskins on TV, if I get that chance, I'm going to watch the Redskins," he said. "Sometimes you just have to stick with your team."

For reporters, quality locker-room time with players was winding down. Capers already had told the players they could clean out their lockers ahead of time, so they wouldn't have to return to Rock Hill after the game. That would give them the opportunity to go wherever they wanted to spend what would be left of the holidays.

Fullback Bob Christian talked about how excited he was for his alma mater, Northwestern. The Wildcats were preparing to represent the Big Ten in the Rose Bowl for the first time since 1949, making Christian smile widely as he thought back to Capers' slip of the tongue during those first few days of training camp, when Capers told the players there would be no laughers like Penn State against Northwestern on a given week in the NFL.

"Dom was talking about parity in the NFL, and he used Northwestern as an example of a team that couldn't compete," Christian said. "It was fun after that because every week, except one, I could rub it in by saying, 'Hey coach, what about Northwestern now?'

"I especially enjoyed raising the topic when Northwestern beat Penn State and handled them so easily."

Chris Low of the *Rock Hill Herald* mentioned to Tim McKyer that he saw McKyer featured on a ESPN segment about NFL cornerbacks.

"It was well done," Low said.

"Did they show any highlights?" McKyer wanted to know.

"They did, didn't they? I'll bet they showed me getting beat by Tony Martin. That's what they showed, wasn't it? Wasn't it? They could have shown any highlight, but you just knew that was the one they would show."

"I really don't remember what they showed, Tim," said Low, stammering. "I'm just not sure."

"Tony Martin. You know it had to be," muttered McKyer, obviously disgusted.

Another reporter asked McKyer what his finest memory of the first season would be.

"I've got 96 best little memories," said McKyer, referring to his 96-yard interception return for a touchdown against the 49ers in San Francisco.

"But you guys won't want to remember that. All you'll want to remember is Tony Martin."

Meanwhile, Lamar Lathon sat brooding in one corner of the locker room when a reporter approached.

"Hey Lamar," the reporter said nonchalantly.

"I ain't talkin'," Lathon shot back.

"Come on. It's the last day we're in here," the reporter said.

Lathon stared.

Then he said, "Maybe you didn't hear me. I ain't fuckin' talkin'."

Someone from a nearby locker stall happened to mention the large number of sacks Bryce Paup of Buffalo had piled up during the season. Paup eventually led the NFL with 17.5.

"That's what I could be doing if they used me right," Lathon grumbled. "If they used me here the same way they used Paup there, that could be me."

Lathon was heading into the season finale with seven sacks and a deteriorating attitude. He wasn't thrilled with Capers' thinking-man's defense, preferring instead to be turned loose with reckless abandon in a manner that required minimal reading of situations.

Some within the organization were beginning to monitor this potential problem with increasing awareness and frustration. In truth, they had believed Lathon would be a better fit for Capers' defense and could only hope he would be in the long run.

Others were in a better mood on their final meet-the-press afternoon.

Derrick Moore, as usual, drew a crowd and had them laughing. He talked about how he wanted to return to Carolina in 1996, but admitted contract talks already had broken down between the Panthers and his agent (whom he eventually would fire and replace with a new one). He admitted there was a chance he would exercise his right to become an unrestricted free agent and sign with another team.

But mostly, Moore talked about his morning drives to the team's temporary practice facility.

Next season the Panthers would be practicing adjacent to new Carolinas Stadium in uptown Charlotte, where they would play their home games. Moore was asked what he would miss most about Rock Hill, since he wouldn't be back there even if he remained with the Panthers.

"What will I remember most about Rock Hill? How I can't turn out of my Paces River apartment complex when I'm trying to get to practice in the morning, that's what!" he bellowed.

"They need a traffic light there. I've been meaning to call the commissioner or the mayor or someone because they need a traffic light there. I can never get out of there.

It's terrible, just terrible! . . . I sit there so long some mornings I don't even have time to get me a sausage biscuit, and that's a tradition for me. I got to have a sausage biscuit from McDonald's in the morning. But when I can't get out of Paces River, I have to make this big loop turn and come all the way back around to get to McDonald's. I get so angry when I have to do that! And sometimes I just don't have the time to do it. That upsets me even more because I got to have my sausage biscuit from McDonald's in the morning!"

After listening to this outburst, someone told Moore maybe he should be doing McDonald's commercials instead of his old buddy from Detroit, Barry Sanders.

"Hey, you've got a point there," he said, flashing his trademark gap-toothed grin. "Maybe you're right."

Across the way, Willie Green was talking about how he had yet another reason to be thankful this Christmas. He revealed he recently had been granted custody of his seven-year-old son, Dontellis, who had been living with his mother—a former acquaintance of Green's—in their hometown of Athens, Georgia. The only debate now, Green said, was whether to enroll Dontellis in school in Atlanta, where Green made his off-season home, or near Rock Hill or Charlotte, where Green was fairly certain he would be back next season after resurrecting his career at age 29.

All along, Green had maintained a cordial relationship with Dontellis' mother. But both parents agreed that the boy needed to be closer to his father.

"I've missed a lot of his football games and basketball games," Green said. "My mom and his mom have camcorded them for me to see later, but it's not the same as being there."

Green recalled how his father had attended all of his games until his father died suddenly of a heart attack during Green's freshman year in college at Mississippi.

"My father never missed one of my games growing up. I'm still happy that he got to see me play my first game in college before he passed," Green said. "You would have never known my father was there at any of those games because he never made any noise. But it meant a lot to me to see him up there in the stands.

"I want to do the same for my son, too. But I won't be one of those parents carrying on all the time about things. I'll be quiet like my father was."

As much as Green liked to talk, the last bit was a little difficult to believe. But the wide receiver obviously was pleased and excited about the future with his son.

"I've already got his room decked out in Carolina Panther stuff," Green said.

Fellow wide receiver Don Beebe talked nearby about how he was convinced he would not be back to play the first season in Carolinas Stadium. He was sure the Panthers planned to release him.

"I did whatever they asked me to do this season. It's just that they didn't ask me to do very much," Beebe said.

Capers said he would miss the down-home feel of Rock Hill, where he enjoyed jogging in Cherry Park and meeting friendly people. He would miss the routine of stopping every morning at a Circle K convenience store on the eight-minute drive from his condominium on Lake Wylie to Winthrop, where he would pick up an orange juice and newspaper and sign autographs.

"Every morning, they have something different for me to sign," Capers said. "I know the people there by first name now."

Finally, some players discussed what they considered an awful bathroom situation in their Winthrop locker room. There were four stalls available for 53 players, which created some problems because they were in almost constant demand.

"If you've ever seen the movie *Outbreak,* you almost don't want to go in that bathroom because you're afraid you'll catch some disease," Frank Garcia said.

"You don't even have to spray for bugs. No self-respecting bug would ever go in there," Mark Rodenhauser added. "They feed us all this food every day. We're all big guys and we all eat a lot; where do they expect us to go? If the health department went into that bathroom, they'd probably order to shut it down."

Upon first glance, Hazel David looked like a typical Washington fan as she boarded the Metro train headed in the direction of RFK Stadium at about 2 P.M. on Christmas Eve. From head to toe, she was dressed in Washington Redskins gear.

But what made her stand out, even aside from the fact that she revealed she was a resident of Winston-Salem, North Carolina, were her two companions—oldest daughter Yvette Hentz and friend Tammy Manuel, both of Greensboro, North Carolina. Hentz and Manuel boarded the train with David and sat just behind her, but they wore Panthers gear.

This was the kind of hybrid group of fans the NFL must of had in mind for the Carolinas when they awarded Jerry Richardson his franchise, and the threesome offered quite a contrast.

David, 50, wore a Redskins sweater, Redskins sweatpants, Redskins socks, a Redskins parka and red gloves. She even opened the hood on her parka to reveal she was wearing Redskins earrings. She carried a Redskins blanket and a Redskins seat cushion. She said she had been a hard-core fan of the team since she was 18 years old, despite living in North Carolina.

Her daughter said she was trying to get her mother to switch allegiances to the Panthers.

"It's only a matter of time," she said.

"Never," David insisted. "Never, never, never. I have no intention of switching teams."

She was, however, carrying a black-and-blue Carolina sign that read PANTHERS ON THE PROWL. But she had no intention of carrying it to her seat in RFK.

"I'm just holding it for them," she said, pointing to her companions. "I'm not even going to sit with them."

David sat instead with her sister, Loretta Johnson, a Washington resident with whom she hadn't shared Christmas Eve in 34 years. David said it would be a special Christmas, shared with Johnson and her beloved Redskins. All other holiday plans at the David home in Winston-Salem already had been set in motion.

"I precooked the Christmas dinner so I could come to this game," she said. "I made my collard greens, my chitlins and my sweet potato pie. I'm going to call my one daughter Christmas morning to tell her when to put the turkey in the oven. I've got everything covered."

Except the fact that she hadn't been able to convert her sister, Loretta, into a Redskins fan.

"She's a Cowboys fan," said David, looking disgusted. "But I guess I'll sit next to her at the game anyway."

———————————

Dom Capers' old baseball coach and assistant football coach from Mount Union College did not appreciate the Carolina Panthers hats Capers sent his two young sons earlier in the season. In fact, he told his sons they couldn't wear them. That was because Capers' old coach from Mount Union was Ron Lynn, who now served as defensive coordinator of the Redskins.

It added one more touch to the season finale.

Lynn had served as best man in Capers' wedding to his current wife, Karen, and the two were best of friends. Lynn told Charles Chandler of the *Observer* that he had a surefire way of keeping Capers in line if the head-coaching position started to go to his head.

"I'll just call him E. Dominic, like I always do when I want to get his goat," Lynn said. "He doesn't like it because his real first name is Ernest and he doesn't want people calling him that."

Ernest Dominic Capers and the Panthers entered the game with the noble goal of becoming the first expansion team in the history of modern major sports leagues to finish with a .500 record. The franchise that previously had come the closest, appropriately enough, also was nicknamed the Panthers—the Florida Panthers of the National Hockey League, who went 33–34–17 during the 1993–94 season.

"Many people might look at this week and say, 'You're out of the playoffs. What incentive do you have?'" Capers said. "But I think there is a tremendous difference between finishing 8–8 and 7–9. If you're 7–9, you've got a losing record.

"It would be a real credit to our players and our team to finish .500. And when you think in terms of having the opportunity to have the best record of any sports expansion franchise in history, that's an accomplishment our guys could really be proud of. I think that's our incentive."

It wasn't meant to be.

The Panthers were winning a war of field position late in the third quarter of a 10–10 ball game when the Redskins took control and did not let go. Backed up to their own seven-yard line after a Tommy Barnhardt punt, the Redskins nonetheless needed only three plays to strike for the touchdown that put them ahead for good in a 20–17 victory. Included in the brief "drive" were a 59-yard pass play from quarterback Gus Frerotte to wide receiver Henry Ellard and a 33-yard run on a reverse to wide receiver Michael Westbrook.

They were the type of big plays the Panthers' defense hadn't given up with any regularity since the 0–5 start to the season.

After the Redskins went up 20–10, the Carolina offense did put together a scoring drive to cut the lead to three with 39 seconds left on a two-yard touchdown pass to Willie Green from Collins.

"Way to scrap! Way to scrap, baby!" yelled McKyer along the sideline after the score. He ran up to pat Collins on the back—the cool 10-year veteran excitedly reaching out to touch the rookie who only five months earlier had been throwing all kinds of mistakes in training camp.

"Great pass," McKyer told Collins. "That's all we needed."

The Panthers then attempted an onside kick, but the Redskins recovered—suddenly making the 1995 season nothing but a satisfying memory, despite the defeat.

Green, dogged by double coverage all afternoon, said later, "I just wish we could have recovered the onsides kick and gotten one last shot at it. I would have liked for them to have been able to throw it to me one more time and had the outcome rest on my shoulders."

No one laughed. Green not only was serious, he was being taken seriously. Who would have thought that would have been possible a little over a year earlier, when Green was one of the Original 10 to sign with the Panthers and was given little chance of even making the team?

The Panthers regretted the loss to the Redskins, but they didn't let it ruin their budding holiday spirits. They obviously were proud of their accomplishments during their first season, which included

➤ A 7–9 record—best in NFL history for an expansion team. It also was leaps and bounds ahead of previous expansion franchises like Dallas. The Cowboys didn't win seven games until their sixth season. New Orleans actually waited 12 years to enjoy such a winning abundance.

➤ A four-game winning streak—the longest ever for an expansion team.

➤ The first victory for an expansion team over a defending Super Bowl champion, which the Panthers achieved with their 13–7 victory at San Francisco on November 5.

➤ Moore, who carried 14 times for 47 yards and one touchdown in the season finale, finished the season with 740 yards rushing to surpass the previous NFL expansion high of 722 by Junior Coffey of Atlanta in 1966.

➤ Mark Carrier, the team's leading receiver who had seven catches for 101 yards against Washington, finished the year with 1,002 yards receiving—something no receiver on an expansion team had previously achieved.

"We didn't turn in that .500 season," said linebacker and undisputed team leader Sam Mills. "That's what's rough about this loss. To be so close and not get there is frustrating.

"At the same time, this team came together more quickly and played better than anyone thought possible. I think we can all be proud of that."

The roster facing Washington included 11 rookies, as the Carolina front office attempted to keep tabs on young players who might fill any gaps left by the off-season's looming free-agent scramble. Bill Polian said he feared a 30-percent turnover of the Carolina roster, but then Polian seemed the man best qualified to handle such a dilemma.

Earlier in the day on *The Sports Reporters*, an ESPN talk show, New York news-paper columnist Mike Lupica called Polian "the year's smartest shopper in the NFL," pointing out the number of quality free agents Polian had signed and the draft the Panthers enjoyed. He called the Panthers the best news story to come out of the NFL in 1995.

"In a year of celebrated disappointments," said Lupica, "the best story came out of what was supposed to be a thrift shop."

The next day in the *Washington Post,* coverage was complimentary toward the losing Panthers. They appeared to have gained in a final defeat what they could not gain from earlier victories: nationwide respect.

One article in the *Post* began, "The Carolina Panthers have 61 fewer years of tradition than the Washington Redskins—and one more victory this season."

McKyer, who had questioned the team's heart more than once during the opening five-game losing streak, pronounced the Panthers a bonafide heart-pumping NFL ballclub.

"Overall this year, we have a lot to feel good about," McKyer said. "We earned a lot of respect around the league, and we deserved it.

"Building and developing, that's old terminology now in the NFL. Free agency has changed the way the entire game is played. The old expansion teams wouldn't have had quality players like we have.

"Now you have to win right away because everyone might be gone next year. I'm personally disappointed. I really thought we should have had nine or 10 wins and maybe made the playoffs."

Christian, the soft-spoken and pragmatic fullback, discussed the team's close losses and how the Panthers bounced back so impressively from the dismal first five games. He also mentioned Northwestern again, as one might have expected.

"What happened in training camp with Coach Capers was understandable because of the perception people have had of Northwestern as a football team," Christian said. "We were really bad for a lot of years. We hardly ever won a game when I was there.

"But what they've done this year just goes to show you that any team or program can turn it around and accomplish great things if it just believes in itself. It doesn't matter what the perception is. You can break it. That's what happened this year at Northwestern. That's kind of what we've done here, too, because most people thought we would be pretty bad because we were a first-year team."

Then Christian paused.

"Now I'm planning to go to the Rose Bowl. I can't wait," he said.

The last of the players started filing out of the visitors locker room at RFK. Blake Brockermeyer left limping and wearing sandals to accommodate the injury to his foot. Collins handed his game jersey to the 12-year-old son of a friend who had stopped by to say hello. Lamar Lathon and Darion Conner walked out together, with Lathon draping one of his long arms around the shoulder of his teammate. Owner Jerry Richardson was having a private talk with Sam Mills, over whom he looked nearly a foot taller.

For his part, Capers was disappointed in the final loss, but hardly found it disheartening.

"Anytime you work hard at something and come up short, it leaves an empty feeling," Capers said. "But one thing I don't what to do is have today's loss distract from some of the things our team accomplished this year.

"When we started, no one really knew anything about the Panthers. One of our goals was to establish an identity and gain some respect in the NFL. I think, as a team, we did that. The best thing we did was pick ourselves up off the ground when we were down and come back from it."

Richardson looked around the locker room and felt a deep sense of pride and accomplishment.

"Some announcer was talking on television the other day about how Ray Rhodes had to adjust to having something like 33 new players on his roster with the Philadelphia Eagles," Richardson said. "I thought to myself, 'Give me a break!' All our players were new, and look what we did."

Richardson was asked about his prediction—made long before the Panthers ever played a game—that the franchise would win a Super Bowl within 10 years.

"I don't think I went out on a limb at all with that one," Richardson said. "In fact, I may have been a little conservative."

Final Score

20 Washington   **17** Carolina

Epilogue

T he greatest challenge facing the Panthers after their wildly successful first season was the same thing that made them the best expansion team in NFL history: free agency. At season's end, the Panthers had 18 players who would be unrestricted free agents and seven who would be restricted if they didn't re-sign by February 16, including seven starters on offense and four on defense.

"The best free agents you can sign are your own," Bill Polian said. "You can go out and get guys to try and plug holes, but you build winners from within. You don't collect people and expect them to win. This has been proven in every sport where there is free agency as the years have gone by."

"The fantasy football approach is wonderful for cocktail conversation, but it doesn't work in the real world in any sport. We want to create a team, not collect a bunch of individuals."

Polian's favorite highlight of the first season was the victory over Atlanta at Clemson in Week 15, when the Falcons seemingly had everything to play for and the Panthers were coming off a lopsided loss to San Francisco that had eliminated them from the playoffs. Coach Dom Capers' most satisfying victory may have been the one over Indianapolis three weeks earlier, when he kept telling everyone the Colts were an outstanding football team; they bore that out by advancing all the way to the AFC Championship game in the playoffs, where they nearly beat the Pittsburgh Steelers. Owner Jerry Richardson said nothing could top the very first victory over the New York Jets at Clemson on October 15, snapping a five-game losing streak. And Mike McCormack, the venerable team president, insisted that beating the defending Super Bowl champion 49ers in San Francisco on November 5 was the thrill of the season for him.

That an expansion team could have so many pleasing moments to choose from for a highlight reel was amazing in itself. Capers credits the players, especially the collection of veterans led by guys like Sam Mills and Brett Maxie who kept the team from falling apart during the 0-5 start.

"When you talk about the football players we had on our football team, we talked a lot about how we wanted to be known as a first-class organization, a classy outfit," Capers said. "We don't want to have guys who are cheap-shot artists. We don't want a lot of trash-talking. We're more concerned about doing our talking on the field."

The same philosophy would be used to build the second-year Panthers, according to Polian, the man who holds what he calls "football temperment" in higher regard than a player's time in the 40-yard dash.

"We're not looking for 49 altar boys," said Polian, "but we are looking for guys who have reasonably strong character."

They started by signing Maxie to a two-year contract extension before the season ended. Mills would be back for another year, probably his last before retiring. And Greg Kragen, one of the aforementioned free agents-to-be, signed on for another year as soon as the Panthers mailed him a contract and he could look it over. Like Maxie, he didn't even bother hiring an agent to read the fine print because he felt he was intelligent enough to comprehend it for himself.

The off-season did not proceed as smoothly for some others. Despite switching agents, Derrick Moore, the team's leading rusher, could not come to an agreement with the Panthers. They eventually agreed to part ways, and the Panthers used their first pick in the April draft, the eighth overall, to select highly-rated running back Tim Biakabutuka of Michigan—who informed the media that he no longer wanted to be called Tim, but would rather be referred to by his given name, Tshimanga (his full name is pronounced Ti-MONG-ah Bee-ock-ah-buh-TWO-kah).

Willie Green was to return for another season of entertaining on the field and in the locker room, as was Mark Carrier, who had become a free agent. The Panthers also added some other promising wide-receiver prospects via free agency and the draft, particulary in second-round draft choice Muhsin Muhammed of Michigan State.

Tim McKyer, who started all 16 games at cornerback, fired one agent and hired another after turning down a substantial offer to return to the team. His first agent, Steve Weinberg, said McKyer was crazy to turn the original offer down and added, "I've represented Tim McKyer for 10 years in this league, and it hasn't always been easy. When you call some teams and tell them you represent Tim McKyer, they hang up on you."

McKyer was still looking for work (and presumably Tony Martin) as of this writing.

The Panthers made McKyer expendable by signing All-Pro cornerback Eric Davis, an unrestricted free agent who started the previous four seasons for the 49ers. Capers said he expected Davis to team with Tyrone Poole to give the Panthers one of the league's top cornerback tandems for years to come.

Also signed from other teams as unrestricted free agents were tight end Wesley Walls, who burned the Panthers for eight catches and 115 yards in two games last season as a New Orleans Saint; outside linebacker Kevin Greene, the former Pittsburgh Steeler All-Pro who became reunited with Capers; backup quarterback Steve Beuerlein, who spent last season with the other expansion team in Jacksonville; another former All-Pro outside linebacker in Duane Bickett, who played last season with Seattle; and huge offensive tackle Greg Skrepenak, who goes 6-7 and 330 pounds and spent the first four seasons of his NFL career with the Oakland Raiders.

Greene is a wild man of sorts who promised fans he "would come with the heat" on opposing quarterbacks. He was slated to start at left outside linebacker while the coaches experimented with moving Lamar Lathon to right. Bickett was to provide depth behind both of them while Darion Conner remained unsigned as training camp approached.

Beuerlein signed as the No. 2 quarterback behind Collins after the Panthers decided not to pursue re-signing Frank Reich or Jack Trudeau. (They might have signed Trudeau had Beuerlein not come aboard, but felt Reich had "lost the zip" in his throwing arm.) Reich later signed on as a backup with the New York Jets.

"I found a way to get on the trivia board again," said Beuerlein, who will now be remembered for becoming the first player to play quarterback for both 1995 expansion teams, in addition to being the first player selected (by Jacksonville, of course) in the allocation draft. The Panthers said they would have taken Beuerlein in that draft, too, had they owned the first pick.

Asked about the differences between the two teams, Beuerlein was frank.

"Coach Coughlin (of the Jaguars) wanted to be the first expansion team to win a game, the first to win two games, the first to reach .500 . . . he wanted to be the first of the two expansion teams to do everything," Beuerlein said. "There was tension in the air every time we lost and Carolina won last year. You wondered what coach Coughlin was going to do next.

"It was a big competition down there. From what I can tell here, there is a big difference. It's like they never really wanted to consider themselves an expansion team at all. They just want to win games, period."

Walls was signed to replace Pete Metzelaars; Skrepenak to replace Derrick Graham. Both Metzelaars, the aging warrior who simply had little left at age 35 by 1995, and Graham, who was haunted by one fateful play in the regular-season opener, were waived shortly after the season. So was Don Beebe, who was not surprised in the least.

In a mild surprise, though, the Panthers did not tender an offer to restricted free agent Eric Guliford, who proved a valuable receiver and punt returner during the first season. They also severed ties with Kevin Farkas, the big offensive tackle whose massive size could not make up for the fact that he continued to encounter difficulty comprehending all of Jim "Mouse" McNally's blocking schemes. And, regrettably, with Paul Butcher, the special-teams maniac who earned the nickname Dr. Psycho by sacrificing his body (he needed postseason shoulder and knee surgery) on every play.

Quarterback Kerry Collins, who no longer can be called a rookie, applauded the Panthers' offseason moves and proved he was truly a Southern convert when he revealed he had become an avid fan of NASCAR racing. He also spent some of that $7 million signing bonus by buying a home in South Charlotte, purchasing a condominium on South Beach in Miami, and taking a trip to Las Vegas with buddy Blake Brockermeyer, where he lost an undetermined sum, but had fun doing it. Then Collins and offensive lineman Frank Garcia served as ushers in Brockermeyer's wedding. (Collins remained a bachelor, but did find a new roommate—a yellow labrador puppy that he aptly named "Dude.")

Brockermeyer's left foot was not broken, as he had feared that last day of the season in Washington. But it was severely sprained, and required some extensive rehabilitation in the offseason.

Curtis Whitley, the soul of the offensive line if Brockermeyer was its heart, was perhaps the most important Panther free agent re-signed in the offseason. Pat Terrell, who made the game-saving play against Atlanta in Week 15 and proved himself the hardest hitter in the secondary throughout the season, was another important free agent guided back into the fold by Polian.

And Mike Fox, the intimidating defensive end who said little but anchored the defense along with Mills, Kragen and the rest, quietly used some of the big money awarded him by the Panthers to establish a scholarship fund for four high-school seniors—two from each of the Carolinas. He sought little publicity for the gesture and received little, as was his style. On the field, though, he continued to bring to mind former Giants teammate Lawrence Taylor's one-time description of him: "Mike is Mike. Nobody messes with Mike."

Elsewhere in the NFL as the offseason progressed, Buddy Ryan got fired as coach of the Arizona Cardinals, Sam Wyche got fired as coach of the Tampa Bay Buccaneers, and Barry Foster plotted another comeback.

Foster, it should be noted, accused the Panthers of "blackballing" him by telling other teams he wasn't motivated, wasn't a great practice player and probably couldn't finish a season healthy. Privately, Panthers' officials snickered at this. The comment was made one month after Foster's release in Carolina and one month before he signed with the Cincinnati Bengals and then abruptly "retired" two days later, causing Mike Brown, general manager of the Bengals, to observe: "He came. He saw. He left."

Foster's agent, Jordan Woy, eventually claimed medical tests revealed the running back had mononucleosis during his brief stints with the Panthers and Bengals. By late February, he claimed Foster was fine and was ready to come out of retirement. He planned a private workout for interested NFL teams to prove Foster was ready to go. The Panthers did not attend.

Capers did not win the major NFL Coach of the Year awards (there are several). Usually, he finished second to Philadelphia's Ray Rhodes.

Polian, who at times one figured might have had a coronary, never did and continued to prove himself one of the league's shrewdest evaluators of talent. He was voted NFL Executive of the Year by his peers. McCormack, the benevolent mild-mannered man who you never would figure to have heart problems but did, is one year closer to retirement and can take satisfaction in the fact that he had as much to do with the success of the first year as Polian or Jerry Richardson or anyone else.

Richardson, who received a scare when he underwent successful prostate surgery in late May, is eagerly awaiting the first game to be played at Carolinas Stadium, which will then leave only one goal left unachieved to complete his NFL dream. Eric Davis, one of the newest Panthers, already knows what it is.

"I worked real hard to get this," said Davis, fingering a championship ring he won two years ago with the 49ers. "And I'm going to wear it until I get another one. After getting a closer look at the way this organization is run and the people running it, I figure that won't be too long. I think it will happen soon."

ACKNOWLEDGMENTS

More than anything, the story of the Carolina Panthers' first season was about teamwork and coming together. This book followed the same path. The two of us didn't even know each other when this project began, which seemed fitting as we watched some Carolina starters sneaking a peek at the back of teammates' jerseys when yelling encouragement during the second half of the Hall of Fame Game in Canton, Ohio.

We witnessed many lifelong friendships develop, including our own. You might say we were like a veteran quarterback and star running back during the process of reporting and writing. Sometimes you have to risk a pass over the middle, other times just hand off the ball to the big guy.

It has been a pleasure to be part of the historical first season, and our hope is this book does some justice to the entertaining blend of players, coaches, front-office executives, support staff, media, and fans who formed the 1995 Carolina Panthers team experience.

We appreciated the time afforded us by everyone, especially Dom Capers, who did not have to invite us to take a look at one of his truly fascinating game plans, but added to our effort by permitting it and taking painstaking efforts to decipher it so we could comprehend it. If there is one hero in this book, it is Capers. He took a bunch of guys who had no familiarity whatsoever with one another, including much of his own coaching staff, and forged a group that operated as a true team at the highest level of professionalism. His dealings with the media were forthright and honest and even funny at times, if not all that revealing by design on other occasions (coaches never reveal everything to the media).

We also would like to thank Jerry Richardson and every member of the Panthers front office, especially Mike McCormack, Bill Polian, Joe Mack and Dom Anile. The public relations staff of Charlie Dayton, Bruce Speight and Lex Sant, as well as their horde of capable interns, was always cheerful and helpful.

The 1995 Panthers were an interesting group of men. The locker room would have been a whole lot less lively without Willie Green, Derrick Moore or even Tim McKyer, although McKyer's perceptions of the media's role in his life grew tiresome at times. (Remember, Tim, we weren't the guys guarding Tony Martin that day in Pittsburgh, nor are we the ones who keep bringing it up.)

Sam Mills and Brett Maxie are two of the classiest men to play any professional sport. Kerry Collins is just a kid, prone to describe spotting favorable pass coverage by saying something like, "It was just really cool, you know." But he grew up a lot and will continue to do so, especially with guys like Mills and Maxie around to help show him the way.

For the most part, the rest of the players were enjoyable to deal with (even Lamar Lathon was usually polite on those many days when he was in a bad mood and declined to talk). We thank them all.

Thanks also to all the beat writers, and the Panthers have more following them on a daily basis than every other NFL team except the Jets, Giants and 49ers. Columnist Lenox Rawlings of the *Winston-Salem Journal* was especially insightful during several of the home games, while sports editor Terry Oberle of the *Journal* permitted pursuit of this project in the first place and then offered support and guidance throughout the season. Charles Chandler and Scott Fowler of the *Charlotte Observer* were helpful, as were Steve Reed of the *Gaston Gazette,* Chris Low of the *Rock Hill Herald,* Ed Hardin of the *Greensboro News and Record,* Willie Smith of the *Greenville News,* Joe Macenka of the Associated Press, David Newton of the State newspaper in Columbia, South Carolina, Dane Huffman of the *Raleigh News & Observer,* Andy Friedlander of the *Spartanburg Herald,* Denny Seitz of Thompson Newspapers and Brett Allen Turner of *Panthers Insider.* For simply putting up with each other day after endless day in the "bunker" at Winthrop Coliseum without any fights breaking out, all should receive commendations.

We also would like to thank Lou D'Ermilio of Fox Sports, and Terry Bradshaw for his unique brand of counseling and insight. Plus Don Pierson of the *Chicago Tribune,* a role model among NFL writers even if he did (correctly) question the wisdom of producing this book after witnessing back-to-back debacles at Clemson early in the season.

We owe a huge thanks to Tony Seidl, who brought this idea and deal to us; to Shari Lesser Wenk, who advised us along the way as it became reality; and to Sam Smith of the *Chicago Tribune,* who introduced us to each other in between phone calls to NBA general managers. John Clark of the *Gaston Gazette* did a fine job providing us with the wonderful photographs in this book. And, of course, the entire project could not have come off without the able editing of Traci Cothran and others at Macmillan Books.

Finally, to our families for putting up with the evenings and nights away from home that come with covering a football team—as well as the ringing phones at odd hours that come with a partnership forged across the miles and the formidable number of hours we spent preoccupied with the minutia of this book while other more important and heart-touching life matters were happening all around us. Not surprisingly, our wives, Sarah and Mary, once again proved to be our best editors and confidence boosters. We love them dearly for this and for so many other reasons.

—Joe Menzer and Bob Condor

The Carolina Panthers Roster*

No	Name	Pos	Ht	Wt	Age	College
54	Bailey, Carlton	LB	6-3	242	30	North Carolina
23	Baldwin, Randy	RB	5-10	220	28	Mississippi
6	Barnhardt, Tommy	P	6-2	218	32	North Carolina
82	Beebe, Don	WR	5-11	185	30	Chadron State
68	Brockermeyer, Blake	T	6-4	300	22	Texas
53	Butcher, Paul	LB	6-0	233	31	Wayne State
32	By'not'e, Butler	RB	5-9	190	22	Ohio State
87	Campbell, Mathew	TE	6-4	270	23	South Carolina
83	Carrier, Mark	WR	6-0	186	29	Nicholls State
76	Childs, Jason	T	6-4	292	26	North Dakota
44	Christian, Bob	RB	5-10	230	26	Northwestern
12	Collins, Kerry	QB	6-5	240	22	Penn State
56	Conner, Darion	LB	6-2	250	27	Jackson State
37	Cota, Chad	S	6-1	195	24	Oregon
62	Dennis, Mark	T	6-6	288	30	Illinois
52	Elliott, Matt	C/G	6-3	295	26	Michigan
89	Ellis, Elbert	WR	6-5	216	26	Pittsburgh
70	Farkas, Kevin	T	6-9	350	24	Appalachian State
55	Faryniarz, Brett	LB	6-3	230	30	San Diego State
93	Fox, Mike	DE	6-8	295	28	West Virginia
65	Garcia, Frank	C	6-1	295	23	Washington
74	Graham, Derrick	T	6-4	315	28	Appalachian State
86	Green, Willie	WR	6-4	185	29	Mississippi
30	Griffith, Howard	FB	6-0	240	27	Illinois
84	Guliford, Eric	WR	5-8	173	25	Arizona State
94	Hill, Travis	LB	6-2	240	25	Nebraska
4	Kasay, John	K	5-10	198	25	Georgia

* For regular season opening game

No	Name	Pos	Ht	Wt	Age	College
96	King, Shawn	DE	6-3	278	23	NE Louisiana
71	Kragen, Greg	NT	6-3	267	33	Utah State
57	Lathon, Lamar	LB	6-3	260	27	Houston
27	Lofton, Steve	CB	5-9	177	26	Texas A&M
78	Martin, Emerson	G	6-2	300	25	Hampton (VA)
39	Maxie, Brett	S	6-2	210	33	Texas Southern
25	McDowell, Bubba	SS	6-1	206	28	Miami (FL)
22	McKyer, Tim	CB	6-0	184	31	Texas-Arlington
88	Metzelaars, Pete	TE	6-7	250	35	Wabash
51	Mills, Sam	LB	5-9	232	36	Montclair St.
20	Moore, Derrick	RB	6-1	227	27	NE Oklahoma St.
60	Peterson, Andrew	G	6-5	308	23	Washington
29	Pieri, Damon	S	6-0	186	24	San Diego State
38	Poole, Tyrone	CB	5-8	188	23	Fort Valley State
92	Price, Shawn	DE	6-5	275	25	Pacific
45	Reed, Michael	CB	5-9	180	23	Boston College
14	Reich, Frank	QB	6-4	210	33	Maryland
63	Rodenhauser, Mark	C	6-5	280	34	Illinois State
21	Smith, Rod	CB	5-11	194	25	Notre Dame
80	Stone, Dwight	WR	6-0	195	31	Mid. Tenn. St.
40	Terrell, Pat	SS	6-2	210	27	Notre Dame
95	Thomas, Mark	DE	6-5	275	26	NC State
85	Tillman, Lawyer	TE	6-5	252	29	Auburn
10	Trudeau, Jack	QB	6-3	220	32	Illinois
64	Whitley, Curtis	C	6-1	295	26	Clemson
16	Wiggins, Brian	WR	5-11	185	27	Texas Southern
98	Williams, Gerald	DE	6-3	290	31	Auburn
34	Workman, Vince	RB	5-10	205	27	Ohio State
90	Zgonina, Jeff	DL	6-1	284	25	Purdue

Index